THE
PRESIDENTIAL
DEBATES

THE PRESIDENTIAL DEBATES

Media, Electoral, and Policy Perspectives

George F. Bishop
Robert G. Meadow
Marilyn Jackson-Beeck

Editors

PRAEGER PUBLISHERS
Praeger Special Studies

New York • London • Sydney • Toronto

Published in 1980 by Praeger Publishers
CBS Educational and Professional Publishing
A Division of CBS, Inc.
521 Fifth Avenue, New York, New York 10017 U.S.A.

© 1978 by Praeger Publishers

All rights reserved

0123456789 038 987654321

Library of Congress Catalog Card Number: 78-70323

Printed in the United States of America

PREFACE

Gerald Ford, in his acceptance speech following his nomination for the presidency at the Republican Party Convention in August 1976, issued a challenge to his Democratic opponent, Jimmy Carter, to engage in a televised debate. Carter accepted immediately. In the weeks that followed, aides for the two contenders, along with representatives from the networks and the sponsoring League of Women Voters' Education Fund, met to work out the specifics. At the same time, numerous social scientists from the disciplines of mass communication, political science, and social psychology hurried to secure funding and to develop research designs for probing the impact and substance of the presidential (and vice-presidential) debates.

The decision to hold the debates occurred somewhat unexpectedly, in effect precluding the development of large-scale research programs organized specifically to study the debates' influence on the electorate. Many investigators, however, were able to field studies in the short time available between the announcement of the debates and the first Carter-Ford encounter in late September. Although most studies with which we are familiar suffered somewhat because of haste in conception and execution, some managed to transcend temporal constraints. Those that excelled appear in this volume, representing in our estimation some of the best and most useful research on the 1976 debates.

While much has been written about various aspects of the debates by journalists, social scientists, and campaign specialists, other dimensions heretofore have been overlooked. The competing perspectives on the significance of the debates sometimes have limited rather than fostered an exchange of information, findings, and insights. We hope this volume will encourage the long-needed exchange among researchers and political observers and provide an enduring forum for the discussion of the role of presidential debates in the American electoral process and, correspondingly, of the contribution of empirical research on televised debates to the study of mass communication.

Between 1960 and 1976, research on presidential debates took on a new meaning. In 1960, much public discussion focused on the novelty of the debates, and, with rare exception, research was directed at viewers' perceptions of the "winner." Scholars from communication, political science, and other disciplines sought to measure the effects of the debates on such variables as the candidates' personality images and voter preferences. Others considered the effects of technical production and setting. In 1976, with the increased sophistication of social science research and researchers' increased familiarity with televised politics, and with a greater knowledge of the importance of policy issues to both candidates and voters, new research questions emerged. For one thing, scholars had the opportunity to reexamine the conceptual assumptions and methodological techniques of the 1960 studies. Prospects for the institutionalization of presidential debates also raised new questions about their potential role in American politics. In short, a host of new theoretical, empirical, and public policy questions joined the agenda of electoral research.

Because of these changes, two of us (Robert Meadow and Marilyn Jackson-Beeck) convened a research conference in May 1977—the Research Conference on Presidential Debates, 1960 and 1976—to which a limited number of researchers were invited to share their perspectives and findings. Sponsored by the Institute for Applied Communications Studies of the Annenberg School of Communications at the University of Pennsylvania, the conference focused on three main themes: (1) theoretical and methodological issues in the study of the presidential debates; (2) institutional treatment of the debates; and (3) meaning and impact of exposure to the debates for individual citizens. The researchers who participated in the conference included, in alphabetical order: George Bishop, Richard Carter, Steven Chaffee, Dennis Davis, Doris Graber, Marilyn Jackson-Beeck, Jim Karayn, Sidney Kraus, Gladys Engel Lang, Kurt Lang, Robert Meadow, Harold Mendelsohn, Arthur Miller, Dan Nimmo, and Thomas Patterson.

Concerning the first topic addressed at the conference—theoretical and methodological issues—many of the participants argued that previous researchers were so taken with the 1960 debates as novel events that they sometimes failed to use the variety of appropriate methodological tools available for adequately understanding them. (Again, time and funding were problems, too.) One of the principal difficulties with the designs used to investigate the 1960 debates was that they barely considered the political milieu in which the debates took place or the social context in which they were viewed. Moreover, it was evident that researchers took their cues from journalists who made the debates seem like contests in which winners and losers emerged, rather than as political events of consequence to voters needing information or to candidates wishing to clarify their policy positions.

The second theme emphasized in the conference—institutional treatment of the debates—revolved around the coverage of the presidential debates, factors determining production, and, most important, the relationship between the mass media's coverage of the debates and the public's interpretation of these events. Here the participants analyzed the extent to which otherwise informative events were reported noninformatively and the link between this reportage and the political needs of the electorate.

The third theme concentrated on the relevance of the debates to the individual voter—the dominant concerns centering around such phenomena as image formation, attitude change, information processing, and, ultimately, the vote for Carter or Ford. A perhaps unintended subtheme that emerged over and over again in this phase of the conference was the role of policy issues in voter decision making. In the past, political scientists of course had reason to doubt that issues were important in voting, relying as they did on findings from the classic Columbia and Michigan voting studies; however, new evidence from the mid-1960s and 1970s indicates that policy issues had become more salient to the average voter. In this context, then, the 1976 debates—unlike those of 1960—were expected to play a much more important role in shaping the electorate's response.

At the same time the conference was being organized, George Bishop was preparing a collection of research papers on the impact of the debates. The three of us began to discuss the utility of a volume on the debates geared to students and researchers—as well as to policy makers and campaign advisers—from a variety of disciplines. We decided to merge most of the original conference contributions with the outstanding manuscripts in Bishop's collection. Our interest in fostering additional research on the 1976 debates, particularly on their content, also led us to include complete and accurate verbal transcripts of all four televised debates, which were produced by Jackson-Beeck and Meadow in the course of their own research.

The collaborative result, this volume, we feel comprises an informative and useful collection of perspectives and research on the 1976 debates. Each chapter contributes conceptually and empirically; each chapter integrates the concerns of two, if not three, disciplines vitally interested in the presidential debates as communication events in the electoral process. The collection thereby adds to our understanding of the 1976 presidential debates, as well as to the field of political communication research. Of course, most of the credit for this effort goes to the many researchers whose endeavors have brought us to our present state of knowledge. The confluence of research interests has been fortunate and satisfying to us, and we hope to our readers.

ACKNOWLEDGMENTS

There are many people and institutions who merit acknowledgment. First on this list are the contributors, all of whom were cooperative and pleasant despite early deadlines. Other researchers whose work on the debates appears elsewhere also are thanked. Many offered helpful suggestions as this volume evolved. And always there are former teachers, colleagues, and friends who, in direct and profound or subtle and unspecifiable ways, have influenced our thinking.

Our appreciation goes as well to our institutional sponsors: the Behavioral Sciences Laboratory at the University of Cincinnati and the Institute for Applied Communications Studies at the Annenberg School of Communications, University of Pennsylvania. Special thanks are due to the director of the Behavioral Sciences Laboratory, Alfred Tuchfarber, who provided the release time and clerical facilities for the first coeditor's work on the manuscript, and to George Gerbner, Dean of the Annenberg School, for his encouragement and generous support of manuscript preparation by the other coeditors. Josephine Holz, a doctoral student at the University of Pennsylvania, is gratefully acknowledged for her assistance at the Research Conference on Presidential Debates, 1960 and

1976, which was held at the Annenberg School in May 1977, as is the Vanderbilt Television News Archives for supplying videotapes of the presidential and vice-presidential debates.

Institutional and collegial support, however, is rarely enough, and we owe a large debt to those without whom this volume would never have been possible—the candidates, the League of Women Voters, and, perhaps most important, the citizens in whose names the debates were held.

CONTENTS

PREFACE v

ACKNOWLEDGMENTS vii

LIST OF TABLES AND FIGURE xii

INTRODUCTION xvi

PART I: THE SETTING

1 A VERY PECULIAR HORSE RACE 3
   Richard F. Carter

2 THE MAKING OF THE DEBATES 18
   Herbert E. Alexander and Joel Margolis

3 A COMPARATIVE PERSPECTIVE ON PRESIDENTIAL DEBATES:
   ISSUE EVOLUTION IN 1960 AND 1976 33
   Robert G. Meadow and Marilyn Jackson-Beeck

PART II: EFFECTS OF COMMUNICATIONS CONTEXT

4 THE FORMATION OF PUBLIC OPINION: DIRECT AND
   MEDIATED EFFECTS OF THE FIRST DEBATE 61
   Gladys Engel Lang and Kurt Lang

5 PUBLIC RESPONSE TO GERALD FORD'S STATEMENTS
   ON EASTERN EUROPE IN THE SECOND DEBATE 81
   Frederick T. Steeper

PART III: COGNITIVE AND BEHAVIORAL CONSEQUENCES OF THE DEBATES

6 PROBLEMS IN MEASURING AUDIENCE EFFECTS OF
   THE 1976 DEBATES 105
   Doris A. Graber

		Page
7	DEBATES' EFFECTS ON VOTERS' UNDERSTANDING OF CANDIDATES AND ISSUES Lee B. Becker, Idowu A. Sobowale, Robin E. Cobbey, and Chaim H. Eyal	126
8	PERSISTENCE AND CHANGE IN CANDIDATE IMAGES Dan Nimmo, Michael Mansfield, and James Curry	140
9	THE IMPACT OF THE 1976 PRESIDENTIAL DEBATES: CONVERSION OR REINFORCEMENT? Paul R. Hagner and Leroy N. Rieselbach	157
10	THE PRESIDENTIAL DEBATES AS A DEVICE FOR INCREASING THE "RATIONALITY" OF ELECTORAL BEHAVIOR George F. Bishop, Robert W. Oldendick, and Alfred J. Tuchfarber	179
11	SUMMARY AND CONCLUSION	197

PART IV: TRANSCRIPTS OF THE 1976 PRESIDENTIAL AND VICE-PRESIDENTIAL DEBATES

12	ASCERTAINMENT AND ANALYSIS OF DEBATE CONTENT Marilyn Jackson-Beeck and Robert G. Meadow	205

Appendix

A	PARTICIPANTS AND PROCEDURES FOR THE 1960 PRESIDENTIAL DEBATES	211
B	PARTICIPANTS AND PROCEDURES FOR THE 1976 PRESIDENTIAL AND VICE-PRESIDENTIAL DEBATES	212
C	THE FIRST PRESIDENTIAL DEBATE: SEPTEMBER 23, 1976, PHILADELPHIA	213
D	THE SECOND PRESIDENTIAL DEBATE: OCTOBER 6, 1976, SAN FRANCISCO	238
E	THE VICE-PRESIDENTIAL DEBATE: OCTOBER 15, 1976, HOUSTON	261
F	THE THIRD PRESIDENTIAL DEBATE: OCTOBER 22, 1976, WILLIAMSBURG	282

	Page
BIBLIOGRAPHY	306
AUTHOR INDEX	316
SUBJECT INDEX	318
ABOUT THE EDITORS AND CONTRIBUTORS	322

LIST OF TABLES AND FIGURE

Table		Page
2.1	League of Women Voters' Presidential Forums	21
3.1	Issues in the Debates	42
3.2	Subissues in the Debates	43
3.3	Issues Discussed by Candidates	44
3.4	Subissues Mentioned by Candidates Regarding Domestic Government	46
3.5	Subissues Mentioned by Candidates Regarding Economics	48
3.6	Political Actors Mentioned	51
3.7	Economic Actors Mentioned within Issue-Units	52
3.8	Debate News Coverage, in Percent	54
3.9	Public's Perception of Most Important National Issues	55
3.10	Public's Perception of Most Important National Subissues	56
4.1	Vote Preference by Exposure	64
4.2	Persons Who Thought Debate Worth Seeing by Vote Preference and Exposure, in Percent	65
4.3	Rating of Debate as Help in Assessing Candidates and of Debate Format by Voter Preference and Exposure	66
4.4	"Who Did Better" in First Debate by Vote Preference and Exposure, in Percent	69
4.5	"Who Did Better" in First Debate by Expectation and Exposure, in Percent	70
4.6	Candidate Perceptions before and after First Debate, by Preference and Exposure	72
4.7	Perceptions of Issues, Differences between Candidates, and Issues Highlighted in First Debate by Exposure, in Percent	75
4.8	Changes in Vote Preference, Certainty, and Eagerness to Vote after First Debate, by Exposure and Initial Preference, in Percent	77
5.1	Reported Voting Intention, by Time of Interview, in Percent	84
5.2	Perceived Winner of the Debate, by Time of Interview, in Percent	85
5.3	Specific Perceptions of the Debate, by Time of Interview, in Percent	86
5.4	Volunteered Criticisms of Ford's Debate Performance, by Time of Interview, in Percent	88
5.5	Profile of Time Period Subsamples, in Percent	91

Table		Page
5.6	Observed Pro-Ford Responses and Expected Pro-Republican Responses, by Time of Interview, in Percent	93
5.7	Vote Intention and Perceived Winner of the Debate by Sex and Time of Interview, in Percent	95
5.8	Vote Intention and Perceived Winner of the Debate by Education and Time of Interview, in Percent	96
5.9	Observed Pro-Ford Responses and Expected Pro-Republican Responses for Men and Women by Time of Interview, in Percent	98
5.10	Observed Pro-Ford Responses and Expected Pro-Republican Responses for College-Educated and Noncollege-Educated Voters, by Time of Interview, in Percent	100
6.1	Background Characteristics of the Intensive Study Panel	107
6.2	Number of Respondents Who Reported Information Items Learned during First and Second Debate	112
6.3	Number of Respondents Who Attained Various Levels of Learning about Both Candidates' Positions on Selected Issues	114
6.4	Number of Respondents Who Reported Various Degrees of Learning, Measured by Self-Assessment and Objective Scores	118
6.5	Number of Respondents Who Watched Each Debate on Television for Varying Periods of Time	119
6.6	Pearson Correlations between Evaluation of Candidates and Exposure/Learning from the Debates	120
6.7	Pearson Correlations between Prior Interest/Knowledge and Exposure/Learning from the Debates	121
6.8	Pearson Correlations between Sex, Age, Education and Interest/Knowledge/Learning from the Debates	122
7.1	Changes in Understanding of the Candidates, in Percent	132
7.2	Changes in Knowledge of Candidates' Stands on the Issues, in Percent	135
7.3	Changes in Candidate Choice, in Percent	136
8.1	A Q-Sample of Items Representing the Basic Dimensions of Voters' Images of Presidential Candidates	143
8.2	Mean Intrapersonal Correlations for Q-Sorts for Less Active Voters, Members of League of Women Voters, and Total Sample, for Each Debate Period, 1976	146
8.3	Images of Ideal President, Jimmy Carter, and Gerald Ford Constructed by Less Active Voters, Members of the League of Women Voters, and the Total Sample during the Period of the 1976 Presidential Debates	148
9.1	Evaluations of Ford and Carter's Debate Performance across the Three Presidential Debates, in Percent	161

Table		Page
9.2	Shifts in Respondent Evaluations of Ford and Carter's Debate Performances across Debate Dyads, in Percent	162
9.3	Debate Evaluations by Party Identification and September Preference, in Percent	164
9.4	Shifts in Debate Evaluations across Debate Dyads by Party Identification and September Preference, in Percent	166
9.5	Panel's Ratings of Candidates' Image Characteristics, May, September, and November, in Percent	168
9.6	Shifts in Candidate Image Evaluations, September-November, in Percent	170
9.7	Relationship between Total Candidate Image Evaluation (in September) and Debate Evaluations	171
9.8	Relationship between Opinions on Unemployment/Inflation Issue and Defense Spending Issue and Candidate Debate Evaluations	173
9.9	Relationship between Candidate Switching and Debate Evaluations, Summary of T-Tests	175
9.10	September-November Vote Changes for All Voters and Debate-Period Deciders, in Percent	177
10.1	Multiple Regression Analysis of the Effects of the Experimental Treatment on Watching the First Debate, Controlling for Campaign Involvement and Demographic Covariates	184
10.2	Multiple Regression Analysis of the Effects of the Experimental Treatment on Degree of Involvement with the First Debate, Controlling for Campaign Involvement and Demographic Covariates	185
10.3	Multiple Regression Analysis of the Effects of Debate Watching on Knowledge of Candidates' Issue Positions, Controlling for Campaign Involvement, Experimental Treatment, and Demographic Covariates	187
10.4	Multiple Regression Analysis of the Effects of Watching Specific Debates on Knowledge of Specific Issue Positions of Candidates, Controlling for Campaign Involvement, the Experimental Treatment, and Demographic Covariates	188
10.5	Multiple Regression Analysis of the Effects of Debate Watching on Issue versus Party Voting for High- and Low-Exposure Groups	190
10.6	Multiple Regression Analysis of the Effects of Debate Watching on Awareness of Issue Differences between Carter and Ford, Controlling for Campaign Involvement, the Experimental Treatment, and Demographic Covariates	192
10.7	Multiple Regression Analysis of the Effects of Campaign Involvement on Debate Watching, Controlling for Demographic Covariates	193

Table		Page
10.8	Multiple Regression Analysis of the Effects of Education, Age, and Sex on Campaign Involvement	193
12.1	Candidates' Use of Imagery in the First 1976 Debate	208
12.2	Time Frames Referenced in the First 1976 Debate	209
12.3	Candidates' Nonfluencies in the First 1976 Debate	210

Figure		
5.1	Continuous Average Score by Viewers of the Second Debate	90

INTRODUCTION

The steadily increasing influence of behaviorism, as a philosophy of science (compare Skinner 1974), is nowhere more evident to the editors than in the contemporary analysis of American electoral behavior. Where once the locus of causality quite clearly resided within the political actors themselves, whether expressed in terms of the effects of their individual social and demographic attributes or their psychological attachments to the major political parties, it has now moved slowly but surely into the external world of political events. What has changed, in other words, are our attributions about the determinants of political attitudes and behavior, from an earlier emphasis on individual, psychologistic explanations (see, for example, Campbell et al. 1960) to a more recent stress on the truly environmental forces that shape political action (compare Kraus and Davis 1976; Nie, Verba, and Petrocik 1976; Robinson 1977), forces mediated largely through mass communications. And while we have always paid a certain amount of lip service to such forces with our routine measurement and analysis of demographic variables like age, race, sex, socioeconomic status, and the like, not until the past several years or so have we tried to operationalize, independently, the sociocultural context of individual electoral behavior—for example, by linking analyses of the content of the mass media with the responses of individuals to that content as assessed in social surveys.

Concurrent with this shift in the locus of causality has come a new accent on the role of policy issues in voter decision making, a feature that has led many researchers to a rediscovery of "rationality" in American politics and to a search for its causal origins in the changing landscape of the U.S. political environment. In our judgment, television as a medium is the catalytic agent that has probably contributed most to this rediscovery of rationality and the rehabilitated role of external events in American politics, especially in presidential elections. For we have arrived, for better or worse, in an electronic age where it is impossible for presidential candidates to avoid national exposure, and nearly as impossible for the public to avoid news and advertisements about the candidates and the campaign. Added to this already pervasive electronic context in the 1976 presidential campaign were the televised debates between candidates Carter and Ford (and Mondale and Dole), communication events that became the subject of intensive analysis by the contributors to this volume. If there is a common theme among them, aside from general interest in the effects of mass communication on political behavior, it is with the potential of the electronic medium to educate American voters, to heighten awareness of the policy positions of the presidential candidates and their qualifications for office—that is, to increase political "rationality."

Whatever their interest or theoretical stance on the problem of rational political participation, researchers studying the 1976 presidential debates stood to profit considerably from those who had investigated the 1960 debates between Kennedy and Nixon (see Kraus 1962), as well as from recent work on political communication (Chaffee 1975; Kraus and Davis 1976; Seymour-Ure 1974) and issue voting (Miller et al. 1976; Nie, Verba, and Petrocik 1976). For example, several contributors to this volume argue explicitly that the theoretical assumptions sometimes used to justify research on campaign debates are gratuitous, that inappropriate methodology too often has been employed, and that researchers themselves must be on the alert for "media effects" shaping their beliefs about the nature and consequences of the debates. Thus, it is not so surprising that previous research on presidential debates has neglected the impact of issue information on voter perceptions of the electoral choice.

Part of the reason that debate research heretofore has not shared the contemporary rationalist perspective perhaps lies in the fact that there is usually so very little opportunity for voters and candidates to show their colors. In ordinary presidential elections, campaigners are not allowed to address a simultaneous nationwide public alone or in concert, and they do not have the freedom to speak without gatekeepers, except in their own campaign literature and billets-doux. Typically, the public has access instead to three-minute network news summaries; to localized, printed accounts of the candidates' campaign speeches and activities; and to brief televised political advertisements known to be weak on substance (Patterson and McClure 1976).

Another possible explanation stems from the prevalent, but mistaken, notion that mass communication effects necessarily imply persuasion, leading to changes in attitudes and behavior. Since this was found clearly not to be the case for voters exposed to the 1960 presidential debates, researchers in 1976 were faced with a "damned if you do, damned if you don't" situation. To the extent that individuals usually did not change after exposure to the 1960 debates (nor do they after exposure to any specific message, for that matter), stability, of course, was implied. But to the extent that such stability was revealed, it seemed to some that debates must have no effect, or, alternatively, no message, and are therefore not worth studying.

Notably, the validity of this argument depends on individuals and individual change as its ultimate point of reference. In contrast, the rationalist perspective begins with the assumption that individuals are quite certain about their persuasions and that the individual in any case is not so important as such but is more productively viewed as a self-interested actor within the political system. From this perspective, then, the debates signify social and cultural events whose greatest impact may be felt at the level of systems and institutions. Furthermore, the felt impact is not seen so much as a matter of change, but rather as a fix or boost for the common political consciousness.

Still another reason for researchers' previous treatment of candidate debates derives from their location within presidential election campaigns, comprising ritual frenzied periods of hoopla, rabble-rousing, and the exchange of petty insults between candidates. Where normally attacks on compatriates' political preferences are restrained, during election years this barrier is removed. Where normally politicians are polite in their criticisms of each other, almost no campaign tactic is too low. And while there are always some hecklers in the crowd, at no time are they so prevalent as during presidential election years. Thus, it was hard for some researchers to regard the 1976 debates as the very significant and special events that they were and to design the appropriate research strategies for analyzing them.

In this volume we have a group of researchers who did take the debates seriously, not only as unique historical events but also as special hypothesis-testing opportunities. In doing so they applied a great variety of methodological techniques, a number of which were not generally used in studies of the 1960 debates—content analysis (Meadow and Jackson-Beeck), Q-methodology (Nimmo, Mansfield, and Curry), large-scale national surveys and multiwave panel designs (Becker et al., Hagner and Rieselbach, Steeper), field experiments within a panel design (Bishop, Oldendick, and Tuchfarber), quasi-experiments (Lang and Lang), and intensive analysis of small panels of voters, beginning before the first primary in January 1976 (Graber). And complementing this variety of research techniques were an equally variable number of theoretical and practical concerns: agenda setting (Becker et al.), candidate images (Nimmo, Mansfield, and Curry), issue evolution (Meadow and Jackson-Beeck), campaign financing (Alexander and Margolis), conversion versus reinforcement effects (Hagner and Rieselbach), issue voting (Bishop, Oldendick, and Tuchfarber), interpretive effects of the news media (Steeper), "sleeper" effects (Lang and Lang), levels of political learning (Graber), and communication paradigms (Carter).

The research reported here draws likewise upon several major disciplines. The first of these, communication, uniquely focuses on the debates as communication events, on exposure to the debates, and on the match between debate content and news reports. The second discipline, social psychology, concerns itself primarily with viewers' cognitive dynamics during and after exposure to the debates, with a special interest in characterizing these dynamics in terms of learning, understanding, reinforcement, conversion, or selective perception. Finally, we have political scientists, who are especially attracted to the debates as occasions for the discussion of policy issues, which may or may not affect the outcome of the election and, consequently, the course of domestic and foreign affairs, and as opportunities for studying such phenomena as candidate image formation and the effects of partisan predispositions on candidate evaluation.

As we look now at the potential of the debates to enhance voter rationality, it seems strange that so much store was set in them. In many ways, the debates were only partly relevant to the electoral process, as is suggested by much of the research in this volume and elsewhere. Of course, empirical research can never fully reveal the impact and significance of the debates, so we do not and cannot know the true extent of their potential, met or missed. Some questions are too large for research, others are too small, and in between are an array outside mainstream research interests. However, to the extent that research on the 1976 debates came equally well from three disciplines—principally communications, political science, and social psychology—and from a variety of perspectives within these, we have as comprehensive and useful a collection of knowledge as can be assembled. The intersection of interest in the debates resulted in a happy meeting of various research principles and techniques—one that we think can more than adequately sustain future research into campaign debates and political communication events generally.

The blended mixture of theoretical, disciplinary, and empirical questions characterizing research on the 1976 debates is represented in this volume particularly well in Chapter 1 by Richard F. Carter. In this essay, Carter analyzes mass media coverage of campaigns and debates in the metaphoric language of the horse race—in part because candidates perceive the election as such. Ironically, for the candidate pursuing a rationalist strategy it is a contest wherein the aim is to gather the most votes. But for some voters, it is a contest in which the goal is to bet on a winner, while for others it is to express ideological preferences. Using an orientation paradigm, Carter outlines the difficulty of researching debates because those most involved in the campaign—voters, candidates, and mass media (as well as researchers)—have their own conceptions of rationality and characteristic orientations that they bring to bear on the election.

If the debates are hard to deal with for researchers, they are even more complicated for the parties responsible for staging them. Chapter 2, by Herbert E. Alexander and Joel Margolis, traces just how the debates were arranged. The League of Women Voters' Education Fund, which sponsored the debates, was clearly interested in these forums as a means of providing information to the voting public. But the major parties and the party candidates had their own rationales for participation. Something of a clash of interests was inevitable. Furthermore, as Alexander and Margolis explain, there were innumerable legal and financial concerns to be addressed.

The third chapter, by Robert G. Meadow and Marilyn Jackson-Beeck, looks closely at debate content. Here they describe an evolutionary issue approach to political communication research in general and to debate research in particular, one which allows researchers to trace the development of issues over time both in terms of their salience to voters and to the candidates seeking to maximize their votes. In an era of issue-oriented voting but alleged issueless campaigns, Meadow and Jackson-Beeck's empirical findings indicate that indeed there is substantial issue content to be found in televised debates but it is not always reported accurately by the news media and it is generally not parallel to the issues that voters themselves identify as most important in public opinion surveys. The failure of the debaters to address public concerns, of course, has considerable implications for policy makers and the sponsors of campaign debates.

The contribution by Gladys Engel Lang and Kurt Lang (Chapter 4) begins the analysis of the cognitive and behavioral effects of the debates by looking at the total communications context in which they were embedded. Contrasting the immediate with the delayed reactions of those who watched the first presidential debate, they give a new meaning to the classic concept of the "sleeper effect" and develop an explanation of the contextual modification of media messages that will shape the conduct of research on political communication for some time to come. And in doing so, they will have helped restore the social framework to the contemporary study of electoral behavior.

In Chapter 5, Frederick Steeper continues the analysis of the communications context by exploring the reactions, both instantaneous and delayed, to Ford's comment (later referred to popularly as a gaffe) on Eastern Europe during the second debate. His study suggests a certain passivity in the reception of messages during the debate, but attributes a strong influence to later mass media coverage of these events. Unusual data suggest that Ford's comment was seen as erroneous only when mass media analysts and critics reported it as such rather than when viewers first heard the remark. As a result, Ford's "losing" margin increased hour by hour following the debate as more and more viewers were exposed to the information that he erred.

If there has been one overriding concern of debate researchers, it is whether there are any effects on individual audience members. The sixth chapter, by Doris A. Graber, deals with the methodological problems of measuring such effects and calls for more sensitivity on the part of researchers to different types of political learning. In particular, Graber explains how careful definition of measurement targets and refinement of measuring devices can explain conflicting or ambiguous findings. In addition, she develops some fresh insights into the traditional problems of pretest sensitization, question wording variations, and the meaning of respondents' answers to standard survey items. Finally, her political scientist's emphasis on the entire campaign context in which the debates take place is a valuable corrective.

The seventh chapter, by Lee B. Becker, Idowu A. Sobowale, Robin E. Cobbey, and Chaim H. Eyal, focuses more directly on the relationship between debate content and debate effects, and strongly suggests that the debates did indeed serve as a tool for increasing voter rationality. Viewed as a whole, the debates made viewers more knowledgable about issues and more informed about the characteristics of the candidates. However, the evidence is less clear that voting decisions were directly affected by the debates. What Becker and his associates have demonstrated, in other words, is that increased information—the stuff of which rational decisions are made—rather than voting decisions per se follows from exposure to debates.

Dan Nimmo, Michael Mansfield, and James Curry (Chapter 8) tell us that the debates did not appreciably alter the basic images of the candidates held by voters. Using a Q-sort technique, they found, among a sample of League of Women Voters members and nonleague individuals, a basic stability of images, despite exposure to the debates. The implications of such findings, of course, are that the debates, at least those in 1976, do not sell candidates; images are not so malleable.

Chapter 9, by Paul R. Hagner and LeRoy N. Rieselbach, continues the focus on the debates' contributions to voter rationality. Not unexpectedly, perhaps, they report that the debates served largely to reinforce predebate orientations on such variables as party identification, candidate preference, and candidate image. Debates, therefore, are not evaluated tabula rasa by voters, and consequently do not provide totally fresh information upon which voters can act. This is not to argue that no new information is available. It is, depending on the definition of information in use. But whether this new information is consistently put to "rational" use in terms of voting choice is questionable.

The tenth chapter, by George F. Bishop, Robert W. Oldendick, and Alfred J. Tuchfarber, deals with the issue of rationality head-on. In an effort to test whether exposure to the 1976 debates made voters more sensitive to specific political issues, they found that issue awareness was not necessarily prompted — an apparent contradiction to the findings by Becker and his associates, but one that can probably best be resolved in terms of the different criteria they use for "political learning" (compare with Graber, Chapter 6). Instead, the better predictor (and a precondition for) debate effects and voter rationality, they find, is formal education and political motivation.

The chapter by Marilyn Jackson-Beeck and Robert G. Meadow introduces the reader to the transcripts of the debates in the Appendix and describes the obstacles that had to be overcome in achieving an accurate accounting of these events. The authors also provide some valuable guidance on how the transcripts can be used by other researchers to test a wide variety of hypotheses about the verbal behavior of the presidential (and vice-presidential) candidates. The transcripts should, moreover, have special significance for future historians who will want to analyze the 1976 debates from yet another perspective—and for future presidential candidates and their campaign advisers who will surely want to learn from the performance of their predecessors.

In sum, whether or not the 1976 debates could have enhanced voters' rational behavior is a question addressed directly and indirectly throughout this volume. To the extent that the findings generally show little change in voting intentions before and after exposure, the answer might first seem to be an unqualified no. But if we include as rational the growth or deepening of voters' understanding of candidates and issues, the answer is perhaps yes. Actually, it is difficult to say very definitely either yes or no inasmuch as research reveals that candidates spoke rarely to the public and its professed interests. Furthermore, the public was exposed at times to incredible remarks and to substantial incoherency on the part of the candidates, as can be seen by reference to the transcripts in the Appendix. Ford's so-called gaffe concerning the absence of Soviet domination of Eastern Europe is but one example. Once the public became aware of the magnitude of inaccuracy displayed by then-President Ford, was it not most rational to withdraw support?

Another related factor possibly obscuring the debates' potential for increasing voters' rational behavior is that the candidates failed really to debate. In apparent fear of showing weakness by responding to each other, to questioners, or to the moderators' pleas, they spoke quite independently. What then was the public to think, if they expected straight talk, or at least straight answers to questions politely asked? Added to this mismatch between the reality and myth of debates was the transparent lawlessness behind the debate broadcast. To qualify as a bona fide news event now regulated under Section 315 of the Federal Communications Act of 1934, the debates were made out to be a news event covered coincidentally by the networks. But if this ruse was not obvious to the voters from the start (as it was to third party candidates), it surely was clear once the action stopped for nearly half an hour during the first debate in deference to audio failure.

What of the debates' capacity for enhancing the candidates' rational behavior? As we have seen by reference to Ford's outstanding gaffe, again the answer would seem to be in the negative. But insofar as candidates generally were evasive, we could call this rational in Downs' (1957) terms. In American politics, as we know, it is a virtue to be forthright and sincere, but politicians who act accordingly are briefly, if ever, in office. Even so, in comparison with 1960, candidates in the first 1976 debate, at least, can be said to have made a poorer showing (see Chapter 3). They were less articulate, and they covered fewer substantive concerns. They were less creative in their imagery and less attuned to the nation's past and future. They spoke of essentially the same topics, despite the passage of some 16 years, so that one might say they played the part not so much of political candidates (as individuals) but a role that time and events had thrust upon them.

As for the rationality and rationale of research on candidate debates, we can say little. The chapters in this volume offer conclusions about the debates and their effects stemming from a variety of research approaches, each with its own merits. But it seems fair to say, collectively, that presidential debates should be viewed as well as researched with care, and that they ought not to be accepted blindly as important events without which the electorate cannot do. Instead, televised debates must be methodically explored and evidence soundly gathered to assist communication scholars, social psychologists, political scientists, sponsors, and policy makers in decisions that will be made about institutionalizing campaign debates and, indirectly, research on these communication events.

PART I

THE SETTING

1

A VERY PECULIAR HORSE RACE

Richard F. Carter

Every four years the American electorate prepares to take an important step, to commit themselves in support of a political administration under the leadership of a president. We prepare for that commitment by participating in a presidential election campaign. We do so on a premise that we should be mentally active in pursuing the most enlightened outcome possible. On those occasions—1960 and 1976—when presidential debates were held, these have been regarded as part of our thinking together about our future.

The political campaign, in its length, and the presidential debates, in their focus, suggest the extent of our concern for an informed citizenry. But realization of our hopes is not yet attained. Criticism of campaign and debates is widespread. Criticism is directed, in large measure, to a lack of informational substance. The campaign is characterized, demeaningly, as a horse race. The debates are said to be a personality contest.

We are strongly attached to a rational approach in these matters. We consider information about issues the most useful content of a campaign. Harold D. Lasswell (1962, p. 20), commenting on the 1960 debates, said:

> *The candidates are expected to serve the electorate . . . by contributing to a process that helps to clarify probable consequences of the policy choices open to the nation.* (italics in original)

That the norm of rationality is often violated is evident. We see caustic titles for several postelection analyses of campaign coverage: "By Trivia Obsessed" (Ungar 1977) and "The Triumph of Junk News" (McCartney 1977). It is not just the media, though. We view them as mirroring what they observe. Candidates and citizens, too, are not all that rational.

But rational consideration of issues is not all there is to thinking, whether individually or collectively. We are very familiar with the techniques of decision making, with the detailing of alternatives and their attributes (favorable and unfavorable). We can conceive of rationality as the gathering of such information

---

A previous version of this chapter was presented at the Research Conference on Presidential Debates, 1960 and 1976, held at the Annenberg School of Communications, University of Pennsylvania, Philadelphia, May 12–13, 1977.

and the weighing of alternatives in the light of this information. And in this light we may well view campaigns as too much devoted to winning per se, and debates as too confrontational in their efforts to test the candidates. But, still, we owe it or ourselves to take another look at the thinking we do during the campaign. Better yet, we can look at the thinking we might do. Could the campaign and/or the debates better serve the electorate other than by being more rational?

Researchers, like the candidates and the media, serve the electorate. Researchers have also been enamored of the rational approach. They have studied the flow of information to voters; they have studied the voters' use of information in their voting decisions. Recent accountings of this research (Chaffee 1975; Becker, McCombs, and McLeod 1975; O'Keefe 1975) suggest that "information processing" is an important citizen behavior. But this is not to say that research can tell us nothing more about the conduct of our campaigns and debates.

Research might well say something of the potential for future campaigns. However, to do so, we must remove our paradigmatic blinders. The notion that thinking is necessarily rational is a narrow perspective. If we are to aid collective thinking, we shall have to broaden our view of thinking in action. To show how this can be done, we shall look first at what is being talked about—the campaign and the debates—to examine just how they deserve the horse race metaphor. For it is a very peculiar horse race. Then we can reexamine our notions of thinking in action, to see the limits of rationality and the prospects of other approaches.

THE RACE

Political observers who characterize the campaign as a horse race seem to have a fairly straightforward notion of that race. When they take the media to task for their coverage, they imply that the media, too, have a very simple notion of a race. Gans (1977, p. 25) said, for instance:

> [They] covered the 1976 campaign primarily as a horse race, constantly assessing who was ahead and behind, and virtually ignoring such judgmental questions as whether the candidates were speaking about the issues that faced the country.

The debates, he said, were part of the same picture:

> Once over, the debates became news and their coverage followed the daily campaign format, for the news media paid major attention to candidate mistakes, and like the pollsters, treated the debates as contests, and thus part of the larger horse race. (p. 25)

This conception of a horse race reminds us of early tribal confrontations. There the champion of one tribe contested the champion of another tribe. Each tribe backed his champion wholeheartedly. There were occasional uproars from backers of one or the other as foul play was suspected. Champions maneuvered for advantage. The roar of the crowd alerted one to changing advantages in position. Today the media and the polls furnish information to those concerned with such conditions who may not be in attendance at the contest struggle itself.

But this is only conception. How accurate is this conception? We would say that the conception is essentially inaccurate. We would say that anyone believing this conception would be grossly misled. The actions of candidate, reporter, and citizen would be misconstrued. We would also say that the researcher cannot fully explore the role of the presidential debates using this conception.

In an earlier day, the political campaign may have been more like this tribal horse race. But now it is significantly different. The first factor that distinguishes our present race is the pure bettor. There may well have been a wayfarer in the past who made some money because tribal passions ran stronger than their champion. However, there were not many. Today we have a major proportion of those attending the race who want themselves to be the winners. The horse race—and the horse—is incidental, though essential, to their aims. Indeed, the necessary evil of depending upon a horse to win for one may bring to the scene a striking distrust for the race itself, impatience with its preliminary aspects, and fury rather than sympathy for a defeated champion.

A second factor distinguishes our current campaign as horse race, altering the conception drastically. At the horse track, the horses determine the winner and the bettors determine the payoffs. In the political campaign, the bettors determine the winner and the candidates determine the payoffs—usually much later.

Under these conditions, the candidates play to an audience looking for a winner. The horse, we might say, is in the unenviable position of running forward while looking backward. How, then, is an issue to be any more important than any other factor disposing toward victory? How can the candidate not make promises, to somehow allude to the future as site of any payoff? Somehow, bettors must be brought to the candidate's side. There may be appeals to specific interest, on the one hand; on the other, general concerns may be approached. Any basis for securing votes becomes a de facto issue. The prospective policy becomes a special kind of issue, one that must be scrutinized carefully to see if its consequences could possibly offend anyone. No-loss issues, such as national unity, are the more tractable.

Presidential debates are not always a popular track with candidates. They seem designed more for the bettors than the candidates. The candidates, after all, still regard it as paramount that they—not the bettors—win out. The political folk wisdom is that one cannot serve, however well, without first being elected.

When the debates are staged, it seems to be because neither major candidate sees an intolerable disadvantage in running head-to-head. But the stage set, a tension between candidate and bettor points of view appears. The bettor wants only to be able to pick a winner. For this a contest—a "trial by fire" (Mears

1977)—makes it easier for the bettor. In the 1960 debate research, it was found that viewers preferred the later, less issue-oriented, debates (Carter 1962). The candidate wants to be the winner. Under the trying conditions of the confrontation, there must be concentrated preparation to avoid any sign of failing. One must be seen to run well. That the media note candidate mishaps—and even seem preoccupied in searching for them—is not strange, given that for which the bettors are looking. But is hard on the candidates.

Attention to the bettors—pursuit of the "independent voter"—does not exhaust the story of a major change in candidate campaigning. The backer is still important, a principal source of resources with which to conduct the campaign, a member of the voting bloc who must not be lost. But both backer and bettor must be accommodated. Coalitions must be constructed. Many issues must be localized. A "pragmatic" campaign is to be waged, with quick changes if the race seems to be going badly. One avoids extremes (the danger of doctrinal candidacy) but goes to extremes (dumping, if need be, the vice-presidential nominee). Mass media messages can be risky; both bettors and backers are in the audience.

What about the electorate? There are getting to be more bettors. There are more of the type we call independents. There are also more nonvoters; they are bettors, too. The nonvoter bets that it makes no difference which candidate wins, that the payoffs will not differ materially. The nonvoter tends to be younger, and is increasing in number if not in proportion.

Where do bettors come from? Are some reformed backers? Has the era of management and its technology of decision making produced bettors by convincing them that choices should always be made, by teaching them decision making? And would they then become frustrated by the difficulty of making a decision and abandon voting, to let someone else bet for them, to rationalize that there is no difference between candidates? How many bettors are competent, habitual decision makers? The "compleat dopester" is a recognized figure, but how typical a bettor? Are not bettors more disposed to judging on familiar grounds, comparing on pertinent attributes, or even looking for signs?

What about the backers? Their wager is often the largest. They are apprehensive of how the campaign is being waged, and must back a candidate who is a good campaigner (Seldes 1962). If their commitment to a candidate is predicated on doctrine, how do they feel about the concessions made and agreements sought by the candidate hunting for votes? What kind of a payoff do they anticipate—that such means could be justified by the end? Have they no questions (in the language of decision making, no uncertainty)?

Then there is the history of events, the experiences and associations the bettor and/or backer may have had with the candidate. As O'Keefe (1975, p. 153) said:

> The voter may react in an election to what was experienced over the
> period since the last election; the vote cast likewise leaves its mark

on how the next between-election period is going to be interpreted.

To all of this, the media and researchers pay avid attention. To the consternation of those who call for an informed, policy-relevant discussion of issues, the media recognize the campaign for what it is, keep track of developments, and treat the race as the major theme. Any issue, policy of otherwise, is viewed in the context of the race. They see the self-serving aspects of platform, pronouncements, private polls, and the like. Can we expect them to ignore all this? Reporters say they admire candidates who give us policy issues to consider; but, meanwhile, they monitor the strategies being used by the candidates to win the voters. Researchers, too, pay a lot of attention to the race, to studying conditions that may predict election outcomes. They have found that party affiliation is not so important as it once was—that bettors are replacing backers. They find that policy issues are not critical determinants of voting preferences. Yet, they persist in examining voter behavior within a framework of rationality—that bettors think and choose, even if they do it inadequately.

There is a certain condescension among media personnel and a parallel plaintiveness among researchers that bear on the perceived irrationality of candidate and voter behavior. What these views may very well show instead is a rather restricted notion of how thinking, and especially collective thinking, can and could operate.

AN INCOMPLETE PARADIGM

After the fact, when the voters have marked their ballots or pulled one of several levers, we find little difficulty in viewing what has happened as decision making. A choice has evidently been made. Those who did not vote made a different kind of choice. So we have a comfortable sense of knowing what is going on when we talk of our decision-making responsibilities as voters and of the relevance of various campaign events to that decision making (see, for example, Becker and Lower 1962).

But has decision making been used? Have the voters been adding up attributional information about the alternative choices, sifting through possible sources of more information, and weighing the informational increments to arrive at a final choice? As bettors, we argued, they are not all that impressive in this light. Further, the image of an informed voter choosing rationally does not do justice to the strategies that voters do apply. It is not just that voters may seem to fail in rationality; it is also possible that rationality may fail in presenting the thinking of voters.

Decision making is one way of operating under an orientation paradigm. In an orientation paradigm, the dominant postulate is that behavior is best characterized by the direction taken in any step. The researcher using this paradigm tries to find out which direction the voter goes, and the conditions that influence that direction. Thus, a choice indicates the direction taken. The research problem, then, is to find the sources of that directed step.

Another, earlier version of the orientation paradigm in use by researchers (and casual observers, too) was the notion of determinism. Here the view was that any directed step was necessarily caused—strictly determined. Just how was not very obvious, but notions that reflect the presumption are common. An "attitude," for instance, is defined as a disposition or predisposition (Green 1954) to direct one's behavior in a certain direction. When it was the case that party affiliation, and especially party affiliation of one's parents, too, was correlated with candidate choices, this variant of the orientation paradigm was commonly asserted to explain how voters operated.

The choice variant represents a development from the blunter determinism. It allows for the consequences of many steps having been taken, not just by each voter but by the collectivity. The experiences of this previous behavior are brought into the current situation as attributes assigned to the various alternatives. Then the strategy is to orient anew (even to resisting "unconscious" temptations or "drives" in one or another direction). The experience-founded attributes are values; they attract. The voter is drawn in to a new orientation.

The campaign norm shows the impact of this orientation paradigm throughout our culture. The behaviors of those in the campaign are supposed to be viewed in an orientational context. The candidates orient themselves; then they are to inform us of their "stands" or "positions." Voters are supposed to make use of all the information the media can bring them about the candidates and their positions. They are expected to have informed opinions about the candidates and their stands on significant issues.

The communication researcher has been much affected by the orientation paradigm. As scientists, they are themselves exposed to a widespread view that there is a general order to all things, a unity expressable in laws of behavior. Surely, then, anything said to be behavioral must have an orientation of some kind. For example, the question is raised of behavior: Nature or nurture? What is the source of instruction for the direction our behavior takes? What is most significant about this question is the assumption that orientation is the kind of question to be asked.

If a question is raised as to evident disorder or lack of order, then unity—and laws of orientational behavior—are pursued to the extent that they do obtain. The norm remains. It has been evident all along that things are not fully ordered. They collide and some may cease to exist. But science has a wonderfully imaginative answer to that dilemma: If things are not fully ordered, then attributes may be. So, as researchers, we try to relate attributes to each other (Carter 1977). The presumption of order is maintained. Attributes of things are assumed constrained by that order; things are necessarily "informed" by their attributes. And, living things are informed by observing the attributes of other things.

The orientation paradigm is so strong that we are likely to accord more reality to a "space-time universe" than to the things for which that positional idea was invented. We are also much enamored of measurement, another orientation aspect imposed on things.

We have had our difficulties in communication research with the orientation paradigm. We looked to see what instruction people got from attending to communication messages. Did the direction of their behavior change after reading something? Not unless this was a novel situation—that was the general answer (Klapper 1960). A popular orientation model was: attention—comprehension—acceptance (Hovland, Janis, and Kelley 1953).

Actually, it was fairly easy to show attention and comprehension. There were message effects. What was difficult to show was that people operated in accord with the orientation paradigm's expectation of how they should. They sometimes did (research hypotheses sometimes beat chance, but in the restricted conditions of laboratory or in unique field situations). Lazarsfeld saw the nature of the trouble. People acted differently under less restrictive conditions (Hovland, Janis, and Kelley 1953, p. 16).

Yet, true to paradigmatic inertia (Kuhn 1962), researchers reworked the orientation approach rather than abandoned it. The archetypic mode of orientation is the orbit or reflex. Things behave very regularly because of the structural constraints involved. In human behavior, "rut" or "habit" are suggestive of this line. But people are far from being so regular in the direction of their behavior. We say they vary from situation to situation. Thus, "situation" gives us the opportunity to talk about orientation being renewed. But to show us that orientation is still paramount, behavior is construed in "stimulus-response" steps. Instruction is said to come to us in our attending to things, not from instruction being resident within us.

An immediate problem is the multitude of sources for instruction in a situation; stimuli are everywhere. For all the depreciation of issues in a campaign, there is no shortage of things to which to attend. The orientation paradigm can be modified, then, to accommodate the elector's relation to several situational things rather than just one. One such model (Carter 1965) suggests a double paradigm of orientation, with two modes: goal-seeking (one-object situation) and evaluation (two-object situation). Orientation behavior would be different as each mode was applicable.

Such a two-object orientation approach does show up some differences in information processing behavior (Jacoubovitch 1977), but it does not generalize to more than two objects all that well. For a two-object situation (for example, the two major presidential candidates), the orientation approach can work fairly well as long as the attributes that characterize the alternatives are shared— though not to the same degree, of course. The voter can sum over attributes to come to a choice, in the manner of decision making. For some two-object situations, voters simply do not (and perhaps cannot) produce such comparative arrays of attributes. So we have come to say that they orient themselves in special ways. Voters may employ "qualitative reduction" (Carter and Sweigert 1963), stripping away potentially informing attributes, perhaps even discarding alternatives, until they get a simpler situation. They may never have tolerated such a situation to the extent that qualitative reduction (as opposed to the quantitative reduction of decision making) was needed. They could have used a "discriminating attribute" to bring focus to the situation, judging things only in that context (Chaffee et al. 1969, pp. 77-80).

Another modification of the orientation approach is to view the voters as somehow affected by things in their situations. This is a "field" theory of orientation behavior. In this view, the instruction of the various things is exercised by their attracting the voters—through the "valences" of the situational things (Lewin 1935).

These attempts to work within the orientation paradigm do not nearly exhaust the modifications advanced by social scientists. They are characteristic of those attempted by communication researchers. The point in bringing these up is that for us to have made such attempts tended to make it less likely that we would seek a better way to study behavior in general, and voters' behavior in particular. There is something to be said for an orientation approach; but it has limited applicability because it is an incomplete paradigm. To improve the paradigm we must add to it, and not just sharpen it.

Operating wholly within an orientation paradigm, it may well seem to some critics of the campaign that the "more informed" of the voters should exert the most influence on presidential selection. Indeed, it may be thought that the campaign—and the debates—are wasted effort, that those most informed might better do the selecting. These views, however, serve to point up a danger of the orientation paradigm. Freedom may be eroded while we sow a field of certainty. Other ways of thinking about presidential candidacies become forfeit, as we attempt to straighten out the flaws of orientation rather than to develop the campaign and the debates to better serve the thinking of the electorate.

Two other modes of thinking are used by the candidates and the electorate. We need to look at them, as they are used separately and in conjunction with orientation. All three taken together are more promising in prospect, and together they emphasize individual freedom.

A MORE COMPLETE PARADIGM

Before the fact, when voters have not committed themselves in any direction, it becomes clearer that orientation is not the only way to proceed. An option to choice is construction, to build a new future rather than to choose among alternatives representing past features. Another option to information gathering and choice is that of continuation. The question is just that of whether to keep on going along the same path. The answer to this can be considered a special kind of choice; but the difference is too great for us to so neglect its characteristics—mainly, that voters so opting do not have to be informed beyond "I know how I feel" or "This is the way I want to go." The paradigm in the latter case is that of reorientation.

Candidates are aware of these other ways of thinking. They use them, too. An incumbent candidate will shy away from a contest with a less known candidate. This has been a problem for those seeking regular presidential debates. The incumbent would prefer that voters thought in terms of a continuing term of office, reviewing the accomplishments of the past term. A comparison on other grounds is not preferred strategy. The incumbent prefers that the voters' consideration be that of reorientation rather than orientation. A candidate who is new to the voters' eye, and who cannot secure an orientational confrontation, may attempt to "capture the imagination" of the voters. The attempt here is to associate with the voters in constructing a future.

Communication research has become more familiar with reorientation than with construction. The difficulties with the orientation paradigm forced us to take heed of reorientation. Behavior often seems based on very little information, whether by voters in campaigns or elsewhere. But the behavior is not without reason. There has been satisfactory experience with steps taken. The term "feedback" is sometimes used loosely to suggest such grounds for continuance of behavior.

Several perspectives have been introduced to discuss reorientation phenomena. Behavior can be analyzed as a guidance question, via cybernetics (Wiener 1950). Here orientation is minimal; the direction taken can be fortuitous in origin. What is important is that information is received (through a feedback mechanism) that alerts us that we are off course; otherwise, we continue on.

Reorientation is important in the operant conditioning model (Skinner 1953). The stimulus-response approach was altered to include the reinforcement providing the response. In this sense, reinforcements may seem significant only for fixing orientations, producing continuance. However, what is also accomplished by each reinforcement (introducing a reward or removing a punishment) is the stopping of the response. A step is ended as another step in the same direction is encouraged.

For reorientation to be possible, steps must be taken. The one step of an orbit would not allow reorientation. That is how the phenomenon was slighted originally, by focusing on one-step things. Behavior as it involves steps must then by concerned with stopping. Stops are controlled by signals (as with reinforcements) or by perceived discrepancies (Carter et al. 1973). There is much in campaign tactics that seems responsive to the latter—as when candidates imply that a voter's course is as simple as following a garden path.

Fundamentally, reorientation addresses the problem of an incomplete ordering of things. This is a problem in that we are subject to collisions, and we have to produce our unity if we are to have it. The same incomplete ordering that yields the lack of orbit is party to our having freedom. There is some (orientational) information available through our experience of things per se. Reorientation adds another kind of available information; it gives us guidance to wherever we were already headed. However, orientation and reorientation are not enough with which to face the nature of things. They are applied to orderings, to available information—albeit of different kinds. But behavior occurs partially in regard to the fact of nonordering per se (Carter 1978). Behavior is sometimes constructive, producing new ordering.

Construction works because our thinking capability includes a way of adducing structure to things, so as to have ideas about them as well as of them (Carter 1977). The kinds of structure contained in ideas are simple: they allow us to locate one thing in respect of another; and they allow us to do this before the fact, as well as afterward. The power of imagination is not merely an ability to accurately recapitulate, even though the notion of "image" suggests otherwise. Cognitive structure has been an important feature of orientation approaches, but in the sense of imaged things (objectively and/or subjectively). Construction in that context is gratuitous. The "how" of construction has not been made evident (McLeod and Chaffee 1972).

The concept of "system" shows this imaginative capability. The concept can be used after the fact, to describe an interdependence of things. But it also can be used before the fact, to prescribe a unity to be attained through interdependence. System entails producing ordering in addition to describing it. We seem to be recognizing that we, as scientists, not only can discover missing links; we also can handle those links that are missing and have always been missing, which were never there and must be supplied by us.

There is, then, a fundamental condition of discontinuity. This is in addition to whatever continuities or orderings there are. Construction is responsive to discontinuity as orientation and reorientation are responsive to available information. A comprehensive paradigm of behavior must contain all three. Orientation, reorientation, and construction all have their parts to play. Candidates use them; voters use them; researchers must use them all if they are to be helpful—especially in such matters as collective thinking before the fact of presidential election.

For convenience, we shall use the acronym ROC to represent this more complete paradigm. First, we shall want to examine more closely how voters and candidates make use of all three thinking modes in their campaign behavior. Then, in a final section, we shall consider how this paradigm might enable researchers to explore more fruitfully the potential of presidential debates.

As formal observers of the horse race, researchers are akin to the reporter. Both purport to "call it the way they see it," to "tell it as it is." So let us look at what candidates and electors are doing, from the ROC perspective.

We shall introduce the ROC paradigm by giving example activities for the candidate that involve two of the three in combination. This in itself argues for the significance of construction in behavior, for the nesting of one in the service of the other is constructive. The candidate may:

ascertain conditions in various sectors before announcing formal candidacy (orientation for reorientation)
analyze needs and resources before putting together a campaign organization (orientation for construction)
see how various trial balloons go before taking a position (reorientation for orientation)
pretest reaction to several planks before putting together the platform (reorientation for construction)
put together an early warning system to alert for possible adjustments in campaign strategy (construction for reorientation)
tie together some issues, in several speeches, to see if this gives comprehensive coverage (construction for orientation)

Generally, with the electorate free to cope with the campaign as it will, the candidate has to be careful not to communicate just an orientational capability and concern—to debate narrowly. A show of strength is necessary; a weak president would be a disaster (Siepmann 1962). What seems to be a personality blitz can be a demonstration of constructive and reorientational potential—a candidate able to develop in dealing with unforeseen events, a candidate able to produce national unity (Lasswell 1962, p. 22).

There is an interesting difference of scale between the control problem of the candidate and that of the citizen. The candidate is immersed in campaigning; the citizen takes some time from other activities to engage in the campaign. One might account the candidate's use of ROC in monies spent; there must be visible evidence to backers and bettors of capability to construct, to reorient, and to be informed. The citizen's efforts are harder to account for; they are particularly hard to observe in the context of the final vote. That vote is constraining; an election has to be made. But it is sheer imputation to think that the election reflects only orientation behavior.

We can see fairly clear evidence of ROC in these citizen activities:

check whether other supporters of candidate are still holding before backing (orientation for reorientation)
ascertain attributes necessary in president before forming notion of ideal candidate (orientation for construction)
try arguing for each of the candidates, to see how it feels, before making up own mind (reorientation for orientation)
find out which rationales work before putting together own rationalization for

choice (reorientation for construction)

devise a means to know when you have not got enough campaign information (construction for reorientation)

establish a frame of reference within which to apply criteria to candidates (construction for orientation)

The communication researcher, if looking for evidence of all three thinking modes, can probably find plenty. After the 1960 debates, Katz and Feldman (1962, p. 216) summarized the research conducted, and remarked: "And did people actually 'use' the debates in their daily lives?" The research, it seems, reflected the orientational concerns of the researchers. The debates need not have been studied only in the perspective of providing attributional information about presidential alternatives. Is this horse race just a difficult orientation question for the researcher? Or is it difficult for the researcher because investigation follows an orientation paradigm while the participants are engaging in all of ROC? We suggest the latter.

THE NEXT DEBATE

What can the ROC paradigm tell us as we prepare for the next presidential debate? In the spirit of construction, we should have no doubt that opportunities for enlightenment are to be found in the debates. In the context of the paradigm, the range of opportunities is broad—surely not restricted to information about policies. The avenues for research are several, extending beyond those of 1960:

> The pity is that in their concentration on the combat, the studies failed to get so much of either the context or the latent consequences *of the institution of the debates.* (Katz and Feldman 1962, p. 219; italics added)

Research in 1976 was not appreciably different. But it can be. And the debates could be different.

As the campaign is conducted—the horse race run—it is doubtful that the candidate or the media can be singlemindedly concerned with policy issues. The candidate enjoys more freedom in reorienting and constructing maneuvers than in orientational messages. Polls, for example, are as often used with respect to, "How am I doing?" as "What should I be doing?" When it comes to constructing, old hands are valuable; their experience is needed to get things and people together.

Nor is it all that fair to citizens to offer them just policy issue information. Four years is a long time. Some living demonstration of candidate capabilities, and not just of the platforms on which they stand, is germane to the elector's questioning stance.

A Very Peculiar Horse Race

The presidential debate is an institution intruded upon recent campaign practice. It is considered to be useful to the electorate. How about further intrusion? Would that be useful? Perhaps it would be possible to examine the capabilities of the candidates even more thoroughly. Some possibilities might include:

A different kind of debate when one candidate is an incumbent. The thrust of reporter questioning would be to examine also the orientational, issue material that the incumbent would prefer to set aside for "running on the record"—and thus hewing to a private agenda.

A different kind of debate for the primaries. More candidates would be involved. Emphasis here might be more on matters of previous record, and on constructive initiatives contemplated for the role of leadership. Most issues could be set aside for treatment after the nominations and party platforms had been made.

A different kind of debate prior to primaries. This would be a time to bring in candidates from nonmajor parties. Emphasis might well be on what the major parties had been accomplishing during the past four years, preparatory to forging an agenda for media surveillance during the ensuing campaign.

A documentary presentation on how some respected citizens go about picking their president. They would tell us what they look for in a candidate and where they obtain the evidence that a candidate "has the goods." We could use something analogous to, but better than, a way of telling who was the better debater. The role of "pathfinder" is honored, but neglected.

A documentary of an interesting historical figure describing the various approaches to campaigning and voting during our country's history.

We might consider expanding on the idea that a tax write-off could be used to support the debates (Mears 1977, p. 22). We might have taxpayers elect to support one or several different campaign events that have been designed to help them in probing their options. We could achieve a reliable poll of how useful various campaign institutions are perceived to be, if we had such a procedure. And campaign events could be compared to write-offs for the candidates themselves (as now), or perhaps to an organization entrusted to provide debates regularly (such as the League of Women Voters in 1976). Most important, there would be money available with which to undertake, constructively, the enrichment of our campaigns.

Not all developments have to be initiated via national media coverage. But unless some development is undertaken, it becomes more difficult for research to assist in producing coverage that reaches into constructive and reorientational, as well as orientational, aspects.

Then, too, there is the possibility that coverage extensions and innovations could lead to a better liking for participation by citizens. The ominous demand by decision making for full information and calculation of values might have something to do with apparent voter apathy.

Citizen participation and particular institutional developments in the campaign would both benefit if we were to broaden our scope as communication researchers, to the extent implied by the ROC paradigm. Then we would be able to take the point of view of citizens, as they try to cope with the election before the fact. Then we may be more understanding of those who are unskilled in decision making or who place themselves apart from the selection offered by the major party nominees.

From the point of view of citizens before an election, the first stage of their step toward commitment to a candidate (or act of commitment to a position of their own) is a questioning stage. Thinking begins here. We can quickly leap ahead in our thinking to say that what is involved is simply a choice among alternatives, thereby reducing our options to which direction we shall take. But we can question in many other ways. Doing so will include construction and reorientation in our approaches, as well as orientation. Decision making is one questioning strategy. Some others are:

Trial and error—we shall give someone new a chance and see how it works out;
Screening—we know what kind of a leader we need; we can sort through the candidates until we find one;
Following—we always follow the lead of this person; watch now;
Seeking—this is impossible to make sense of, we shall have to get help, somewhere and somehow;
Searching—we can look for the perfect candidate;
Pointed questioning—we shall ask about these conditions in particular, because we know what we want to know;
Judging—we shall weigh how we feel about this against how we feel about that;
Problem solving—we can define the situation as a problem, then see what solution is necessitated by that definition;
Checking—we know how we feel about things, but we had better check before proceeding;
Hypothesis testing—we seem to need a leader of this type—so let's test that possibility;
Discussing—we collectively can better comprehend our situation if we share various kinds of information;
Debating—we collectively can sharpen our options if we subject them to mutual analysis.

Some of these strategies are largely orientational (seeking, searching, asking a pointed question, following, decision making, judging). Some make use of reorientation (checking, trial and error, debating). Construction seems involved in several (problem solving, hypothesis testing, screening). Clearly, these strategies were never formulated to provide examples of the various ways of thinking; rather experience and initiative in thinking has produced a number of ways to try to handle the imposing challenge of freedom inherent in taking steps. Lines of demarcation are not clear-cut. But it is not important that they should be. It is not a content analysis of activities that we envision. What we want to accomplish is a wider sweep of research on the behavior of citizens coming to the election campaign in their various ways. Then research can make evident the usage and the utilities of usage for these various ways. From this, citizens may improve their questioning repertoire, so they need not feel trapped by decision making (liking neither the alternatives nor the mechanism itself). From this, we can better know what it is about these modes of questioning that seems productive, so that we can construct new communicative institutions for our election campaigns, to be tried out in turn (like the suggested debate variations).

Citizens who are unprepared for, or dissatisfied with, the decision-making approach to campaigning may well find our peculiar horse race to be a shallow game. They may opt to manage themselves, using their intellectual resources (especially of reorientation and construction) on private undertakings. They live inside the economy and geography of the country, so to speak, but outside the polity. This does not produce the collective strength on which a free people must occasionally rely.

Communication research has an inside track in furthering a productive democracy and protecting our freedom. Collective behavior is produced by communicating. When we study communicating, before the fact, we must see construction at work—along with orientation and reorientation. As we study communicating in the perspective of this ROC paradigm, we are more likely to come up with findings applicable to societal needs.

2

THE MAKING OF THE DEBATES

Herbert E. Alexander and Joel Margolis

The Federal Communications Act of 1934 stated that if broadcasters allowed a political candidate to "use" their stations, the latter had to give "equal time opportunities" to all other candidates for that office. In 1959, Congress passed an amendment to the 1934 act that exempted bona fide newscasts, news interviews, news documentaries, and on-the-spot coverage of news events from the equal-time rule.

One year later, Congress suspended Section 315, the so-called equal-time section of the act, but only for that year and only for the presidential campaigns. The three major television networks had sought repeal of Section 315, but Congress would agree only to a one-year suspension; key members of Congress had voiced the fear that the networks would have an undue influence on political campaigns in this country. Upon winning the Democratic presidential nomination, Senator John F. Kennedy challenged Vice-President Richard Nixon, the Republican party's nominee, to a series of debates. After some hesitation, Nixon agreed, and four one-hour debates were held in September and October 1960.

Following his inauguration, John Kennedy had promised to debate his opponent in 1964, but his assassination intervened. In 1964, Senate Democrats defeated a resolution suspending the equal-time provision on the grounds that it would be unwise for an incumbent president, Lyndon Johnson, to engage in televised debates. Interestingly, Senator Barry Goldwater, President Johnson's opponent, agreed that there was a danger that an incumbent might reveal foreign policy secrets during debates.

In 1968, House and Senate Republicans prevented passage of a resolution suspending the equal-time provision. Vice-President Hubert Humphrey, who had avoided debates with Senators Robert Kennedy and Eugene McCarthy in the prenomination period, sought one with Richard Nixon in the general election.

Nixon said that he would agree to the debates only if Governor George Wallace were included; Humphrey refused this condition, and no debates took place. (Nixon led in the polls and presumably thought debates might upset his lead.)

In 1972, the Senate repealed the equal-time provision for the presidential election but the House killed it. President Nixon stated he opposed repeal of the provision unless it applied to congressional, as well as presidential, candidates. Nixon refused to debate his Democratic opponent, Senator George McGovern.

In sum, in the three presidential elections after 1960, the candidates who led in the polls (Lyndon Johnson in 1964 and Richard Nixon in 1968 and 1972) avoided debates with their opponents, and their party members in Congress prevented suspension of Section 315. In 1968 and 1972, the trailing major party candidates sought them, while the favored candidate usually hid behind the equal-time provision.

On September 25, 1975, the ground rules were changed. The Aspen Institute Program on Communications and Society petitioned the Federal Communications Commission (FCC) to exempt presidential debates from the equal-time provision if the debates were: (1) covered live and completely and (2) sponsored by an organization other than the networks. The FCC ruled that such political debates were bona fide news events and thus exempt from the equal-time law. This reversed a 1962 ruling. In addition, the commission altered its position on candidates' news conferences. Reversing a 1964 decision, the FCC excluded these, too, from the equal-time requirement.

LEAGUE OF WOMEN VOTERS' PRESIDENTIAL FORUMS

In the spring of 1975, Marjorie and Charles Benton and Gene Pokorny developed a proposal for a series of "presidential forums" to be held during the presidential primaries in the winter and spring of 1976. In July 1975, the William Benton Foundation authorized a planning grant of $50,000 to develop the idea on condition that the program was certain to be implemented. The money was to be made available in October 1975. James Karayn, former head of National Public Affairs Center for Television, was, through its Education Fund, a consultant to the Benton Foundation, and discussion began with several major organizations involved in public television. Following the September 1975 ruling, Karayn and Charles Benton suggested to the League of Women Voters that it sponsor a series of forums with the various presidential candidates during the primaries.

With a subsequent grant of $150,000 from the William Benton Foundation, the League's Presidential Forums were launched in the prenomination period, with Karayn as the director of the project. The forums were directed jointly by the League, Karayn, and a steering committee that included the forums' prominent public officials and private citizens. The forums resembled town meetings, and they were held in public meeting places with live audiences of between 500 and 1,000 persons. All presidential candidates who had qualified for public funding under the Federal Election Commission's ruling and were on the ballot in primaries grouped by region were invited to participate. Since both President Gerald Ford and Governor Ronald Reagan declined to participate, the forums turned out to be all-Democratic events. The president's advisers considered, and then rejected, a Ford-Reagan debate. The president argued that debates were useful only if the views of the candidates were not well known. This, he said, was not the case for either Governor Reagan or himself.

Originally, the League had arranged five forums, each dealing with a separate and important political topic. The final forum, scheduled for Los Angeles, was canceled because none of the candidates agreed to participate, an indication of the low priority most of them placed on the California primary; Carter's nomination seemed certain by then.

The forums were moderated by Elie Abel, dean of Columbia University's Graduate School of Journalism, and ran from one and one-half to two and one-half hours in length. Questions were posed by a regional panel of individuals knowledgeable about the topic under discussion. Queries from the audiences were used, although they were screened before being asked. The forums were carried live and in their entirety by whichever stations in the Public Broadcasting System accepted them; National Public Radio also offered the forums to their stations.

From the data available, it appears that only a small proportion of the potential audience watched the programs. In New York City, for example, approximately 3.5 percent of the television audience watched the forum held in that city (New York *Times* April 1, 1976); about the same proportion of viewers tuned in to watch the debate in Miami. The viewer audience for the Boston program was too small to register on the Nielsen ratings. None of the commercial networks carried any of the forums, although they were offered them.

Each of the major Democratic candidates, with the exception of George Wallace, participated in at least one debate (Table 2.1). Jimmy Carter participated in three of the four. Whether or not a candidate participated in a given debate seemed to be an indication of how well he thought he would do in the corresponding primary or primaries, and the importance he attached to the outcome.

It is hard to determine what impact, if any, the forums had on the outcome of the primaries or the convention. As to the League, it had previous experience in presenting candidates' night programs. While the forums preceded serious thought of general election debates, the fact that they generally were well received enhanced the legitimacy of the League's later proposal for debates between the two major presidential candidates in the general election.

TABLE 2.1

League of Women Voters' Presidential Forums

Date	City	Topic	Participants
February 23	Boston	High Employment, Low Inflation and Cheap Energy: Can We Have Them All?	Bayh, Carter, Harris, Jackson, Shapp, Shriver, Udall
March 1	Miami	From Social Security to Welfare: What's the National Responsibility?	Carter, Church, Harris, Jackson, Udall
March 28	New York City	Who Is Responsible for the Cities?	Carter, Church, Harris, Jackson, Udall
May 3	Chicago	Defense, Detente and Trade: What Are Our Goals?	Church, Udall
May 24	Los Angeles	Growth and the Environment: How Much Can We Control?	Canceled

Source: Compiled by the authors.

ARRANGING THE DEBATES

In April 1976, Jim Karayn, Ruth Clausen, chairman of the League of Women Voters' Education Fund, and Peggy Lampl, executive director of the League, met with network representatives and learned that they did not plan to sponsor debates between the Democratic and Republican presidential candidates in the fall. As a result, on May 5, the League of Women Voters announced that it would sponsor such a series of four debates and that it had initiated a drive to collect 4,000,000 signatures on petitions urging the major party presidential candidates to participate in a series of face-to-face debates.

The League's efforts were supported by many newspaper editorials, business and professional leaders, and, judging from the results of several public opinion polls, the general public. During the primary election period, League officials spoke with representatives of each of the major presidential contenders and sought promises that the candidates would agree to participate in a series of general election debates.

On August 19, 1976, the League sent telegrams to both President Ford and Jimmy Carter formally inviting them to debate. That evening, in his speech accepting the Republican nomination, the president declared: "I am ready, I am eager to go before the American people and debate the real issues, face to face, with Jimmy Carter." Candidate Carter soon accepted the president's challenge and stated that he had planned to issue a similar statement the day following the president's nomination speech.

Why did the 1976 debates take place? These were only the second set of televised presidential debates in American history, the first in 16 years. Lyndon Johnson and Richard Nixon could use Section 315 of the Federal Communications Act to avoid debating their opponents; Gerald Ford did not have this advantage. Johnson and Nixon were comforted by the fact that they had large leads over their opponents in nearly all the polls; Gerald Ford did not have that advantage.

President Ford, the first chief executive in American history to enter the office as a result of a resignation by his predecessor, trailed in the polls by a wide margin. His party was associated in the public's mind with economic recession, and in 1976 the nation was in the midst of one. Only one in five Americans called himself a Republican. Gerald Ford, who had entered the presidency with the nation's best wishes, had seen his support plummet after his unexpected pardon of Richard Nixon. From his perspective, the prospect of challenging his opponent to a series of debates seemed to be a good idea. He may have agreed with one of his assistant who argued that the president had nowhere to go but up in the polls. Moreover, by issuing the challenge, instead of merely responding to one from Jimmy Carter (which is what would have happened had he waited only 12 more hours), he gained some public support.

Why did Jimmy Carter accept? Despite his massive lead in the polls, the Democratic nominee was not as well known as the president. In addition, he was concerned about charges that he was not specific on the issues but rather sought to appeal to a broad coalition with only vague generalities. While the president's camp viewed the debates as an opportunity to force Carter to take clear and specific positions on a host of controversial issues, the Democratic nominee felt that they would show the contrast between the Ford record (numerous vetoes of social programs) and the president's rhetoric (an improved economy). Moreover, Carter as well as Ford confronted an electorate that contained the largest percentage of independent and undecided voters in American history. Thus, from both candidates' perspectives, there were incentives to accept the League of Women Voters' offer of a series of face-to-face debates. But, in addition to all of the reasons why the candidates agreed, there was another, and perhaps controlling, factor—the Federal Election Campaign Act Amendments of 1974; this connection will be noted shortly.

The League moved rapidly to set up the debates. On August 26, only one week after the president had issued his challenge, representatives from the Ford and Carter camps met with League representatives to begin negotiations. On September 1, the two sides announced their acceptance of League sponsorhip of the debates. In contrast to 1960, when more than a dozen meetings over a three-week period were held before agreement could be reached, in 1976 the two sides seemed eager to make arrangements for the confrontations. During the discussions, the Ford and Carter representatives compromised on the number, the length, and the dates and sites of the debates, as well as the topics to be covered in each debate. At no time did either side adopt a "take-or-or-leave-it" attitude.

RESPONSE OF THE COMMERCIAL TELEVISION NETWORKS

In contrast to the candidates' willingness, the three major commercial television networks were unhappy with the proposed arrangements. After President Ford and Governor Carter had agreed to debate, NBC and CBS sought to have Congress suspend the equal-time provision of the 1934 Federal Communications Act, as was done in 1960. Senator John Pastore, chairman of the Communications Subcommittee of the Senate Commerce Committee, and probably the most influential legislator in the area of communications, refused on the grounds that the League's plans were well advanced. Pastore's views were echoed by Representative Lionel Van Deelin, his House counterpart. Thus, the League's early development of a plan to hold the debates helped it overcome a potential source of trouble.

The networks complained that they would not, under the League's ground rules, be able to show audience reaction. The League had taken this position because neither of the candidates wanted shots panning the audience, feeling that the audience's reactions could influence home viewers. The networks felt that this restricted their liberties and was a form of prior censorship. CBS threatened to boycott the debates and, in an October letter to the New York *Times*, Reuven Frank, former president of NBC News, criticized the League for allowing the candidates to control the debates. The League replied that the charges were false. Further, they noted that in 1960, when the networks supposedly were running the show, the candidates were in a far more dominant position than in 1976. For instance, during the Kennedy-Nixon debates, representatives from each of the two sides were in the control rooms directing which camera shots should be shown on the air. In the end, the networks (as well as foreign broadcasters, and the USIA [United States Information Agency]) acquiesced and agreed to broadcast the debates. Each major network expected more than $2 million in unrecouped revenue loss from airing the debates. Since nearly all the advertising time for programs displaced by the debates had been sold, commercial time lost during the debates could not be made up later.

Another contention of the networks was that the candidates had vetoed some of the panelists. The League retorted that each of the candidates had agreed to submit a list of 45 names—15 print journalists, 15 television journalists, and 15 editorial writers or columnists—for each debate. These were added to other names of possible panelists. Then a six-person committee, composed of the three steering committee chairs—Rita Hauser, a prominent New York attorney, Charles Walker, former deputy secretary of the treasury, Newton

Minow, a former charman of the Federal Communications Commission—and League representatives—Ruth Clausen, Peggy Lampl, and James Karayn—made the final choices. The League stated that neither candidate exercised a veto over any panelist. Several CBS correspondents were invited to participate but declined because of their network's disagreement with ground rules.

THE LEGAL BATTLES

While the League sought to have President Ford and Governor Carter agree to a series of debates, the Federal Election Commission—after questioning by a reporter triggered a controversy—began to consider the question of whether the funding for the programs, or the presentations themselves, would constitute an illegal contribution during the general election.

The television networks' attempts to alter the technical aspects of televising the debates were not the only efforts made either to change them or to prevent them from being held at all. Other groups filed challenges relying on various legal arguments and appealed to several authorities, including the FCC. While most were divided as to the reasons for their suits, in the end all of them lost.

The League argued that the expenditure of funds for the debates was not a contribution, as the term is used in the Federal Election Campaign Act, because the debates were not designed to advance the candidacy of either Gerald Ford or Jimmy Carter, would serve an educational and informational purpose, and would advance the cause of free and robust speech. Furthermore, the League's Education Fund, by its by-laws, was prohibited from supporting candidates. In addition, the League's attorney contended that the term "contribution" in the Federal Election Campaign Act derived from the same term in the Federal Corrupt Practices Act. Under the latter act, the courts consistently had held that funds from labor unions and corporations were barred if they were given for the purpose of "active electioneering" on behalf of a candidate or party, but not if they were provided for information activities.

The Federal Election Commission (1976) in its August 30 ruling put the matter in a similar light. It ruled:

> In the limited circumstance of presidential debate, the costs incident thereto which will be incurred by the [League of Women Voters Education] Fund are neither contributions nor expenditures under 2 U.S.C. 441a and 431 of the Federal Election Campaign Act of 1971, as amended.

The Federal Election Commission (FEC) stated that it based its ruling on the League's history of nonpartisanship and educational activities and the fact that neither candidate was particularly advantaged by the debates. The FEC went on

The Making of the Debates

to allow the League to receive tax deductible funds from individual and corporate and labor political action committees, but it banned direct contributions from labor unions or corporations. The FEC reasoned as follows:

> The disbursements by the League Education Fund are nonetheless "in connection with" a Federal election and accordingly may not be made with funds from corporate or labor organization treasuries . . . or made by other persons forbidden to participate in the Federal election process by the Act.

The League, as might be expected, was upset with the FEC ruling, feeling that it might harm future nonpartison efforts to educate the electorate. As a result of the FEC's decision, the League, on September 11, was forced to issue a public appeal for funds to pay the cost of debates. Although permitted to do so, the League decided against accepting money from political action acommittees, on the grounds that the committees were established for campaign purposes; the League maintained that the debates were an educational, not a political, activity. The organization placed advertisements in a number of newspapers—including the New York *Times*, the Washington *Post*, the *Wall Street Journal*, the Los Angeles *Times*, and the *Christian Science Monitor*—and conducted a direct mail campaign. As of the end of 1977, the League had spent approximately $325,000 in connection with the debates—$233,000 from contributions and more than $92,000 from reserves and the operating budget of the Education Fund treasury.

Long after the debates were held, the legal battles continued. On February 9, 1977, the League, the Education Fund, and the League of Women Voters of Los Angeles, Inc. brought suit against the FEC in the U.S. District Court for the District of Columbia. The plaintiffs sought to have the court declare invalid that part of the FEC ruling that barred corporations and unions from contributing to the League to pay for the expenses of the debates.

The League noted that because the FEC ruling preventing it from accepting corporate and union offers made prior to the issuance of the policy statement to provide financial assistance in connection with the debates, it was required to incur expenses that it would not otherwise have incurred in attempting to raise funds from other sources. In addition, the League, as a corporation, was precluded from lending financial support to the Education Fund to defray the costs of those debates. Furthermore, since many of the League's state and local affiliates are incorporated, they presumably could not provide financial assistance to the fund either.

The FEC ruling not only prevented corporations and unions from contributing but also it forced several major incorporated foundations to rescind their promises to assist the League in paying the costs of the 1976 debates. In addition, the League argued in its suit that foundations, corporations, and unions would be unable to contribute if similar programs were held in the future.

The FEC asked the court to dismiss the League's complaint on April 12, 1977. Furthermore, it asked dismissal on the grounds that the "court had no jurisdiction over this matter because the Commission's policy statement is not a final action . . . but represents an attempt . . . to give informal advice in an uncharted area of the law."

After the suit and the FEC answer were filed, the FEC decided to reexamine its policy and called a hearing for comment. In testimony before the FEC in September 1977, the League argued that the ruling had a "chilling effect" on the organization's efforts to raise money to pay for the debates. As a result, the League fell short of its need to pay the bills. Education Fund Chairman Ruth Clausen stated that organizations might be reluctant to sponsor future debates unless the decision was overruled.

A former staff attorney for the FEC, Benjamin M. Vandegrift, explained the ruling and said the FEC "simply had not had enough experience with the political industry to understand the scope of what we were doing . . . . Stories about corporate political contributions, both foreign and domestic, were everyday occurrences . . . . It seemed better to err on the side of caution."

Charles Benton, president of the William Benton Foundation, testified that "Public financing imposes a new responsibility and mandate on candidates to make their views public . . . . Sooner or later you will have to tie together public financing and getting information . . . to the public."

Considerable time was spent during the hearing discussing the role of minor and independent candidates in future television debates. Nicholas Johnson, former member of the FCC, noted that some Democratic voters might have been influenced had McCarthy been allowed to participate in the Ford-Carter debates. "Television is the ballgame in politics . . . . If minor parties are kept off television, they will be weak. If they are given access to it, they will be strong."

A memorandum was submitted by the Chamber of Commerce of the United States commenting on the FEC policy and seeking to permit corporations to lend assistance in the future for nonpartisan activities that facilitate an informed and educated electorate.

In December 1977, the FEC approved a proposed regulation that would allow corporations and labor unions to donate funds to certain nonprofit groups to pay for the costs of sponsoring candidate debates. The contributions would be restricted to those nonprofit organizations that are exempt from federal taxation, that have a history of neither supporting nor endorsing candidates or political parties, and that administer the debates. The definition clearly applies to the League of Women Voters.

The proposed regulation was considered by the League as a limited reversal by the FEC, probably aimed at mooting the League's suit. However, the League felt the policy was still too restrictive, especially since it did not address the minor party or independent candidate issue or funding by lobby-type organizations covered by IRS ruling 501(C)(4). In any case, the proposed regulation is subject to congressional veto within 30 legislative days—as are all FEC regulations—once it is submitted in 1978 to Congress for consideration. At this writing, the League suit still stands.

We return now to the sequence of events in 1976. With the announcement that the president and his Democratic opponent had agreed to a series of televised debates, a number of challenges were filed to block or alter the programs. On September 17, Judge Aubrey E. Robinson, Jr., of the U.S. District Court, dismissed law suits brought by American party presidential candidate Tom Anderson and Independent presidential candidate Eugene McCarthy. The American party's suit contended that the debates were merely panel discussions and thus not exempt from the equal-time provision. In addition, the American party argued that sponsorship by the League of Women Voters was the equivalent of an illegal contribution to, and expenditure on behalf of, the two major party presidential candidates.

Five days later, the U.S. Court of Appeals for the District of Columbia upheld Judge Robinson. On September 24, the FCC refused to accept McCarthy's arguments that: (1) the League, in contradistinction to the FCC's 1975 ruling, were merely acting as an agent for the networks in arranging the debates, and thus the programs were not exempt from the equal-time provision as a bona fide news event; and (2) the debates were a violation of the fairness doctrine, since they would give the impression that McCarthy was not a bona fide candidate.

During this time, Lester Maddox, American Independent party candidate for President, sought relief as well. He, too, was unsuccessful. On September 20, the FCC rebuffed his petition for inclusion in the debates. One the same day, the FCC denied the request of the Socialist Workers party that its presidential candidate, Peter Camejo, be included. Later, attorneys for McCarthy and Camejo argued that during the first debate the program was stopped when a mechanical failure caused a 26-minute delay, contending that in a true news event the program would have continued. They overlooked the fact that the League had attempted to continue the debate but was unable to do so since the public address system for the Walnut Street Theatre was connected to the television feed system. As a result, in each of the subsequent debates, there were two separate systems; thus, if a similar problem arose, President Ford and Governor Carter could have continued their debate before the live audience.

On October 12, the United States Supreme Court refused to review three petitions that had been filed concerning the FCC's 1975 rulings. The plaintiffs included those groups that had lost in April before the U.S. Court of Appeals in the District of Columbia, plus the Socialist Workers party. Each of these petitions was opposed by the FCC, the League, the three networks, and the federal government. Finally, on October 22, Chief Justice Burger denied Eugene McCarthy extraordinary relief and refused to enjoin the debates. In sum, the debates, though challenged, were upheld.

FINANCIAL INCENTIVES TO DEBATE

For the first time in American history no private contributions were permitted in the general presidential election campaigns, and the candidates were under rigid financial limitations. Each major party candidate could spend, with party support, no more than a total of $25 million. This necessitated revisions in traditional campaign strategies. In particular, the media became an even more important tool. As Gerald Rafshoon (*Broadcasting* 1977), head of the Carter advertising team, put it: "You can control your dollars better with media. A couple of hundred thousand in a state doesn't buy a whole lot of workers or a lot of headquarters." But such a sum of money can have a significant impact if it is used for media expenditures.

Both the Ford and Carter campaigns spent close to one-half of their allotted funds on media efforts. The new campaign law seemed to encourage such activities, but for Jimmy Carter this was a natural outgrowth of previous political experience. Ever since he first ran for governor in 1966, the Democratic nominee had placed a heavy emphasis on television. During this entire period Gerald Rafshoon had been his key media adviser. Rafshoon was particularly attracted to five-minute television programs. During the campaign, he devoted a considerable part of the media budget to televising five-minute snippets of the Carter biography.

On the Republican side, Douglas Bailey and John Deardouff, codirectors of the Ford advertising campaign, signed on after the Republican national convention. In contrast to the Democrats' continuity, the Ford team was hired at the last minute, seemingly indicating a lack of advance planning on the president's part. Concentration on winning the nomination perhaps made planning difficult.

The 1971 and 1974 federal legislation had another impact on the presidential campaigns. It accelerated a trend that had been developing over the past several elections, namely, a centralization of broadcasting expenditures controlled by the national presidential organization. The 1972 Nixon campaign, for different reasons, exemplified this pattern and the 1976 Carter and Ford campaigns continued the tradition. There were severe political and legal consequences if candidates failed to account for each dollar spent.

COMPARING THE 1960 AND 1976 DEBATES

In general, the process of organizing and staging the debates was completed more easily and rapidly in 1976 than in 1960. Perhaps it was the nature of the two candidates compared with their counterparts in 1960, or perhaps it was the evolution of television and the political sophistication of both the candidates and the public that caused the 1976 discussions with the League to move so swiftly and smoothly.

Obviously, a key difference in the two elections was the basis for the debates. In 1960, it took an amendment to the 1934 Federal Communications Act to enable Kennedy and Nixon to meet. The 1976 contests grew out of a ruling by the FCC. As a consequence, the Ford-Carter debates were sponsored by an outside organization, the League of Women Voters' Education Fund, whereas in 1960 the networks had run the shows. While the 1960 contents had been held in television studios without live audiences, the 1976 debates were held on a specially designed set that was moved to each of the four locations, none of which was a studio. Each of the 1976 programs was presented before a live audience.

In terms of length, each of the Kennedy-Nixon debates ran for one hour. In 1976, the three presidential debates lasted for 90 minutes, while the vice-presidential program was 15 minutes shorter. In general, the candidates in 1976 had more time to answer the questions posed than did their 1960 counterparts.

In 1960, the broadcast journalists who participated had been selected by the networks and the print journalists included had been chosen by lot. In 1976, the League of Women Voters sought panelists from a broader selection pool, including regional as well as national correspondents.

The League's efforts reflected lessons learned from the 1960 debates. Moreover, in 1976, the Presidential Forums held in the spring gave experience in planning and handling such matters. The networks 16 years earlier had no unified plan for the debates, while the League did. Despite the early preparations, the attendant publicity, and the League's efforts, the proportion of households that watched the first debate in 1976 was smaller than the percentage that had viewed the initial Kennedy-Nixon confrontation. Nevertheless, from the data available, it appears that about 75 to 95 million Americans viewed each program. According to Nielsen figures, the proportion of households watching declined from the first (53.5 percent) through the second (52.49 percent) and third (47.79 percent) presidential debates, with the smallest audience, 35.5 percent of the households, tuning in for the Dole-Mondale contests. In all, 90 percent of households saw at least one debate. The average household in the United States saw 2.8 of the debates. The viewing figures for the debates were, nevertheless, considerably higher than for the highest rated television shows (League of Women Voters 1977).

RESPONSE TO THE DEBATES: CANDIDATES AND VOTERS

How did the two candidates view the debates? Both considered them to be crucial to their campaigns—they both prepped for them, with Ford going through several full-scale mock rehearsals. Both thought the debates were good for the American public. In an October press conference, the president remarked,

"I think [the debates] have been very wholesome. I think they've been constructive." Shortly after the election, Jimmy Carter echoed a similar sentiment, "The debates were good for the country. They were a good educational process and gave the people a good look at us and how we handled the issues." James Karayn, director of the debates, agreed: "The public won on this one as far as I'm concerned" (*Broadcasting* October 18, 1976: p. 26).

Of course not everyone voiced the same sentiments. Some individuals contended that the debates had too much image, not enough focus on the issues. Obviously, the debates were not truly debates in the sense that forensic specialists use the term. There was not a stated proposition on which the two candidates took opposing sides. However, they did provide the American public with an opportunity to see the two major candidates face-to-face, answering the same questions sequentially. In most campaigns, the public has no such advantage. Normally, voters are exposed to messages from one or the other candidate, carefully controlled to present a point of view or to eliminate completely any possibility of a mistake. The League of Women Voters noted, "The debates . . . may have counterbalanced the effect of the candidates' own television presentations . . . . The debates presented the candidates in a neutral setting." They also provided the candidates with the largest possible audience. Moreover, the president and his challenger used each of the debates as the basis for subsequent campaign remarks.

Ironically, in the end, the debates may have benefited Ford as well as Carter. Important supporters of both candidates, as well as at least one of the candidates, seem to agree.

Patrick Caddell, Carter's pollster, stated that the debates helped Carter win by interrupting the presidential campaign at three key points. In each case, Ford was closing in on Carter and the debates seemed to slow down or reverse the president's momentum. Carter was even more explicit:

> There was a general feeling that I had lost the first debate because of what I subjectively analyzed as an overly deferential attitude toward Mr. Ford.
>
> I think the debates let the American people be kind of reassured that "well, at least, Jimmy Carter has some judgment about foreign affairs and defense and all" (Wooten 1976).
>
> I have a feeling that had it not been for the debates, I would have lost (*Broadcasting* January 3, 1977a).

There is no public statement on whether Ford thought the debates had helped or hurt his campaign. But his staff believed they gave his campaign a lift by, in effect downgrading all the campaign activity between the Republican presidential convention and the first debate, thus giving the Republican side a chance to get organized following a close contest through the time of the convention.

Tens of millions of potential voters watched the programs. But what actual impact did they have? The League of Women Voters (1977) noted:

> The effect of the debates on the election is far from simple. They are knitted into the whole campaign and it is difficult to unravel the different strands. Their impact was felt in the image they formed in the public's mind about the characters of the candidates, the hard substantive information they provided the voters on issues, the generation of public excitement in the debates as a "sporting event" with a winner and a loser, information and blunders made by the candidates becoming the fodder for further campaign stands and statements, and the fact that the debates took the place of other traditional campaign strategy.

Several polls indicated that the public's interest in the campaign increased as it developed; the debates may have contributed, although the same result can be seen in presidential elections in which there were no debates. Some surveys showed an increase in the electorate's level of information about the campaign. Here, the impact of the debates is probably more certain. But, judging from earlier studies, it is likely that the debates reinforced, rather than converted, many voters. Given the closeness of the election, it is conceivable that Governor Carter's margin was dependent on his showing in the debates, as he himself claimed.

Two election-day polls give some food for thought. A CBS poll found that 10 percent of its sample agreed with the following statement: "I was impressed by [my candidate] in the debates"; 12 percent stated that they had made up their minds about whom to vote for during the debates. No data were provided on the distribution of Ford and Carter voters on this question.

The results of an NBC survey were different. One-third of its sample stated that they had made up their minds during the debates, while one-half of the sample said that the debates had had no impact on their vote. Of the individuals interviewed, 3 percent stated that they had switched their choice as a result of the debate; again, no data were provided on Ford and Carter voters separately.

Whatever their impact, the debates were, in a sense, extralegal. The 1974 Amendments to the Federal Election Campaign Act provided that no presidential candidate, including party support, could spend more than $25 million in the general election. Yet, the debates gave the candidates an immense exposure to the electorate not contemplated by the election law, and thus could be considered an evasion of the expenditure limits. The debates were thought by many to have discriminated against minor party and independent candidates.

Of course, the debates were sanctioned by key members of Congress, the FCC, the FEC, a federal district judge, a federal court of appeals, and the United

States Supreme Court. Nevertheless, they raise serious issues about the future of presidential elections in this country. If such programs were to become a permanent fixture on the American political landscape, they would benefit the two major parties at the expense of other organized political entities in the country. They would further enhance the role of television and the three commercial networks, as well as the League of Women Voters, if it remains as the sponsor. Although President Carter has not committed himself to appearing in 1980, Gerald Ford's actions, while an incumbent president, will make it difficult for him to avoid them.

The debates point to the problem of using ceilings rather than floors in regulating campaign expenditures. With limitations on expenditures, it is essential that candidates not go over the allocated maximum. They and their supporters have incentives to seek ways of receiving assistance in a manner that will not be counted against their totals (for example, using volunteer rather than paid workers). The debates produced a similar outcome, an activity not counted against the limits, yet providing exposure worth many dollars.

3

A COMPARATIVE PERSPECTIVE ON PRESIDENTIAL DEBATES: ISSUE EVOLUTION IN 1960 AND 1976

Robert G. Meadow and Marilyn Jackson-Beeck

In all but two presidential elections, nearly all voters were informed about candidates and issues indirectly and sporadically, as relevant information happened their way through conversations, pamphlets, posters, advertisements, news, and editorials. Typically, the public was forced into a condition of dependency on gatekeepers working within mass media institutions, within localities. But of course the situation was different in the 1960 and 1976 elections, for those campaign periods were marked, if not defined, by nationally televised presidential debates featuring the presidential and vice-presidential candidates.

In 1960 and 1976, the public was thus afforded rare opportunities to escape the typical pattern of dependency on secondhand accounts of campaign events. It had opportunities to see and hear the candidates directly present themselves and their issue positions in response to each other, within the context of journalists' questions and specified time limits, on network television.

Tens of millions of voters in 1960 and 1976 saw and heard the major party candidates as they acted, interacted, and exposed their persons, ideas, and nerves. As a result, voters had the raw material from which to assess similarities

---

The authors wish to thank the Institute for Applied Communications Studies for research support. Survey data in this chapter were made available by the Inter-University Consortium for Political and Social Research, via the University of Pennsylvania Social Science Data Center. The 1976 data were originally collected by the Center for Political Studies of the Institute for Social Research, the University of Michigan, under a grant from the National Science Foundation. Neither the original collectors of the data nor the consortium bear any responsibility for the analyses and interpretations presented here.

or differences between Kennedy and Nixon, and Carter and Ford. At the same time, voters exposed to both debate series had an opportunity to consider the samenesses and differences characterizing politics and presidential elections across the span of 16 years, 1960-76.

While each election seems so very special, with its own unique characteristics encapsulating four-year chunks of history, the similarities of debate format and, as we shall see, discussion imply the opposite. Aside from improved technology and sophistication of production and packaging, differences between the 1960 and 1976 debate series were fairly minor. What distinguishes the 1976 debates is that they took place in an atmosphere structured by the mythology surrounding recollections of the "great" (Siepmann 1962) 1960 debates. The experiences of the 1960 debates—for candidates, producers, and voters—were largely responsible for what occurred in 1976.

The first debates in both the 1960 and 1976 series, widely held to have been the most important in each grouping, were expressly presented as vehicles for informing the electorate. For example, in 1976, Edwin Newman, moderator, said the debates were arranged "in the hope of promoting a wider and better informed participation by the American People in the election in November." In 1960, Howard K. Smith, moderator, stated that television and radio stations provided "facilities for a discussion of issues in the current political campaign." These two debates were held at about the same point in the campaign, late in September, about three weeks after the beginning of the campaign season (Labor Day).

Both debate series were born of delicate negotiations among the candidates, lawmakers, citizen groups, and the networks (compare Chapter 2 in this volume and Kraus 1962). In both cases, candidates' preparations were exhausting, as they strove to learn new material and to present themselves in the best way possible. Nixon's poor appearance in the first 1960 debate was widely referenced, so much so that the candidates in 1976 were extraordinarily careful to look and try to do their best. Observers also noted that the candidates debated each other in 1960, to the exclusion of the viewing audience; this was changed in 1976, as the candidates were viewed addressing the audience. To some extent, the candidates of 1976 had "come of age" in the electronic era of politics begun with the televised convention of 1952 (Lang and Lang, 1968).

HISTORICAL SETTING OF THE DEBATES

The time frames in which the 1960 and 1976 debates occurred were not altogether different. In 1960, the United States was just emerging from an economic recession that had begun during the latter years of the 1953-61 Republican administration. The country had been at peace for eight years following the conclusion of hostilities in Korea under Eisenhower, yet the cold war was raging.

The civil rights movement had yet to get under way. Government spending for social services was relatively low, and inflation was scarcely a problem. In short, while these were indeed crucial issues of the day, they had not reached the public agenda.

In 1976, economic difficulties also were present. During the last years of the Nixon administration, and through the Ford administration, there was an economic recession, this time accompanied by high levels of inflation. Again the country was at peace following the troop withdrawals from South Vietnam, again under a Republican president. But there were some differences compared with 1960. The cold war had been replaced by detente. Resources were in short supply; indeed, belief in unlimited economic growth and American global supremacy was no longer firmly held. The turmoil of the 1960s in urban areas and on the campuses had taken its toll. And, in 1976, Watergate was not too far distant.

As for the candidates, both major party nominees in 1960 were non-incumbents. The Republican candidate, Richard M. Nixon, was vice-president for two terms previous. He was widely known, and secured the nomination with little difficulty. Nixon was considered to be an effective debater following his "kitchen debate" with Nikita Khrushchev in 1959. Furthermore, based on his "Checkers" speech in 1952, he had earned a reputation as an effective television performer (Lang and Lang 1968). Senator John F. Kennedy was lesser known, despite the long primary and state caucus battles prior to his nomination. Although he had been a member of Congress for 14 years and was briefly considered for the vice-presidential nomination in 1956, he had considerably less national stature than Nixon. Nevertheless, each candidate saw advantages to debating. Nixon seemed to approach it as an opportunity to reinforce his experience and presidential bearing; Kennedy may have had foreseen a chance to become better known and dispel impressions that he was too young and too Catholic to be president.

In 1976, Gerald R. Ford was an incumbent president, but had not been elected. He was appointed by his predecessor and fellow debater (in 1960) Richard M. Nixon, following the resignation of Nixon's first vice-president, Spiro T. Agnew. As the Watergate scandal unfolded and Nixon's role was exposed, Nixon resigned, and thus Ford, in August 1974, became the only president to succeed to the presidency without having been nationally elected. Ford seemed to restore a degree of public confidence in government during his two-year tenure prior to the 1976 election. His demeanor, if ordinary, was countered by a presidency not uneventful: the pardon of Richard Nixon; continued economic recession; the fall of South Vietnam and its neighbors following the American troop withdrawal. Within the Republican party, Ford faced a stiff and serious challenge from a conservative Republican, Ronald Reagan, before winning the nomination by a thin margin. It was in his acceptance speech at the convention that the challenge to debate was issued to the Democratic nominee, Jimmy Carter.

Jimmy Carter was virtually an unknown before 1976, having been a governor of Georgia but out of office for over a year. Yet, after a long, successful primary election campaign, he emerged with the Democratic nomination by a sound majority of convention delegates. Perhaps as a result of extensive television coverage of the numerous primaries, he was far better known to the public by the time of the Democratic convention than other contenders had been in earlier elections. His famous smile and earnest speech made him appear fresh, positive, and enthusiastic. Moreover, he was a smart politician who developed a lead in the omnipresent "trial heats" of the polling organizations.

As for the debates, there were only minor differences between 1960 and 1976. The equal-time requirements of Section 315 of the Federal Communications Act of 1934 had been suspended in 1960, but not in 1976. However, in practice this imposed no constraints on the 1976 debates. In 1960, there were four debates, including one—a split-screen debate—in which Nixon responded to questions from a studio in Los Angeles, while Kennedy responded from a studio in New York. The debates in 1960 were 60 minutes long compared with 90 minutes in 1976. Finally, in the first 1960 debate, the candidates were allowed opening statements of eight minutes each, while there were no opening statements in 1976—although both in 1960 and 1976 there were closing statements.

In light of the many similarities in 1960 and 1976 debate format and context, it seems only reasonable to expect debate content to be much the same despite the passage of sixteen years. The process we call "issue evolution," in other words, would be reflected by mostly parallel debate discussion at the two time points, combined with some predictable but unparalleled discussion appropriate to time and speaker idiosyncracy. However, in the absence of systematic and comparable content analysis of 1960 and 1976 debate issues, there is no scientific means of supporting this contention.

Until our own comparative content analysis of 1960 and 1976 debate content, beginning in 1977, the necessary content data were not available. Why would this be? One reason is that political scientists, until recently, had reason to doubt that issue discussion is terribly important. The classic voting studies (Lazarsfeld, Berelson, and Gaudet 1948; Berelson, Lazarsfeld, and McPhee 1954) suggested, instead, that social characteristics and party identification or candidate image determine the vote (Campbell, Gurin, and Miller 1954; Campbell et al. 1960). But in the past decade, since Key (1966) and others asserted that "voters are no fools," political scientists have awakened to the importance of of candidate- and campaign-specific factors.

For contemporary political communication researchers, the issues and images presented in televised presidential debates are definitely important, for reasons in addition to predicting voters' behavior. Not only do debates provide information on candidates and their issue positions but also their analysis makes it possible to address related questions illuminating the role of mass communication in the political process. One question raised by debates concerns gatekeeping and its sociopolitical meaning. While campaign news is not found to be biased in terms of ideological preference or distribution of coverage (Frank 1973; Meadow 1973; Hofstetter 1976), studies by Graber (1971), Funkhouser (1973), and Meadow (1976) show that only a limited number of issues are reported.

Candidates themselves often discuss many more issues—and those in much greater detail—than media reports indicate, depending on which of two ways mass media institutions choose to present campaign issues. They could present issues discussed by the candidates by printing or broadcasting speeches verbatim and/or by providing detailed, accurate summaries. In this case, voters have nearly direct access to candidates' issue positions. The second, and more typical, method by which mass media operate is to selectively report issues, concentrating on those presumed to be important to the audience or those preferred by gatekeeping editors and publishers. Voters, therefore, have a small "agenda" of media-reported issues (McCombs and Shaw 1972; McLeod, Becker, and Byrnes 1974; Benton and Frazier 1976) that they may view, or about which they can read, during most election campaigns.

If access to issue information is not restricted (as in debates), the public can be expected to enjoy more complete knowledge of candidate positions and policy preferences. Provided that issue-oriented voting occurs, of course, this would fortify popular sovereignty. But to the extent that information is managed by gatekeepers, the situation is reversed. Bases of knowledge are restricted and, therefore, so is popular potential to govern. Whether one or the other system of reporting is maintained is thus a question of public policy at the institutional and social levels.

From a policy perspective, issue evolution analysis can yield insight into yet another question. Are the debates really useful in terms of providing issue information from which potential voters and other audiences can draw? Independent of the uses to which the debates are put by voters and other individuals, the debates may fail to address issues. But with systematically conducted content analysis, the extent to which issues were addressed in 1960 and 1976 can be assessed. Whether issues are or are not addressed, policy makers would have a sound foundation on which to build decisions to institutionalize, expand, or eliminate debates in the future.

ISSUE EVOLUTION IN 1960 AND 1976

From the issue evolutionary perspective taken in this chapter, the presidential debates of 1960 and 1976 are accorded larger meaning than usual. In most debate research (compare Katz and Feldman 1962), the focus is on debates' meaning for individual vote decisions. While an issue evolutionary approach lies within established traditions of debate research (Kraus 1962; Lang and Lang 1961; Ellsworth 1965), it differs somewhat in method and time perspective. Evolutionary treatment of political issues stems from prior analysis of content (in this case, the text of the debates) and a concern for historical comparison. This means, first, that the focus of our research is not so much on individual voters as on the meaning of the debates to the public and public institutions. Second, the research focuses on substantive issues, while providing a context for the analysis of candidates' style.

In our view, issue evolution provides a useful framework for analyzing political communication events. Since it examines debate issues—aspects of the political environment with joint relevance for political scientists and mass communication researchers—we believe it may help to integrate research approaches that often begin with different assumptions and goals.

It is unfortunate, but true, that most social scientists' view of presidential debate content is consistent with popular notions of the debates: since "nothing" was said in the debates, presumably there is no content to analyze. While this lack of content research (save Ellsworth's [1965] effort and recent work by Becker et al., forthcoming, and Miller and MacKuen [1977]) may not have hampered "individual effects" researchers, the absence of knowledge of debate content may not correspond with the needs of those who study the debates as important communication events. It is to us a curious fact that the verbal message partially responsible for any debate effects have so rarely been given sustained, systematic, objective, quantified study. Researchers have acted as if they knew what was said, or could ignore what was said. At the same time, in their efforts to assess the social value of the debates, policy makers apparently have felt unhindered by the absence of reliable data on exactly what was discussed.

We feel that the constitution of the existing body of debate literature is rather weak because of the general absence of relevant content analysis. Lacking objective knowledge of the content, researchers have focused on the debates most often as political events in the context of the presidential campaigns. However, with the fruits of content analysis, research can treat the debates as communication events, in a meaningful way not only for voters and candidates but also for mass media analysts, policy makers, and communication researchers.

In the context of debate research, content analysis offers one means of investigating issue evolution. At the simplest level, it provides a framework for objectively quantifying and otherwise analyzing the characteristics of candidate statements in the debates. Candidate (and questioner) statements can be categorized along numerous dimensions. For example, one can explore the amount of attention given to certain issues in terms of the amount of time, or number of words, devoted to those issues. Or the researcher can construct a mosaic of how the candidate views the political system from the number and type of descriptive references to groups, economic actors or government agencies, and so forth.

More traditional uses of content analytic techniques also contribute to the issue evolutionary perspective. Debates as major events occurring during political campaigns are widely reported in both print and electronic news media. However, it often has been argued and widely documented that mass media report only a limited quantity of information available to them. Through analysis of the manifest content of news media, the extent to which the debates are reported, the issues that are emphasized, the attention given to substance versus styles of the debaters, and so forth can be quantified. In conjunction with a content analysis of the debates, the extent to which media reports deviate from the actual debates in terms of issues emphasized and other dimensions can be measured.

Another way that content analysis is used in debate and issue evolution research is by establishing a basis by which to determine the extent to which issues of concern to the public are addressed. For example, if we assume that public opinion polls ascertaining the issues most important to voters in choosing a candidate are accurate reflections of true voter issue interest, then we have a hierarchical ordering of salient issues. If we can assume further that candidates try to address the issues of concern to the electorate, through analysis of the debates, we can measure the extent to which this goal is met. Of course, it can be argued that candidates in the present debate format are constrained by the questions asked. But there is considerable leeway in responding to questions or rebutting answers, and closing statements exist for the candidates to address whatever issues they desire. At the same time, the questions themselves reveal the extent to which media correspondents perceive issues to be important and reflect the distance of media correspondents' perceptions of the issues from the public's issue conceptions.

METHODS

To address our research questions, a three-phase design was required. In phase one, the first 1960 and 1976 debates were content analyzed, issue by issue, on the basis of accurate transcripts. The 1960 debate transcripts used were provided by Clevenger, Parson, and Polisky (1962). These were prepared by a panel who repeatedly reviewed professional quality audiotapes. The 1976 debate transcripts were prepared by the authors from studio-quality videotapes (see Chapter 12). Each transcript is complete in that it includes all utterances by all the debate participants (moderators, questioners, and candidates), including vocalized pauses such as um, er, uh, and so forth, as well as errors of fluency and nonwords or word fragments. (It is interesting to note that "verbatim" transcripts of the debates appearing in the New York *Times*, besides excluding vocalized pauses and errors of fluency, contained errors and omissions.)

Both debates were coded by a coder-pair using major issues within speaker turns as the unit of analysis. A total of 13 domestic issues paralleling cabinet functions formed the basis for issue identification, plus two nonissue categories covering debate formalities. Within issue units, subissues and other debate content were recorded (for example, references to political officials, ethnic and nationality groups, economic factors, dates and times, political symbols, and metaphoric language). Also, the number of words per issue was noted.

Issues were chosen as the unit of analysis to parallel our interest in issue evolution. First, and most important, was a desire for the maximum amount of information on each major issue raised. Practicality was a second concern as other conceivable coding units such as the sentence, speaker turn, or question-response-follow-up/question-rebuttal cluster were indeterminable. Sentences could not be examined because the 1976 transcribers found no satisfactory method by which to determine where true sentences ended and others began. (Often speakers continued without pause, and many "sentences" ran on or consisted of clauses repeatedly joined by conjunctions.) Speaker turns in many cases covered more than one major issue, which would have inhibited detailed analysis of the specific characteristics associated with each issue. Question clusters were rejected as a unit of analysis because the candidates and questioners so often changed the subject during follow-up and rebuttal.

Debate issues were defined according to the following definition applied by a coder-pair: "topics raised by candidates or questioners relating to substantive areas of controversy or conflict within the social or political system." Multiple issues or units could be housed within individual speaker turns; further, within issue units up to ten "subissues" (that is, substantive concerns) were coded.

Domestic issue categories covered government, transportation and communication, housing, urban problems, health, education, social welfare, economics, foreign affairs, defense, resources, law, and science. Subissues included topics such as federal spending, inflation, unemployment, size and scope of federal government, morality of government, structure of government, candidates' leadership qualifications, energy, crime, urban blight, and so forth. By definition, each speaker turn in the debates housed at least one issue, but the number of subissues varied.

Broad issues in the debates were further examined for subissues, for "discrete" or specific issues, or programs mentioned in passing and in limited detail. For example, in a question or response dealing with programs to stop inflation, the broad issue would be "domestic economics," while the subissue might be "inflation," with discrete issues perhaps including "wage and price controls," "tax reform," and other specifics. A question of government reorganization would be coded under the broad issue "domestic government," with "government reorganization" as a subissue, and discrete issues perhaps of "government employment," "zero-based budgeting," and "bureaucracy." Overall, during the 1960 debate, 80 major issue units were identified during the 65 speaker turns, while in 1976, there were 98 over 86 speaker turns.

Reliability tests conducted up to six months after original coding of the debates showed content data used in our analysis to be satisfactorily reliable. Using Holsti's (1969) percentage of agreement formula, average reliability was 92 percent.

The second phase of the research involved comparing those issues raised in the debates with media accounts of what issues were discussed by the debate participants. This aspect of the design permitted a comparison between objective measure of what transpired—with the luxury of no time deadline and a transcript in hand—with subjective accounts by reporters working without the benefit of transcripts, under nearly instantaneous deadlines. Specifically, the late editions of the New York *Times* for two days following the first 1960 and 1976 debates were content analyzed for debate news, and particularly for the issues that were emphasized. The postdebate edition of two national newsweeklies—*Time Magazine* and *Newsweek*—whose writers had the advantage of more distant deadlines and opportunities to read debate transcripts, were similarly analyzed and compared with our objective issue analysis of the first 1960 and 1976 debates.

The third phase of research involved parallel grouping of discrete issues named by survey respondents interviewed shortly before the 1960 election, and shortly after the 1976 election. Preelection respondents in the 1960 American National Election Study responded to the following open-ended question: What would you personally feel are the most important problems the government should try to take care of when the president and Congress take office in January? When multiple problems were named, the first in order of mention or mention of importance was analyzed after recoding according to the same issue and subissue classification schemes applied to debate content.

Postelection respondents in the 1976 American National Election Study were asked to name the single most important problem the country faces, from among those named in response to the following open-ended question: What do you think are the most important problems facing this country?

With the application of prescribed weighting factors, responses from both election studies can be treated as representative of the views of cross-sections of voting-age citizens living in noninstitutionalized arrangements within the 48 contiguous states.

FINDINGS

Table 3.1 invites comparison of the main issues discussed in the first 1960 presidential debate versus its 1976 parallel. Most striking is the close comparability in terms of the percentages of words devoted to discussion of government and economics. In both cases, slightly more than half of all issue-units related to government, and over one-fourth dealt with economics. At the same time, this table indicates the brief passage of issues more amenable to solution. For

TABLE 3.1

Issues in the Debates

	1960			1976		
	Number of Issues	Number of Words	Percentage of Words	Number of Issues	Number of Words	Percentage of Words
Domestic issues						
Government	20	5,702	53	39	7,500	54
Health	1	147	2	–	–	–
Education	5	582	5	–	–	–
Welfare	1	99	1	–	–	–
Economics	12	2,757	26	25	4,292	31
Foreign affairs, defense	6	932	8	–	–	–
Resources	–	–	–	5	1,210	9
Law	–	–	–	1	143	1
Procedure						
Debate Formalities	34	476	4	28	617	4
Participant Pass	1	4	–	–	–	–
Total	80	10,699	99*	98	13,762	99*

*Numbers do not total one hundred because of rounding.

Note: The data presented here include the questions and statements by the moderator and questioners as well as the responses given by the candidates. The greater number of words and issues in the Carter-Ford debate, of course, reflects the fact that the 1976 debate was 90 minutes long (not including the gap during audio failure) compared with 60 minutes in 1960.

Source: Compiled by the authors.

example, in 1960, defense, foreign affairs, and education were issues occupying 8 percent of the discussion, quite likely as a function of cold war competition and hostilities. They were not concerns in 1976, but discussion of natural resources in the wake of the energy crisis occurred with some frequency. Repeatedly in the 1960 debate, the participants underscored the relationship between domestic policy and foreign policy, hinting that domestic success in the cold war battle with the Russians and Chinese depended on a well-executed foreign policy and a strong defense posture.

Among the issues dying out between 1960 and 1976 are health (government assistance for health, training of health professionals, delivery of services), education (aid to education, quality of schools, busing), and social welfare (quality-of-life programs, civil rights, civil liberties). This is not to argue, of course, that these issues were resolved or that they are no longer appropriate for presidential debates. Rather, in view of the slight increase in discussion of

A Comparative Perspective 43

domestic government and economics in 1976, compared with 1960, it happened that health, education, and welfare were discussed in terms of their costs in a deficit-laden budget (economics) or in terms of the limits to government's provision of social services (government), as indicated in Table 3.2. This table shows the various substantive concerns or subissues raised in the 1960 and 1976 debates. Here is evidence suggesting that the broad issues of health, education, and welfare, in fact, were treated in terms of quality of life and social service in

TABLE 3.2

Subissues in the Debates

	1960 Number	1960 Percent	1976 Number	1976 Percent
Domestic subissues				
Congressional action/inaction	2	2	9	5
Executive action/inaction	9	8	30	17
Preservation of American system	5	4	2	1
Legal rights, justice system	3	3	3	2
Government morality, priorities	1	1	4	2
Partisanship	14	12	18	10
Size, scope of federal government	6	5	4	2
Structure, process of government	–	–	9	5
Candidates' qualifications for office	14	12	12	7
Unemployment	–	–	16	9
Gross national product, economic growth	8	7	3	2
Taxes	–	–	14	8
Economic system	5	4	3	2
Inflation, wages, prices	6	5	9	5
Federal budget, spending	5	4	18	10
Quality-of-life programs, facilities	17	14	10	6
Quality of social services	8	7	–	–
Energy	1	1	5	3
Conservation	2	2	4	2
Foreign subissues				
Potential threats to security	6	5	–	–
Size, scope, strength of defenses	3	2	–	–
Conduct of foreign affairs	3	2	–	–
Total	118	100	173	98*

*Numbers do not total one hundred because of rounding.
Source: Compiled by the authors.

TABLE 3.3

Issues Discussed by Candidates

	1960						1976					
	Kennedy			Nixon			Carter			Ford		
	Number of Issues	Number of Words	Percentage of Words	Number of Issues	Number of Words	Percentage of Words	Number of Issues	Number of Words	Percentage of Words	Number of Issues	Number of Words	Percentage of Words
Domestic issues												
Government	9	2,708	58	6	2,605	55	13	3,271	54	15	3,260	64
Health	—	—	—	1	147	3	—	—	—	—	—	—
Education	2	250	5	1	149	3	—	—	—	—	—	—
Welfare	1	99	2	—	—	—	—	—	—	—	—	—
Economics	3	1,098	24	7	1,455	31	8	1,953	32	7	1,475	29
Foreign affairs, defense	3	512	11	2	371	8	—	—	—	—	—	—
Resources	—	—	—	—	—	—	2	723	12	1	376	7
Law	—	—	—	—	—	—	1	143	2	—	—	—
Procedure												
Debate Formalities	1	4	—	2	10	—	—	—	—	—	—	—
Participant Pass	—	—	—	1	4	—	—	—	—	—	—	—
Total	19	4,671	100	20	4,741	100	24	6,090	100	23	5,111	100

Source: Compiled by the authors.

1960 (21 percent of subissue-level discussion) but as economic questions in 1976. Rather than discussion quality-of-life programs as matters of social welfare, these were more often discussed in terms of the federal budget deficit in 1976. The evolution of health, social welfare, and education as national issues between 1960 and 1976 seems to have moved away from substantive concerns toward illustrative examples of problems in economics or further government.

It is interesting to note also that unemployment and taxes were not treated as substantive concerns in 1960, yet they account for 17 percent of the subissues mentioned in 1976. Another difference is that subissues of economic growth are mentioned only one-third as often as in 1960, while the subissue federal spending occurred with more frequency. From an issue evolution perspective, these examples illustrate how the broad issue "economics" has changed over time. In 1960, following a recession unaccompanied by inflation in 1958, growth was the crucial economic issue. Moreover, growth was emphasized as the key to peace with regard to the Soviet Union. But in 1976, the ability of the economy to sustain growth was no longer a question. Unemployment was high, tax relief was sought, and budget deficits in the tens of billions of dollars were said to contribute to inflation. Thus, while discussion of "economics" appears stable across time (Table 3.1), Table 3.2 reflects considerable differences in the tenor of discussion.

Foreign affairs and defense subissues also dropped out between 1960 and 1976. The timing of the 1960 debate, as well as the easing of cold war tensions, perhaps is reflected in the diminished discussion of defense and foreign policy linkages to domestic problems.

In Table 3.3, illustrating the emphasis given by each candidate separately to the major issues, the two Democratic candidates are revealed to be responsible for the introduction of those issues mentioned only once (compare Table 3.1). Kennedy was the only candidate to pose social welfare as a major issue; Carter was the only one to pose law. Apparently, neither received in-kind response. Yet, there is a similarity of issues presented not only between 1960 and 1976 but also among the debaters. While it might seem that Ford discussed economic issues more frequently (as a percentage of his time) than Carter, this edge is deceiving. Carter, in fact, said more (quantitatively) than Ford because he spoke faster. Over the course of the debate, Carter squeezed in nearly one thousand more words than Ford, despite the fact that Carter was cut off by audio failure during one answer, and spoke only 51 words in that turn, instead of his average 355 words.

Tables 3.4 and 3.5 present subissues discussed in terms of the issue-units "government" and "economics," and thus a more incisive view of candidates' positions can be seen. Although roughly equal amounts of time were spent on domestic government as an issue in 1960 and 1976, the issue was discussed along many more dimensions by candidates in 1960. Nearly one-fourth of Nixon's governmental subissues (24 percent) relate to concrete government action—

TABLE 3.4

Subissues Mentioned by Candidates Regarding Domestic Government

	1960				1976			
	Kennedy		Nixon		Carter		Ford	
	Number	Percent	Number	Percent	Number	Percent	Number	Percent
Action								
Congress	—	—	2	8	1	6	2	10
Executive	1	3	4	16	3	19	1	5
Political system								
Preservation	2	6	1	4	1	6	—	—
Legal rights	3	9	—	—	—	—	2	10
Morality	1	3	—	—	—	—	—	—
Leadership								
Partisanship	6	18	3	10	2	13	3	15
Qualifications	5	15	2	8	2	13	—	—
Scope of Government								
Size	2	6	2	8	—	—	2	10
Structure	—	—	—	—	1	6	2	10

Output									
Programs	2	6	5	20	—	—	2	10
Quality	3	9	1	4	—	—	—	—
Resources								
Energy	—	—	1	4	1	6	—	—
Conservation	1	3	—	—	—	—	—	—
Economics								
Unemployment	—	—	—	—	2	13	2	10
Gross national product, growth	1	3	1	4	1	6	1	5
Taxes	—	—	—	—	—	—	1	5
System	1	3	—	—	—	—	1	—
Inflation	2	6	1	4	1	6	—	—
Federal spending	—	—	1	4	1	6	2	10
Foreign								
Security	1	3	1	4	—	—	—	—
Defense	2	6	—	—	—	—	—	—
Total	33	99*	25	98*	16	100	20	100

*Numbers do not total one hundred because of rounding.
Source: Compiled by the authors.

47

TABLE 3.5

Subissues Mentioned by Candidates Regarding Economics

	1960				1976			
	Kennedy		Nixon		Carter		Ford	
	Number	Percent	Number	Percent	Number	Percent	Number	Percent
Action								
Executive	—	—	1	5	2	9	—	—
System								
Legal rights	—	—	—	—	1	5	—	—
Leadership								
Partisanship	—	—	2	10	2	9	—	—
Qualifications	—	—	2	10	—	—	—	—
Scope of government								
Size	—	—	2	10	3	14	4	24

48

Output							
Programs	1	11	1	5	—	—	1	6
Quality	1	11	—	—	—	—	—	—
Economics								
Unemployment	1	11	5	25	1	5	1	6
Gross national product, growth	1	11	1	5	4	18	2	12
Taxes	2	22	2	10	2	9	—	—
System	1	11	2	10	3	14	3	18
Inflation	1	11	1	5	4	18	5	29
Federal spending	1	11	1	5	—	—	1	6
Foreign								
Security	—	—	1	5	—	—	—	—
Total	9	99*	20	100	22	101*	17	101*

*Numbers do not total one hundred because of rounding.
Source: Compiled by the authors.

49

either congressional or executive. In contrast, Kennedy demonstrates less concern with action (3 percent), concentrating more on abstract topics concerning the nature of the political system and justice within that system. Nixon's concerns and his underlying conception of the political system, in other words, seem to be with processes of political subsystems (such as the executive branch or Congress), while Kennedy is oriented more to the status of the larger political system.

Differences between candidates in 1976 are not so clear-cut as in 1960, but the popular Tweedledum-Tweedledee analogy does not fit either. Carter was more action-oriented than Ford (25 percent compared with 15 percent), and more leadership-oriented (25 percent compared with 15 percent), reflecting greater concern with the processes or "nuts and bolts" of government machinery. Ford, for his part, tended to deal with the scope and structure of government.

In Table 3.5, the four candidates' discussions of economics are seen to cluster around specific aspects of policy, as regarding unemployment and inflation. But differences exist between candidates. For Kennedy, economic issues stand independent of government action, as government subissues accompany his discussion of the issue. This would imply a belief on his part that economic problems can be solved technically, without so much regard for the political processes necessary to deliver solutions. Nixon apparently did not share this view, for fully 35 percent of his subissues are political, reflecting on leadership qualifications and partisan issues. For the 1976 candidates, differences are present, but again to a lesser extent than in 1960. Carter, the Democrat, reveals a greater linkage of economics to political questions than does Ford. Interestingly, across all candidates, with the exception of Nixon's discussion of unemployment, no candidate suggests an economic policy focusing exclusively on one or two economic subissues.

Table 3.6 presents the specific political actors mentioned during the debates by the four candidates. Overall, Kennedy's performance suggests concern for inclusion of numerous and diverse political actors, as he named a total of 40. The other candidates name about the same number of political actors (26 to 27), but they "specialize" in various branches of government. Notably, none of the candidates mentioned "the people" very often as a political force. (In particular, the data do not support Carter's alleged populism.) Of interest, too, is the extent to which the candidates' regard for certain actors in government reflect their own experiences. Kennedy referred to the executive and legislative branches with nearly equal frequency, although he aspired to an executive position. His tenure in Congress, as the source of his qualifications for leadership, might have been the reason. Nixon, as a member of the executive branch, referred to that branch in nearly two-thirds of his specific references to political actors and twice as often as he referred to the legislative branch over which he partially presided as vice-president.

TABLE 3.6

Political Actors Mentioned

	1960		1976	
	Kennedy	Nixon	Carter	Ford
Executive				
Nonspecific	2	2	2	2
President, administration	9	9	4	2
Executive agencies	7	5	5	3
Subtotal	18	16	11	7
Legislative				
Congress	4	1	6	13
Senate	7	3	1	1
House	5	3	1	1
Subtotal	16	7	8	15
Judicial				
Supreme Court	0	0	1	0
Subtotal	0	0	1	0
Nonfederal government				
State and local	3	0	3	1
"The people"	3	4	3	2
Subtotal	6	4	6	3
Total	40	27	26	25

Source: Compiled by the authors.

Both Kennedy and Nixon, having served in both the House and Senate, specifically named these bodies more often than Ford and Carter, who referenced "Congress" more generally. Of course, Carter had no federal legislative experience, and Ford had served as a unifying House minority leader, besides being vice-president and president. Despite the fact that Ford had been president for over two years at the time of the first 1976 debate, he mentioned Congress most often as a political agent relative to issues. Perhaps criticisms of Ford as being unable to rise to the tasks of the presidency were inspired by his own speech; it seems he was oriented to the legislative branch more than the executive. In contrast, Carter, a former state governor, referred more often to the executive branch of federal government, in keeping with his aspirations.

Also with respect to Table 3.6, the infrequency of candidates' mentioning the Supreme Court is striking in light of recent criticism of "activist" courts and the increasing scope of decisions in both the Warren and Burger courts. Through failure (with one exception) to discuss the court, perhaps the candidates reveal a belief in the independence of the judiciary as a third branch of government. Notably, it was the Democratic candidates who displayed greater concern with the state and local levels of government, regardless of popular conceptions that Republicans favor state and local control and decentralized government.

In the listing of economic actors mentioned by the candidates (see Table 3.7), Kennedy is shown to mention economic actors in only five issues, suggesting

TABLE 3.7

Economic Actors Mentioned within Issue-Units

	1960		1976	
	Kennedy	Nixon	Carter	Ford
Private institutions	1	1	2	3
Public institutions	2	6		4
Individuals	1	1	5	2
Private and public institutions	1			1
Public institutions and individuals		1		2
Private institutions and individuals			3	
Private institutions, public institutions, and individuals		1	3	3
Total	5	10	13	15

Source: Compiled by the authors.

A Comparative Perspective 53

an orientation toward political solutions to economic problems. (However, his references to economic actors do apply across private and public institutions and individuals.) Nixon, who mentions economic actors in twice as many issues as Kennedy, seems to be more attuned to the public as an economic actor.

Further analysis of Table 3.7 suggests some support for Carter's alleged populism combined with a commitment to the private sector. He never mentions the public sector alone, and, in 11 of 13 issues referencing economic actors, individuals are referred to specifically. Ford, although he mentions economic actors in more issues than any other candidate, distributes his references across sectors.

But, laying aside our scientific account of the debates' content, just what was reported in print media—from which the interested voter might be expected to gain information? Following each debate, several reports appeared in the New York *Times* and in *Time Magazine* and *Newsweek*; most were concerned with the aspects of the debates other than the issues discussed (Table 3.8). Several articles dealt only with voter reaction and technical aspects of the production. Even in the lead stories, relatively little attention—with one exception—was devoted to substantive issues that were discussed. Most of the articles considered who "won" and who "lost," physical appearance of the candidates, and viewer reactions. In 1960, only the New York *Times* had substantial coverage of the issues, plus a transcript of the debate.

Coverage of the 1976 debates was considerably more issue-oriented across the three print sources, and contained far more words. Nevertheless, substantial portions of the reports were devoted to candidates' physical appearance and performance, studio conditions, and the "winner" and "loser." Again, issue coverage in the New York *Times* was considerably more extensive than in the newsweeklies, despite the fact that *Time Magazine* and *Newsweek* had more time to analyze debate content and effects. The New York *Times* also carried a complete transcript; *Newsweek* had a partial transcript of about half the text.

Were the presidential debates relevant to the public? Did they provide issue-oriented information by which to make an informed voting choice? Tables 3.9 and 3.10 would indicate that many issues of popular concern (as reflected in survey data) were not covered extensively during the first 1960 and 1976 debates.

In 1960, the public most often named foreign affairs and defense as important national issues, followed by economics and social welfare. At the time of the 1976 election, economics was cited by nearly three-fourths of the public, with the remaining percentage divided roughly equally among government, social welfare, foreign/defense, and law-related issues.

Comparison of Tables 3.9 and 3.10 with Tables 3.1 and 3.2 would suggest that many issues occupying so much of the debate dialogue were not particularly salient to the public. For example, government—the most discussed topic in 1960 and 1976—was of little concern as an issue or subissue to the public in

TABLE 3.8

Debate News Coverage, in Percent

	1960			1976		
	Newsweek	Time Magazine	New York Times	Newsweek	Time Magazine	New York Times
Topics						
Preparation	—	—	12	14	—	—
Purpose	—	14	—	1	2	—
Election news	35	32	10	19	11	1
Style	23	—	13	8	12	12
Studio	24	10	6	9	8	4
Rules	5	45	5	2	—	1
Testimony	14	—	53	12	28	4
Issues	101	101	99	36	39	78
Total percent*	863	473	1,338	101	100	100
Total number words				4,178	3,192	2,635
Issues						
Economics	—	—	61	70	47	56
Government	—	—	18	27	49	44
Welfare	—	—	21	—	—	—
Education	—	—	—	—	4	—
Resources	—	—	—	3	—	—
Total percent	—	—	100	100	100	100
Total number words	—	—	693	2,908	1,178	2,066

*Numbers do not total one hundred because of rounding.
Source: Compiled by the authors.

TABLE 3.9

Public's Perception of Most Important National Issues

	Preelection 1960 Number	Preelection 1960 Percent	Postelection 1976 Number	Postelection 1976 Percent
Government	4	0	96	4
Housing	10	0	2	0
Health	42	2	11	0
Education	26	1	7	0
Social welfare	164	9	116	5
Economics	438	25	1,574	73
Foreign affairs/defense	1,048	60	110	5
Resources	0	0	118	5
Law	1	0	133	6
Science	4	0	0	0
Number of respondents (weighted)	1,737	97*	2,167	98*

*Numbers do not total one hundred because of rounding.
Source: Compiled by the authors.

either year. Other issues, such as crime, were cited more often, but went undiscussed in the 1976 debate. The requirement that the first debate in 1960 (as well as in 1976) be limited to questions on internal or domestic matters may be partly responsible for the public's unmatched concern with foreign affairs. However, the flexibility in candidate responses suggests that almost any question on domestic issues could have been answered in terms of foreign affairs or defense. In 1976, economic concerns were named most often by the public, while the debaters often answered questions in political or governmental terms. In other words, the public could not have heard the candidates addressing issues in proportion to their perceived importance.

CONCLUSION

With voting today much less predictable from an individual's social, economic, and political characteristics than in the past, and with mass media a prime potential source of issue information for the public, it is instructive to study issues, presentation of issues by news media, and issues seen as important by the public, within and across time points.

TABLE 3.10

Public's Perception of Most Important National Subissues

	1960 Number	1960 Percent	1976 Number	1976 Percent
Government				
Size, scope, structure of government	4	0	22	1
Preservation of American government and society	0	0	68	3
Qualifications for office	0	0	4	0
Executive action/inaction	0	0	2	0
Economics				
Inflation, wages, prices	45	3	790	37
Unemployment	122	7	679	31
Taxes	54	3	31	1
Gross national product, economic growth	15	1	29	1
Federal spending, monetary policy	52	4	22	1
Commercial/industrial economics	37	2	12	1
Agricultural economics	108	6	12	1
Social Welfare				
Quality of life programs and concerns	67	4	72	3
Health care assistance and services	42	2	11	1
Nature and quality of public education	30	2	7	0
Civil rights, civil liberties	107	6	42	2
Crime, law and order	0	0	133	6
Energy, conservation	0	0	119	5
Defense				
Threats to security	14	1	0	0
Size, scope, strength of equipment and staff	309	18	36	2
Conduct of foreign affairs	382	22	5	0
Diplomatic relations	69	4	23	1
Agreements, treaties, alliances	144	8	37	2
Foreign aid and assistance	131	8	11	1
Number of respondents (weighted)	1,732	100	2,167	100

Source: Compiled by the authors.

The issue evolutionary approach to politics focused on the major political events represented by the first 1960 and 1976 televised presidential debates thus provides information relevant to campaigns and elections as well as on the underlying issue orientations and agencies that shape the ongoing political environment.

Looking back on our findings, the dynamics of issue evolution are suggested by analysis of (1) issues discussed in the first 1960 and 1976 presidential debates, (2) subsequent presentation of debate issues in the news, and (3) the public's conception of important problems facing the nation about the time of these debates. Through content analysis of the debates, overriding emphasis on the same issues (government and economics) was revealed. This implies a certain durability of concern among presidential candidates. Interestingly, the concerns reflected in the debates were not entirely parallel to the public perception of important problems facing the country, which would make it seem that the debates were conducted somewhat outside or aside from popular concerns.

While primarily addressing the evolution of issues, our content data also proved useful toward characterizing the candidates' images and political orientations. Additionally, the application was valuable for looking at debates not only in political terms but also as communication events.

Debate content data supported some of the popular and mass media descriptions concerning debate performance, which implies that at least some aspects of content are accurately perceived and identified. In contrast, our analysis of news reports about the debates showed little correspondence between the topics actually discussed and the issues reported, providing evidence for certain theories of agenda setting. This is rather interesting—to find that communication research has been most concerned with aspects of content (manifest, verbal) not easily discerned even by reporters, highly practiced observers and recorders of communication events. Meanwhile, what is best and accurately remembered—the nervousness of 1976 and the skill of 1960—goes uninvestigated in terms of effects.

In political terms, the implication of these findings is that the course of modern-day politics may be embodied more than before in the candidates as individuals. Although the issues they choose to address in debate may not become salient to the voters for some period of time, it can be argued that the generally discussed issues will be reflected in policy decisions for years. Substantive concerns, as we have seen, will come and go, more or less depending on election winners.

Journalists emerge as a second party with greater implied political power because of the occurrence of presidential debates. It is they who choose the questions roughly delimiting candidates' responses (compare Jackson-Beeck and Meadow 1977). But, more important, they have the power to redefine events (such as the debates), as we observed in our analysis of *Time Magazine, News-*

week, and the New York *Times* debate coverage. What was reported did not fit with debate reality as objectively determined.

To the extent, then, that the public's knowledge and beliefs—if not behavior—are shaped by mass media, reporting strategies may be highly important not only to elections but also to political life as it proceeds from day to day and year to year. If, as in 1960 and 1976, television chooses (and is permitted) to nationally broadcast candidates' unedited remarks in the form of presidential debates, there remains the potential for the public to respond directly to the issue positions and philosophies expressed therein.

PART II

EFFECTS OF COMMUNICATIONS CONTEXT

4

THE FORMATION OF PUBLIC OPINION: DIRECT AND MEDIATED EFFECTS OF THE FIRST DEBATE

Gladys Engel Lang and Kurt Lang

Though almost three decades have passed since Hovland's experiment using army orientation films first made us aware of sleeper effects, few studies of mass communications in the public opinion process have been informed by this concept (see Hovland, Lumsdaine, and Sheffield 1949; Hovland, Janis, and Kelley, 1953; Catton 1960). The distinction between the direct impact of a communication immediately after exposure and its more delayed effects nevertheless remains crucial. The exact meanings of a communication are not always evident in the initial encounter with its text, but take time to evolve. First impressions are often modified when checked out against supplementary information, including the reactions of significant others and of credible mass media sources.

What is true for a particular communication item (like a video commercial) will be equally, if not more, true of a significant communication event (like a televised presidential debate), which invariably elicits a flood of communications, some distinctly partisan and meant to influence reactions. Others, mainly from

---

This study was presented at the Research Conference on Presidential Debates, 1960 and 1976, held at the Annenberg School of Communications, University of Pennsylvania, Philadelphia, May 12-13, 1977. A revised version of this chapter will appear in Kraus (forthcoming).

We wish to thank faculty members Susan Chambre, Tom Jukam, William Linehan, Norman Luttweg, Kristen Monroe, Normal Prusslin, Sasha Weitman, and Gerald Zeitz, at the State University of New York at Stony Brook, for their invaluable assistance in distributing our questionnaires for this project. Special mention is also due Richard Carlson and Richard De Simone, staff members of Stony Brook's Educational Communications Center, who made both the viewing and taping of the debates possible; Carl Roberts, a graduate student in sociology, who joined us in both drawing up the questionnaire and preparing the data for computer analysis; and undergraduate students, Robin Landberg and Merille Newman, who supervised and did a good part of the coding.

the journalistic fraternity, provide contextual (and sometimes corrective) information as well as interpretive comment.

Especially visible in connection with press coverage is the rush toward a definitive public judgment of the event, the "instant news analysis," which the Nixon-Agnew administration attacked as a media plot to neutralize potential political gains from major appearances on television. But another form of instant analysis has by now become something of a science. In election year 1976, newspapers and politicians joined forces with pollsters to employ the newest technology to shorten the time lag between an event and authoritative measure of the public response to that event.

The televised Ford-Carter debates were no exception. When, during the first encounter on September 23, 1976, the sound went dead, network newsmen immediately began to elicit evaluations of performance from partisan spokesmen, even though the debate had not yet officially terminated. Not long after the two candidates had made their final statements, television reporters added their own judgments. All these early appraisals seemed to agree on one point, namely, that neither had gained a clear advantage over his adversary. To be sure, two polls whose results were broadcast that evening (one by Roper, the other by the Associated Press) gave Ford a slight edge, but a New York *Times* headline two days later still read "Debate Viewed as a Draw by Experts in Both Parties," and cited polls to support this view. Yet, a Gallup poll published the following week showed Ford to be the "victor" by a 13-point margin, and the judgment based on a poll conducted on Long Island by *Newsday* was that "Ford's success in the debate seems conclusive." Recapitulations at the end of the three debates unanimously gave the first debate to Ford.

Whatever one's predilections lead one to believe, so far no one has been able to supply any really hard evidence that the reporting of such results swings votes (Mendelsohn and Crespi 1970; Lang and Lang 1968). Be this as it may, such information is definitely not ignored. On the contrary, many members of the electorate are as interested as party strategists in what the polls report about the relative standing of the candidates. This is not only because the public sees the campaign as a "race" but also because a candidate's popularity represents a real political asset, which can help shape policy and persuade a reluctant Congress. Similarly, how well a candidate does in a debate has something to do with the kind of image—as leader, as wise statesman, as "man of the people"— each is trying to project.

This rush to judgment by the media on the 1976 presidential debates afforded an opportunity to assess the extent to which the initial impact was contaminated by other political communications, especially the news commentary on the debates and on "who won." Does the quick verdict become assimilated into how viewers of the debate remember them? If the direct and immediate impact of the first debate differed from its delayed effect, as we shall try to document, this raises the question about the point in time most suitable for measuring public reaction so as to pin down definitively the debate "effect": before viewers have learned the judgments of others or after a lag sufficient for a collective definition to develop?

DESCRIPTION OF THE STUDY

We used a before-and-after design with two exposure conditions. All "before" questionnaires were filled out either on the day of the first debate or the day before. Items covered what respondents were looking for and what each stood for, media exposure to past and current political events, interest in the campaign and in voting, and political preferences.

Our subjects were students at the State University of New York at Stony Brook. Nearly all of them were undergraduates and first-time voters. In a way, the study is a cross between a laboratory and a field experiment. One group—some of whom had completed the predebate questionnaire earlier, some completing it while waiting for the program to start—viewed the first debate under "controlled" conditions in one of three adjoining lecture halls. Interaction could not be altogether prevented but was held to a minimum. Their "after" questionnaires were completed during the 27-minute gap. The other group, having first filled out the predebate questionnaire in a classroom, viewed the debate in whatever setting was available—at home, in their college dormitory, or wherever they happened to be. Since they had time to discuss the debate and to be exposed to press commentary between the time they watched the debate and the time they completed their "after" questionnaires four to seven days following the debate, their responses are considered "contaminated." Indeed, over 90 percent of the latter group said they discussed the debates, over 80 percent said they had learned what the polls said about who "won," and 75 percent said they had read about the debates in the newspapers or newsmagazines. Analysis contrasts the responses of 308 students who viewed the debate in the lecture hall and gave their reactions immediately after with responses of 386 students who viewed elsewhere and gave their reactions only after some delay.* Those who did not view the debate or saw only clips on television news are eliminated from the analysis presented here.

---

*This chapter reports only one aspect of the study that was originally designed to help understand more about so-called political apathy and alienation among young voters. A third brief questionnaire was distributed after the last debate. The need to protect anonymity made it difficult to recontact respondents not originally contacted in classrooms. Still, we have 428 persons filling out three questionnaires; 393, only the first and second, 60, only the first and third; 216, only the prequestionnaire; 125, only the second; and 79, only the final.

Questionnaires were distributed in 13 sociology, political science, and communication classes, most of them at the introductory level, so that all majors were represented among those answering. We also put out publicity urging students to attend the public viewing of the debate and to come early enough to complete our questionnaire beforehand.

Though random assignment was not possible, the two groups are subsamples of the same student population; they are surprisingly well matched on such variables as age, declared academic major, interest in the campaign, mass media exposure, intention to vote, and measures of political efficacy and cynicism. The one exception is candidate preference (Table 4.1). The contaminated exposure group contains more who favored or, if they had not yet definitely made up their minds, were leaning toward Ford and fewer who described themselves as either totally undecided or against both candidates.* Consequently, all comparisons of the amount of change under the two exposure conditions are given separately for the supporters of Ford, of Carter, and all others.

TABLE 4.1

Vote Preference by Exposure

	Immediate		Mediated	
	Percent	Number	Percent	Number
Ford	19	58	30	116
Carter	56	173	53	205
Neither*	25	77	17	65
Total	100	308	100	386

*A large 49 percent said they had definitely *not yet* made up their minds about voting for a president.
Source: Compiled by the authors.

EVALUATIONS OF THE FIRST DEBATE

"Was the debate worth seeing?" As Table 4.2 shows, overwhelming majorities replied affirmatively. Supporters of either Ford or Carter were somewhat

---

*This probably reflects the higher proportion of commuting students who viewed the debate at home. Long Island (Nassau and Suffolk Counties) is still disproportionately Republican.

TABLE 4.2

Persons Who Thought Debate Worth Seeing by Vote Preference and Exposure, in Percent

Exposure	Ford	Carter	Neither	Total
Immediate	95	94	88	93
Mediated	79	77	71	77
Difference	-16	-17	-16	-16

Source: Compiled by the authors.

more enthusiastic than those with no distinct preference between the two. However, responses in the week following the debate, while still favorable, had become somewhat less favorable. The difference persisted across candidate preference. What was it about the debate that elicited this initial favorable response and what elements were the first to erode? Respondents were asked to rate as good, fair, or poor certain aspects of the debate format, what it revealed about the candidates and their stand on issues, and how useful it was in making up one's mind and how to vote. These ratings are summarized in Table 4.3, where the scores represent the proportion rating the debate "good" minus the proportion rating it "poor." Thus, a positive rating indicates the degree to which the balance of evaluation was better than "fair," a negative rating the degree to which it fell below this minimum standard.

As to format, the moderator, Edwin Newman, received the highest marks for his fairness. Respondents also generally approved the questions, which they judged fair and reasonably difficult. But there was less certainty that the debate afforded opportunity to observe a direct give-and-take between the candidates; here the average rating was only "fair." In line with this, we find the debates rather higher on showing where Ford and Carter stood on issues than on the spontaneity of their replies. They were considered even less revealing of what the candidates "were really like." To some extent these ratings follow partisan lines, and those who had expressed no preference for either candidate before the debate tended to be somewhat less approving, though not consistently so.

Overall, the debate was judged least helpful in deciding whether and how to vote. And here again, those leaning toward either Ford or Carter evaluated the debate somewhat more favorably than those who preferred neither. A disproportionate number within this undecided and/or antagonistic group had already indicated before the debate that they neither expected nor would be looking for help in making their vote decisions.

In the controlled exposure group, where responses were obtained immediately after the debate, there were no marked differences in the assessments of

TABLE 4.3

Rating* of Debate as Help in Assessing Candidates and of Debate Format by Voter Preference and Exposure

	Ford			Carter			Neither			Total		
Format	Imme-diate	Medi-ated	Change	Imme-diate	Medi-ated	Change	Imme-diate	Medi-ated	Change	Imme-diate	Medi-ated	Change
Format												
Give and take of debate	9	8	−1	10	−32	−42	1	−13	−14	4	−21	−25
Fairness of questions	62	64	+2	76	59	−17	69	60	−9	71	63	−8
Fairness on part of moderator	88	67	−21	78	72	−6	59	72	+13	77	70	−7
Difficulty of questions	59	47	−12	61	38	−23	37	32	−5	55	40	−15
Mean rating	37	34	−3	45	20	−25	28	17	−11	35	22	−13
Candidates												
What Ford is really like	20	13	−7	20	−3	−23	−9	−5	+4	13	2	−11
What Carter is really like	7	8	+1	32	1	−31	−6	−10	−4	29	1	−28
Ford's stand on issues	56	53	−3	55	24	−31	19	16	−3	41	32	−9
Carter's stand on issues	16	11	−5	59	20	−39	24	0	−24	46	14	−32
Spontaneity of Ford's replies	42	49	+7	16	3	−13	29	19	−10	24	20	−4
Spontaneity of Carter's replies	12	23	+11	41	19	−22	36	2	−34	25	20	−5
Help in Deciding												
Whether to vote	1	−15	−16	+10	−31	−41	−20	−34	−14	−2	−27	−25
How to vote	−3	−22	−19	+5	−44	−49	−23	−44	−21	−3	−37	−34
Number	60	115	—	164	198	—	66	61	—	290	374	—

*Percent rating "good" minus percent rating "poor." A negative "change" means a downgrading, a positive one an improvement between the two exposure conditions.
Source: Compiled by the authors.

the debate format by Ford and Carter supporters. That Ford supporters rated the "fairness" of the moderator somewhat higher while Carter supporters thought reporters' questions somewhat fairer hardly seems significant. It is significant, however, that respondents, asked what the debate revealed about each candidate, split pretty much along partisan lines. Each camp more often saw the debate as showing that its own man was "really like," informing them where he stood on issues, and revealing the spontaneity with which he answered questions. On all these points, Carter supporters tended to rate the debate higher for what it revealed about Ford then Ford supporters rated it with regard to Carter. Yet, despite the greater influence partisan preferences appear to have had on perceptions of Ford supporters, Carter supporters actually saw the debate doing somewhat more for Carter than Ford partisans saw it doing for Ford. Those preferring neither candidate were generally most negative in assessing both the debate format and what it revealed.

These difference also are reflected in immediate reactions to the debate as a help in deciding whether and how to vote. On both these counts, Carter's followers were most inclined to rate the debate better than "fair"—the net approval of help on whether to vote or not was +10; for how to vote, +5. The comparable figures for Ford's following were +1 and -3, respectively, while reactions among the "neither group" were distinctly negative.

Mediated evaluations obtained during the following week—that is, in the delayed response group—were distinctly lower on nearly all counts than in the controlled exposure group. The slippage was far greater among persons who, before the debate, had preferred Carter and whose initial reactions had apparently been most favorable than among those who had preferred Ford. Between the two exposure conditions, the relative positions of Ford and Carter supporters on many measures were, indeed, reversed.

The change measured in Table 4.3 is the simple arithmetic difference between ratings of the controlled and contaminated exposure groups with the sign reversed, so that a negative number indicates a downgrading, a positive one an upgrading in approval of the particular aspect of the debate. Most downgraded by Carter supporters was "helping determine how to vote"—a loss of 49 points. Next, by amount of slippage, were: the give-and-take between the candidates (42), whether to vote (41), and Carter's issues stand (39). Moreover, Carter slipped more than Ford in the eyes of his own followers, whose vision of the debate became blurred in other respects as well. They were less sure they had learned what either Ford or Carter were really like and where each stood on issues, and less likely to consider the questions posed by reporters "difficult" or answers as particularly revealing. The most serious slippage among Ford supporters was with respect to the moderator, whom Ford supporters responding immediately had given unusually high ratings. Among Carter supporters, judgments of Newman remained relatively firm.

Downgrading of the debate among persons leaning toward neither candidate was limited by the comparatively low rating given the debate format and its usefulness under the controlled exposure condition. Yet, between candidates, it points to a slippage in Carter imagery parallel to that which he apparently experienced among his own following. Carter "lost" more than Ford on spontaneity (-34 versus -10), on clarifying where he stood (-24 versus -3), and on revealing what he was really like (-4 versus +4).

DEBATE PERFORMANCE

The question that arises is whether the candidates' performance in the debate had anything to do with this delayed downgrading of the debate, especially among those not supporting Ford. Respondents were asked before the debate, "Whom do you expect to come out best in the first debate—Carter or Ford?" The follow-up question—"Whom do you think came out best in the first debate?"—allowed respondents to indicate, if they wished, that "both did equally well" or "both did equally poorly."

A majority had expected Carter to "win" the debate but, as the last column in Table 4.4 shows, the verdict went to Ford by 31 to 30. Once again there is a sharp contrast between those responding immediately and those responding during the week following. The controlled-exposure group gave the debate to Carter by roughly a seven-to-four margin, and those who saw no clear winner twice as often said both had done well as both had done poorly. The judgments in the contaminated-exposure group went in the opposite direction with Ford leading Carter, though by a somewhat smaller margin, and those seeing a tie becoming somewhat less charitable, more critical of both.

The difference between the two exposure conditions persists when we look separately at responses of Ford and Carter supporters. It is not, in other words, a consequence of the different political complexions of the two groups. The immediately after verdict splits very much along partisan lines, but Carter clearly did better among those partial to neither debater. However, those with no preference who responded after several days' delay were equally clear in believing Ford had done better; the judgments of Carter supporters were far more evenly divided though still favoring their own candidate, while more Ford partisans thought he had won. The percentage of Carter supporters who thought he had done better dropped from 59 to 28 percent; among those with no preference, the drop was from 43 to 15 percent. The last group, in particular, was distinctly more inclined to say that both men had performed poorly.

Nor is this rather striking contrast between exposure conditions accounted for by differences in predebate expectations. An almost identical 64 percent in the immediate response group and 62 percent in the delayed response group expected Carter to win. Nearly two-thirds of all perceptions about who did better were concordant with prior expectations (see Table 4.5). But expectations

TABLE 4.4

"Who Did Better" in First Debate by Vote Preference and Exposure, in Percent

| | Immediate |||| Mediated |||| Total ||||
	Ford	Carter	Neither*	All	Ford	Carter	Neither*	All	Ford	Carter	Neither*	All
Ford better	64	8	16	21	70	22	39	39	68	16	27	31
Carter better	4	59	53	45	6	28	15	19	5	42	30	30
Both well	25	21	27	23	18	29	20	24	21	25	24	24
Both poorly	7	12	14	11	5	22	26	17	6	17	20	15
Total percent	100	100	100	100	100	100	100	100	100	100	100	100
Total number	55	166	73	294	115	205	65	385	170	371	128	679

*The "neither" include undecideds and "antis," who split by party affiliation as follows: Democrat—16 immediate, 19 mediated; Republican—30 immediate, 31 mediated; Indepdent—54 immediate, 50 mediated.
Source: Compiled by the authors.

TABLE 4.5

"Who Did Better" in First Debate by Expectation and Exposure, in Percent

	Expected Ford to Win			Expected Carter to Win		
	Immediate	Mediated	Ford Gain	Immediate	Mediated	Ford Gain
Ford better	38	57	+20	16	31	+15
Both well	27	23	−5	22	23	1
Both poorly	9	8	+1	11	21	−10
Carter better	26	13	+14	51	25	+26
Total percent	100	100		100	100	
Total number	82	122		141	198	

Note: Tau B (Ford by Carter) = .264 (p < .001); Tau B (Ford by Carter) = .325 (p < .001).

Source: Compiled by the authors.

of a Carter win were more often confirmed in the controlled-exposure condition, pro-Ford expectations in the contaminated condition. Furthermore, the Carter confirmation rate drops somewhat more between the two conditions than the Ford confirmation rate rises. Ford's gains were greatest among those who had expected him to do better all along, while Carter's losses concentrated among those who before the debate had expected Ford to lose. We are observing shift and not just erosion.

CANDIDATE IMAGERY

Our prequestionnaire included a list of adjectives culled from the media coverage of the campaign. The respondents were asked to indicate whether each adjective did or did not describe each candidate. The list was repeated on the postquestionnaire. These responses are summarized in Table 4.6. The "before" column shows how the followers of Ford and Carter rated their own candidate on each adjective relative to the other candidate. The values represent differences, not actual ratings, of the candidates. That is to say, they indicate the extent to which each candidate was perceived by his own supporters as having a distinctive image: the smaller the difference (that is, the lower the value) next to a descriptor, the more similar do the candidates appear within the particular constituency. Whether this is because both candidates have equally high or low ratings is not shown. A positive sign in any but the "gain or loss" columns denotes not a gain but merely that respondents are more ready to attribute a particular trait to the candidate they favor than to his opponent. This is usually the case for traits judged positively. When partisans more often pin a label on the other candidate, the characterization usually has negative undertones.

There is, of course, nothing absolute about this tendency. On some labels the consensus cuts across partisan lines. Even before the first debate, Carter and Ford supporters alike considered Ford the clumsier, the more conservative, and the more predictable; Carter was seen as the more religious, liberal, and opportunistic of the two. Ford had higher standing as an administrator but Carter was believed to be better at debating. On nine other descriptors, perceptions of the candidates were distinctly partisan. Before the debate, the favored candidate consistently had the edge on honesty, intelligence, knowledgeability, being presidential, sincerity, and trustworthiness, but Ford supporters seemed to have had none of the doubts that apparently plagued Carter's following about their own candidate's evasiveness and vagueness relative to his opponent.

When viewed in the controlled condition, the first debate tended to accentuate partisan perceptions. Carter generally did better among his potential constituency than Ford did among his. The only descriptor on which he did not improve his standing relative to Ford's was on being presidential. Although the measure shown does not discriminate between gains due to one's candidate's positive projection or his opponent's deficiency, that Ford managed to cash in on his incumbency is clear from other evidence. On other traits, Ford's gains are less consistent than Carter's; but he managed to persuade his following that he could match Carter in debating skill, while the latter merely maintained the advantage his supporters gave him from the beginning.

Yet, insofar as our main analytic problem here is to differentiate between contaminated and controlled exposure, the critical columns for this purpose are those labeled "gain or loss." They sum the difference between perceptions under the two exposure conditions. For example, in both exposure groups, Ford supporters saw Ford as even less evasive relative to Carter than they had prior to the debate. Among Carter supporters, shifts on evasiveness are smaller but tend to favor Carter, because Ford also appeared to be evasive. Most important, time elapsed since viewing changed perceptions of Ford supporters very little (-.09) but caused a significant reversal among Carterites (+.21), with slippage back two-thirds of the way toward parity. Since evasiveness is a negative trait, the net shift among these viewers went against Carter.

The patterns of gains and losses resembles that previously observed for evaluations of the debate. The difference between the immediate and the mediated response is almost invariably in the same direction, regardless of partisan preferences; that is, a gain for Ford among his following goes with a loss for Carter among those leaning toward him before the debate. Ford, who had gained very little in the controlled-exposure condition, managed to improve his standing vis-a-vis Carter where exposure was contaminated. His gains among his own

TABLE 4.6

Candidate Perceptions before and after First Debate, by Preference and Exposure

	Prefer Ford				Prefer Carter			
		Shift				Shift		
	Difference Before	Immediate	Mediated	Gain or Loss	Difference Before	Immediate	Mediated	Gain or Loss
Partisan traits								
Corrupt	-.13	-.05	-.02	+.03	-.31	+.04	+.20	+.16[a]
Evasive	-.49	-.26	-.45	-.19	-.02	-.37	-.04	+.33[b]
Genuine	+.48	-.26	-.08	+.18	+.22	+.40	+.24	-.16
Honest	+.41	-.07	-.02	+.05	+.24	+.28	+.13	-.15
Intelligent	+.06	+.07	+.09	+.02	+.48	+.21	+.03	-.18[b]
Knowledgeable	+.18	+.19	+.27	+.12	+.27	+.03	-.14	-.17
Presidential	+.67	+.32	+.28	-.04	+.36	-.16	-.40	-.24[a]
Sincere	+.53	-.32	-.17	+.15	+.21	+.38	+.22	-.16
Trustworthy	+.45	-.17	-.05	+.12	+.26	+.04	+.01	-.03
All partisan	—	—	—	+.08	—	—	—	-1.58[c]

72

Competence							
Experienced administrator	+.68	+.19	+.40	+.21	-.08	+.30	+.01	-.29[b]
Good debater	-.04	+.26	+.49	+.23	+.40	+.04	-.41	-.45[c]
Combined	—	—	—	+.45[b]	—	—	—	-.74[c]
Ford traits								
Clumsy	+.62	-.49	-.49	00	-1.00	+.60	+.55	-.05
Conservative	+.64	+.25	+.23	-.02	-.68	-.44	-.61	-.17
Predictable	+.44	-.49	-.14	+.35[a]	-.38	-.04	-.25	-.29
Carter traits								
Liberal	-.49	-.04	-.49	-.45[b]	+.65	+.27	+.17	-.10
Opportunistic	-.38	+.02	-.11	-.13	+.20	+.02	-.01	-.03
Religious	-.41	+.12	-.06	-.18	+.64	-.27	-.03	+.24[b]
Vague	-.60	-.05	-.36	-.31	+.07	-.25	-.08	+.17

[a]$p \leq .05$.
[b]$p \leq .01$.
[c]$p \leq .001$.
Source: Compiled by the authors.

followers were on being trustworthy, a "good debater," sincere, presidential, intelligent, and genuine; his "losses" were on being vague and evasive. On knowledgeability there was no change, but Ford's admirers had scored him high on this trait before the debate.

While the image of Ford improved within his own constituency, Carter lost ground with his. Those responding days after the debate gave him relatively lower ratings on being a "good debater," intelligent, knowledgeable, presidential, honest, genuine, sincere, and trustworthy; "gains" on being evasive and vague were, in fact, political losses. Respondents were also asked which traits had been highlighted by the debate. Most often mentioned was Ford's conservatism; Carter's liberal views also ranked high, being cited by slightly over one-third of the respondents. But in the week after the debate, it was the Ford supporters who developed a clearer conception of ideological differences between the candidates: Ford gained 11 points as being the more conservative and 32 as being the less liberal. No parallel changes occurred within the Carter group; indeed, there was a slight loss in perceiving him as liberal relative to Ford.

ISSUES

In the main the debate highlighted candidate differences on issues students had chosen, before the debate, as important in making up their minds (Table 4.7). An exception was the candidates' stand on amnesty for draft evaders; but 65 percent of the respondents had been aware of differences on this issue beforehand, and it had not ranked particularly high as an issue that would determine how to vote. Respondents were very much aware of differences on four other issues highlighted by the debate; namely, level of government spending, unemployment, the tax burden on the middle classes, and inflation, which were considered important for one's vote.

On the other hand, abortion, an issue where a majority saw significant differences between the candidates, did not surface in the first debate, and no noticeable changes in perceptions followed. On abortion, as on five other issues— equal rights for minorities, farm subsidies, church-state relations, marijuana, and aid to Israel—there was a slight decline in the number perceiving significant differences, probably because the issue was not discussed, not because the two candidates sounded so much alike. Among the issues not highlighted, invasion of privacy was the only one with a modest, but unexplained, increase of differences that cannot be attributed to the debate.

On issues, we find noticeably less differences between the two exposure conditions than we found on performance and candidate imagery. The biggest difference occurred with regard to protection of the environment—one of the more salient issues, but one where only a minority had seen a significant difference between the two candidates before the debate. The debate seems to have

The Formation of Public Opinion

TABLE 4.7

Perceptions of Issues, Differences between Candidates, and Issues Highlighted in First Debate by Exposure, in Percent

Issue (in Order of Declining Importance)[a]	Significant Difference Before Debate	Increase after Debate Who See Significant Difference — Immediate	Increase after Debate Who See Significant Difference — Mediated	Highlighted in Debate — Immediate	Highlighted in Debate — Mediated
Unemployment	52	29	28	81	79
Inflation	58	23	19	60	60
Tax on middle class	49	25	24	74	71
Federal aid to education	44	21	18	48	41
Environment	34	32	4	32	4
Government spending	70	19	15	88	86
Rights for minorities	30	0	-4	10	12
Invasions of privacy	21	10	12	b	5
Military outlays	62	-7	11	16	50
Urban aid	59	3	11	35	40
National health insurance	48	3	9	30	29
Abortion	53	-10	6	1	10
Draft amnesty	65	24	21	92	83
Aid to Israel	39	-11	-10	b	5
Church-state	22	-13	-8	0	3
Marijuana	30	-9	-3	0	1
Farm subsidies	45	-11	5	8	23

[a]Importance = percentage who said the stand taken by either candidate would be important in making up their mind.

[b]Less than 0.5 percent.

Source: Compiled by the authors.

enhanced perceptions of a difference among the controlled-exposure group; but any such change appears to have been dissipated within the week following, when few people acknowledged that the debate highlighted this difference. Those who cared about the environment may have been scrutinizing the debate for clues about the candidate's stand on this issue, but the lack of emphasis in the postdebate commentary helped condemn it to oblivion.

With regard to military spending, constitutional amendment on abortion, and farm subsidies, the trend is the other way around. An initial decrease in perceived differences immediately after the debate is followed by a recovery beyond the original level. Although the recovery is accompanied by an increase in the number who "saw" the difference highlighted in the debate, the fact that only 16, 1, and 8 percent, respectively, of the controlled exposure group made this connection speaks against the debate as a direct influence. The increase in perceived difference is probably attributable to commentary and other communications about the debate.

LANDSLIDE AND UNDERDOG PERCEPTIONS

The contrast between the immediate impact of the debate and the mediated responses obtained after several days' delay point to the attenuation of some short-run effects. There was, as we observed, a general downgrading of the debate, less approval of its format, of its usefulness, and of the information it provided. Also, evaluations of the relative performance of the two candidates differed. Within the controlled-exposure group, Carter was perceived as the winner; for those responding in the week following, he had become the loser. During the same interval, Carter's personal image also suffered some erosion, but there was little change in the number perceiving significant differences between the candidates on those issues highlighted by the first debate.

Were these changes translatable into a movement of votes that almost gained Ford the election? Did the support for Carter soften as a result?

Obviously, one would not expect many changes in vote intention in so short a span of time, and the large majority with a preference before the debate, no matter how weak, did not switch or waver. The dominant change, if it is a change, was in the direction of reinforcement; that is, persons became "more certain" and "more eager" to vote rather than the reverse (Table 4.8). Also, a considerable number of crystallizations occurred among those initially unwilling to state a preference between the two major candidates. Here Carter gained slightly more than Ford. But comparison of the two exposure conditions suggests once again that some of the Carter gains immediately following the debate may have eroded. The erosion, however subtle, mainifests itself in a number of ways. First, there are the actual changes in preference. Those responding immediately less often switched away from Carter or wavered in their preference for the Georgia governor than those responding during the week after. Also, crystallization among those initially behind neither candidate favored Carter in the immediate response group and Ford in the delayed condition. Second, among Carter supporters the net increase in both certainty of preference and eagerness to vote was greater than among the Ford constituency; days later changes favored Ford. Whatever losses Ford seems to have suffered immediately after the debate were recouped.

These findings must nevertheless be qualified. The changes observed are perceptions and preferences, not definite vote intention, and the sample is atypical even though a student population without long-standing political

TABLE 4.8

Changes in Vote Preference, Certainty, and Eagerness to Vote after First Debate, by Exposure and Initial Preference, in Percent

	Ford Immediate	Ford Mediated	Carter Immediate	Carter Mediated	Neither Immediate	Neither Mediated
No change	70	78	80	76	53	58
Wavered[a]	16	10	9	11	—	—
Switch	14	12	11	13	—	—
Crystallized						
Ford	—	—	—	—	11	26
Carter	—	—	—	—	37	16
Number	58	114	168	203	68	62
More certain	38	22	37	22	27	13
No change	49	71	55	59	56	75
Less certain	13	7	8	19	17	13
Number	61	117	170	202	70	63
More eager to vote	42	22	39	21	32	14
No change	42	70	54	59	58	72
Less eager	16	8	7	20	10	14
Number	50[b]	98[b]	148[b]	179[b]	31[b]	43[b]

[a] Now "undecided."
[b] Eligible to vote only.

Note: The overall differences on certainty and eagerness between the two conditions are significant (Tau C) beyond .001; they approach significance for Carter voters. The differential crystallizations among the "neither" (chi-square) is significant beyond the .001 level.

Source: Compiled by the authors.

loyalties and civic commitments may be an unusually sensitive indicator of shifting sentiment. In addition, there is an underlying consistency about all the data together. They indicate a gradually developing feeling that Carter, unlike John F. Kennedy in 1960, had not scored heavily and that, regardless of one's personal reaction, Ford had therefore improved his chances for election by the debate. Respondents were very much aware that Ford had trailed badly in the polls. In response to a direct question, more respondents pinned the underdog label on Ford (29 percent) than on Carter (17 percent); the rest had no clear perception of either. Among those responding immediately after the debate, there was a slight, but insignificant, increase in underdog perceptions of Ford. The contaminated-exposure group was as likely to think of Carter as of Ford as underdog. This label is, of course, related to a person's expectation of who would win in November. By and large, the followers of each candidate considered his prospects better than his opponent's. Therefore, those with no candidate preference before the debate provide the best indications of changing perceptions. Within this group, there was a sharp contrast between those responding immediately after and those responding some days later. A clear majority in the controlled-exposure group expected Carter to win; in the contaminated-exposure group, this expectation was reversed.

IMPLICATIONS OF THE STUDY

There are several alternative explanations for our findings. The question here is: Which accords most closely with the data presented? A first explanation relates to the nature of the two exposure conditions. Unless experimental contamination is ruled out as a cause of variation, no other explanation has any credence.

All persons who filled out questionnaires distributed during the 27-minute sound gap had witnessed this first debate from its beginning. We can be less certain about exposure to the debate among those responding later—we had to rely on their self-reports. Only those saying they watched the debate "live" were included. Of these, 84 percent definitely had seen the beginning of the debate and 79 percent indicated they had kept watching during the gap. However, even when responses of those who did not see both the beginning and the gap are omitted from the analysis, the contrast between the immediate and mediated response group remains.

Still, the difference in reaction may be a function of viewing in a group versus viewing as individuals (see Weiss 1969). The debate, for students in the lecture hall, was a spectacle luring people from their dorms and "digs" to a public "happening"; for those watching the debate under other conditions, viewing was a far more routine event. While we cannot completely ignore the possible influence of the viewing situation, we nevertheless discount it—for several reasons—its significance. First, we were able to minimize interaction among the lecture hall audience, so much so that any group effect was probably weaker than that found among those viewing in the residence halls (where one-third of the later response group watched). It is also probable that most of those viewing at home also viewed in groups and so were subject to group effects. Be this as it may, in what direction might group viewing influence response? Possibly, those at the public viewing might have come prepared for more of a spectacle and, thus, have been more susceptible to disappointment than those whose viewing was more routine. But we have no evidence that the two groups differed in what they wanted to see or expected to see.

A second line of explanation focuses on erosion over time. If erosion were a matter of mere forgetting, any initial effect of the debate would wear off. Both candidates would soon revert to their predebate standing. But this is not what happened. Some of the initial gains—that is, Ford's—were selectively reinforced between the two conditions. It was the candidates' personal images and evaluations of their performance, which are less subject to "forgetting" than overall impressions, that changed more in favor of Ford than perceptions of how the two had differed on some particular issue during the debate.

Third, differences over time might be explained as a strain toward cognitive consistency to redress a short-run imbalance between partisan preferences and perceptions of the candidates created by the debate. This is to say, as the week wore on the perceptions of Carter by Carter's following should have become more favorable, and Ford should also have been defined more positively by his potential supporters. Yet, our findings provide no evidence that the short-run effect of viewing was to increase imbalance. Immediate changes in candidate perceptions were, by and large, along partisan lines, with an increase in consistency translated into greater certainty about one's preference and greater eagerness to vote. What remains unexplained is the one-sided difference between the controlled and contaminated conditions, with cognitions of Carter supporters becoming less, not more, consistent with time.

Specificically political factors suggest still a fourth line of explanation. Carter's support among college students had been generally diagnosed as "soft." Our own subjects were no exception. Yet, inasmuch as the proportion "certain" relative to "undecided but leaning toward" was the same for Carter as for Ford, supporters of both seemed equally open to persuasive influence from the debate, except that pro-Republican pressure on those contaminated, who apparently moved in a more Republican milieu, may have been greater than that holding those within or hovering about the Carter camp. In this way, an initial response favorable to Carter could have been neutralized by competitive campaign influences. This explanation can satisfactorily account for certain changes in imagery but not for other attitudinal shifts, such as downgrading the debate as useful in arriving at a decision on voting. It is plausible only if we make the additional assumption that what persons "saw" or "learned from" the debate was effectively counteracted by communications to which persons were exposed in the week following.

This brings us to the fifth explanation, the one that strikes us as most satisfactory: The contaminated group must have been influenced by communications about the debate to which no one in the controlled exposure condition could possibly have been exposed. The collective definition of the debate—the way it emerged in the public mind—did not depend solely on what each viewer had experienced by himself or herself in intimate communion with the tube. Rather, it developed over time by way of a process in which each person's impressions were constantly tested against those of others, including interpretative and analytic commentaries offered by authoritative mass media sources. Impressions gained directly from the debate were accordingly modified and elaborated.

Those that diverged too much from this consensus enjoyed little support and, consequently, were apt to lose out until they were no longer expressed. Persons within the controlled exposure conditions had given their evaluations without the benefit of any such give-and-take.

Taken together, our findings suggest that most respondents were aware of the drift in sentiment. There was a feeling that Carter was slipping and that Ford, who was rapidly closing the gap, could no longer be considered the underdog. The awareness that the debate contributed to this shift was pronounced in the contaminated-exposure group. As yet, no bandwagon for Ford was about to roll, but the belief that the debate had improved Ford's chances was gaining ground. Such "landslide" perceptions apparently had their origin in media reports.

Less than systematic analysis of media debate coverage supports this contention. One recurrent theme, largely based on polls but also expressed as private estimates, was that Ford had "won" the first debate. This view predominated among the delayed-response group but not those responding directly. The difference could be designated a "polling effect," but is more correctly a reflection of the overall image conveyed by the media. A second theme casts doubts on the efficacy of the debate as a campaign device. Before the debate, both electronic and print press invoked the image of Kennedy skillfully using this format to turn the tide against Nixon. By contrast, Carter had failed dismally. His "failure" as a debate performer spilled over to other aspects of his image. Negative evaluations dampened enthusiasm not only for the candidate but also for the debate as conducted. Unfavorable comparisons with 1960 were common even though the 1976 debate had lasted longer, had involved more penetrating questioning of the candidates, and had forced them to stick closer to the point than had Kennedy and Nixon.

The comparison between the more positive response immediately after the debate and the more negative delayed response suggests that, if Carter was judged wanting, this was mostly against the background of high expectations shaped by the relevant past. The press did its part in deploring the lackluster performance of both Carter and Ford, calling how either handled himself irrelevant to his ability to meet the requirement of office and thereby, inadvertently, helping Ford exploit the advantage of his incumbency. But which candidate gained more from the debate and why is hardly the point. What matters is that the impact of the 1976 debates cannot be assessed without taking full cognizance of the context provided by other and less dramatic communications.

5

PUBLIC RESPONSE TO GERALD FORD'S STATEMENTS ON EASTERN EUROPE IN THE SECOND DEBATE

Frederick T. Steeper

BACKGROUND

The formation of a public image is an asymmetrical process. While the positive side almost always is built over a long period of time involving many actions and accomplishments, the negative side can form suddenly from a single action or statement. Two famous examples of these assertions happened during the New Hampshire presidential primary campaigns: the publication of George Romney's statement that he had been "brainwashed on Vietnam" and U.S. Senator Edmund Muskie's tear-shedding scene before the Manchester *Union* building. Each man, after making significant progress in become a legitimate presidential candidate, fell from that achieved status overnight. (Romney was far behind Richard Nixon in New Hampshire when the brainwashing statement was publicized, and his candidacy probably would have ended in New Hampshire, anyway. Muskie, on the other hand, was the Democratic front-runner at the time of his statement.)

The easy potential for damaging a candidacy is well appreciated by candidates and their campaign strategists. It has even been fashioned into something called the "Romney Rule" by political consultants: "Penalize bloopers severely, irrespective of their real importance" with a corollary "let it (early blooper) sit for a while then beat them to death with it in the final two weeks" (Parkinson 1977).

There are severe limits, however, on how effectively candidates can penalize opponents because of danger to their own credibility. Voters associate

---

This is a revised version of a paper prepared for the Annual Convention of the American Association for Public Opinion Research, Buck Hill Falls, Pennsylvania, May 1977.

mudslinging with campaigns and can discount such attacks as "just politics." Mistakes or bloopers are more likely to become a significant factor in the outcome when they are publicized in news stories by the mass media. The news media are considered a neutral source, therefore more trustworthy than the candidates, and are credited with some expertise. In short, they are a more credible source than the actual combatants in the campaign.

The power of the news media to "penalize bloopers severely" was amply demonstrated in the cases of Romney and Muskie. It was also the case with Gerald Ford's statement on Eastern Europe's freedom from Soviet domination during the second presidential debate on foreign policy. The data to be presented in this chapter suggest that the general public did not know that the president had made an "error" until they were told so by the news media during the following day.

Ford's publicized statement did not cause his candidacy to collapse; the 1976 presidential election was one of our closest elections. However, the two-month trend toward Ford recorded in the public polls came to a halt in the wake of the foreign policy debate. The Ford campaign was put on the defensive for several valuable campaigning days, while the media pressed Ford for a restatement of his position. In the intricate process of building and maintaining an overall positive image, the Ford campaign had suffered a serious setback. The seriousness was compounded by the facts that the foreign policy debate was to have been a trump card for Ford, yet it seemed to give evidence for a perception that some Democrats had tried to foster—that Ford was not smart enough to be a great president.

President Ford's remarks occurred about 25 minutes into the debate when Max Frankel of the New York *Times* asked President Ford if it were not true that communism, as Khrushchev had predicted, had gained the upper hand over the West. Frankel reeled off alleged examples of growing communist influence and negotiating prowess, including the Helsinki agreement by which, he suggested, the United States virtually recognized the Soviet Union's right to dominate Eastern Europe. (The complete transcript of this portion of the debate can be found in Appendix D.)

In responding, President Ford gave his own examples and interpretations of the U.S. dealings with the Soviet Union beginning with his 1974 Vladivostok meeting with Brezhnev, which Ford contended placed important caps on Soviet missile capabilities and the grain sales to the Soviet Union—which he defended as benefiting American agriculture. Ford, then, turned to the Helsinki agreement and tripped over it. Frankel's critique of the Helsinki agreement was not new, and one can speculate, given the extensive preparations the participants made for the 1976 debates, that Ford had prepared for Frankel's particular charge. Ford said that the Vatican had signed the Helsinki agreement and that the Pope would not have approved an agreement that turned over the domination of Eastern Europe to the Soviet Union. One of Ford's last remarks in this sequence is intriguing as he suddenly draws Carter's name into the argument (suggesting a planned tactic to head off an anticipated Carter attack on the Helsinki agreement).

METHODOLOGY

The President Ford Committee commissioned Market Opinion Research to impanel viewers during the debate and to survey a national sample of registered voters by telephone after the debate. The panel consisted of 52 adults in Seattle, Washington.* The national survey began immediately after the debate (11:00 p.m. EST), with 101 interviews completed by 1:00 a.m. and 397 interviews completed through the following day (October 7) ending at midnight.

The purpose of the Seattle panel was to learn what specific parts of the debate, if any, helped or hurt each candidate. Each panelist had a circular dial ranging from 0 to 100. They were instructed to turn it toward 100 if what they were hearing made them feel more favorable about President Ford or less favorable about Carter and toward 0 if what they were hearing made them feel more favorable about Jimmy Carter or less favorable toward Ford. The dials were connected to a computer that kept a running average for all the panelists and for two subgroups: those who said they leaned toward Ford and those who said they leaned toward Carter. The running average was synchronized with a videotape of the debate for analysis afterward.

The primary purpose of the telephone survey was to measure the postdebate voting intentions and candidate perceptions of a representative sample of the national electorate. In addition to asking them who won the debate, they were also asked to rate Carter and Ford on a series of issues and personal qualities. However, the survey was not purposely designed to measure the mediating effects of the news media.

Evidence of some crucial interviewing variable between the debate and the following night is chiefly provided by an analysis of the voters' responses in the national survey by time of interviewing. The respondents were divided into four time periods according to the time they were interviewed: 11:00 p.m., October 6 to 1:00 a.m., October 7; 9:00 a.m. to noon; noon to 5:00 p.m.; and 5:00 p.m. to midnight, October 7. All times are eastern standard time. The intervening variable is presumed to be the dissemination of the information—by the news media on the day following the debate—that President Ford had made an incorrect statement about Eastern Europe.

---

*The panel portion of the research was conducted by Tell-Back, Inc., Spokane, Washington, for Market Opinion Research.

RAW FINDINGS BY TIME OF INTERVIEWING

Among 101 voters interviewed Wednesday night immediately following the debate, Ford had a 54-to-36 percent lead in their stated voting intentions. During the next evening the 121 voters interviewed were "voting" for Carter by a 54-to-37 percent count (Table 5.1). Thus, in only 25 hours, our raw data was showing an 18 percent majority lead for Ford turning completely around and giving a +17 percent lead for Carter for a remarkable point total change. In addition, there appeared to be a progressive movement to Carter, although at uneven rates, during the following day. The change was already apparent in the interviewing done between 9 a.m. and noon. Ford's +18 percent lead had been reduced to only +3 percent. At this point an obvious intervening event was the appearance of the morning newspapers and the telecasting of the morning news programs. The noon-to-5 p.m. interviewing yielded an insignificant change from the morning although in the same direction. Ford's lead had closed to 1 percentage point. The evening interviewing, which overlapped and extended beyond the evening news programs and presumably the reading of the afternoon newspaper by people returning from work, showed the largest change from its adjacent time period. Compared to his already reduced 1 point lead in the afternoon, Ford fell -17 percent behind Carter among the voters interviewed between 5 p.m. and midnight Thursday.

TABLE 5.1

Reported Voting Intention, by Time of Interview, in Percent*

	Total	Oct. 6, 11:00 p.m. to 1:00 a.m.	October 7 9:00 a.m. to noon	October 7 Noon to 5:00 p.m.	October 7 5:00 p.m. to midnight
Ford	45	54	45	45	37
Carter	44	36	42	44	54
Undecided	11	10	13	12	9
Total	100	100	100	100	100
Number of cases	498	101	125	151	121

*The question asked was: "If the presidential election were being held today, which candidate would you vote for—Ford, the Republican, or Carter, the Democrat?" Results are for the entire sample 70 percent of whom saw or listened to the debate.

Source: Compiled by the author.

TABLE 5.2

Perceived Winner of the Debate, by Time of Interview, in Percent*

	Total	Oct. 6 1:00 p.m. to 11:00 a.m.	October 7 9:00 to noon	October 7 Noon to 5:00 p.m.	October 7 5:00 p.m. to 5:00 midnight
Ford	28	44	31	22	19
Carter	48	35	44	48	61
Both	9	7	12	12	5
Neither	5	3	4	6	4
Don't know	10	12	8	11	10
Total	100	100	100	100	100
Number of cases	348	67	92	103	85

*The question asked was, "Who do you think did the 'better job' in this debate—Gerald Ford or Jimmy Carter?" The question was asked only of those respondents who reported they saw or listened to the debate.

Source: Compiled by the author.

The voters' perceptions of the debate itself showed an even greater change than was appearing in their voting intentions (Table 5.2). There was a huge 51 percent change between late Wednesday and Thursday nights in the voters' perceptions of who had done the "better" job in the debate. Ford was the +9 percent plurality choice Wednesday night, but, on Thursday night, a 61 percent to 19 percent majority said Jimmy Carter had done the "better job." With this perception a more even progression toward Carter is evident. There was a 22 percentage-point change between Wednesday night and immediately after the dissemination of the morning news. There was a 13 percentage-point change between the morning and afternoon. Finally, there was a 16 percentage-point change between Thursday afternoon and night. Again, the largest spurts to the trend came immediately after the morning and evening news periods.

Three specific perceptions of the debate were measured and, of the three, the one substantively closest to Ford's overstatements about Eastern Europe registered the largest reversal. Accidental to what was to happen that night, we asked, "Generally, do you think that Jimmy Carter's or Gerald answers were more believable?" On this question there was a 48 percentage-point change during the 25 hours following the debate. In contrast, there was noticeably less change on which candidate the voters most "agreed with" (35 percentage points)

TABLE 5.3

Specific Perceptions of the Debate, by Time of Interview, in Percent

	Total	Oct. 6 11:00 p.m. to 1:00 a.m.	October 7 9:00 a.m. to Noon	October 7 Noon to 5:00 p.m.	October 7 5:00 p.m. to Midnight
Credibility[a]					
Ford	39	52	42	40	26
Carter	37	27	31	39	49
Both	11	11	15	9	9
Neither	1	3	–	2	1
Don't know	11	7	11	11	15
Agreement with[b]					
Ford	40	48	46	40	30
Carter	42	36	40	39	53
Both	6	5	5	10	4
Neither	2	3	1	3	3
Don't know	9	8	8	10	10
Directness[c]					
Ford	41	42	49	42	31
Carter	34	31	33	31	40
Both	13	13	9	15	14
Neither	4	4	5	3	3
Don't know	8	8	4	9	11
Total	100	100	100	100	100
Number of cases	348	67	92	103	85

[a]"Generally, do you think that Jimmy Carter's or Gerald Ford's answers were more believable?"

[b]"Personally, did you most agree with Gerald Ford's or Jimmy Carter's statements during this debate?"

[c]"Overall, who do you think answered their questions more directly–Jimmy Carter or Gerald Ford?"

Source: Compiled by the author.

and which candidate they thought answered his questions "more directly" (20 percentage points). Ford's statement on Eastern Europe was "direct" if nothing else and the voters appeared to be responding to that observation. Possibly reflecting the double meaning of the question, on the perception of who gave the more "direct answers," Ford gained among the morning voters over the Wednesday night voters—the only such instance of a countermovement in the four measures discussed thus far (Table 5.3).

DIRECT EVIDENCE OF THE VOTERS' LEARNING ABOUT FORD'S MISTAKE

Fortunately, we are able to make a direct tie between these movements and Ford's misstatement on Eastern Europe. The voters were asked to volunteer what they thought were the "main things" each candidate had done "well" and and "not [done] well during the debate." On Wednesday night not a single respondent mentioned Ford's statements about Eastern Europe. But the next morning the mentions began to appear (Table 5.4): 12 percent of the voters in the morning, 12 percent in the afternoon, and 20 percent after 5:00 p.m. cited Ford's Eastern Europe pronouncement as one of the "things" he "did not do well during the debate."

Moreover, additional voters gave such responses as, "Ford had unorganized facts" or "Ford was mixed up on his facts." There is no way of knowing now whether or not these voters had in mind Ford's misstatement on Eastern Europe. It is very tantalizing to draw that conclusion because these responses are found only in the interviewing done after 12:00 noon the next day; that is, 3 percent of the noon-to-5:00-p.m. respondents and 6 percent of the 5:00-p.m.-to-midnight respondents. In any event, the total absence of explicit or implicit criticisms of Ford's statement on Eastern Europe in the interviews immediately after the debate and the growing appearance of those criticisms the next day is very impressive evidence that the true status of Eastern Europe was not clear to many Americans until they learned it the next day, presumably from the news media.

The Seattle panelists provide direct evidence of initial nonrecognition of Ford's overstatements. They did not react one way or the other during this part of the debate in which Ford made his comments about Eastern Europe. Their running average score changed frequently during the debate, ranging from 29 (pro-Carter), when Carter was criticizing U.S. arms sales to Iran, to 64 (pro-Ford), when Ford was defending his actions in the Mayaguez rescue mission. Nevertheless, there was little movement during the segment in which Ford made his statements about Eastern Europe. When Ford started the sequence by referring to the Helsinki agreement, the group average was 45. It increased mildly to 49 when Ford opened the door for his interrogator, Frankel, by saying

TABLE 5.4

Volunteered Criticisms of Ford's Debate Performance, by Time of Interview, in Percent

	Total Sample	Oct. 6 11:00 p.m. to 1:00 a.m.	October 7 9:00 a.m. to Noon	Noon to 5:00 p.m.	5:00 p.m. to Midnight
Eastern Europe/complete domination of Eastern Europe/goofed on Eastern Europe	9	—	10	10	13
Indirect answers/answers weren't good	4	4	3	5	5
Evaded the issue/did't address himself to the issue	4	10	5	3	—
Could have done better	4	3	3	4	7
Not a clear speaker/delivery faded	4	7	3	5	1
Ford on defensive	4	7	3	4	1
Scared/nervous/worried	3	6	—	4	4
Russian issue/statement on Russia	3	—	2	2	7
Not specific enough	3	4	1	1	5
Unorganized facts/mixed up on facts	2	—	—	3	6
Not aggressive/forceful/did not push hard enough	2	1	5	1	—
Everything OK	1	1	—	1	1
Tearing down Carter/talk about Carter	1	—	1	1	1
No warmth/sober/stoneface	1	1	—	2	—
Unemployment issues/creating jobs	1	—	—	2	—
Explaining the economy issue	a	—	—	1	—
Was not dramatic like Reagan	a	—	—	—	1
Not constructive/cut down everything Carter said	a	—	—	1	—
Other negative Ford responses	5	6	2	8	3
None/nothing	21	23	34	13	14
Don't know	33	33	29	37	34
Number of cases	348	67	92	103	85

[a]The question asked was, "What are the main things you think President Ford did not do well during the debates?" *Source*: Compiled by the author.

that the Pope would not sign an agreement that turned over to the Warsaw Pact nations the domination of Eastern Europe. The group average held to 48 as Frankel finished his follow-up question in astonishment at the implication of Ford's previous remarks. As Ford began his reply, the group average dropped slightly to 46, and then to 44, when Ford included the Poles. The group average held to 44 throughout the last 30 seconds of Ford's reply. The Seattle panelists did not react at all. Moreover, the earlier decline from 48 to 44 is mild compared to the movements recorded during other parts of be debate, as can be seen in Figure 5.1.

Jimmy Carter obliquely challenged Ford's statements by a response that would have been unclear and unappreciated by that portion of the listening public that initially did not consider Ford's remarks erroneous. Moreover, Carter delayed his reply to Ford's references to the autonomy of Yugoslavia, Romania, and Poland until the second part of his response. Carter's behavior in this regard is very important for it allowed the "no reaction" phenomenon to persist. Evidently, for most of the Seattle panelists, if an authority figure such as the president of the United States said Eastern Europe was free from Soviet domination, then it might be true. It was not until the following day that we find evidence of the public doubting the credibility of the President's pronouncements; that came about by the media directly taking Ford to task.

THE PROBLEM OF POST FACTO DATA

In spite of the magnitude of the national survey changes and the direct confirmation by the volunteered remarks and by the Seattle panelists, there are problems with our analysis that must be addressed before the conclusion of a media effect can be entertained. The samples falling in the four time periods were not matched national samples. Instead, interviewing necessities dictated the selection of respondents in the four time periods. Two biases in the subsamples directly resulted from the constraints on the interviewing. First, most of the interviewing Wednesday night (79 percent) was done in the West because the hour was too late to telephone in the eastern and central time zones. Second, the interviews completed Thursday night were mostly with men (94 percent). The sex biases by time period were necessary to avoid the unacceptable alternative of overrepresenting daytime at-home males, especially retirees.

An inspection of the demographic profile of the four samples (Table 5.5) uncovers one additional bias, although a moderate one. The voters interviewed Wednesday night more frequently were college-educated (55 percent with some college education or more) compared with the voters interviewed Thursday (45 percent with some college education or more). The education bias is directly related to the regional bias already described.

FIGURE 5.1
Continuous Average Score by Viewers of the Second Debate

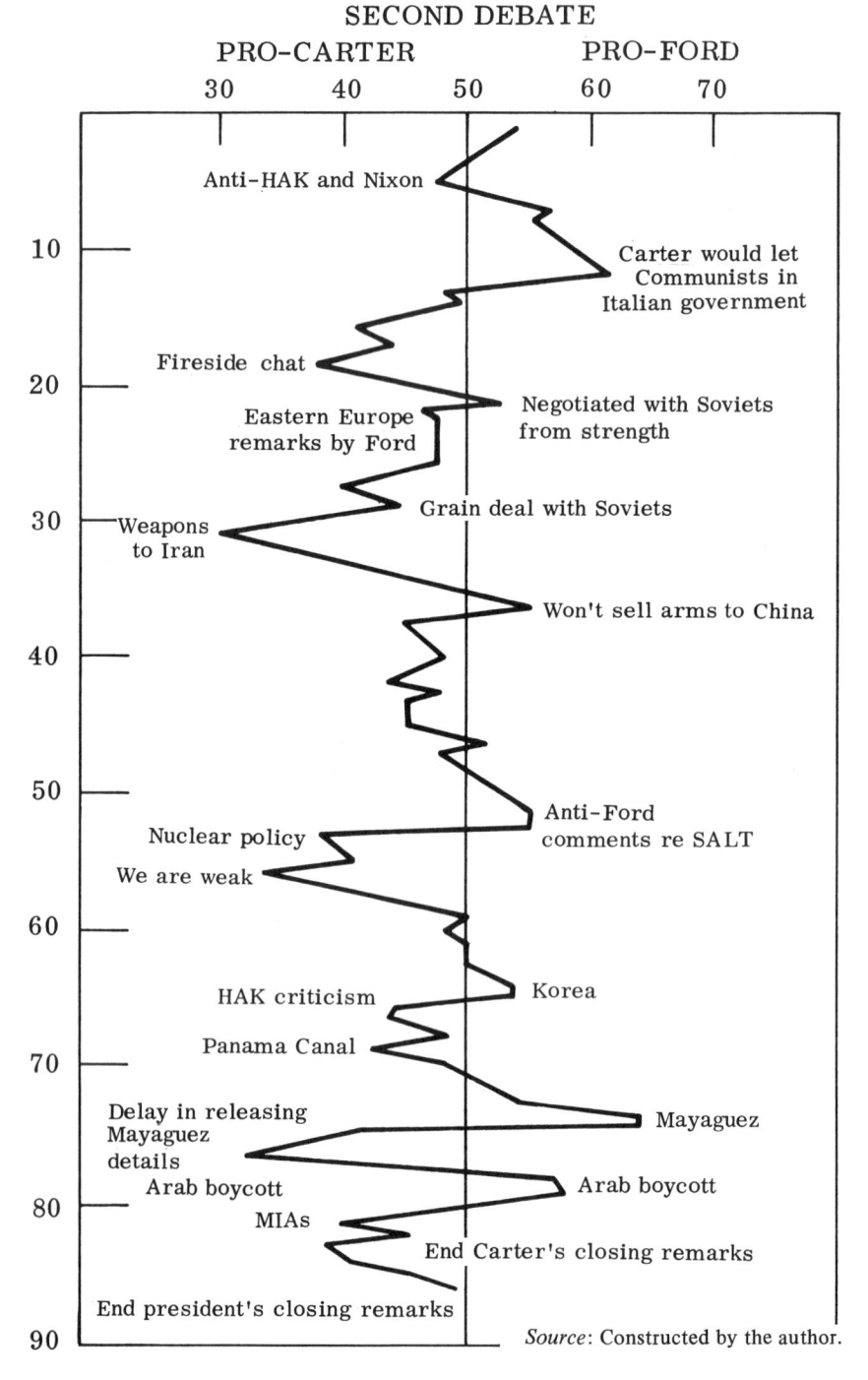

SECOND DEBATE
PRO-CARTER   PRO-FORD
30   40   50   60   70

- Anti-HAK and Nixon
- Carter would let Communists in Italian government
- Fireside chat
- Eastern Europe remarks by Ford
- Negotiated with Soviets from strength
- Grain deal with Soviets
- Weapons to Iran
- Won't sell arms to China
- Anti-Ford comments re SALT
- Nuclear policy
- We are weak
- HAK criticism
- Korea
- Panama Canal
- Delay in releasing Mayaguez details
- Mayaguez
- Arab boycott
- Arab boycott
- MIAs
- End Carter's closing remarks
- End president's closing remarks

Source: Constructed by the author.

TABLE 5.5

Profile of Time Period Subsamples, in Percent*

	Total	Oct. 6 11:00 p.m. to 1:00 a.m.	October 7 9:00 a.m. to Noon	Noon to 5:00 p.m.	5:00 p.m. to Midnight
Party identification					
Republican	21	24	13	28	18
Democrat	37	34	39	34	42
Independent	42	42	48	38	40
Region					
East	23	3	21	36	30
Midwest	27	1	33	30	37
South	31	17	46	32	25
West	18	79	–	2	8
Education					
Less than high school	16	14	14	19	16
High school	36	29	44	33	38
Some college or more	47	55	42	46	45
Sex					
Men	52	50	26	41	94
Women	48	50	74	59	6
Race					
Nonblack	90	95	93	88	89
Black	7	5	5	11	7
Total	100	100	100	100	100

*There were no significant differences by age, union membership, or religion; therefore, those results are not listed.

Source: Compiled by the author.

The regional biases present the possibility that the more favorable results for Ford on Wednesday night were entirely due to interviewing a more Republican subsample from the West compared with the interviewing done on Thursday in the more Democratic South, East, and Midwest. Consequently, it is necessary to place a control for partisan loyalties on the raw data to see if the original pattern holds or vanishes. The control for the partisan loyalties of the voters in each time period must serve as a substitute test for the effects of the regional biases. It is impossible to control on region directly because there were almost no interviews done in the West the next day on which to compare with those done Wednesday night. The control for partisan loyalties also is mandatory because of the general influence of party identification on perceptual results of this kind quite apart from the regional bias in this study. To account for that portion of the change due to partisan differences in the subsamples, the expected Republican response for each subsample will be calculated and the observed deviation will be reported. (The expected Republican response is an adaptation of Converse's "normal vote" concept [1966].) If there was a media effect, then the deviations from the expected Republican response should become more unfavorable for Ford the further in time from the debate the respondents were interviewed. If the observed or raw pattern was due only to partisan biases in the subsamples, then the deviations will be the same for each time period. Theoretically, this analysis also could uncover a favorable trend to Ford that was smothered by the sampling biases.

The degree to which the raw results can be explained away by sex and education biases in the four time periods will be answered by the straightforward method of breaking the results by sex and education within each time period. The observed pattern will be further tested by requiring that the deviations from the expected Republican responses show a decline for Ford among men, women, the college-educated, and the noncollege-educated across the four time periods.

THE EFFECT OF PARTY IDENTIFICATION ON THE OBSERVED CHANGES

As Table 5.5 shows, the voters interviewed late Wednesday night were more Republican than the nation as a whole, but only moderately so. Moreover, the voters interviewed between noon and 5:00 p.m. Thursday were just as Republican as those interviewed Wednesday night. Instead of interviewing fewer and fewer Republicans as time went on, the partisan composition of the four time periods actually follows a zigzag pattern. In terms of the expected Republican response for each time period, there is a 47 percent expected pro-Republican response by the respondents interviewed Wednesday night, 40 percent by those interviewed Thursday morning, 47 percent by those interviewed Thursday afternoon, and 40 percent by those interviewed Thursday evening and night.

Most of the decline in Ford's intended vote between Wednesday night and Thursday morning can be accounted for by the interviewing of a less Republican sample Thursday morning. However, the lack of an observed raw change between the morning and afternoon proves to be misleading. The afternoon respondents were more favorably predisposed to a Republican candidate than the morning respondents, but Ford's vote did not increase accordingly. By remaining the same in the two time periods, Ford's deviation from the expected Republican vote fell from +14 percent to +7 percent. This measures a real trend

TABLE 5.6

Observed Pro-Ford Responses and Expected Pro-Republican Responses, by Time of Interview, in Percent

	Observed Response	Expected Pro-Republican Response	Deviation	Adjusted Trend	Number of Cases
Ford's committed vote*					
Total listener sample	52	44	+8	–	348
October 6, 11:00 p.m. to 1:00 a.m.	63	47	+16	–	67
October 7, 9:00 a.m. to noon	54	40	+14	-2	92
October 7, noon to 5:00 p.m.	54	47	+7	-7	103
October 7, 5:00 p.m. to midnight	38	40	-2	-9	85
Total decline	-25	-7	-18	-18	
Ford did better job					
Total listener sample	37	44	-7	–	348
October 6, 11:00 p.m. to 1:00 a.m.	56	47	+9	–	67
October 7, 9:00 a.m. to noon	41	40	+1	-8	92
October 7, noon to 5:00 p.m.	32	47	-15	-16	103
October 7, 5:00 p.m. to midnight	24	40	-16	-1	85
Total decline	-32	-7	-25	-25	

*The committed vote differs from Table 5.1 in that the undecided voters have been dropped from the base. Also, Ford's vote in this table and succeeding tables uses the stated intentions of the viewers and listeners of the debate rather than the total sample.

Source: Compiled by the author.

away from Ford between the two daytime periods. With the Thursday night respondents, Ford's vote fell another 16 percentage points, 7 points of which is due to the less pro-Republican composition of the sample, but leaving 9 percentage points of the decline not accounted for by differences in party strengths. As summarized in Table 5.6, there is an adjusted trend against Ford across the four time periods of a -2 percent between Wednesday night and Thursday morning, -7 percent between the morning and afternoon on Thursday, and -9 percent between the afternoon and night on Thursday. The total decline in

Ford's vote that cannot be accounted for by partisan sampling differences is −18 percent. These deviations measure declines in Ford's strength between time periods without an exception and at an accelerated rate.

Similarly, there is a total −25 percent decline in the proportion of voters saying Ford did the "better job" in the debate that cannot be accounted for by the partisan differences between the four subsamples. In contrast to the voting intention data, very little of the −25 percent decline for Ford occurred with the Thursday night respondents; instead, 16 percentage points of the 25 percentage-point drop ocurred between the morning and afternoon on Thursday. Again, the deviations show continued declines for Ford between time periods, without an exception.

The differing rates of change on the two dependent variables fit a theoretical expectation. First, the direct measure of the stimulus object—that is, who did the better job in the debate—underwent the largest and fastest change. Vote intention, which would be a consequence of the perceptual change, lagged behind the rate of change in the antecedent measure. An intuitively appealing reason the perceptions of the debate winner slowed in their trend away from Ford is that by 5:00 p.m. they already had reached a theoretical minimum level, that is, the "hard-core" Ford proportion in the electorate. By remaining at that low point, however, the unfavorable perceptions of Ford's performance continued to pull down his ballot support in the electorate.

THE EFFECTS OF SEX AND EDUCATION ON THE OBSERVED CHANGES

The declines in the voters' preferences for Ford are still present in the data when the sex and education of the respondents are held constant. The sampling differences on these demographics do not explain away the changes. In fact, cutting the data by these demographics leads to some additional findings. While Ford's declines are present in each case, they are much larger with women than with men, and with college-educated voters than with noncollege-educated voters.

As can be seen in Table 5.7, men undergo a 31 percentage-point change to Carter as their vote choice, and a 28 percentage-point change to Carter as doing the best job in the debate. The women switch to Carter by 40 percentage points for their vote choice, and by 65 percentage points for doing the best job in the debate. (The changes for women are based on the first three time periods. There were only six interviews with women in the last time period.) The results by sex are close for vote intention, but there is a big difference between men and wonen in the changes in their perceptions of who won the debate. Also suggesting that women, more so than men, were the focus of the media's educating role on Ford's statements about Eastern Europe is the impressive consistency in the

TABLE 5.7

Vote Intention and Perceived Winner of the Debate by Sex and Time of Interview, in Percent (viewers and listeners of the debate only)

	Total Sample	Men					Women				
		Total Men	11:00 p.m. to 1:00 a.m.	9:00 a.m. to Noon	Noon to 5:00 p.m.	5:00 p.m. to Midnight	Total Women	11:00 p.m. to 1:00 a.m.	9:00 a.m. to Noon	Noon to 5:00 p.m.	5:00 p.m. to Midnight
Vote intention											
Gerald Ford	47	46	50	55	56	36	47	63	47	42	18
Jimmy Carter	44	46	39	42	35	56	41	26	42	45	65
Refused	1	1	2	4	–	1	1	–	–	3	–
Don't know	8	6	9	–	9	6	11	11	11	10	18
Who did better job											
Gerald Ford	28	25	30	29	29	19	31	57	32	18	18
Jimmy Carter	48	52	43	54	43	60	43	26	41	52	82
Both did a good job (volunteered)	9	9	8	9	15	6	10	6	13	9	–
Neither did a good job (volunteered)	5	6	6	8	8	5	3	–	3	5	–
Don't know	10	8	13	–	4	11	13	11	11	17	–
Total	100	100	100	100	100	100	100	100	100	100	100
Number of Cases	348	180	34	24	43	80	168	34	68	60	6

Source: Compiled by the author.

TABLE 5.8

Vote Intention and Perceived Winner of the Debate by Education and Time of Interview, in Percent
(viewers and listeners of the debate only)

	Total Sample	High School and Vocational or Less						Some College or More				
		Total	11:00 p.m. to 1:00 a.m.	9:00 a.m. to Noon	Noon to 5:00 p.m.	5:00 p.m. to Midnight	Total	11:00 p.m. to 1:00 a.m.	9:00 a.m. to Noon	Noon to 5:00 p.m.	5:00 p.m. to Midnight
Vote intention											
Gerald Ford	47	45	57	44	44	40	48	54	56	51	30
Jimmy Carter	44	46	34	50	46	50	41	33	32	36	65
Refused	1	1	3	2	2	–	1	–	–	3	2
Don't know	8	8	6	5	9	10	10	13	12	10	3
Who did better job	28										
Gerald Ford	28	24	41	26	15	20	32	48	38	28	18
Jimmy Carter	46	52	37	55	50	59	44	34	29	49	63
Both did a good job (volunteered)	9	8	6	8	14	4	11	8	18	10	8
Neither did a good job (volunteered)	5	4	3	4	5	4	5	3	5	8	5
Don't know	10	12	13	7	17	13	7	7	10	6	7
Total	100	100	100	100	100	100	100	100	100	100	100
Number of Cases	348	181	29	53	53	46	162	37	39	48	38

Source: Compiled by the author.

decline of Ford across the three time periods in which there are between 34 and 68 interviews with women voters. The men, on the other hand, do not display a monotonic change.

In Table 5.8, Ford's decline and Carter's increase in public favor can be traced for college and noncollege voters by time of interview. The college voters exhibit the greater change of the two: 56 percentage points on vote intention and 59 percentage points on who did the better job in the debate. Noncollege voters changed by 33 and 43 percentage points on vote intention and perceived winner of the debate, respectively. For both groups, their raw pattern is monotonic across the 25 hours for the perceived winner of the debate. On vote intention, both groups have one countermovement to the overall trend by time period.

The final step taken in the analysis was to calculate the expected Republican responses for the four demographic control groups for each time period and then calculate the deviations of the observed or raw pro-Ford responses from the expected proportions. This was done, first, to confirm that the basic finding could withstand the simultaneous control of party and demographic characteristics and, second, to possibly iron out the few countermovements existing in the raw data. Tables 5.9 and 5.10 present the results of this analysis. The basic finding withstands this test very well. Moreover, all the apparent countermovements in the raw data can be accounted for by an increase in the pro-Republican bias of the sample in the time period causing the exception. When that factor is taken into account, the demographic group's pattern returns to the monotonic decline of pro-Ford responses observed in the sample as a whole.

This analysis also uncovers two important countermovements that cannot be seen in the raw data. The new exceptions involve the noncollege voters on both dependent variables between the afternoon interviewing and the evening interviewing on Thursday. On each variable Ford does less well than expected with the afternoon respondents than with the evening respondents, and, thereby, the monotonic pattern that exists everywhere else in the data breaks down among the noncollege voters at one point. There is still a total drop for Ford among the noncollege voters from Wednesday night to Thursday night. The noted inconsistency does not negate the basic relationship, but it does indicate a weaker impact of the news stories on the less educated voter.

The larger total change in the raw data for college voters also exists in the adjusted results. Coupled with the perfectly consistent pattern exhibited by the college voters, the magnitude of the change for college voters surprisingly suggests that the news commentaries the next day had a much greater impact on them than on noncollege voters. Among college voters Wednesday night, Ford was running +14 percent ahead of the expected proportion that would choose the Republican as doing the better job in the debate. The observed Ford proportion dropped to a +11 percent over the expected on Thursday morning, plunged

TABLE 5.9

Observed Pro-Ford Responses and Expected Pro-Republican Responses for Men and Women by Time of Interview, in Percent

	Observed Response	Expected Pro-Republican Response	Deviation	Adjusted Trend	Number of Cases
Ford's committed vote					
Total male listeners	50	43	+7	—	180
October 6, 11:00 p.m. to 1:00 a.m.	56	39	+17	—	34
October 7, 9:00 a.m. to noon	57	40	+17	0	24
October 7, noon to 5:00 p.m.	62	51	+11	-6	43
October 7, 5:00 p.m. to midnight	39	41	-2	-13	80
Total decline	-17	+2	-19	-19	
Total female listeners	54	44	+10	—	168
October 6, 11:00 p.m. to 1:00 a.m.	71	51	+20	—	34
October 7, 9:00 a.m. to noon	52	40	+12	-8	68
October 7, noon to 5:00 p.m.	49	46	+3	-9	60
October 7, 5:00 p.m. to midnight	21	32	-11	-14	6
Total decline*	-22	-5	-17	-17	
Ford did better job					
Total male listeners	32	43	-11	—	180
October 6, 11:00 p.m. to 1:00 a.m.	42	39	+3	—	34
October 7, 9:00 a.m. to noon	35	40	-5	-8	24
October 7, noon to 5:00 p.m.	39	51	-12	-7	43
October 7, 5:00 p.m. to midnight	24	41	-17	-5	80
Total decline	-18	+2	-20	-20	

TABLE 5.9 (Continued)

	Observed Response	Expected Pro-Republican Response	Deviation	Adjusted Trend	Number of Cases
Total female listeners	42	44	-2	—	168
October 6, 11:00 p.m. to 1:00 a.m.	68	51	+17	—	34
October 7, 9:00 a.m. to noon	44	40	+4	-13	68
October 7, noon to 5:00 p.m.	26	46	-20	-24	60
October 7, 5:00 p.m. to midnight	18	32	-14	-6	6
Total decline*	-50	-19	-37	-37	

*Total decline for women is for the first three time periods.
Source: Compiled by the author.

to a -12 percent on Thursday afternoon, and ended at -23 percent on Thursday night. This is a total adjusted change of -37 percent in the proportion choosing Ford over Carter as the winner of the debate. In contrast, the total adjusted change for noncollege voters is -14 percent. Even if the lowest point for Ford is used among the noncollege voters—that is, from noon to 5:00 p.m.—the adjusted change from Wednesday night is still less than the total change among the college voters. The difference between college and noncollege voters is even greater in their respective changes in voting preferences. Stated intention to vote for Ford drops an adjusted -32 percent among college voters, but it drops only -5 percent among noncollege voters across the four time periods.

The comparison of the adjusted changes for men and women must be limited to the first three time periods because of the lack of interviews with women in the final time period. The three-period change for women in their choice of Ford as doing the best job in the debate is -37 percent compared to a lesser -15 percent drop for Ford among men. Stated intention to vote for Ford drops an adjusted -17 percent for women and a -6 percent for men across the first three time periods.

TABLE 5.10

Observed Pro-Ford Responses and Expected Pro-Republican Responses for College-Educated and Noncollege-Educated Voters, by Time of Interview, in Percent

	Observed Response	Expected Pro-Republican Response	Deviation	Adjusted Trend	Number of Cases
Ford's Committed Vote					
Total noncollege listeners	49	41	+8	–	181
October 6, 11:00 p.m. to 1:00 a.m.	63	49	+14	–	29
October 7, 9:00 a.m. to noon	47	34	+13	–1	53
October 7, noon to 5:00 p.m.	49	47	+2	–11	53
October 7, 5:00 p.m. to midnight	45	36	+9	+7	46
Total decline	–18	–13	–5	–5	
Total college listeners	54	46	+8	–	162
October 6, 11:00 p.m. to 1:00 a.m.	62	44	+18	–	37
October 7, 9:00 a.m. to noon	64	47	+17	–1	39
October 7, noon to 5:00 p.m.	58	48	+10	–7	48
October 7, 5:00 p.m. to midnight	32	46	–14	–24	38
Total decline	–30	+2	–32	–32	
Ford Did Better Job					
Total noncollege listeners	31	41	–10	–	181
October 6, 11:00 p.m. to 1:00 a.m.	52	49	+3	–	29
October 7, 9:00 a.m. to noon	33	34	–1	–4	53
October 7, noon to 5:00 p.m.	23	47	–24	–23	53
October 7, 5:00 p.m. to midnight	25	36	–11	+13	46
Total decline	–27	–13	–14	–14	
Total college listeners	43	46	–3	–	162
October 6, 11:00 p.m. to 1:00 a.m.	58	44	+14	–	37
October 7, 9:00 a.m. to noon	58	47	+11	–3	39
October 7, noon to 5:00 p.m.	36	48	–12	–23	48
October 7, 5:00 p.m. to midnight	23	46	–23	–11	38
Total decline	–35	+2	–37	–37	

Source: Complied by the author.

SUMMARY AND CONCLUSIONS

Pro-Ford responses after the second debate declined steadily through the following day. The observed declines were not due to the known sampling biases in the data used to measure Ford's decline. The volunteered descriptions of the debate by the voters surveyed immediately after the debate included no mentions of Ford's statement on Eastern Europe. Not until the afternoon of the next day did such references appear, and by Thursday night they were the most frequent criticism given of Ford's performance. Similarly, the panelists monitored during the debate gave no indication of an unfavorable reaction at the time they heard Ford's Eastern European remarks. The conclusion is that the preponderance of viewers of the second debate most likely were not certain of the true status of Eastern Europe or, less likely, did not consider Ford's error important. Given the amount of publicity given to Ford's East European statements the next day by the news media and the concomitant change that took place, it is concluded that this publicity caused the change. The change probably was too rapid to be caused by interpersonal influence or by the classic two-step process. Rather, this is evidence of direct media influence.

College-educated voters appeared to be a major group affected by the next-day publicity. A possible reason for this is that they are more attentive to political news and commentary than the noncollege voters and, consequently, were more likely to learn of the scope of Ford's error. Women also seemed to be disproportionately affected by the next-day publicity. This would suggest that women had fewer and/or less intense perceptions of Ford and Carter beforehand than did men; thus, the women were less resistant to the flow of bad information about Ford the next day. (Different explanations are given for the same change by college-educated voters and women because of the wide differences in general political interest associated with each group.)

Finally, the voting intention data used in the analysis are not meant to imply that Carter surged to a lasting 17 percentage-point lead on October 7. He obviously did not. It is not clear why the voting intention measure should have been as sensitive as it was to the publicity following the debate. However, its change did lag behind the change registered by the measure of the voters' perceptions of the winner of the debate as would be expected. Possibly, the voting intention change reflects the extreme softness in each candidate's vote throughout the campaign. Voters were easily deflected from Ford by a surge of "bad news" about him, but, because of other factors, many snapped back to him when the initial trauma of their candidate's statement faded in their minds. However, it generally has been observed that Ford's second debate "blooper" did halt a two-month trend toward him, a trend that he never was able to start again at a rate sufficient to win.

PART III

COGNITIVE AND BEHAVIORAL CONSEQUENCES OF THE DEBATES

6

PROBLEMS IN MEASURING AUDIENCE EFFECTS OF THE 1976 DEBATES

Doris A. Graber

The 1976 presidential debates, like their 1960 counterparts, have become a much-frequented happy hunting ground for mass communication scholars in search of audience effects. The circumstances seemed ideal: here was a much-publicized event, attended simultaneously by an average of 85 million Americans, for periods up to 270 minutes of television time. Presumably, the vast audience for whom the League of Women Voters' Educational Fund staged this campaign information project was motivated by similar goals. Viewers, it was hoped, wanted to learn more about the presidential candidates to refresh, corroborate, deepen, or supplement what they already knew. They also wanted to form or change impressions that would guide them in appraising the candidates and in making or confirming voting decisions. The researcher simply had to select a sample of people from this vast audience, compare the respondents' pre- and postdebate views, and record the changes as debate "effects."

Alas, what seemed so simple turned out to be extremely difficult. There were methodological reefs galore to make the research ship founder, along with whirlpools of imprecision ready to trap unwary scholars and mar their findings. As one who has traveled the rough seas, I want to point out a few of the treacherous reefs that have not yet been adequately marked by buoys set out by the research community. Specifically, I want to examine problems encountered in setting a base line against which learning can be measured and those that spring from a failure to distinguish various levels of learning. I will also briefly

---

An earlier version of this chapter was presented at the Research Conference on Presidential Debates, 1960 and 1976, held at the Annenberg School of Communications, University of Pennsylvania, Philadelphia, May 12–13, 1977.

assess the soundness of a number of widely used measuring instruments and the effects of instrument deficiencies on the accuracy of debate effects findings. Last, I will explore the difficulties that spring from separating debate analysis from the matrix of prior election learning and from the general political context in which the debates occurred.

THE DATA BASE

The data from which these observations are drawn come from the responses of a small panel of voters who were intensively interviewed at roughly five-week intervals, between January 1976 and January 1977. The panel was part of a larger study that investigated political learning, including agenda setting, by a combination of content analyses of media used by the respondents and interviews that tested the nature of learning about political figures and issues throughout the election year.*

The small panel, made up of 21 voters in Evanston, Illinois, a town adjacent to Chicago, was selected from a randomly drawn sample of registered voters. The panel was composed to reflect a demographic cross-section as well as different levels of interest in politics, availability of time for exposure to news, and attention to print and/or electronic media. Various comparisons between the characteristics and attitudes of the Evanston panel and those of larger, randomly selected panels indicated no significant discrepancies except for the fact that the Evanston panel had a higher than average number of college graduates.† The descriptive data about political learning should be interpreted in that light. The background characteristics of the panel are shown in Table 6.1.

Members of the Evanston intensive study panel were personally interviewed in their homes ten times throughout the election year. The interviews, which ran between one and two and one-half hours in length, were tape-recorded. Most questions were open-ended and designed to permit the respondent to formulate the major outlines of the answers as she or he perceived them. These broad questions were followed by more focused questions designed to get

---

*In addition to the intensive study panel, panels of 48 respondents were interviewed nine times throughout the election year in Evanston, Illinois; Indianapolis, Indiana; and Lebanon, New Hampshire. Most of the questions asked of the larger panels were also asked of the intensive study panel. Coinvestigators in this project are Maxwell McCombs and associates, Syracuse University, and David Weaver and associates, Indiana University. Young Yun Kim, Governors State University, participated significantly in the analysis of the debate data from the study.

†The data have been compared with all 1976 debate studies cited in the references throughout this chapter, with the three larger panels that form part of this study, and with relevant Gallup and Roper and CBS-New York *Times* polls.

TABLE 6.1

Background Characteristics of the Intensive Study Panel

	Age	Sex	Education[a]	Occupation	Marital Status[b]
High interest, high availability group	25	M	College	Research engineer	Single
	38	M	College	Administrator	Married
	45	M	College	Academic	Married
	74	M	College	Lawyer	Married
	75	M	Grade school	Blue collar	Married
High interest, low availability group	28	F	College	Home/child care	Married
	28	F	College	Corporation executive	Single
	30	F	College	Job/home/child care	Married
	33	M	College	Government administrator	Married
Low interest, high availability group	36	M	College	Editor	Married
	25	M	College	Grocery clerk	Single
	46	F	High school	Dress shop owner	Married
	50	F	College	Homemaker	Widowed
	65	F	High school	Bookkeeper	Widowed
	78	F	High school	Homemaker	Widowed
Low interest, low availability group	23	M	College	Hospital clerk	Single
	27	M	College	Retail sales	Single
	28	F	High school	Insurance clerk	Single
	36	F	High school	Nurse	Married
	56	F	Third grade	Maid	Widowed
	62	M	College	Plant manager	Married

[a] The designations indicate completion of degree requirements.
[b] Occupational needs, and social needs related to marital status, had a strong impact on frequencies of political discussion.

Note: Group assignments are based on replies to nine questions that ascertained interest and participation in politics and media-use patterns and life-style characteristics. The latter two gave clues to the availability of mass media information for particular respondents. Scores were based on a combination of self-assessment and objective measures.

Source: Compiled by the author.

all the respondents to cover the same knowledge areas. To elicit as broad and complete a response as possible, probes and follow-up questions were unlimited. Probes routinely asked for the reasons that had prompted particular answers. When the thrust of questions was obviously misconstrued by a particular respondent, the question was reworded to convey its meaning more effectively to that particular respondent. When questions appeared to be ambiguous to a respondent, we asked for her/his range of interpretations and for the answers to each of these interpretations.

The members of the intensive panel also completed daily diaries throughout the year. Here they recorded news stories that had come to their attention from the mass media or through personal contacts. They were instructed to enter any news story that they remembered at the time set aside for diary completion, noting briefly the main theme, the source, the length of the story, the reasons for their interest in the story, and their reactions to it. A minimum of 30 minutes was to elapse between story exposure and diary entry to allow normal forgetting processes to operate. In most instances, the actual interval was four hours or more. In addition, members of the intensive panel were questioned during each interview about an array of 20 to 30 news stories that had been covered by the newspapers and/or television news programs to which they normally paid attention.

To detect possible sensitization effects that might appear in the repeated interviews and in the diaries, news story recall tests were administered to control subjects who had not been previously interviewed. Recall of stories was scored on a four-point scale, ranging from 1 for "none" to 4 for "a lot." The latter rating was awarded whenever respondents could spontaneously relate three or more aspects of a news story. Comparisons of the mean recall scores showed no significant difference ($p < .05$) between the mean scores of news awareness of panel members ($\bar{x} = 2.3$) and the control group ($\bar{x} = 2.4$).

The reason for the small panel was the desire to investigate the political learning process intensively, over an extended period of time. The nature of the investigation—which demanded close and prolonged monitoring of the entire information supply of specific respondents, collecting daily diaries in writing or by telephone, and researching life-style details of panel members—made it mandatory to limit the number of respondents under study. As numerous other intensive studies of small numbers of individuals have shown, this does not preclude making generalizable findings about human behavior. With proper controls, these can be projected to larger populations (Lane 1962, pp. 1-11; Keniston 1968; Kerlinger 1972; Brown 1974; Lamb 1975, pp. vii-xiii, 3-23). The reward of this intensive analysis is far more intimate knowledge of respondents, their learning behaviors, and their perceptions of, and reactions to, various research instruments than is possible when large panels are used.

MEASURING "LEARNING": BASE LINES AND LEVELS

Judging from the extensive reports on research about the 1960 presidential debates, and the early reports on research about the 1976 debates, most such studies deal with the same narrow spectrum of effects (Kraus 1962; forthcoming). Researchers have focused on the audience's evaluation of the candidates' performance in the debates and its designations of "winners" and "losers." They have investigated whether viewing the debates changed attitudes regarding the qualities and qualifications of the candidates, and whether changes in evaluations altered the viewer's reactions to the candidates and their political parties (Cantrall, Colella, and Monroe 1976; chapter 7 in this volume; chapter 9 in this volume; Miller and MacKuen 1977; McLeod et al. 1977; Morrison, Steeper, and Greendale 1977; Becker et al. 1978). Researchers also have attempted to judge whether the attitudes resulting from perceptions of the debates had an impact on voting intentions and the actual vote. Likewise, attention has been paid to debate effects on cognitions, such as salience of candidates and issues and general learning about candidates and issues (chapter 7 in this volume; Graber and Kim 1977, 1978; Morrison, Steeper, and Greendale 1977; Becker et al. 1978).

While the findings from these studies generally point in the same direction, there is considerable variability in the strength of effects that have been reported. Our intensive study points to methodological divergencies and problems as the major source of discrepancies. Findings about "learning" from the debates about candidates and issues will serve as an example. Investigations of learning during the 1976 debates have yielded reports that learning was substantial, as well as reports that learning was minimal (chapter 7 in this volume; chapter 10 in this volume; Graber and Kim 1977, 1978; Miller and MacKuen 1977). Two methodological problems account for the differences. The first relates to the problem of establishing a base line from which to measure learning. One cannot observe postdebate changes without knowing what respondents had already learned prior to the debates. Since there is little agreement on the proper procedures for establishing base lines, techniques vary and yield different results, which, in turn, yield different learning measures.

Base Line Establishment and Sensitization Effects

Base lines have been established most simply by asking respondents to assess their predebate knowledge after the debates and compare it to their postdebate knowledge. Alternatively, predebate knowledge has been formally tested prior to the debates and the results have been compared with postdebate tests.

Reliance on self-evaluation is problematical because the flow of election information is continuous and repetitive throughout the campaign. This makes it extremely difficult for respondents to remember at what point in time and from what specific source they acquired a particular bit of information. For instance, when we asked our respondents repeatedly throughout the interview year to identify the specific news story from which recalled information originated, they were unable to do so for at least 80 percent of the information they had acquired. Other researchers have reported similar findings (McClure and Patterson 1973). Because of the difficulty of establishing a base line through informal self-evaluation, findings about debate learning based on this procedure are unreliable and often discrepant from study to study. This also holds true of findings based on self-evaluation of the separate effects of each debate, particularly if assessment is made collectively, after all of the debates, rather than seriatim, after each debate.

Formal pretesting presents even more serious problems. For example, several well-conceived and -executed debate studies involve interviews with panels of voters immediately prior to the first presidential debate, and again after the first debate, to establish a knowledge base from which to gauge knowledge gains. Respondents' predebate knowledge was determined by supplying them with statements of particular issue positions on topics such as unemployment, abortion, tax reform, federal reorganization, and the like. Respondents were asked whether each candidate favored or opposed the given stand. At a later date, following one or more debates, the questions were repeated to check whether the respondents' ability to identify the position of each candidate had changed in any way. The findings from such studies often indicated substantial learning. Panel members significantly improved their ability to identify candidate positions for issues covered during the debates. When the issue was not covered, no improvement occurred.

However, the validity of these findings is marred because the pretest procedure was likely to spur learning beyond normal levels. Respondents who are asked about the candidates' positions shortly before they have an opportunity to hear these positions expounded are sensitized to the information in question and are likely to learn at abnormally high rates.

Our Evanston study provides supporting evidence for this phenomenon. In answer to a series of questions that probed the effects of interviewing on our respondents' interest in current political events, attention to these events, and learning from them, we found that the most frequent effect was temporarily heightened interest in questions raised during the interviews.

Respondents reported discussing the questions and appropriate answers with family, friends, and associates in the immediate postinterview period. If the media carried relevant stories within a span of one to three days of the interview, these were likely to be read with above-average attention. Likewise, compared to subject areas that had not been covered, interview discussion topics were more likely to appear in the respondents' diaries in the days following an interview, if there were corresponding events in the news. The correlations were significant at the .001 level. Recall of stories to which respondents had been alerted also was higher and more sustained after a lapse of time than recall of stories that had not been a part of interviews within the preceding 60 days.

Since a pretest immediately prior to debate effects measurements is inadvisable, how early can one test and still avoid sensitization? Our findings indicate that the impact of prior questioning regarding election issues tends to be pronounced for up to two months and declines thereafter. This observation is based on a study of memory spans for news stories that we undertook as part of our research. During each interview, we routinely tested the recall by respondents of 20 to 30 news stories that had been prominently featured in the news to which they had been exposed one to five weeks earlier. We retested memory of a sample of these stories after lapses ranging from two to nine months. Our findings indicate that 70 percent of election stories were remembered to varying degrees for roughly a 60-day span, with respondents recalling substantial amounts of information for from 12 to 18 percent of the stories. Beyond the 60 days, memory rates dropped rapidly and details vanished.

The answer to the question of a safe time span for administering a pretest, then, is, "60 days prior to the stimulus whose effects are to be measured." This is obviously unsatisfactory, since a pretest that is far removed from stimulus administration fails to capture important changes that may occur between the pretest and the stimulus situation. A better solution is to structure the pretest in a way in which the thrust of posttest questions is not obvious. Alternatively, one can desensitize respondents by frequent administration of tests. We used both approaches with our Evanston panel, with partial success. The debate interviews followed after seven prior interviews that had somewhat blurred the novelty of the test situation and hence its sensitizing effects. We also included so many questions in our lengthy interviews that it became a chore for respondents to try to keep informed about the many areas that had been covered. This reduced their attempts to pay particular attention to matters mentioned in the interviews.

Learning Levels: Aided versus Spontaneous Recall

The second major reason for differential findings regarding the amount and nature of debate learning is the failure to define what is meant by "learning." Some researchers are satisfied that learning has occurred if respondents are able to judge the correctness of a statement about an item of information that was transmitted during the debates. Other researchers believe that this requirement is too low and insist that learning scores be based on the ability to recall information spontaneously, without extensive memory aids. Unfortunately,

TABLE 6.2

Number of Respondents Who Reported Information Items Learned during First and Second Debate
(n = 21)

	First Debate		Second Debate	
	None	Three or More Items	None	Three or More Items
Spontaneous recall	21	0	8	1
Aided recall*				
Jobs/Africa	3	7	6	3
Taxes/Soviet	3	10	5	7
Draft/defense	1	17	3	16

*First debate/second debate.
Source: Compiled by the author.

the nature of the standards used to determine whether learning has occurred is often blurred in research reports, particularly when findings are compared. Consequently, the reasons for discrepant findings are obscured.

Our study of the debates and other types of political learning disclosed large differences in learning scores, depending on whether the questions asked panel members for spontaneous reports about the sorts of theings they had learned about candidates and issues or they aided memory by mentioning specific events and asking respondents if they recalled them. Table 6.2 provides examples.

After the first debate, in which 16 policy issues were prominently discussed, our panel members could not spontaneously recall a single "new" item of information that they had learned from the debate. But when the interviewer reminded them that each candidate had spelled out a variety of positions on tax reform, plans to increase jobs, and the treatment of draft evaders, nearly the entire panel could recall at least one new item. In fact, anywhere from a one-third to four-fifths of the panel members had learned enough to be able to cite three or more new items of information on one of the three issues. Job creation policies had been discussed extensively by the candidates in eight answers, tax reform in seven, and the treatment of draft evaders in two, counting each candidate's answers separately.

Spontaneous recall was better for the second debate in which 13 issues were examined. Only eight respondents were unable to recall spontaneously any new information. Recall improved moderately or greatly, depending on the issue, when the interviewers asked specifically about new information learned about American policy in Africa, American relations with the Soviet Union, and the defense policies advocated by the candidates.

The differences in aided and spontaneous recall were greatest when one looks at the ability to report several information items about a topic. Only one respondent could spontaneously report three or more items of information about an issue. When memory was aided, 3, 7, and 16 respondents, respectively, displayed fairly extensive knowledge about American defense policies and American relations with the Soviet Union and Africa. Defense policy had been discussed extensively by the candidates in eight debate answers, relations with the Soviet Union in seven, and Africa policy in five, counting each candidate's answers separately.

Learning Levels: Degrees of Knowledge

The concept of "learning" is further obscured because most studies fail to distinguish among various degrees of knowledge acquisition and among bases for knowledge display. To deal with these problems, we distinguished four levels of knowledge acquisition for debate learning. These were "awareness," which meant that a respondent recalled that the information was mentioned without remembering what was said or who said it. A second level was "recall with facts," which entailed familiarity with various policy options or presidential qualifications, without knowing to which candidate they pertained. A third level of knowledge was recorded when a respondent was able to link specific information to one of the candidates; a fourth level entailed ability to correctly link both presidential candidates to various issue stands. Depending on whether one makes the judgment of knowledge or learning on the basis of mere awareness, recall with facts, or ability to link political information to one or both candidates, knowledge and learning scores will differ.

Distinguishing learning levels is intrinsically as well as practically important. Intrinsically, knowledge about political learning will remain extremely crude if we fail to refine our learning measures. Practically, we cannot tell whether the debate sponsors' objectives of facilitating intelligent voting were achieved, without knowing what level of learning was attained. If the debates simply made voters aware that the defense budget was a controversial issue, this helped them little in determining how to square this information with their voting decision. Table 6.3 presents information on the level of learning attained by our respondents about various issues. It is based on aided rather than spontaneous recall.

TABLE 6.3

Number of Respondents Who Attained Various Levels of Learning about Both Candidates' Positions on Selected Issues
(n = 21)

Issue	No Awareness	Awareness	Know Issue Only	Know Issue Plus One Candidate's Stand	Know Issue Plus Two Candidates' Stands
Jobs	3	4	4	3	7
Taxes	3	3	0	5	10
Draft	1	0	1	2	17
Africa	6	2	4	6	3
Soviet	5	0	5	4	7
Defense	3	0	2	0	16

Source: Compiled by the author.

LEARNING LEVELS: CONTAMINATION OF LEARNING SCORES

The bases for knowledge display need to be distinguished as well. A good bit of political knowledge reflects past learning and reasoning ability, along with fortuitous guessing. If learning tests fail to sort out such guessed and inferred knowledge from knowledge flowing from the particular stimulus that is under investigation, learning scores will be exaggerated. Our respondents freely admitted on numerous occasions that they did not have candidate or issue information but were willing to make a guess. The politically astute frequently were able to infer information from a general knowledge of party stands or the candidates' performances in the past. In most instances, these inferences were correct. Interestingly, the ability to make correct inferences about the candidates increased markedly after the first debate had brought election information into sharp focus. We had observed similar peaks in political astuteness when the primary elections and the conventions served as refresher courses for political information.

A related problem concerns the handling of knowledge instability. Much political learning is extremely fleeting, so much so that people who have just finished watching a telecast or reading the paper often cannot recall what they have heard or read, if questioned within minutes of completing reading or viewing. The greater the interval between exposure to information and questions about the information, the less, in general, is the recall. Given such high instability in knowledge retention, it seems advisable to reserve terms like "learning" and "knowledge " for information acquisition that is retained and readily recallable for more than a few hours. At the very least, studies should report the interval between exposure to the stimulus and measurement of the effects to alert the reader to assess how much forgetting has already taken place and how much more might normally be expected within a brief period of time.

The importance of clearly establishing interview timing for proper assessment of debate impact can be demonstrated in other contexts as well. The problem of contaminating the initial effects of a communication event through intervening media commentary is one example. Speculations about the impact of the debates appeared in the press and on television well before the first debate, possibly conditioning debate effects. Appraisals, instant and otherwise, followed each debate event and apparently influenced reader judgments. For instance, pollster Robert Teeter, who analyzed responses to the second debate, which contained the much-criticized Ford remarks on Eastern Europe, reported that immediate postdebate phone calls, prior to media commentary, showed a 9 percent margin in favor of Ford as the debate winner. Following media commentary, the winner label was transferred to Carter a few hours later. Carter's winning margins rose steadily from interview to interview. Within 24 hours, after the evening news, the Carter advantage had risen to 42 percentage points (chapter 5 in this volume; Teeter 1977). Given the fact that the earlier opinion revisions occurred before attempts by the Ford camp to explain what had happened, it seems clear that media commentary was largely responsible for the change.

Should one record the ephemeral Ford "victory" as learning emerging from the debates? Or should that designation go to the Carter "victory" recorded later? The answer, of course, depends on interview timing, which must be clearly specified, and on the researcher's inclination to accept or discount media-induced changes as genuine debate effects.

EFFECTS OF VARIOUS MEASURING INSTRUMENTS

Question Wording

When events, such as the presidential debates, spark a large array of parallel studies, the impact of question wording on findings becomes readily apparent. For example, findings will vary when respondents in one study are asked generally, "Who won the presidential debates?", while those in another study are queried more specifically about who won the first, second, and third debate, and the individual judgments are averaged. It also makes a difference whether respondents are asked who "won" or who "did a better job" or "who showed the best debate style." All too often, these distinctions are ignored when findings are compared. The consequences can be unfortunate.

Aside from these well-known difficulties, intensive work with our small panel of voters has convinced us that there is little merit in the hallowed rule that dictates identical question wording for every respondent. Identically worded questions rarely gave us appropriate answers for all of our respondents, particularly those at the lower end of the educational spectrum. When a respondent who is asked whether President Ford wants to increase or decrease the defense budget replies that Ford is bad for welfare, it is clear that the question has not been understood and needs to be rephrased in simpler language. Equivalence of conveyed information, rather than equivalence of wording, is important whenever the latter means inequivalence of conveyed information.

Just as researchers are willing to translate questionnaires into foreign languages and accept interlanguage equivalence, so one needs to accept intralanguage equivalence. If a respondent does not understand terms like "budget" and "increase" and "decrease," a translation of these terms into "spending more or less money" may be sensible and appropriate.

A second problem concerns the latitude of meanings that are embedded in many questions, including amply pretested ones. Failure to specify the intended meaning may yield answers that are useless because the analyst does not know which meaning particular respondents had in mind. For instance, a question asking respondents to express agreement or disagreement on a seven-point scale with the statement that "Ford, as president, would reduce unemployment" produced three different ratings from one respondent. Ford's desire to reduce unemployment was given the highest positive rating; his ability to do so, given an obstreperous Congress and economic realities, was evaluated at the midpoint; and his anticipated performance, compared to Carter, was rated at the most negative end of the scale. Without specifying which meaning was desired, it would have been impossible to produce comparable scoring for the respondents in our study.

A simple rating question, such as the request to rate the debate performance of each candidate as good, bad, or indifferent, turned out to be highly ambiguous. Respondents inquired, among other things, whether the ratings were to be made (1) in comparison with other, unspecified, political debates that they had witnessed; (2) in comparison with the Kennedy-Nixon debates; (3) by comparing the candidates to each other; or (4) by measuring the candidates against the respondent's predebate expectations. When asked to respond to all four options, one respondent stated that performance had been good for both candidates, compared to most other debates; bad for both, compared to the Kennedy-Nixon debates; good for Carter, compared to Ford, and indifferent for Ford, compared to Carter; and good for Ford and indifferent for Carter, when compared to the respondent's expectations.

The meaning of "performance" also caused some consternation. Did this mean style, substance, poise, "presidential" demeanor, or what? Some respondents found it difficult to make a combined judgment, claiming that the imaginary scores on the various dimensions were so wide apart that averaging them out seemed inappropriate.

The Meaning of Answers

Another common methodological problem relates to the comparability of answers when self-evaluation or answers based on objective tests are used as measuring instruments. To appraise the difference between these measuring devices, we asked our panel members to evaluate the extent of their learning about the candidates and issues for each debate. If learning was claimed, we then asked what the new information was, probing for as much detail as the respondent could recall. The self-assessment measure and the objective measure, represented by the item count of information actually recalled, were highly correlated ($p < .001$). Table 6.4 presents this information. However, any conclusion that the two measures are indeed equivalent must be tempered by noting that our respondents had been conditioned to strive for accurate self-assessments. They knew from previous interviews that their self-appraisals would be followed by specific questions designed to substantiate or refute the self-approasal. This knowledge may have kept them from exaggerating or underestimating learning to the greater degree that we noted during the earliest phases of our study. However, the data in Table 6.4 provide evidence that accurate self-appraisal is quite possible. (To avoid tailoring of later responses to earlier self-appraisals, we repeatedly separated the two types of questions in hopes that self-appraisals would be forgotten after a lapse of time.)

Drawing correct inferences from answers may also be fraught with difficulties that indicate the need for clusters of questions to put answers into proper perspective. For example, most respondents expressed high interest in the debates. But this could not be construed as a harbinger for faithful attention to them. As Table 6.5 shows, a third of the respondents were dropouts in each presidential debate and one-half missed the vice-presidential debates altogether.*　Only half of those who watched the debates paid attention to the entire broadcast; only six individuals saw portions of all four debates.

Examination of interview transcripts shows that high interest was readily counteracted by other, often trivial, demands on the respondent's time. This indicates that expressions of great interest in politics need to be cast into the

---

*The extent to which the respondents exposed themselves to each of the live telecasts of the presidential debates was measured by six levels. None = 1; less than thirty minutes = 2; 30–45 minutes = 3; 45–60 minutes = 4; 61–75 minutes = 5; more than 75 minutes = 6. The sum of the scores for the presidential debates was counted as each respondent's degree of exposure to the presidential debates on television.

TABLE 6.4

Number of Respondents Who Reported Various Degrees of Learning, Measured by Self-Assessment and Objective Scores
(n = 21)

Subject	Debate	Self-Assessment			Objective Scores		
		None	Some	Lot	None	Some	Lot
Ford	First	11	10	0	11	10	0
Ford	Second	9	11	1	8	13	0
Ford	Third	12	9	0	11	10	0
Dole	Vice-presidential	11	7	3	10	11	0
Carter	First	12	9	0	12	9	0
Carter	Second	7	14	0	6	15	0
Carter	Third	9	11	1	9	12	0
Mondale	Vice-presidential	12	7	2	11	10	0
Issues	First	21	0	0	21	0	0
Issues	Second	9	12	0	8	12	1
Issues	Third	15	4	2	13	4	3
Issues	Vice-presidential	14	6	1	14	7	0

Note: Some = one or two items; lot = three or more items.
Source: Compiled by the author.

TABLE 6.5

Number of Respondents Who Watched Each Debate on
Television for Varying Periods of Time
(n = 21)

	None	1–29 Minutes	30–59 Minutes	60–90 Minutes
First debate	6	6	2	7
Second debate	7	3	4	7
Third debate	7	3	3	8
Vice-presidential debate	11	1	2	7

Source: Compiled by the author.

context of competing interests in the respondent's life. Compared to these other interests, the concern with politics tended to be low, when judged by willingness to spend time to gather political information.

Similarly, it was difficult to interpret the degree to which the debates bored or excited our respondents. The vast majority of respondents labeled the debates as somewhat or very interesting when asked to make a specific rating. But these judgments were contradicted by the bulk of reasons cited for watching only a part of each debate broadcast. Respondents explained their high dropout rates by calling large portions of the debates dull, repetitive, hard to follow, and sleep-inducing. Hence it seems that an overall judgment that the debates were interesting, or even somewhat interesting, masked strong impressions that dullness was the predominant quality.

THE CONTEXTS OF DEBATE STUDIES

Our year-long perspective on political learning has convinced us that the debates cannot be studied properly as isolated events. Rather, they must be viewed as integral parts of a continuous flow of election information that interacts with a multiplicity of factors in the political environment. Three major types of contextual factors have a strong impact on debate effects and confound measurement accuracy. First, respondents' susceptibility to debate influence varies, depending on predebate conditioning factors. Second, the nature of the debates, as such—including substance, format, and execution—is bound to mediate debate effects. Third, the general political climate into which the debate stimulus is injected affects the impact of the debates. Researchers must exercise extreme caution to avoid crediting the debates with effects that have been produced by other forces present during the debate time span.

Respondents as Context

A study of various factors that influenced how much or how little our respondents learned from the debates indicated substantial impact of some predebate factors on learning scores. Tables 6.6, 6.7, and 6.8 present an overview. For instance, watching the televised debates, rather than merely reading about them, markedly affected the amount of learning. The correlation coefficient between television watching and issue learning was .41 ($p < .05$); for learning about the candidates, it was .45 ($p < .05$). The decision to watch the debates hinged on the individual's general interest in the election. Those who had the greatest interest in the election, for a variety of reasons unrelated to the debates, were more likely to expose themselves extensively to the debates and somewhat more likely to learn from them. The correlation between prior interest and learning about the candidates was .37, significant at the .10 level; however, for issue learning, the correlation was not significant (.21, $p > .10$). The level of interest in the election was measured by the frequency of election stories in each respondent's diary. Greater interest was linked to the level of education, earlier political experiences, the interest generated in the campaign through prior campaign events, and the manner in which campaign events were reported by the mass media. Demographic factors, such as age, sex, and occupation, appeared to have little impact on the interest level.

There also was a strong relationship between education, and the knowledge level reached by the time the debates were held, and additional learning

TABLE 6.6

Pearson Correlations between Evaluation of Candidates and Exposure/Learning from the Debates

	Evaluation of Ford	Evaluation of Carter
Degree of exposure to television debates	-.01	-.16
Learning about Ford (self-assessment)	-.04	-.05
Learning about Ford (number of qualities)	-.04	-.04
Learning about Carter (self-assessment)	-.52*	-.29
Learning about Carter (number of qualities)	-.14	-.09
Learning about issues (self-assessment)	-.09	-.07
Learning about issues (number of issues)	-.12	.21

*Significant at the .05 level. All other correlation coefficients are not statistically significant at the .10 level.

Source: Compiled by the author.

TABLE 6.7

Pearson Correlations between Prior Interest/Knowledge and Exposure/Learning from the Debates

	Prior Interest	Prior Knowledge
Degree of television exposure	.35	.34
Learning about issues (self-assessment)	.20	.35
Learning about issues (number of issues)	.21	.56[b]
Learning about candidates (self-assessment)	.43[a]	.68[c]
Learning about candidates (number of qualities)	.37[a]	.67[c]

[a]Significant at the .10 level.
[b]Significant at the .05 level.
[c]Significant at the .001 level.
Source: Compiled by the author.

from the debates (r = .59 and .67, p < .001 for learning about candidates; r = .47 and .56, p < .05 for learning about issues). Knowledge level was scored by the extent of recall of election stories in response to questions in each of the ten interviews. Debate learning was assessed by the following questions: (1) "How much did you learn from the debates about Ford/Carter?"; (2) "How much did you learn from the debates about the candidates' issue stands?"; (3) "What specific things about Ford/Carter did you learn from the debate?"; and (4) "What specific knowledge did you gain in terms of each candidate's issue stands?" Those who had previously learned the most, also learned most from the debates, even though they had less to learn than those who had previously learned little.* Thus, since debate effects were contingent on predebate events that affected various audience members in different ways, consideration of these earlier conditioning factors was essential for appraising debate effects.

Debates as Context

One of the most important predebate factors that must form part of debate effects studies is an analysis of the content of the debates in light of

---

*However, in the group of those whose prior learning had been comparatively small, those who were highly interested, but prevented by time pressures from learning much, seemed to use the debates as a way to catch up with knowledge missed earlier.

TABLE 6.8

Pearson Correlations between Sex, Age, Education and Interest/Knowledge/Learning from the Debates

	Sex	Age	Education
Prior interest	.04	.18	-.01
Prior knowledge	-.21	-.07	.34[a]
Learning about issues (self-assessment)	.01	.00	.31[a]
Learning about issues (number of issues)	.05	-.29[a]	.47[b]
Learning about candidates (self-assessment)	.10	.02	.53[c]
Learning about candidates (number of qualities)	-.08	.03	.59[c]

[a]Significant at the .10 level.
[b]Significant at the .05 level.
[c]Significant at the .01 level.
Source: Compiled by the author.

predebate information. How much new can be learned from a particular event depends on how much new information is presented. The debates came late in the campaign and contained comparatively little information that had not been widely available in the predebate period and repeatedly presented to the voters. This was true of explicit and implicit information about the personalities and qualifications of the candidates, as well as about campaign issues.

Moreover, predebate cognitions and attitudes in many instances predetermined the manner in which the debates were perceived. Based on prior information, the debate audience already had formed firm notions about the respective integrity, ability, charisma, and intelligence of the candidates and about their positions on a few issues salient to each respondent. Most voters also had made a firm or tentative electoral choice.

Even when debate appraisal contradicted previous image formation, voters did not change their images substantially in the wake of the debates (Hagner and Rieselbach 1977). Our panel members indicated that they were unwilling to reopen their image judgments in major ways, or to revise their firm or tentative voting decisions, unless some extraordinary disclosure sprang from the debates. Nothing that occurred during the debates, not even President Ford's infelicitous remark about the status of Eastern Europe, was construed as an extraordinary disclosure.*

---

*The 1960 debates made a greater impact on voters because opinions were less well

Debate impact was further reduced because the audience deemed much or all of the performance a dull show, as well as confusing and difficult to grasp. Media commentary enhanced the impression that the debates were a lackluster affair. There also was disappointment that the event was conducted more like a press conference than a point-counterpoint debate in which the candidates would interact directly. The comment that the debates were political "rhetoric" that should not be taken seriously was heard often. The first debate, which elicited the largest number of complaints about format, also produced the lowest rate of learning. Waning disapproval in subsequent debates was accompanied by increased learning rates.

Political Climate as Context

For practitioners of politics—particularly the handlers of the candidates— and for many ordinary citizens, the crucial question is not what kind of new cognitions the debates produced, or how they changed attitudes and feelings. Rather, the big question is whether the debates changed votes and whether this affected the outcome of the election. Unfortunately, measurement of vote effects is fraught with some of the same difficulties we already have noted, such as assessing the diminution of debate impact due to debate format and timing.

Even when a voting decision was made, affirmed, or altered subsequent to a particular debate, there is no assurance that the debate produced the change. We have evidence to the contrary. Several of our panel members, for instance, delayed their voting decision in hopes that the debates would provide solid guidelines. When this did not occur, they made their decision after the debates on the basis of predebate considerations.

Another dubious claim about debate effects is the contention that the debates contributed to Carter's victory because 55 percent of the voters who had not made a firm voting decision by debate time finally voted for Carter rather than Ford. This contention is tenuous when one looks at the context of party alignments. The undecided group included a much larger number of Democrats than Republicans. The bulk of these voters would still have chosen Carter because of their basic political orientations, even if there had been no debates.

---

formed. Voters' predebate exposure to John F. Kennedy was far less than Jimmy Carter's predebate exposure in 1976. Predebate evaluations of the candidates were assessed through a series of questions that asked respondents to use a seven-point scale to indicate various degrees of agreement or disagreement with the following four statements: (1) "Ford/Carter, as President, could be trusted"; (2) "Ford/Carter has the kind of personality a President ought to have"; (3) "Ford/Carter, as President, would reduce unemployment"; and (4) "Ford/Carter, as President, would make the government run better and make it more efficient." The respondent's composite score from these four items was used as a measure of her/his attitude toward Ford and Carter prior to the debates.

Trends concurrent with the debates also may explain away a number of other widely publicized "debate effects." For instance, George Gallup has contended that the debates were a turning point in the election because they halted the surge in pro-Ford voting intentions. This surge, which had sharply reduced the number of voters who had preferred Carter in the late summer of 1976, stopped after the second debate (Gallup 1977). While Gallup attributed the halt to debate impact, Robert Teeter, who had been Ford's pollster, has argued that Ford had attained the maximum support level possible for him by early October. Victory hinged on losses by Carter, possibly via the debates, and not on further surges in support for Ford (Teeter 1977). Regardless of the merits of the respective arguments, the conflicting views illustrate how difficult it is to distinguish "debate effects" from the effects of long-term trends that continue throughout the debate period.

SUMMARY AND CONCLUSIONS

We have examined a number of the methodological problems that explain differences in findings regarding the impact of the presidential debates on American audiences. These methodological problems include the difficult task of establishing base lines for measuring change without sensitizing subjects and making their behavior abnormal following the base-line procedures. They also include the problem of identifying and measuring various substantively different levels of the same behavior so that unambiguous reports and accurate comparisons become possible.

We have pointed out the large response differences that spring from questions based on spontaneous recall, compared to questions that include various types of memory aids. We also have indicated the great need to further clarify the meanings that questions and answers have for specific respondents. Without such clarifications, which are all too rarely undertaken, intelligent interpretations and comparisons cannot be made.

A number of contextual factors were identified as crucial determinants of the impact of political events. These factors, which must be encompassed in political communication effects studies, include the respondent's psychosocial setting, such as prior knowledge of and interest in an event and capacity to recall newly learned facts over a lengthy time span. They also include the form that a particular stimulus event has taken that may enhance or diminish its impact on various respondents. Finally, care must be taken to avoid the dangerous practice of crediting stimulus events with producing the changes that follow them, without ascertaining whether other past or concurrent or immediately subsequent events could be responsible.

Current social science knowledge permits us to avoid or ameliorate many of the pitfalls that we have described. Unfortunately, this knowledge is too seldom applied. The consequences are poor data and improper data analysis. This situation could be greatly improved through more comprehensive, broadly gauged research, focused on long- and short-term effects in wider contexts, and using more delicate and continuously readjusted research instruments. These methodological improvements cannot be achieved without increased and well-organized cooperation among many researchers. Efforts to create the formal and informal institutions to make such cooperation feasible should therefore be high on the agenda of social scientists interested in methodological excellence for the profession at large.

7

DEBATES' EFFECTS ON VOTERS' UNDERSTANDING OF CANDIDATES AND ISSUES

Lee B. Becker, Idowu A. Sobowale,
Robin E. Cobbey, and Chaim H. Eyal

When in late August of 1976 it began to appear likely that presidential debates, absent from the U.S. political scene for 16 years, might again be held, the speculation in the press began. For the most part, the speculation centered on two related questions: Who would win the debates? What would be the effects of the debates on the decision voters would be making on election day? Almost without exception, those posing the questions were seeking simple answers. Either the debates would change people's evaluations of the candidates, and thereby the election outcome, or they would not.

While that perspective may seem to have much merit—and it certainly reflected the concerns of the candidates involved—it ignored several important lessons that have been learned in the years following the 1960 debates. The media, it is now clear, are much more likely to influence what people know about the candidates and the issues than to change voting decisions (Becker, McCombs, and McLeod 1975). The voting act is a complex one, owing much to factors as diverse as family background and contemporary friendship networks (Sears 1969). As a consequence, campaign events seldom seem to have unmitigated effects on voter decisions.

In fact, the research conducted during the 1960 campaign provided ambiguous answers to questions of the debates' effects on vote outcome. Katz and Feldman (1962, p. 211), after an examination of the data gathered, concluded:

> Did the debates really affect the final outcome? Apart from strengthening Democratic convictions about their candidate, it is very difficult to say conclusively.

One of the ironies of the preoccupation in 1976 with the debates' effects on vote outcome is that the project's sponsors were not concerned with that at all. While the 1960 encounters took place in a television studio and were produced by the networks, those in 1976 were staged by the nonpartisan League of Women Voters. The sponsoring of the debates was considered by the League to be a continuation of its long tradition of providing educational materials to the electorate. The League's intent, quite clearly, was to inform—not convert—the audience members.

The League stood a fair chance of succeeding. The 1960 data showed that viewers learned both about the issues and the candidates from the debates (Katz and Feldman 1962). Research that has been conducted in the fields of mass communications and public opinion within the last two decades has demonstrated quite convincingly that the media, through their campaign reportage, influence to a considerable degree what the people know about the details of the election process (McCombs and Shaw 1972; Becker, McCombs and McLeod 1975; Palmgreen and Clarke 1977; Shaw and McCombs 1977). The media are, after all, the only link most voters have to the actual events and activities of a political campaign. Few voters meet the candidates or even see them in the flesh on the campaign trail. Only through the media do most voters have contact with the campaign.

To argue that the media serve more of an informational than persuasive function in most campaigns is not to relegate them to a trivial role. Most voters probably evaluate the information they obtain from the media against other information held, use it in discussions with friends and family, and weigh it when they make the final voting decision. In this view, the media serve an important informational function and can have at least indirect effects on election outcomes.

The range of what people can learn from media coverage of campaigns is quite extensive. For example, the 1976 debates provided audience members opportunities to judge which of the two candidates performed better under pressure. In short, each debate allowed listeners and viewers to judge who won. Those in the debate listening or viewing audience also could learn about general differences that existed between the candidates' views on political and social matters as well as the ideological orientations of the candidates. The debates also provided audience members opportunities to learn about the candidates, their training and background, and their personalities. Finally, the debates allowed audience members to learn about the various issues in the campaign and the positions the two candidates were taking on those issues.

In summary, the media, through their coverage of the campaign, provide audience members with a great deal of information about the actors in, and issues of, the campaign. In 1976, much of this information was transmitted by way of the debates. Through broadcast coverage of the debates, the media offered audience members unusual opportunities to learn about the candidates and issues. Whether the audience members did in fact use these opportunities to learn about the candidates and issues is the empirical question that this study addresses.

Preliminary evidence that the voters did gain information from the debates would be seen in any change in what the voters knew about the candidates and issues from before to after each of the debates. For example, change in the percentage of voters thinking a given candidate won from debate to debate would be evidence that the debates were providing new information that was being received by the voters. Similarly, changes in the percentage of voters seeing a difference between the candidates or thinking a candidate held a particular ideological stance would be preliminary evidence of the debates' effects. Finally, if the debates had an effect on what voters knew of the campaign, there should be seen a change in the percentage of respondents able to describe those candidates and correctly identify their issue stands as the debates progressed. These changes, of course, ought to be concentrated among those voters who actually listened to or viewed the debates. Only if the effects are concentrated among those exposed to the debates is it possible to argue that the debates per se had the effects. Since debate viewers are likely to be somewhat better educated and informed, even before the encounters, than those who do not attend to the debates, it also is necessary to make sure that the debates had effects distinct from the effects of education. In other words, education of the respondent must be used as a control.

STUDY DESIGN

Data gathered in an upstate New York study in the fall of 1976 tend to support this expectation of cognitive effects of the debates. The study consisted of five waves of telephone interviews in Onondaga County, a metropolitan region located approximately in the center of the state. The first wave of interviewing was conducted immediately prior to the initial presidential debate on September 22. Subsequent waves were fielded after each of the four debates, with the final wave ending on election eve. In all, over 1300 interviews were conducted with the probability samples of registered voters.

Onandaga County, which includes the city of Syracuse, historically has voted in much the same way as most other upstate New York counties. In 1976, when Jimmy Carter received 52 percent of the vote statewide, he carried only seven of New York's 62 counties. Four of the seven were in New York City. The 60-to-40 percent split of votes in Onondaga County—in favor of incumbent Gerald Ford—is fairly typical of the ratio for Ford in upstate New York. Onondaga County has approximately twice as many registered Republicans as Democrats. The county gave 68 percent of its vote to Richard Nixon in 1972 and 50 percent of its vote to Nixon in the three-way 1968 race.

Effects on Voters' Understanding

Respondents in the 1976 study were asked who they thought had won the debate that had occurred immediately prior to the interview. For the first two debates, this question focused on presidential candidates Jimmy Carter and Gerald Ford. The question after the third debate—the first ever televised between two vice-presidential candidates—dealt with Republican Robert Dole and Democrat Walter Mondale. The question on the final wave dealt with the presidential candidates.

An additional question, used only on the final three waves of the study, asked "how much of a difference" the respondents thought there was between the candidates' stands on most issues. Again, the fourth wave of the study (fielded after the debate between Dole and Mondale) focused on differences between vice-presidential candidates. The other waves focused on presidential candidates.

Respondents also were asked to indicate whether they considered the presidential candidates (vice-presidential candidates in wave four) to be conservative, moderate, or liberal "on most political matters."

In order to gain additional information on how much the voters had learned about the candidates from the debates, the following questions were included in each of the five waves: "Suppose you had a friend who was unfamiliar with the presidential candidates for some reason or other. If your friend asked you about (Gerald Ford/Jimmy Carter), what would be the most important thing you would want to say about (Ford/Carter)? Now what would be the next most important thing you would want to say about (Ford/Carter)?" In the fourth wave of the study, these questions were asked for the vice-presidential as well as the presidential candidates. For the analyses reported here, respondents were grouped according to whether they could provide at least two distinct characteristics of the candidate under consideration or were unable to list two such characteristics.

Finally, the predebate and first postdebate waves of the study included various questions designed to determine how knowledgeable respondents were regarding the stands candidates were taking on the issues. Issues discussed in the popular press and on which the candidates had taken clear stands were selected for inclusion. Two types of issues were selected: those that would be covered by the first presidential debate and those that were unlikely to be discussed in that first interaction. For each issue selected, respondents were read a particular issue stand and asked to indicate whether each candidate favored or opposed that stand.

Additional questions on each of the postdebate interview schedules were designed to determine whether respondents had listened to the most recent debate on radio, watched it on television, done both, or neither watched or listened to the debate. The 1960 debate data suggested some differences in reactions to the debates for those who watched them on television and those who listened to them on radio (Lang and Lang 1968, p. 296). However, the number of persons in the Onondaga County study who listened to even part of the debates on radio was so small (averaging 3 percent) that separate analyses of viewers and listeners was not practical. In the analyses reported here, viewers and listeners have been grouped together. The label of the dominant group—viewers—has been used throughout.

Each wave of the study also included an additional question that serves as a comparison against which changes in understanding of the candidates and issues can be gauged. The question is fairly typical of those used to determine vote choice: "If the election were held tomorrow, would you vote for Gerald Ford, Jimmy Carter, one of the other candidates, or wouldn't you vote? Or maybe you haven't made up your mind yet."

A subsample of those persons interviewed after the first, second, and third presidential debates had been interviewed in the previous wave. No individual, however, was interviewed more than twice. No distinction is made in the analyses that follow between persons interviewed in the previous wave and those not interviewed earlier since analyses of the two groups showed no noticeable effect of prior interviewing.

RESULTS

It is clear the debates were a significant part of the 1976 campaign for most Onondaga County voters. According to the survey estimates, 78 percent of the county voters watched or listened to part of the first debate, a figure somewhat higher than the 67 percent national voters estimated by the Gallup Poll to have watched that first encounter (Gallup 1976). Viewing of the subsequent debates fell off somewhat, with approximately 60 percent of those surveyed indicating they saw each, including the debate between the vice-presidential candidates. The Gallup data do not show a drop-off for the second and third presidential debates; Gallup did not report an estimate for the vice-presidential debate, which came after the first two presidential debates but before the final presidential debate. The Onondaga County data show that almost 28 percent of the voters locally watched some part of all four debates, and only 9 percent watched none of them.

While that high level of exposure to the debates may seem to argue in and of itself for debate effects, that is a conclusion that could be premature. It is at least possible that the debates added little information not already a part of the campaign. If that is true, the debates per se would not have produced noticeable effects.

To guard against an erroneous interpretation that the debates had effects, respondents are divided, in Table 7.1 and subsequent tables, into two groups: those who watched or listened to at least 15 minutes of the debate in question and those who watched or listened to less than that or did not watch at all. The decision to include persons having watched less than 15 minutes with those having watched none of the particular debate is predicated on the assumption that little of consequence could have been learned from so little exposure.

Gallup data indicate that Ford was picked more often than Carter as the winner of the first debate, while Carter was picked more often than Ford as the winner of the second encounter (Gallup 1976). No Gallup data were reported regarding the winner of the third debate to which Dole and Mondale were parties. Gallup reported Carter had a slight advantage nationally in the final debate. Onondaga County voters seem to have had much the same reactions, as Table 7.1 indicates. The vice-presidential debate, according to these data, was won by Democrat Mondale.

The general fluctuation across the debates in the percentage of respondents picking Carter or his vice-presidential candidate as the winner is preliminary evidence that the debates had some impact on voters. Had respondents been picking a debate winner solely in terms of their own partisan sentiments, such fluctuation would not have been expected. Shifts in partisan sentiments during the debate period simply were not so dramatic. The evidence, then, is that the debates matter, at least as far as choice of a winner was concerned.

This interpretation is reinforced by the comparisons of viewers and nonviewers of each of the contests. Viewers of the first debate, for example, were more likely to pick Ford as the winner than nonviewers. In the second debate, viewers were more likely to pick Carter as the winner than nonviewers. Mondale was more likely to be chosen winner by viewers than nonviewers of the third debate. Only in the final debate, which was judged pretty much of a draw, is the difference between viewers and nonviewers rather small.

In addition, the shifts that surface after each of the debates are generally greatest for viewers. After the first debate, an equal percentage of viewers and nonviewers thought Carter had won. After the second debate, this percentage had increased most markedly for the viewers, though the nonviewer percentage increased as well. Again, after the third presidential debate, the change was greatest for the viewers. In other words, shift in views of who won the debates tends to be associated with viewing itself.

It is worth noting, of course, that not all change is attributable to debate viewing. In fact, it seems that the total debate environment may produce some change. Most likely interpersonal discussion of the debates as well as subsequent media coverage of the encounters produced effects that filtered down to those who did not see or listen to the live encounter. But the evidence is that those who were in the initial broadcast audience showed the most change.

Contrary to many popular reports on voter reactions to the 1976 election, the Onondaga County electorate saw differences between the candidates. The debates, however, seem not to be the determinant of this view. Since this measure was not used in the early waves of the study, it is possible that the first debate, which produced some of the most dramatic shifts in other questions

TABLE 7.1

Changes in Understanding of the Candidates, in Percent

Measure	Pre-debate (n=104)	Postdebate 1[a] Total (n=297)	Postdebate 1[a] Viewers (n=215)	Postdebate 1[a] Non-viewers (n=82)	Postdebate 2 Total (n=256)	Postdebate 2 Viewers (n=148)	Postdebate 2 Non-viewers (n=108)	Postdebate 3 Total (n=427)	Postdebate 3 Viewers (n=231)	Postdebate 3 Non-viewers (n=196)	Postdebate 4 Total (n=233)	Postdebate 4 Viewers (n=124)	Postdebate 4 Non-viewers (n=109)
Debate winner[b]													
Picking Carter (Mondale)	—	7.8	7.9	7.6	41.8[c]	51.0[c]	30.2[c]	27.0	39.4	12.8	23.6[c]	28.2[c]	18.3[c]
Picking Ford (Dole)	—	40.8	43.7	32.9	13.0	13.6	12.3	16.2	20.4	11.3	16.3	21.0	11.0
Difference between candidates													
Seeing "a lot" (Carter/Ford)	—	—	—	—	39.7	39.7	39.6	45.0	47.3	42.1	39.9	41.0	38.7
(Mondale/Dole)	—	—	—	—				37.0	44.5	27.3			

Ideology of candidates												
Thinking Carter liberal (Mondale)	30.8	30.8	30.7	31.3	40.7[c]	36.7	46.2[c]	40.0	42.9	36.7	36.2	37.4	34.9
								39.9	50.4	27.6			
Thinking Ford conservative (Dole)	41.3	50.3	54.0[c]	40.7	51.4	51.0	51.9	49.1	52.2	45.4	50.9	53.7	47.7
								37.3	46.1	27.0			
Detailed knowledge of candidates												
Able to describe Carter (Mondale)	72.1	82.5[c]	88.4[c]	67.1	78.1	81.8	73.1	71.0	77.1	63.8	73.4	79.8	66.1
								41.5	54.1	26.5			
Able to describe Ford (Dole)	75.0	81.5	87.4[c]	65.9	84.8	87.2	81.5[c]	76.6	83.1	68.9	77.7	84.7	69.7
								43.6	57.6	27.0			

[a]Viewers are persons either viewing or listening to at least 15 minutes of the debate. Nonviewers are all others.
[b]Only the differences for the Carter responses were tested since response categories are not independent.
[c]The probability of the difference between the group and the comparable group in the previous wave occurring by chance is less than .05. For the postdebate 1 comparisons, viewers as well as nonviewers were compared with all predebate respondents.

Source: Compiled by the authors.

examined, did have some effect. The last three debates, however, seem not to have mattered much. In the final wave, it is worth noting, only 15 percent of those surveyed said there was "very little difference" between the candidates' stands on most issues.

There is evidence in Table 7.1 that voters began to see President Ford as more conservative after the first debate and continued to see him that way throughout the campaign. Indeed, it was the viewers who changed most as a result of that first encounter, which dealt with domestic issues.

For Carter, however, the evidence is that voters began to see him as more liberal after the second debate, which focused on foreign affairs. Here, however, the nonviewers, rather than the viewers, showed the greatest changes, so exposure to the debate per se cannot easily be the cause of the shift. It is worth noting, however, that viewers showed slight shifts in terms of seeing Carter as a liberal after each of the first three debates, while there was an increase in nonviewers viewing Carter as liberal only after the second debate. After that point, the percentage began to decline again.

Finally, there is evidence in Table 7.1 that the first debate increased voter knowledge about the candidates. The level of knowledge about both Carter and Ford increased from the predebate to postdebate 1 wave, though only significantly for the Carter descriptions. And the increase in each case was greatest for those who watched the first debate. The first debate, the data suggest, helped the voters learn the backgrounds and characteristics of the candidates.

After the first debate, there is little evidence of any gain in knowledge about the presidential candidates attributable to the encounters. In fact, there is some evidence of movement in the opposite direction as voters apparently forgot some of the details they had learned earlier or found them less worthy of mention.

The vice-presidential debate, however, seemed to play much the same role for Mondale and Dole as the first debate played for Carter and Ford. While the overall level of knowledge for the two vice-presidential candidates is considerably lower than for the presidential candidates, the comparison of viewers and nonviewers of the debate indicates that the lower level of knowledge is attributable to a very large degree to the lack of knowledge on the part of the nonviewers. Those who watched the debate were better able to provide concrete information on the vice-presidential candidates.

Perhaps the most dramatic evidence of the debates' effects is shown in Table 7.2. Here, respondents to the predebate wave and the postdebate 1 wave are compared in terms of their understanding of the candidates' stands on the issues. For each of the three issues covered in the first debate—unemployment, tax reform, and federal reorganization—the level of knowledge increases significantly from the first interview wave to the second. For the three issues not discussed in the first debate—abortion, armed crime, and the B-1 Bomber—level

TABLE 7.2

Changes in Knowledge of Candidates' Stands on the Issues, in Percent

		Postdebate 1		
Issue	Predebate (n = 104)	Total (n = 297)	Viewers[a] (n = 215)	Nonviewers (n = 82)
Federal unemployment programs[b]				
Knowing Carter's stand	57.7	73.4[c]	76.3[c]	65.9
Knowing Ford's stand	28.8	43.6[c]	47.4[c]	33.3
Abortion amendment				
Knowing Carter's stand	30.8	34.7	38.1	25.6
Knowing Ford's stand	32.7	36.7	40.5	26.8
Tax reform[b]				
Knowing Carter's stand	59.6	75.4[c]	80.9[c]	61.0
Knowing Ford's stand	22.1	35.1[c]	35.5[c]	34.1
Controlling armed crime				
Knowing Carter's stand	21.2	25.9	26.5	24.4
Knowing Ford's stand	28.8	33.7	35.3	29.3
Federal reorganization[b]				
Knowing Carter's stand	50.0	75.4[c]	79.5[c]	64.6[c]
Knowing Ford's stand	23.1	41.1[c]	43.3[c]	35.4
Construction of B-1 bomber				
Knowing Carter's stand	43.3	36.0	37.7	31.7
Knowing Ford's stand	36.5	34.0	37.2	25.6

[a]Viewers are persons either viewing or listening to at least 15 minutes of the debate. Nonviewers are all others.

[b]Issue was discussed in the first debate; the others were not.

[c]The probability of the difference between the predebate wave and postdebate 1 wave occurring by chance is less than .05.

Source: Compiled by the authors.

of knowledge increased very slightly or showed a slight decline. This finding holds whether knowledge of Carter's or Ford's stands is examined.

What is more important, when the postdebate 1 sample is divided into those who viewed or listened to the debate and those who listened to or watched less than 15 minutes or none of it, it is clear that those who tuned into the debate showed the greatest increase in level of knowledge. Only for one issue is there a significant increase in knowledge in evidence when the nonviewers are examined. The nonviewers did seem to gain in knowledge of Carter's stand on

TABLE 7.3

Changes in Candidate Choice, in Percent

	Pre-debate (n=104)	Postdebate 1[a] Total (n=297)	Postdebate 1[a] Viewers (n=215)	Postdebate 1[a] Non-viewers (n=82)	Postdebate 2 Total (n=256)	Postdebate 2 Viewers (n=148)	Postdebate 2 Non-viewers (n=108)	Postdebate 3 Total (n=427)	Postdebate 3 Viewers (n=231)	Postdebate 3 Non-viewers (n=196)	Postdebate 4 Total (n=233)	Postdebate 4 Viewers (n=124)	Postdebate 4 Non-viewers (n=109)
Candidate choice[b]													
Choosing Carter	20.2	23.6	24.7	20.7	26.3	30.6	20.2	24.8	30.6	18.1	26.9	31.7	21.5
Choosing Ford	27.9	40.4[c]	41.4[c]	37.8	39.4	33.3	48.1	40.3	39.6	40.9	42.7	41.7	43.9
Undecided	51.9	36.0	34.0	41.5	34.3	36.1	31.7	34.9	29.7	40.9	30.4	26.7	34.6

[a]Viewers are persons either viewing or listening to at least 15 minutes of the debate. Nonviewers are all others.
[b]Only the differences for the Ford responses were tested since response categories are not independent. Ford carried Onondaga County on election day.
[c]The probability of the difference between the group and the comparable group in the previous wave occurring by chance is less than .05. For the postdebate 1 comparisons, viewers as well as nonviewers were compared with all predebate respondents.

Source: Compiled by the authors.

reorganization. But those who watched the debates seemed to gain more dramatically, in keeping with the inference that the debates, rather than other aspects of the campaign, caused the greatest increase in knowledge.

A partitioning of the postdebate 1 sample into two groups, based on amount of formal education, shows that the better-educated sample members were in fact the ones most able to tell the candidates' stands on the issues, as would be expected. But even members of this group benefited from debate exposure. In other words, the debates had effects on audience members regardless of educational level. For several issues, the analyses make clear, the debates tended to help the less well educated audience members catch up with the better educated in the community. In other words, the less well-educated, who had most to learn about the issues, tended to get more information from debate viewing or listening than did the better-educated. But both groups seem to have gained from the experience.

In fact, the introduction of an education control for the analyses reported in Tables 7.1 and 7.2 indicates that variable does not explain the debate effects. For example, the educational control did not alter the interpretation that the first debate increased voter knowledge about the candidates. Nor did education explain away the finding that those persons who exposed themselves to the vice-presidential debate were more knowledgeable about each of the candidates than those persons who did not attend to the debates. To be sure, there was an educational difference, in that the better-educated members of the sample were able to provide more information about the candidates. But within education groups, debate viewing seemed to increase knowledge.

Viewed as a whole, the data in Tables 7.1 and 7.2 present rather strong evidence that the debates had an effect on viewers. They made them more knowledgeable about the issues and more informed of the backgrounds and characteristics of the candidates. There is some evidence, as well, that they helped the viewers understand the ideological aspects of the campaign. Without a doubt, they led those viewing the debates to differing interpretations of who had won the encounters. The evidence is less clear, however, that the debates actually affected the decisions Onondaga County voters made on election day. While the data shown in Table 7.3 indicate that there was movement in the county toward support of Ford after the first debate, which a plurality thought he won, those who viewed or listened to the debate were no more likely to show this movement than were those who watched or listened to little or none of the first debate. So it is difficult to argue that the debate per se caused the change. In addition, the second presidential debate, which a plurality of local voters thought was won by Carter, produced no statistically significant movement to the Democratic candidate, though such movement would be expected if the debate influenced voter choice. For the most part, the percentage of voters picking Carter and the percentage picking Ford remained constant after the initial encounter.

Perhaps the most logical explanation for the movement to Ford in Onondaga County after the first debate is that the debate allowed those inclined to vote Republican to feel more confident about the choice of the party's 1976 nominee. This is an interpretation reinforced by a closer examination of the postdebate 2 data. When respondents were grouped according to their official party registration, obtained from the county board of election, it was clear that some differences between viewers and nonviewers of the first debate existed. But the differences were masked to some degree by party. Those Republicans who watched the first debate were more likely than other Republicans to indicate support of Ford after the encounter. Democratic viewers and nonviewers, however, supported Ford in approximately equal proportions. And independents, or those not in either of these parties, tended to support Ford over Carter regardless of whether they had seen or listened to the debate. The margin of difference was less, however, if the independents actually had seen or heard the first debate.

The conclusion is much like the one reached after the 1960 debates. The 1976 debates might have led some people, uncertain about their party's candidate, to feel more confident with him; but there is little evidence of massive conversion attributable to the debates.

CONCLUSION

These data argue that the debates did in fact increase voters' understanding of the candidates and the issues in 1976. Voters were better able to describe the candidates as a result of the first presidential debate and the vice-presidential encounter, and they were better informed about the issues dealt with in the first presidential debate. The debates had other effects as well, but they were less dramatic.

The debates, of course, did not provide all of the information introduced into the 1976 campaign. The usual media coverage of the candidates and the issues no doubt had some effects as well. But the data in Table 7.2 show that those issues covered in the first debate were the ones on which there was an increase in knowledge. Little gain in knowledge is shown for the abortion issue, in particular, which played an important part in the early coverage of the campaign but was not included in the first debate. Additional analyses, not shown here, also indicate that the debates helped voters in their descriptions of the candidates even after considering what they learned from their usual media-use behaviors. In other words, the debates had an effect on this measure even after controlling for normal media use.

The measures employed here to gauge the effects of the debates on voters' understanding of the candidates and issues are not the only ones that could have been selected. Other, more demanding, criteria exist. Graber and her colleagues have concluded that the debates had little effect in terms of their criteria (see chapter 6). There is no simple way of assessing which of the various criteria is most appropriate.

The Onondaga County data indicate the debates made some voters better able to describe the candidates and better informed on the candidates' stands on some of the issues. In that sense, at least, the debates were successful in doing what their sponsors had intended: to produce a better-informed electorate.

8

PERSISTENCE AND CHANGE IN CANDIDATE IMAGES

Dan Nimmo, Michael Mansfield, and James Curry

Studies of the 1960 presidential debates focused upon a variety of questions, especially shifts in voting intentions, voters' positions on issues, and the debates' effects on the electoral outcome. One line of inquiry, of primary concern to us here, examined the relationship of televised confrontations to the images voters constructed of the presidential contenders. Studies drew such conclusions as: individual debates contributed to marginal shifts in viewers' biases, but basic thoughts about the candidates remained the same (Kraus and Smith 1962); the debates clarified the image some voters held of the candidates, especially the undecided (Katz and Feldman 1962; Lang and Lang 1968); and voters responded more to personal qualities projected by the candidates than to political attributes (Land and Lang 1968; Nimmo and Savage 1976).

Before the 1976 presidential debates, there were reasons to speculate that the televised confrontations might have a greater role in aiding voters to construct images of the contenders than had been the case 16 years earlier. For example, despite polls reporting a sizable lead for Jimmy Carter over Gerald Ford in early "trial heats," the same polls indicated far more potential fluidity in voters' perceptions of the two candidates than of Kennedy and Nixon in 1960. Thus, in reporting the results of the Stapel Scalometer in 1960—a device obtaining voters' ratings of candidates on a scale ranging from +5 to -5—the Gallup poll indicated that both candidates had "highly favorable" ratings from 42 to 43

The authors gratefully acknowledge the support of the University Research Committee, Baylor University, Waco, Texas.

An earlier version of this chapter was presented at the Research Conference on Presidential Debates, 1960 and 1976, held at the Annenberg School of Communications, University of Pennsylvania, Philadelphia, May 12-13, 1977.

percent of the respondents; less than one-half of the voters were in the "mildly favorable," "mildly unfavorable," or "don't know" categories and thereby likely to shift images as a result of the debates (Gallup 1972). Compare these data with those of 1976, when Gallup found one-half to two-thirds of voters located in the scalometer range subject to potential shifts in ratings (Gallup 1976). Moreover, a variety of predebate polls reported that two to three times as many voters were "undecided" between the two candidates than was normal for comparable periods in previous presidential campaigns.

Our purpose here is to build upon earlier studies of the relationship between candidate images and televised presidential debates by exploring the stability and change in images across the 1976 confrontations. In addition, we draw upon a related line of research suggesting that campaign communication works fewer changes in the images of involved than noninvolved voters (Converse 1962; Sherif, Sherif, and Nebergall 1965).

DESIGN OF THE STUDY

Previous research has convinced us of the utility of employing Q-methodology to explore the types of images people construct of political objects, especially political candidates (Nimmo and Savage 1976). Unlike survey research or opinion polls that derive their rationale from large sample doctrine (with sample sizes normally ranging from n = 400 to n = 1,500 or more), Q-methodology typically uses small samples of respondents, rarely working with more than n = 100. Whereas survey research frequently uses probability techniques to assure representativeness of samples, Q-methods obtain samples of respondents (called P-samples) and of stimuli (called Q-samples) through balanced and/or factorial designs. The respondents in a small P-sample rank order the opinion statements comprising the Q-sample (each statement typed on a separate card) along a continuum (say, for example, from most to least characteristic, or most to least agree) under a condition of instruction stated by the investigator. Thus, for instance, a researcher might ask a respondent to sort a series of adjectives, first, to describe the respondent; again, to describe the respondent's father; again, to describe the respondent's mother; again, the respondent's spouse, and the like. Q-method thus permits repeated, intensive study of small number of people who operantly model their views of various stimuli. Because of the nature of the forced-choice distribution that comprises the continuum along which each respondent sorts the Q-statements, the numerical value assigned to each statement through the sorting process can be treated as interval rather than ordinal datum. Sorts for all respondents are intercorrelated and the correlation matrix submitted to a Q-factor analysis to produce clusters of persons (Q-factors) rather than clusters of test items, as in R-factor analysis. Each Q-factor consists of respondents who have sorted the Q-statements in similar ways under a given condition of instruction. By examining the characteristics of respondents loading on a factor and by studying the typical ordering of Q-statements of persons comprising that factor, it is possible to describe the nature of each factor (Stephenson 1953). One way to think of each factor is to consider it as a distinct image of the object modeled through respondents' sortings (Stephenson 1967, p. 41).

In this study we employed a matched sample, purposively not randomly drawn, of two categories of citizens. The first consisted of 30 members of a local chapter of the League of Women Voters. For each League member we also included in the sample a subject from the general citizenry of the local community who was not a member of that organization and who professed being relatively inactive in politics beyond voting.

Our Q-sample of opinion statements consisted of 52 items employed in previous research, most notably in a study of images of the 1972 presidential candidates (see Nimmo and Savage 1976). The Q-sample was developed in a balanced design to represent four basic dimensions of voters' images of candidates; that is, 13 statements each representing voters' perceptions of the qualities of a candidate's characteristics as a party politician, the personal qualities of the candidate, and the qualities of the candidate as a television performer. The number items representing the four dimensions of the Q-sample are listed in Table 8.1.

Each of our 60 respondents sorted the 52 Q-statements at six widely spaced times during the 1976 presidential campaign. The sequence was as follows:

Sort 1: prior to the first presidential debate, before the election campaign had become heated
Sort 2: immediately following the first televised debate, between the presidential candidates
Sort 3: immediately after the second presidential debate
Sort 4: immediately following the televised debate between the vice-presidential contenders
Sort 5: after the third presidential debate
Sort 6: immediately after the election

At each period respondents sorted the statements three times—once to describe their views of the ideal president, once to portray Jimmy Carter, and once to portray Gerald Ford. Respondents sorted the 52 Q-statements along a forced-choice nine-point continuum from "most" to "least" characteristic of the object in question:

TABLE 8.1

A Q-Sample of Items Representing the Basic Dimensions of Voters' Images of Presidential Candidates

Traits as a public official
1. He is a good administrator.
2. He can unite people in support of his policies.
3. He is not fearful of criticism.
4. His words, actions, and manner always reflect the dignity and honor of the office.
5. He takes a firm stand on pertinent issues but does not disregard the views of others.
6. He is concerned with the public as a whole, not a collection of minority and majority groups.
7. He is a statesman and a leader who explains to the people as much as possible the reasons behind his actions or proposals.
8. He arrives at decisions through careful consideration and analysis of all available information.
9. He sticks to his decisions once they are made.
10. He is a middle-of-the-roader.
11. He attempts to bring people together in common goals.
12. While qualified in terms of education, he has common sense.
13. He makes only those promises he has the ability to keep.

Traits as a party leader
14. He articulates what his party stands for and always tries to show how each action or proposal is moving toward that goal.
15. He is capable of maintaining party unity on major issues.
16. He carries the image and platform of his party to the people.
17. He represents the major policy stands of his party but he is flexible as the situation and public mood change.
18. He has a record of good honest service to his party.
19. He is grateful for his party's support but not controlled by their demands.
20. He is a leader and open-minded when it comes to his party's varying membership and interests.
21. He is able to get things done, and this means charming and motivating people.
22. He does not mirror the policies of any one party.
23. He should be elected as a result of his party allegiance because talk is cheap and all candidates promise great things.
24. He makes deals without compromising his principles.
25. He listens to other advisers' opinions first, then feels free to do what he thinks is best for everyone.
26. He does not sling mud at his fellow party members or members of the opposing party whose ideas do not coincide with his own.

TABLE 8.1 (Continued)

Traits as a person
27. He has the highest degree of honesty, integrity, and intelligence.
28. When he is wrong, he admits it.
29. He is calm, analytical, and cautious, yet bold and decisive in carrying out his plans.
30. He earnestly wants to be liked and respected.
31. He has a faith in God and is not afraid to express it.
32. He is a good family man.
33. He is of high moral character.
34. He is imaginative, experimental, and hip.
35. He is natural and sincere and does not appear to be trying to impress people.
36. He has a sense of humor.
37. He is ambitious.
38. He is a person capable of deep emotion and warmth.
39. The central quality that gives depth and substance to all the others is his quality of caring.

Traits as a television performer
40. He is cool, calm, and collected in front of an audience.
41. He does not read his speeches; he delivers them.
42. He exhibits warmth and personal appeal on television.
43. His personal magnetism and physical attractiveness are positive assets.
44. He is expressive but not overdramatic.
45. He expresses himself intelligently and clearly so that the educated and uneducated alike understand what is said.
46. His perseverance, firmness, coolness, and aggressiveness clearly project a take-charge image.
47. He is sure of what he is saying and ready for anything.
48. He is himself; he is genuine in television appearances since people today sense insincerity.
49. He is able to hold his audience's interest.
50. His voice, speech patterns, expressions, and cool appearance are more important than the mere words of his speech.
51. He is proof that Madison Avenue advertising techniques make television appearances more effective.
52. He appeals to reason rather than people's emotions and prejudices.

Source: Compiled by the authors.

		Most Characteristic				Least Characteristic			
Score	+4	+3	+2	+1	0	-1	-2	-3	-4
Number of items	4	5	6	7	8	7	6	5	4

Given the small sample characteristic of Q-studies and that they are purposively, rather than randomly, drawn, our findings cannot be generated to a larger universe. Moreover, our study is not of the panel or experimental variety that permits us to control for repeated measurements. Yet, given our balanced samples of two contrasting voting groups and the intensive analysis employed in Q-techniques, we can describe the images held by two sets of voters, compare these images as the campaign developed, and speculate about the effects of the presidential and vice-presidential debates upon image construction.

PERSISTENCIES IN THE PERCEPTIONS OF PRESIDENTIAL CANDIDATES

Our data permit us to examine the persistency of individual perceptions of the ideal president, Jimmy Carter and Gerald Ford, respectively. For this purpose we look at the correlation of each person's sort under a given condition at one time period with his/her sort at another period. It is not practical to present here the full matrix of all intrapersonal correlations for each of the three sorts at each of six time periods. Therefore, we limit ourselves in Table 8.2 to displaying the mean intrapersonal correlations for the total sample, the subsample of League members, and the subsample of less active voters. We recognize that there are problems associated with interpreting mean correlations—not the least of which is the masking of individual changes—but the patterns revealed in Table 8.2 are sufficiently typical of insights offered by individual respondents.

It is apparent at the outset that perceptions of the ideal president were more stable across the campaign than were those of either of the two candidates. This finding squares well with the results of earlier research (Nimmo and Savage 1976). This greater stability in how people perceived their ideal president appears within the total sample and for both of the League and non-League subsamples. Correlations among members of the League of Women Voters are higher than those for our less active voters, but the differences between mean correlations are not statistically significant. We conclude that there was relatively little difference in the stability of the perceptions of League and non-League members with respect to their views of the ideal president.

Note that there is a "firming" of the ideal image over time, that is, the mean correlations for each subgroup's perceptions at sorting period to the postelection sort increases for each postdebate sort. Thus, the correlations of the sorts following the first debate to the postelection sorts are higher than the pre- to postelection sorts; the postsecond debate to postelection correlations

TABLE 8.2

Mean Intrapersonal Correlations for Q-Sorts for Less Active Voters, Members of League of Women Voters, and Total Sample, for Each Debate Period, 1976

	Debate Period															
	Predebates to				Postdebate 1 to				Postdebate 2 to			Postdebate 3 to		Postdebate 4 to
Sort Condition	Postdebate			Post- election	Postdebate			Post- election	Postdebate		Post- election	Postde- bate 4	Post- election	Postelection
	1	2	3	4		2	3	4		3	4				
Ideal president															
Less actives	.66	.60	.60	.56	.60	.69	.64	.59	.61	.68	.64	.66	.72	.70	.69
League members	.83	.79	.79	.77	.76	.82	.80	.82	.78	.80	.80	.80	.83	.81	.83
Total	.75	.70	.70	.68	.69	.76	.73	.72	.71	.75	.74	.73	.78	.76	.77
Jimmy Carter															
Less actives	.52	.43	.46	.42	.46	.43	.54	.47	.54	.52	.46	.48	.64	.63	.65
League members	.57	.56	.54	.51	.56	.64	.61	.62	.65	.67	.64	.69	.69	.69	.74
Total	.55	.53	.50	.47	.51	.55	.57	.54	.60	.60	.56	.59	.67	.66	.70
Gerald Ford															
Less actives	.47	.40	.42	.45	.41	.46	.47	.49	.51	.54	.45	.45	.58	.55	.56
League members	.57	.52	.52	.53	.53	.64	.62	.66	.61	.66	.67	.67	.72	.69	.72
Total	.62	.46	.48	.49	.57	.56	.55	.58	.57	.60	.56	.57	.66	.63	.59

Note: For less active voters, n = 30; for members of League of Women Voters, n = 30; for total sample, n = 60.
Source: Compiled by the authors.

exceed those of postfirst debate to postelection sorts, and the like. We cannot say how much of this firming of images of the ideal president is an artifact of repeated measurement effects, because our design had no controls permitting the detection of such effects. However, on the basis of earlier research—using both Q-techniques and the semantic differential—revealing that images people have of ideal officeholders are more clear-cut than those of actual candidates, and that there is some sharpening of images of both ideal and actual candidates from pre- to postelection periods (Nimmo and Savage 1976), we hypothesize that the firming was more than a measurement artifact.

Differences in the persistency of the perceptions of League and non-League members with respect to each of the two candidates are smaller than with respect to views of the ideal president. Again, the differences are not significant, and we usually observe a firming process. It is also interesting that in the case of the candidate sorts (and with respect to sorts on the ideal as well) pre- to postelection correlations are generally lower than those between preelection sorts and those following the first debate. Thus, our subjects in both subgroups approached the campaign with their individual perceptions of what they wanted in a president and of what each candidate possessed. As the campaign progressed through the debates, these preelection orderings of perceptions generally became less predictive of subjects' perceptions at successively later periods. In short, whether viewed as a firming process whereby correlations between each successive sort and the postelection sort increased or as a reordering process whereby preelection rankings are less and less consistent with later ones, the inference from mean intrapersonal correlations is that changes in our voters' images were taking place. Looking at the images themselves helps us to see how this is so.

THE CHARACTER OF CANDIDATE IMAGES, 1976

Given the three conditions of instruction (to sort on the ideal president and on each of the two candidates) for each of the six time periods, our respondents sorted the Q-sample of image statements 18 times. We factor-analyzed each of these sorts in a variety of ways, using different criteria for extracting factors. With a host of statistical tests—including the scree test, common variance tests, and Humphrey's test—and a desire to enhance comparisons across our selected time periods, we decided upon two-factor solutions for each set of sorts. We rotated factors to simple structure by means of the varimax method and calculated significant factor loadings by using the standard error for a zero correlation coefficient: $SE = 1/\sqrt{n}$, where n = number of statements, 52. Loadings significant at the .01 level are 2.5 × SE, or .35. All findings appearing in Table 8.3—which reports the number of respondents comprising the two images of the ideal president, two of Jimmy Carter, and two of Gerald Ford—meet the criterion for significance.

TABLE 8.3

Images of Ideal President, Jimmy Carter, and Gerald Ford
Constructed by Less Active Voters, Members
of the League of Women Voters, and
the Total Sample during the Period
of the 1976 Presidential Debates

	\multicolumn{6}{c}{Images}
	Ideal President		Jimmy Carter		Gerald Ford	
Debate Period	Able States-man	Moral Leader	Moral Leader	Ambitious Leader	Good Man	Party Leader
Preelection						
Less actives	7	21	15	12	16	5
League members	23	6	18	11	14	13
Total	30	27	33	23	30	18
After first debate						
Less actives	8	20	10	15	17	3
League members	22	7	14	14	9	18
Total	30	27	24	29	26	21
After second debate						
Less actives	7	22	15	9	20	5
League members	24	6	19	7	14	14
Total	31	28	34	16	34	19
After third debate						
Less actives	7	22	16	8	18	6
League members	22	7	24	3	13	13
Total	29	29	40	11	31	19
After fourth debate						
Less actives	8	19	18	8	19	4
League members	26	1	24	4	16	14
Total	34	20	42	12	35	18
Postelection						
Less actives	11	19	14	11	21	4
League members	20	9	23	5	17	11
Total	31	28	37	16	38	15

Source: Compiled by the authors.

The Ideals of Able Statesman and Moral Leader

Consider first images of the ideal president. The two images are distinct, both with respect to the type of respondents loading on the factors that define them and with respect to the ordering of Q-statements that discriminate between those factors. At each election period the bulk of the League of Women Voters subsample load on one factor; the bulk of our subsample of less active voters on the other. In fact, the distribution of the two types of respondents between the two factors is in all cases significant at the .01 level of significance. We are clearly justified, for each period of the campaign, in speaking of distinct, separate League and non-League images of the ideal president.

What are these two images of the ideal president and how can we characterize them? Our factor analysis provides us with a typal array of Q-statements representing each factor, or image. This typal array is, in effect, a Q-sort representing the most typical way all persons loading on a given factor sorted the 52 Q-statements. By comparing the typal arrays, or typical Q-sorts, we can see what the two images of the ideal president are and can describe the differences between them. For the sake of brevity we will examine only the statements that discriminate clearly between the two images. What we find are two images that existed across the entire campaign but differed markedly from one another.

The Able Statesman

The statements ranked as most characteristic (scored +4 in the Q-sort) of their ideal president by persons loading on the factor comprised chiefly of members of the League of Women Voters were:

7. He is a statesman and a leader who explains to the people as much as possible the reasons behind his actions or proposals.
8. He arrives at decisions through careful consideration and analysis of all available information.
28. When he is wrong he admits it.

What begins to emerge is the picture of an open, cautious, candid statesman. That image is rounded out by examining the statements comprising the least characteristic (a -4 score) attributes of the ideal president:

23. He should be elected as a result of his party allegiance because talk is cheap and all candidates promise great things.
50. His voice, speech patterns, expressions, and cool appearance are more important than the mere words of his speech.
51. He is proof that Madison Avenue advertising techniques make television appearances more effective.

This image, then, emphasizes ability, but not ability as a partisan, stylist, or television performer. Content of policy and utterances are key emphases, not cosmetic qualities. The image stresses qualities of leadership in an official capacity and traits as a person, but not party ties or television acumen. We label this image that of the "able statesman," the image of the ideal president held by members of the League of Women Voters throughout the 1976 campaign.

The Moral Leader

Our subsample of less active voters agrees with League members in what they find least characteristic in their ideal president. They too give a –4 ranking to the same Q-items 23, 50, and 51. But they add another item they find least characteristic of their ideal: "He is imaginative, experimental, and hip." Where this alternative image of the ideal president sharply differs from that of the able statesman is in the Q-items most characteristic of the image:

1. He is a good administrator.
27. He has the highest degree of honesty, integrity, and intelligence.
31. He has a faith in God and is not afraid to express it.
33. He is of high moral character.

With the exception of the item praising administrative ability, the non-League image concentrates on personal traits defining an ideal president, particularly those associated with morals and religious faith. What emerges is the image of the ideal president as "moral leader."

Table 8.3 indicates that there was some shifting by respondents between able statesman and moral leader images during the campaign. This is most notable in the shift of League members late in the campaign and after the election. Yet, the two images remain distinct in their primary composition: League members want an able statesman, less active voters want a moral leader. Such distinctiveness in images, at least as associated with League or non-League affiliations, is not the case when examining the images of Jimmy Carter and Gerald Ford.

JIMMY CARTER: MORAL OR AMBITIOUS LEADER?

As with the case of the ideal president, the images of Jimmy Carter and Gerald Ford that emerged in preelection sorts retained their character throughout the campaign, as evidenced by the results of Q-factor analysis of sorts in each time frame of the campaign. Turning first to the case of Jimmy Carter, it is apparent that one of the emergent images of him is virtually a restatement of the non-League, moral leader image of the ideal president. Thus, three of the items ranked +4 as most characteristic of Carter in the Q-sort typical of this image were statements 27, 31, and 33, precisely the three items that emerge with +4 rankings in the moral leader image. And what of the attributes least characteristic of Carter as seen by persons holding this image? They are the same traits least characteristic of the ideal president in the moral leader image, that is, 23, 50, and 51. In sum, Carter came across to many respondents in our sample as authentic in personal traits, not as a product of television style.

With the exception of sorts following the first debate, the plurality of our respondents conceived Carter as moral leader. Moreover, this image gained adherents through the debates, followed by a shift away of some respondents to an alternative view after the election. The image of Carter as moral leader was attractive to both members of the League of Women Voters and to less active voters; no significant differences appear between the numbers of respondents in the two subsamples loading on the moral leader image as contrasted with its alternative.

And what was the alternative image of Carter in 1976? It is highly personalized with respect to attributes demed most characteristic of Carter. Although all respondents holding this alternative image recognized Carter's faith in God (Q-item 31) as characteristic, they also gave +4 scores to the following:

30. He earnestly wants to be liked and respected.
32. He is a good family man.
37. He is ambitious.

Such traits yield a mixed picture, that is, positive traits regarding Carter's religious and family ties, but a hint of a negative assessment regarding his ambition and desire to be liked and respected. Added evidence of a negative coloring in the image comes from inspecting the traits deemed least characteristic of Carter:

7. He is a statesman and a leader who explains to the people as much as possible the reasons behind his actions and proposals.
8. He arrives at decisions through careful consideration and analysis of all available information.
9. He sticks to his decisions once they are made.
10. He makes only those promises he has the ability to keep.

Ranked only slightly less characteristic of Carter (-3) in the typical Q-sort describing this alternative image are references that "he does not mirror the policies of one party" and "he does not sling mud."

In sum, persons holding this second image of Jimmy Carter found that he did not measure up to the able statesman image of the ideal president. The negative quality of the image suggests it proper to label it the image of Carter as an "ambitious leader." If we do this, then we note that the only shift away (see Table 8.3) from the view of Carter as moral leader to ambitious leader among our respondents came after the first presidential debate (the debate publically trumpeted in the press and polls as "won" by Gerald Ford). The setback was temporary. Persons returned to the moral emphasis in Carter's image after the second debate. After that point an increasing number of our respondents came to regard Carter as moral leader, a suggestion of image changes taking place throughout the campaign.

Gerald Ford: Good Man and Party Leader

The two leading images of Gerald Ford derived from our Q-study are more difficult to label. The first, which we shall refer to as the "good man" image, shares some of the characteristics of the non-League, moral leader conception of the ideal president. Thus, Q-statement 33 describing Ford as of high moral character is ranked as most characteristic in the good man image. However, another item ranked characteristic (scored +4 or +3) emphasizes Ford's careful processes of decision making (Q-item 8), a trait crucial to the definition of the able statesman view of the ideal president. Other traits ranked most characteristic of Ford by respondents fashioning the good man image include:

4. His words, actions, and manner always reflect the dignity and honor of the office.
18. He has a record of good, honest service for his party.

With respect to attributes deemed least characteristic of Ford in the good man image, Q-statements 50 and 51 appeared. Thus, respondents did not believe Ford a product of Madison Avenue nor one inclined to have more style than substance. Nor did holders of the good man image find Ford imaginative, experimental, and hip (Q-item 34) or overly beholden to the Republican party (Q-item 23).

In sum, the good man image of Gerald Ford appeared as very much like the view portrayed in the press of the incumbent from the time he had first been selected for the vice-presidency by Richard Nixon, that is, an honest, decent, deliberative man without great imagination or engaging style. Ford the good man resembled what his campaing advertising said, "He made us proud again."

An alternative image of Ford, however, emphasized personal and partisan qualities. It is of Gerald Ford as "party leader." Of the four traits given +4 rankings in this image, two stress partisan and two personal attributes:

16. He carries the image and platform of his party to the people.
18. He has a record of good, honest service for his party.
30. He earnestly wants to be liked and respected.
32. He is a good family man.

Ranked least characteristic of Ford by the respondents associated with the party leader image are qualities of nonpartisanship, effectiveness in getting things done, being willing to admit he is wrong, boldness, and decisiveness. The image is one of a sound party man but not of an outstanding president.

Both the image of Gerald Ford as a good man and as party leader stress reliability and dependability. In this respect the images are distinct. For example, the correlation between the two images revealed by the factor analysis was never more than .17 for any sorting period during the campaign. As Table 8.3 indicates, the image of Ford the good man was most popular with members of our sample. There was but one significant difference between League and non-League respondents with respect to aligning with these images. After the first debate, the good man image of Ford was a non-League view, while Ford the party leader was the view of a significant proportion of our respondents from the League of Women Voters.

As the debates wore on, as in the case of Carter's images, one of the two Ford images emerged as dominant. As the first debate receded into the past, the image of Ford the good man began to take over. Following the third presidential debate more than two-thirds of our respondents had settled on Jimmy Carter as a moral leader, Gerald Ford as a good man. The remaining one-third held more negative views of both candidates. As might be expected, there were respondents who constructed a positive image of one candidate, a negative image of the other. But, given the fact that so many of our respondents held positive views of both candidates, the fashioning of images of the presidential candidates was something more than a mere exercise in praising one's preference and damning the opposition.

THE IMAGES OF THE VICE-PRESIDENTIAL CANDIDATES

In addition to their cooperation in sorting Q-items pertaining to the presidential contest, 57 of our subjects (27 League members and 30 non-League) agreed to sort the Q-statements following the debates between vice-presidential candidates Robert Dole and Walter Mondale (designated the third debate in reporting sorts on presidential candidates). Again we extracted two-factor solutions.

With respect to Dole one image is distinctly positive, the other slightly negative. The positive image emphasizes Dole's service to his political party and his governmental experience. Thus, among the statements ranked most characteristic of Dole (+4) we find:

    3. He is not fearful of criticism.
    8. He arrives at decisions through careful consideration and analysis of all available information.
    12. While qualified in terms of education, he has common sense.
    18. He has a record of good, honest service for his party.

Persons loading on this factor ranked as least characteristic such qualities as the candidate being a Madison Avenue product, engaging in cheap talk by promising great things, being hip, or being a mudslinger.

Dole's more negative image stressed such traits as "he is ambitious" (+4); "he does not sling mud" (-4); and "his words, actions, and manner always reflect the dignity and honor of his office" (-4). But the image is not strictly negative. Thus, we encounter the following items:

    36. He has a sense of humor (+3).
    40. He is cool, calm and collected in front of an audience (+4).
    41. He does not read his speeches, he delivers them (+3).
    49. He is able to hold his audience's interest (+3).

By and large, Dole's qualities as a television performer and speaker dominate this image, personal traits and partisanship come next, and perceptions of his experience as a public official occupy midpoints in the forced-sort Q-distributions.

Among our respondents, only 12 had significant loadings on the positive Dole image; 42 comprised the image of Dole the performer. Of those 42 there were 22 League members and 18 non-League members, a distribution revealing no significant difference among members of the two subgroups in images of the Republican candidate.

The two Mondale images are relatively easy to interpret. The first—loading 32 respondents—emphasizes the candidate's positive personal qualities and record of public service while minimizing his partisanship and style as a television performer. Thus, for example,"he has the highest degree of honesty, integrity, and intelligence," "he is of high moral character," "he is a statesman and leader," and "his words, actions, and manner reflect the dignity and honor of his office" all receive +4 rankings. References to his being a product of Madison Avenue techniques rank least characteristic of Mondale.

The second image—loading 24 respondents—notes negative personal and partisan qualities. People constructing this image find Mondale "ambitious," devoted to the party line, promising more than he can deliver, something of a mudslinger, and a person who wants to be liked and respected. Traits as a television performer, however, are respected—for example, his ability to hold his audience, to express himself so that educated and uneducated alike understand him, and to be cool and collected.

What is most distinctive about the Mondale images, however, is that they divide League and non-League respondents in a significant (at the .01 level) fashion: 22 of our 27 League subjects comprise the positive Mondale image; 19 of 30 non-League respondents comprise the slightly more negative view.

CANDIDATE IMAGES AS PERSONAL CONSTRUCTIONS

A view of image analysis borrowed from symbolic interaction is that people respond to objects on the basis of the meanings those objects have for them, that is, meanings are constructed through responses (Blumer 1959). We have explored the meanings that a small set of respondents constructed for selected political objects during the course of the 1976 presidential debates. We have sought those meanings, or images, in responses displayed through subjectively derived Q-sortings. By extracting those images we have found that—at least in the cases of ideal president, the images of Gerald Ford after the first debate, and the images of Walter Mondale—that our politically involved and less involved subjects held distinctly different views of ideal and actual candidates.

One might argue, of course, that the differences we found among League and non-League respondents' images could be accounted for by other factors than League membership or level of voter involvement. Our search for these other factors, however, has not been rewarding. In our pre- and postelection interviews we gathered information about several aspects of respondents' backgrounds influencing party identification, 1972 and 1976 presidential voting behavior, perception of how respondents thought they were influenced by the debates, perceptions of the influence of campaign events, and standard social and demographic data. Although all League members were, except one, female, and were predominantly Democrat and favorable to Carter, the League sample did not differ all that much from the non-League sample in these respects. Moreover, our analysis revealed no significant differences in images associated with differences in measured predispositions, preferences, or attributes. As far as we can discern, therefore, the League and non-League images were attributable to membership rather than to differing partisan loyalties, candidate preferences, or socioeconomic characteristics of respondents.

Although basic images of the ideal president and actual candidates remained the same (a finding consonant with those from the research surrounding the 1960 debates), individual members of our sample did shift from image to image as the campaign progressed. In part, this shifting (the full magnitude of which is masked in Table 8.3 due to many subjects canceling out one another's shifts in the aggregate figures reported there) may reflect a clarifying and firming process revealed in earlier studies. Through attitional analysis we hope to explore this question by identifying shifters and persistents and factor-analyzing all of each respondent's 18 sorts in a series of n = 1 studies. Such a procedure enables us to explore the dimensions of each voter's images using in-depth procedures not normally available in survey or experimental research. We also plan to explore another question hinted at but not elaborated on in this report, namely, to what degree are images of actual candidates the results of voters projecting their ideal visions upon available choices or do images of the ideal reflect perceptions of the candidates observed by voters?

In short, the obvious implication of this line of inquiry is that candidate imagery is a highly personalized phenomenon. This is not, however, to say it is idiosyncratic and beyond explanation. Additional in-depth studies may provide the opportunity to ferret out the patterns of image construction that transcend individual subjects.

9

THE IMPACT OF
THE 1976 PRESIDENTIAL DEBATES:
CONVERSION OR REINFORCEMENT?

Paul R. Hagner and Leroy N. Rieselbach

Although modern electoral analysis is well into its fourth decade, it has provided relatively little insight into the possible effects of compaign events and stimuli on the citizen's political decision making. The central reason is that the classic studies of voting behavior concentrate on the importance of long-term political predispositions rather than shorter term, campaign-related phenomena (Converse 1966). From this theoretical perspective, the campaign is the mechanism by which long-term dispositions are linked, or transmitted, to the specific problem of choosing between two or more candidates (Farley and Marks 1974), and specific campaign events usually are evaluated in terms of the way in which they reinforce these political predispositions (Lazarsfeld, Berelson, and Gaudet 1948).

Conceptualizing the campaign as a period in which long-term predispositions are linked to a specific political choice tends to divert researchers from examining political campaigns as periods in which new political information is learned and new political attitudes formed. Likewise, the importance and impact of the carriers of this new political information, the mass media, also have been largely overlooked (Kraus and Davis 1976). As a result of these and other omissions, more emphasis has been placed upon the continuity that exists among elections than upon changes that occur within the election periods themselves.

We gratefully acknowledge the support of the Knight-Ridder Newspapers and the Deans of Research and Graduate Development and the College of Arts and Sciences of Indiana University. Though these organizations and individuals bear no responsibility for our arguments and interpretations, the research could not have been conducted without their assistance. An earlier version of this study was presented at the 1977 Annual Meeting of the Midwest Political Science Association, Chicago, Illinois.

Another, more concrete, set of explanations for the lack of emphasis given to the campaign derives from the fact that campaigns themselves present difficult research quandaries. For one thing, it is not always easy to delineate what constitutes a "campaign period." In the past two presidential elections, candidates have been announced more than six months before the first primary election. A second problem inheres in the primary system itself. In numerous states voters do not cast ballots directly for presidential aspirants; where they do, there should be more direct political communication than in those states that operate under state convention systems. Similarly, a third problem with campaign analysis results from the electoral college system. Given the lure of states with large electoral vote blocs, the general political campaign will be fought harder and the public bombarded with more pleas for support in some areas than in others.

The consequence of these and related factors is that national political campaigns tend to be open-ended affairs largely concentrated at the state and local levels rather than at the nationwide level. There are actually very few campaign events directed to a nationwide audience. Political advertising sometimes focuses on the nation, but much of it, especially in the more recent campaigns, has become more and more regionalized. The party conventions certainly seek a nationwide audience, but, given their length and the many conflicting stimuli they emit, their impact may be negligible. Thus, for the most part, research on campaign effects is more suited to regional, rather than national, studies.

In 1960 and 1976, however, there occurred campaign events specifically directed at a nationwide audience and intended to foster each candidate's electoral fortunes. We refer, of course, to the presidential debates. The debates provide an escape from the limitations of regional analysis. They do not incorporate widely diffused stimuli, they engender a relatively high degree of citizen interest and participation, and they avoid regional constraints. For these reasons we have chosen the presidential debates as the focusing agents of the national presidential campaign. The general purpose of the following analysis is to examine the effect the debates had on voter orientations toward the candidates and issues in the 1976 campaign. Specifically, we wish to examine the debates both as events that reinforced previously existing political orientations and as phenomena that redirected or converted those predispositions.

METHOD OF STUDY

To gauge the impact of the debates upon such things as vote intention and candidate image, we must be able to measure the respondent's pre- and postdebate attitudinal positions. Trend analysis is inadequate since stable cross-time measures may conceal considerable individual fluctuation. To compare pre- and postdebate attitudes and the evaluation of candidate performance in the debates themselves, it is essential to have data from a panel of respondents.

Our data come from a study conducted by Knight-Ridder Newspapers and Indiana University. The study features a nationwide panel of respondents, all of whom were interviewed in May, early September, and the day after the election (n = 442). For present purposes we will be most interested in the September-November panel, which will make up our pre- and postdebate comparisons. After weighting on sex and education, the two-wave panel closely approximates the original national sample. The only major differences between the original sample and the panel occur with respect to whether the respondents are registered to vote and whether they voted in the 1972 election. Members of the panel were more likely to be registered to vote (86 percent versus 79 percent) and reported voting in 1972 more frequently (81 percent versus 72 percent). On all standard demographic characteristics, as well as party identification, political ideology, and political efficacy, there were minimal or no differences.

In the September wave, respondents were asked to (1) evaluate both Ford and Carter along four different image dimensions, (2) respond to a number of issue questions, and (3) indicate their intended vote and the certainty of their decision. In the November administration, respondents were asked the same image and issue questions as in September: how they voted; whether they watched or listened to each debate; and, if they had watched or listened, how they evaluated each candidate's performance in that debate.

It would have been preferable to have immediate evaluations of each debate, but we did find substantial variation in evaluations across each debate dyad. On the average, 60 percent of our sample gave different evaluations to the same candidate between the debates, indicating there was a process of differentiation taking place. Additionally, the November evaluations of the first debate were correlated with the respondents' evaluations of that debate measured the day after the debate took place (in a panel wave not used in this chapter). The high level of first-debate evaluation consistency over this six-week period (phi = .88) and the between-debate variation permit considerable confidence in the reliability of the debate evaluation measures we use here.

The interaction between campaign events and the individual's political perceptions is a double-edged sword. Individuals' evaluations of a candidate's debate performance may influence their perceptions of that candidate's image, their opinion on a key debate issue, or even their vote intention. However, it is also plausible that individuals' prior attitudinal dispositions influence their evaluations of each candidate's debate performance. That is, as the pioneering studies of Lazarsfeld, Berelson, and their collaborators suggested more than three decades ago, the campaign may alter voters' feelings about candidates and issues (may convert them) or it may reinforce those prior feelings (Lazarsfeld, Berelson, and Gaudet 1948).

We infer converting effects—where the campaign changes previously held positions—when there is a congruent shift in respondents' debate evaluations, on the one hand, and their candidate images, vote intentions, and issue orientations, on the other. We recognize that such shifts do not prove that the debates caused opinions to change; we only can point out that evaluation and opinion move together. On the other hand, if the analysis shows that changes in debate performance evaluations to not covary, it should strengthen arguments that suggest that the debates did not play a significant role in the citizen's campaign decision making.

We infer reinforcing effects—where the campaign preserves or sustains previously held views—when preexisting dispositions seem to influence debate evaluations, for example, when response to the debates is consistent with earlier partisan identification or candidate preference. We would expect, in this case, Democratic identifiers or Jimmy Carter supporters to rate Carter's debate performance superior to that of Gerald Ford.

Our analysis will proceed as follows: In the first section we look at the reinforcing effect of party identification and candidate preferences upon the evaluation of the debate performances. The second section examines the role of candidate image as an agent of reinforcement as well as the object of conversion. In the third section we examine two key debate issues—unemployment versus inflation and defense spending—for both converting and reinforcing effects. In the final section, we analyze the relationship between candidate selection and the debates from both converting and reinforcing perspectives.

PARTY IDENTIFICATION, CANDIDATE PREFERENCE, AND DEBATE EVALUATION

Here we deal with the possible reinforcing effects of party identification and candidate preference on the individual's evaluation of each candidate's performance in the presidential debates. In the November interview, each respondent was asked to evaluate the performance of both candidates in the debates that the respondent watched. Table 9.1 shows the aggregated responses for each debate, and the results confirm press accounts of the three debates. Clearly, Carter's aggregated evaluations rose across the three debates, while Ford's performance evaluations dropped in the second debate and did not improve in the third. In sum, Carter "lost" the first debate, but "won" the last two. His most significant gain came in the second debate, and he sustained that level in the third. The most interesting aspect of this table is that the percentage of neutral evaluations decreased for both candidates across the three debates, especially for Carter. It appears that the respondents became more opinionated about the contenders' performances as the debates progressed.

The importance of the first and second debates is further emphasized when we examine the changes in individual evaluations across the debates (Table 9.2). Between the first and second debates, and the first and third, Carter made substantial gains in his debate performance evaluations, while Ford's losses

TABLE 9.1

Evaluations of Ford's and Carter's Debate Performance across the Three Presidential Debates, in Percent

Evaluation	Ford Debate 1 (n=321)	Ford Debate 2 (n=285)	Ford Debate 3 (n=273)	Carter Debate 1 (n=321)	Carter Debate 2 (n=285)	Carter Debate 3 (n=273)
High						
1	7	7	6	9	15	15
2	12	9	13	5	16	15
3	18	18	19	14	15	19
4	15	14	14	10	8	10
Neutral						
5	28	26	22	35	23	21
6	5	7	9	10	7	4
7	5	5	5	6	6	7
8	5	6	7	7	5	6
9	1	2	2	1	1	1
Low						
10	2	4	4	4	4	2

Note: The question was asked, "How would you rate _____'s overall performance in the _____ debate on a scale from 1 to 10 with "1" being very favorable and "10" being very unfavorable?"

Source: Compiled by the authors.

overshadowed his gains. This pattern does not hold for evaluations across the second and third debates, each candidate sustaining roughly equal losses and gains. One explanation for this is that while Ford had the initial advantage, probably as a result of his familiarity and his incumbency, the first debate had a "leveling out" effect for both candidates—Carter gained in status and exposure by debating a president and Ford lost ground by being forced to debate Carter as an equal.

Having established that respondents differentiated candidate performance for each debate and that substantial evaluative shifts occurred between debates, we can begin to examine some of the sources of this variation. Table 9.3 presents the debate evaluations first presented in Table 9.1 (collapsed into "approve," "neutral," and "disapprove") broken down by the predebate (September) party identification and candidate preferences. According to the reinforcing effect hypothesis, we should expect Republicans and Democrats and Carter and Ford

TABLE 9.2

Shifts in Respondent Evaluations of Ford's and Carter's Debate Performances across Debate Dyads, in Percent

		Debates 1 and 2[a]		Debates 2 and 3[b]		Debates 1 and 3[c]	
		Ford	Carter	Ford	Carter	Ford	Carter
Loss	−3 to −8	11	3	5	4	10	5
	−1 to −2	26	12	18	17	20	10
No Change	0	42	37	44	47	40	33
	+1 to +2	19	37	26	25	26	37
Gain	+3 to +8	2	11	7	7	4	15

[a] Only those who watched debates 1 and 2 (n = 237).
[b] Only those who watched debates 2 and 3 (n = 209).
[c] Only those who watched debates 1 and 3 (n = 233).
Source: Compiled by the authors.

supporters to have different evaluations of the debate performance of Ford and Carter.

A quick examination of Table 9.3 confirms the self-apparent hypothesis that partisans and supporters of candidates differed significantly in their evaluations of each candidate's debate performance. Party identification, for instance, clearly influenced debate evaluations. Republicans and Democrats were predictably partisan in their evaluation of Ford's and Carter's performances. The evaluations of the Independent voters are interesting. Their evaluations of Ford's debate performances closely resemble those of the Democrats; their evaluations of Carter, while resembling Republican evaluations in the first and third debates, differ considerably from Republican evaluations of Carter's performance in the second. More significantly, on the average, Independents gave the same percentage of neutral evaluations of Ford as did the Democrats. This implies that, lacking the reinforcing effect of partisanship, the Independents were less extreme in their evaluations of each candidate's performance.

Table 9.3 also shows the reinforcing effect of candidate preference to be as strong as party identification. Those who expressed a definite preference before the debates tended to evaluate each candidate's debate performance according to that preference. Those respondents who were unsure of their final vote tended to look like Republicans in their evaluations of Ford and like Democrats in their evaluations of Carter. Here again we see the importance of the reinforcing effect of initial candidate preference upon debate evaluations.

It seems that, on the aggregate level, the reinforcing effect of party identification and candidate preference is pronounced. However, when we examine individual changes across the debates, the reinforcing effect of party identification and candidate preferences becomes much less clear. According to the reinforcing effect hypothesis, we should expect across-debate evaluations of Ford by Democrats either to remain stable or to drop in comparison with across-debate evaluations of Ford by Republicans. Table 9.4, however, does not show this to be the case. Surprisingly, Democrats generally showed higher cross-debate evaluations of Ford than did Republicans. The same pattern is evident for the Republican evaluation of Carter.* An examination of the relationship between changes in debate evaluations and candidate preference shows the same pattern witnessed for party identification. For the cross-debate comparisons, candidate preference was not consistently related to changes in candidate debate evaluations.

Roberta Sigel (1964, p. 496) wrote:

> In 1960 millions of Americans got a close personal look at both candidates via the TV cameras and thus were in an excellent position to be affected by the candidate's image and to lose sight of the candidate's party. . . . And yet our data bring out that, even in a highly personalized campaign, party image featured prominently in the sample's political perception.

Our findings support those of Sigel in the area of overall debate evaluations. Additionally, candidate preference exerts a similar effect on the evaluation of candidate debate performance. The reinforcing effect of party identification and candidate preference was not, however, found to operate at the level of individual shifts in debate evaluations. What emerges is that, while partisan attitudes and candidate preferences may determine initial levels of candidate evaluation, they cannot explain evaluative shifts across the debates.

CANDIDATE IMAGES AND THE DEBATES

It is widely accepted that one of the main reasons each candidate agreed to debate was the hope that he could project a positive image that would translate into votes in November. This section examines the hypothesis that the debates had a converting effect upon the citizen's evaluations of each candidate's image over the debate period. In addition, we will look at the effect the individuals' predebate image evaluations had on their later evaluations of the candidates' debate performances.

---

*This pattern cannot be explained by the fact that Democratic ratings of Ford had "no place to go but up." If there was a reinforcing effect, then the low Ford ratings for the first debate should have remained stable across the second and third debates. For the majority of the respondents, this was not the case.

TABLE 9.3

Debate Evaluations by Party Identification and September Preference, in Percent

	All Respondents	All Democrats	All Independents	All Republicans	September Preference		
					Support Carter	Unsure	Support Ford
Debate 1							
Ford evaluations							
Approve	37	31	34	60	23	51	48
Neutral	48	57	43	33	59	39	41
Disapprove	15	12	18	7	18	10	11
Number	315	130	125	60	127	41	131
Carter evaluations							
Approve	28	40	21	20	43	34	11
Neutral	52	46	57	57	47	58	57
Disapprove	19	14	22	23	10	7	32
Number	314	129	125	60	126	41	131

164

Debate 2							
Ford evaluations							
Approve	36	31	32	55	25	44	46
Neutral	46	51	48	33	51	50	41
Disapprove	18	18	20	12	24	6	13
Number	270	110	111	49	116	34	111
Carter evaluations							
Approve	45	57	42	26	65	51	23
Neutral	37	29	39	50	28	37	46
Disapprove	18	14	19	24	7	11	31
Number	271	110	111	50	116	35	111
Debate 3							
Ford evaluations							
Approve	38	34	34	54	25	45	53
Neutral	44	42	54	31	51	47	35
Disapprove	17	24	12	15	24	8	12
Number	265	110	103	52	118	38	97
Carter evaluations							
Approve	49	64	36	41	71	55	21
Neutral	34	22	47	37	23	34	49
Disapprove	17	14	18	22	6	10	30
Number	264	110	103	51	118	38	96

Source: Compiled by the authors.

TABLE 9.4

Shifts in Debate Evaluations across Debate Dyads by Party Identification and September Preference, in Percent

	All Respondents	All Democrats	All Independents	All Republicans	September Preference		
					Support Carter	Unsure	Support Ford
Debates 1 and 2							
Ford							
Loss	37	38	41	27	40	39	32
No change	43	35	46	52	35	42	48
Gain	20	27	13	20	24	19	19
Number	237	95	98	44	94	31	99
Carter							
Loss	16	17	12	20	14	13	17
No change	37	36	37	39	34	32	41
Gain	48	47	51	41	52	55	41
Number	237	95	98	44	94	31	99

Debates 2 and 3							
Ford							
Loss	23	26	23	18	28	17	20
No change	44	39	41	65	42	40	49
Gain	32	35	36	18	30	43	31
Number	209	83	86	40	95	30	74
Carter							
Loss	21	23	20	18	14	20	27
No change	48	53	46	40	53	50	40
Gain	32	24	34	42	34	30	32
Number	209	83	86	40	95	30	74
Debates 1 and 3							
Ford							
Loss	30	31	34	20	35	24	26
No change	41	36	37	56	36	46	45
Gain	30	33	29	24	29	30	29
Number	233	94	89	50	97	33	89
Carter							
Loss	15	15	18	8	10	18	16
No change	34	33	30	44	28	30	44
Gain	51	52	52	48	62	52	40
Number	233	94	89	50	97	33	89

Source: Compiled by the authors.

TABLE 9.5

Panel's Ratings of Candidates' Image Characteristics,
May, September, and November, in Percent
(n = 442)

		Ford May	Ford September	Ford November	Carter May	Carter September	Carter November
Personal Appeal							
High	1	26	13	21	24	36	27
	2	32	41	38	34	29	39
	3	28	32	32	29	20	24
	4	8	9	5	6	9	6
Low	5	7	4	4	7	6	4
Total[a]		100	100	100	100	100	100
Ability							
High	1	14	14	19	10	16	18
	2	36	40	40	29	34	35
	3	35	32	33	42	35	35
	4	10	7	4	12	8	8
Low	5	7	6	4	7	6	4
Total[a]		100	100	100	100	100	100
Honesty							
High	1	33	33	38	21	33	32
	2	33	31	37	30	27	33
	3	23	26	17	35	29	26
	4	7	5	6	8	6	6
Low	5	5	5	3	5	4	3
Total[a]		100	100	100	100	100	100
Intelligence							
High	1	b	26	30	b	35	34
	2	b	43	48	b	37	41
	3	b	22	23	b	23	21
	4	b	7	2	b	3	2
Low	5	b	3	2	b	2	3
Total[a]			100	100		100	100
Total Image[c]							
High	1	17	17	21	13	28	25
	2	43	54	56	39	41	47
	3	30	21	19	34	23	23
	4	8	8	3	11	6	4
Low	5	3	1	1	3	1	1
Total[a]		100	100	100	100	100	100

[a]Numbers may not total 100 because of rounding.
[b]No measurement taken in May.
[c]Scale comprised of four image dimension items.

Note: The question asked was, "We are now going to ask you to fill out a 'report card' for both Ford and Carter. What grade would give give _____ for (appeal, honesty, intelligence, ability) with 1 being the highest grade and 5 being the lowest?"

Source: Compiled by the authors.

The panel respondents were asked in May, September, and November to "grade" both Ford and Carter on four image characteristics: honesty, intelligence, personal appeal, and ability. Table 9.5 shows the aggregated rankings of each candidate along each image dimension for May, September, and November. In addition, Table 9.5 presents a total image measure, created by combining the individual measures. The total image evaluation measures are Likert-type scales averaged by number of items to compensate for the fact that an intelligence question was not asked in May. The alphas for these scales were all acceptable: May—.756, September—.86, and November—.92.

It is interesting to observe, looking at Table 9.5, that both Ford and Carter received small but noticeable increases in individual and overall image evaluations from May to November. In all categories except ability Ford was given a slight edge over Carter. However, it is fair to say that the campaign period aided both candidates in the "selling" of their respective images

When we look at the individual image evaluation shifts from September to November (Table 9.6),* we see that Carter was definitely losing the image battle with Ford when that battle is defined in terms of gains and losses. A closer examination of Table 9.5 will show that Carter made his most important gains between May and September and maintained a relatively stable overall image evaluation through November, with his September-November losses and gains canceling out. Ford, on the other hand, increased his evaluations through November across each image characteristic.

Having described the patterns of image evaluation for each candidate, we turn to an examination of the reinforcing effect individuals' predebate evaluations of a candidate's image have on their evaluation of the candidate's debate performance. As before, the reinforcement hypothesis would predict significant differences in evaluation of debate performance between those who gave a candidate high image ratings and those who gave that candidate low marks.

The comparisons, summarized in Table 9.7, were operationalized in the following manner. The debate evaluation rankings (originally scaled from 1 to 10) were trichotomized. The total image evaluations for each candidate were collapsed into five classifications to approximate the scales of the original items. The debate evaluations for each candidate were then cross-tabulated with both candidate total image measures, with chi-square used as the test of significance. The measure of association, Tau C, was chosen because of the rectangular tabular design, the ordinal level of measurement, and because its underlying model produces a more conservative estimate of the relationship.

---

*The loss/stable/gain classifications in this table were derived from the comparison of September and November image evaluation ratings. Since the ratings were based on a five-point scale (A, B, C. D, F), the range in absolute magnitude for losses and gains went from 1 to 4.

TABLE 9.6

Shifts in Candidate Image Evaluations, September-November, in Percent

(n = 442)

	Appeal Ford	Appeal Carter	Ability Ford	Ability Carter	Honesty Ford	Honesty Carter	Intelligence Ford	Intelligence Carter	Total Image Ford	Total Image Carter
Loss	21	30	19	23	18	27	19	25	28	41
No change	46	45	49	48	49	45	54	51	22	18
Gain	32	25	31	28	33	29	27	24	50	41
Total	100	100	100	100	100	100	100	100	100	100

Note: Numbers may not total 100 because of rounding.
Source: Compiled by the authors.

TABLE 9.7

Relationship between Total Candidate Image Evaluation
(in September) and Debate Evaluations

	Ford Total Image Evaluation, Tau C	Carter Total Image Evaluation, Tau C
Debate 1		
Ford	+.23*	−.06
Carter	−.02	+.31*
Debate 2		
Ford	+.33*	−.08
Carter	−.16*	+.39*
Debate 3		
Ford	+.30*	−.02
Carter	−.04	+.32*

*p < .05.
Source: Compiled by the authors.

The reinforcing hypothesis was confirmed in each case where a candidate's image evaluations were compared to his debate evaluations. In those cases where one candidate's image evaluations were compared to the other candidate's debate performance, only one comparison (again involving Ford's second-debate performance) yielded a significant relationship. Thus, except for that one case, respondents' evaluations of one participant's debate performance were not influenced by their evaluations of the image of the opponent.

Looking at the relationship between the predebate image evaluations and shifts in evaluations across the debates, we found, as before, no significant relationship between the two (data not shown), again minimizing the role of predebate orientations as effects on evaluations of debate performance. We then turned to an examination of the conversion hypothesis involving debate evaluations and image evaluations. If individuals' evaluations of a candidate's performance in the debates had a converting effect on their evaluations of that candidate's image, we should expect to see congruent shifts in debate evaluations and image evaluations (compared in September and November). We compared each image characteristic (honesty, intelligence, ability, appeal) and the total image measure with the dyadic debate evaluation shifts. There was not one significant relationship in all of these comparisons (data not shown). The total lack of confirmation of the converting effect hypothesis in these comparisons suggests strongly that the shifts in image evaluations and debate evaluations represent two separate and orthogonal processes. It is apparent that the goal of image improvement, which, in part, served to motivate debate participation for the candidates, was unattained.

It is not immediately apparent how to square these findings with those of researchers who looked at image patterns and the 1960 debates. Several researchers found that the debates had some converting effect on image evaluations, especially those of Kennedy (Kraus 1962). One possible explanation lies in the fact that the media coverage of the 1960 and 1976 presidential elections differed markedly in predebate examination of the candidates. To many 1960 voters, the debates provided their first real look at Kennedy. By contrast, media coverage of Jimmy Carter was, by any standard, extremely thorough after Iowa, seven months before the first debate. We suggest that a large majority of the public had had time to develop relatively strong opinions on the images of Carter and Ford and that it took more than staged debates to change them.

ISSUES AND THE DEBATES

While most research on the 1960 debate effects concerned candidate image evaluations and vote choice, a few studies suggested that the debates may have provided a forum for learning about various issues (Middleton 1962). We now look at the possible reinforcing and converting relationships between two debate issues and candidate debate evaluations.

For our examination we chose two issues that (1) figured prominently throughout the debates and (2) tended to differentiate Carter voters from Ford voters: opinions on the amount of money that should be spent on defense and opinions on whether inflation was a more important problem than unemployment. In the debates, each candidate made it quite clear where he stood on the two issues: Carter favored reduced defense spending and emphasized unemployment; Ford supported maintenance of defense spending levels and expressed concern about inflation. Our examination of the data shows quite clearly that those who voted for each candidate also reflected their candidate's stand on each issue. On the question of whether the United States should reduce defense spending, 73 percent of the Carter voters wanted to see less spending compared with only 27 percent of the Ford voters. On the question of which problem, unemployment or inflation, should be of most concern to the government, 67 percent of the Carter voters but only 33 percent of those who voted for Ford were more concerned with the unemployment problem. It appears that there was a clear differentiation between both candidates and their supporters on these two issues.

Given this, did respondents' opinions on the two issues have a reinforcing effect on their evaluations of each candidate's debate performance? The summaries in Table 9.8 indicate that, for the most part, they did not. The com-

TABLE 9.8

Relationship between Opinions on Unemployment/Inflation Issue and Defense Spending Issue and Candidate Debate Evaluations

	Defense Spending (Cramer's V)	Unemployment/Inflation (Cramer's V)
Debate 1		
Ford	.14*	.05
Carter	.03	.08
Debate 2		
Ford	.07	.03
Carter	.06	.03
Debate 3		
Ford	.01	.04
Carter	.16*	.05

*p < .05.
Source: Compiled by the authors.

parisons were operationalized as follows. The candidate debate evaluations were trichotomized as before. The responses to the two issue questions (excluding all "don't knows" or missing responses) retain their original dichotomous categories ("agree"/"disagree" for defense spending and "unemployment/inflation" for the unemployment-inflation question). Significance tests are again based on the chi-square distribution of the cross-tabular comparisons. Cramer's V, a variant of phi that corrects for an inflated coefficient value that could be the result of 2 by N analysis, was chosen as the measure of association for the nominal and ordinal comparisons.

Opinions on the unemployment-inflation issue did not influence the evaluations of either candidate's debate performance. Opinions on the defense spending issue were only weakly related to evaluations of Ford's first-debate performance and Carter's performance in the third debate. This is interesting, for while the second debate concentrated on foreign affairs and dealt most directly with the defense spending issue, respondents' opinions on that issue did not influence their debate evaluations. We also examined the possibility that individuals' opinions on both issues might influence change in evaluation of each candidate's debate performances across the debates. Here we found no significant relationship between the two across all of the debate pairings. It seems that the individuals' opinions on these two issues had little or no reinforcing effect on their evaluations of each candidate's performance in the debates.

If the debates had a converting effect on the respondents' issue positions we should expect that those individuals who changed their positions on either the unemployment-inflation or the defense-spending issue might have done so as a result of their evaluations of each candidate's performance in the debates where the issues were discussed. During the period from September to November, while a large majority of the respondents did not change their opinions on either issue, 29 percent did give a response to the unemployment-inflation question in November that differed from the one given in September. Similarly, 24 percent shifted their opinion on the defense-spending issue during the same time period.

We then examined the converting effect hypothesis, comparing the respondent's evaluation of each candidate's performance across each debate pairing with the pattern of change in his/her September-November opinions on each issue. Our expectations were, for example, that increasingly positive evaluations of Carter's debate performance might induce shifts toward Carter's positions on the two issues. For every comparison, for both candidates across each debate dyad, we found no support for the converting effect hypothesis (data not shown); indeed, for most of the opinion shifters, the changes in each candidate's debate evaluations were almost identical—that is, those who changed their minds about this country's defense expenditures were just as likely to improve their evaluation of Carter as they were to improve their evaluation of Ford.

Thus, we conclude that, for these issues, there was little evidence to support either of the effect hypotheses. This conclusion cannot, of course, be extended to all issues of the 1976 campaign, but, given the clear differentiation in candidate choice associated with each issue, the findings are not unimportant. (For a more extended discussion of shifts in issue opinions over the 1976 campaign period, see Hagner and McIver [1976].)

THE DEBATES AND THE VOTE

Here we deal with what is perhaps the most important dimension of debate effects: their influence on the individual's actual voting behavior. We have already examined the reinforcing effect of candidate preferences on debate evaluations and have found significant effects present. In this section we assess the converting effect hypothesis that individuals' evaluations of each candidate's debate performance has a determining effect on their votes in November.

Comparing respondents' vote intentions, as reported in September, with their reported November vote (removing all nonvoters and refusals from the analysis), we found that 80 percent of the respondents actually voted for their September choice, 12 percent shifted from Carter to Ford, and 8 percent went from Ford to Carter. The first question to be raised is: Did those who switched

TABLE 9.9

Relationship between Candidate Switching and Debate Evaluations, Summary of T-Tests

Debate Performance Evaluation	Difference in Means Test (T-Test) between Those Who Switched to Carter and Those Who Switched to Ford
Debate 1	
Ford	$p > .05$
Carter	$p < .05$
Debate 2	
Ford	$p > .05$
Carter	$p < .05$
Debate 3	
Ford	$p > .05$
Carter	$p < .05$

Source: Compiled by the authors.

from Ford to Carter and those who switched from Carter to Ford differ in their evaluations of each candidate's debate performance? The results presented in Table 9.9 show that the two switching groups differed significantly on each of Carter's debate performances but did not differ significantly on Ford's. It is apparent that, for those who switched between September and November, Carter's debate performances were definitely an issue while Ford's were not. This finding has many interesting features, not the least of which is that Ford's well-publicized error in the second debate did not appear to be a factor in the switching of candidate allegiances.

Even though there is a clear relationship between vote switching and evaluations of Carter's debate performance, we would be stretching our data to say that the debate evaluations caused the shift to occur. There may have been numerous other factors that influenced both the debate evaluations and the changes in voting intention. With this in mind, we devised an alternate test of the converting effect hypothesis.

All respondents who voted were asked to specify the campaign event, or time period, closest to the time they made their decision to vote for Ford or Carter. The interviewers were specifically instructed to ask the respondents to name a campaign event that occurred just before the time they made up their minds. In postinterview debriefings, the interviewers reported that most respondents readily associated their decisions with campaign events, including the debates. Of all those who voted, 6 percent specified the period immediately following the first debate as the time at which they decided; 7 percent cited the period following the second debate; and 4 percent, the period following the third debate. Thus, 17 percent of all the respondents who voted identified the debate period as the time during which they decided for which candidate to vote.

It is interesting to look at the composition of this group. They represented 22 percent of the Democrats, 17 percent of the Independents, and 11 percent of the Republicans. More important, 38 percent of those who were unsure of their choice in September made their decisions during this time period, as compared with 17 percent of Carter supporters and 15 percent of Ford supporters. It appears that the stimulation of the debate period affected both Democrats and undecided voters more than the other groups.

The next logical question is: How did this 17 percent vote? For all voters who stated that they made up their minds during the debate period, 55 percent voted for Carter and 45 percent for Ford. This finding, in conjunction with our previous results, indicates that Carter's vote advantage resulted from the disproportionate number of Democrats who made up their minds during the debate period.

The evidence seems to indicate that there was some degree of conversion taking place over the debate period. What was the nature of that conversion? Was it a conversion from weak support of a candidate to actual participant support of that candidate, or was it a conversion to support for another candidate entirely? We can ascertain this by comparing the September and November candidate choices of the 17 percent who said that their final decision came during the debates. Table 9.10 shows that those who made up their minds during the debate period were less stable in their vote choice than other voters and, in contrast to all voters, favored Carter over Ford by a slim margin. These figures indicate that those respondents who decided for (or against) a candidate during the debate period exhibited higher degrees of conversion than those who made up their minds during other periods of the campaign. While we still cannot say with absolute certainty that the debates caused this conversion, the fact that these voters cited the debate period as the time of their decision lends credence to that supposition.

There is some basis for saying that the debates did have a converting effect on a small part of the electorate. While it would be hazardous to state that the debates were a key factor in Carter's victory, the evidence presented above does indicate that Carter benefited more, in terms of vote switching, than Ford and that this margin of benefit approximated his victory margin in the general election.

TABLE 9.10

September–November Vote Changes for All Voters and Debate-Period Deciders, in Percent

	All Voters (n = 342)	Debate Deciders (n = 62)
Stable voter intentions	80	66
Switched from Ford to Carter	8	18
Switch from Carter to Ford	12	16
Total	100	100

Source: Compiled by the authors.

CONCLUSION

At the beginning of this chapter, we presented two sets of hypotheses about the role of the presidential debates in the campaign of 1976. We suggested that predebate orientations on party identification, candidate preference, candidate image, and issues might be reinforced in the evaluations of each candidate's performance in the debates. We found confirmation for all but the reinforcing effect of issues on debate evaluations. We found that respondents' party identification, candidate preferences, and evaluations of the candidate's image all had a significant impact on how they viewed each candiate's debate performance. The implication of this finding is that the debates were by no means evaluated tabula rasa by the majority of the respondents; instead, they were evaluated as extensions of partisan and candidate predispositions. Since evaluations of the debates were so closely linked to the respondents' predispositional states, on the whole it is doubtful that the debates played an important informational role within the 1976 campaign. Their influence more closely resembles that found to be associated with certain forms of political advertising (Agranoff 1976; Patterson and McClure 1976). This suggests the relative unimportance of the debates as sources of "new" political information.

The second set of hypotheses concerned the converting effect of debate evaluations on the respondents' orientations to the candidates' images, issues, and vote intentions. The evidence suggests that, while there is no relationship between debate evaluations and changes in image and issue positions, there does exist a small, but substantial in a close election, converting influence on some respondents' vote intentions. The interesting observation here is that those changes in vote intention flowing from the debates were unrelated to changes in the evaluations of the candidates' images or issue positions. Thus, the influence of the debates appears to be direct—that is, not the indirect result of changes in candidate image or issue evaluations. Those who altered their vote intentions seem to have done so as a direct result of viewing the debates. All of this, however, must be kept in proper perspective. Only a small percentage of the voters, after all, switched candidate allegiance between September and November. Thus, for the large question of the debates' overall impact, we conclude that the debates reinforced existing predispositions considerably but actually changed them very little.

10

THE PRESIDENTIAL DEBATES AS A DEVICE FOR INCREASING THE "RATIONALITY" OF ELECTORAL BEHAVIOR

George F. Bishop, Robert W. Oldendick, and Alfred J. Tuchfarber

The revival of presidential debates in the 1976 election campaign created a rather special opportunity to test not only many of the original generalizations derived from studies of the 1960 presidential debates (Kraus 1962) but also a number of classic and contemporary models of the effects of mass communication on political behavior: the agenda-setting function of the mass media (McCombs and Shaw 1972; Shaw and McCombs 1977), the social influence model (Berelson, Lazarsfeld, and McPhee 1954; Lazarsfeld, Berelson, and Gaudet 1944), the two-step flow hypothesis (Katz and Lazarsfeld 1955; Robinson 1976), the selective exposure thesis (Sears and Freedman 1967), the uses and gratifications approach (Katz, Blumler, and Gurevitch 1974), and consistency theories of attitude change (Abelson et al. 1968). We also looked upon the staging of the debates as an appropriate occasion for resolving some of the recent theoretical controversies in the electoral behavior literature about the degree to which the American voter had become more "rational" and sophisticated, ideologically and otherwise, since the supposedly nonideological 1950s (compare Niemi and Weisberg 1976). From the seminal studies of this period (Berelson, Lazarsfeld, and McPhee 1954; Campbell, et al. 1960; Converse 1964; Lazarsfeld, Berelson, and Gaudet 1948), we had inherited a portrait of the average citizen that was rather unflattering, to say the least, not to mention the severe contra-

---

The authors wish to thank the University of Cincinnati's Research Council for supporting this project. An earlier version of this study was presented at the Research Conference on Presidential Debates, 1960 and 1976, held at the Annenberg School of Communications, University of Pennsylvania, Philadelphia, May 12-13, 1977.

dictions it created for the requirements of normative democratic theories. He or she, we were told, had little or no interest in politics; their beliefs and attitudes on a given public policy issue—for example, governmental responsibility for reducing unemployment—correlated hardly at all with their position on issues in the same general domain (domestic affairs), not to mention voting behavior or issues in other domains (foreign affairs); and when they bothered to vote, they did little more than reaffirm unthinking allegiance to one of the two major parties, casting a vote that was relatively devoid of issue content. These classic descriptions had likewise led us to believe that the mass media were essentially impotent; that if they did reach the voter, it was through that most traditional medium—interpersonal communication—that is, through what Katz and Lazarsfeld (1955) called the "two-step flow"; and that, when they did occasionally break through, their effects were rather limited to "reinforcing" partisan predispositions (Katz and Feldman 1962; Klapper 1960; Kraus and Davis 1976; Chapter 9 in this volume). Some of the features we have described may be a bit overdrawn, but the overall image is a good approximation of that found in the conventional literature on the American voter.

Beginning in the mid-1960s, however, a number of political scientists and other researchers began to suspect that many of these propositions about the American voter, based as they were on data mostly from the 1950s, had become, in a word, "time-bound." The sources of the suspicion were varied, but one likely factor may have been the unexpected sociopolitical changes and events that transpired during this period—the growth of the civil rights movement, the Vietnam War and the protest it generated, the assassinations of the Kennedys and Martin Luther King, Jr., and the black rebellions in many of our major cities, to mention only the most prominent. Thus, it probably was reasoned that politics and public affairs had become more salient to the mass electorate. And if this were true, it would make good theoretical sense to predict that the growing political awareness of the average citizen would lead to a corresponding increase in his or her ability to integrate various political beliefs with one another and with voting behavior—that is, to predict greater ideological sophistication. Whatever the theoretical or psychological sources, the availability of the ever-expanding Michigan time series on American electoral behavior provided an opportunity to subject these suspicions to an empirical test (Inter-University Consortium for Political and Social Research 1976). And in the last several years or so, there has been a deluge of data that, on first glance, appeared to confirm what a growing number of political behavioralists had already come to believe—namely, that the American voter had changed and radically so (Bennett 1973; Kirkpatrick, Lyons, and Fitzgerald 1975; Miller at al. 1976; Miller and Levitin 1976; Nie and Andersen 1974; Nie, Verba, and Petrocik 1976; Pomper, 1972; Repass, 1971).

Unlike his or her counterpart of the 1950s, the newly reconstructed voter of the 1960s and 1970s had, in contemporary lingo, "put it all together"; beliefs on various policy issues had now become more consistent with those on other issues. In turn, much greater weight was evidently placed on issues and much less on political party affiliation in deciding how to vote, a change that many have traced to the growing mass media penetration of American politics since the 1950s (Kraus and Davis 1976; Mendelsohn and Crespi 1970; Mendelsohn and O'Keefe 1976; Robinson 1976). Though this performance might not elevate citizens to the status of ideologues in the traditional sense, and while many political theorists would not regard higher correlations of issues with voting as satisfactory evidence of "rationality" (Converse 1975; Patterson, McLure, and Meier 1974), in comparison with predecessors from the 1950s, voters looked downright sophisticated.

As often happens in the survey business, however, the impressions from the first look at the new data proved to be illusory. In fact, just recently we have uncovered some fairly convincing evidence (Bishop et al. 1977; Bishop, Oldendick, and Tuchfarber 1978a; Bishop, Tuchfarber, and Oldendick, 1978b), which has been independently confirmed by other researchers (Sullivan, Piereson, and Marcus 1978; Brunk 1978; Darcy 1977), that almost all of the changes in mass political sophistication since the 1950s are due not to the rising salience of political events but to a fundamental methodological artifact: changes in question wording and format. We have summarized these findings elsewhere and mention them here largely as an indicator of the pessimism that formed the background for the present investigation. For we looked at the debates as a fortuitous situation for testing whether the mass media could indeed upgrade the quality of electoral behavior by increasing the role of issue content in the calculus of voter decisions, or whether the authors of *The American Voter* (Campbell et al. 1960) were fundamentally correct after all in their dour assessment of the "inherent limitations" of the general electorate. Our recent analysis of the Michigan national election series, taking into account the modifications in wording and format, told us that they were. Yet, we wanted to believe, like the League of Women Voters and the many others who supported and contributed to the staging of the debates, that this encounter between the candidates might break down many of the psychological barriers to informed participation, which stem from selective exposure and political apathy, and thereby improve the quality of the electoral response.

At the same time, though, we wanted to do more than just another panel study of the presidential debates. In addition, we felt that merely watching the debates might be too passive for effective political learning, especially for the less involved citizen (see Chapter 6). So we introduced an experimental manipulation that we thought would heighten the salience and significance of the debates to the respondents, which would, in turn, increase their interest and involvement in the campaign, their issue awareness, and, ultimately, the impact of issues on their final vote decision. We then superimposed this artificial experiment upon the natural experiment created by the occurrence of the presidential (and vice-presidential) debates for a very explicit, substantive purpose: to see if we could enhance the quality of political participation, despite the negative indications from our recent secondary analyses of the Michigan election surveys and over and above any "naturally occurring" effects generated by the debates themselves. We will now describe this experiment and our findings.

RESEARCH DESIGN

Using random digit dialing to select a probability sample of telephone households (Tuchfarber and Klecka 1976), we completed interviews during the course of the study with 898 adult respondents (18 years and over) living in the Greater Cincinnati Metropolitan area. This group consisted of 480 panel respondents who were interviewed just prior to the first presidential debate, 138 subjects who served as controls for effects of repeated measurement in the second wave of interviewing, which we carried out between the first and second debates, and another (independent) control group of 280 subjects interviewed only during the final wave after the election—again, for the purpose of partialing out any influences arising from repeated measurements. Altogether, there were three waves to the panel.

The Experimental Manipulation

As already noted, within the overall framework of the panel design we added an experimental variation. This consisted of randomly assigning half of the 480 panel members (n = 240) to a "salience-of-debate" condition and the other 240 respondents to a control or "natural" panel condition. The manipulation we used was fairly straightforward and, as we shall see, rather mild in intensity. The experimental and control groups both received an identical set of questions about their interest and involvement in the campaign, their perceptions of selected candidate attributes, their positions on various issues, their party identification, their candidate preferences, and the like—with no mention, however, of the upcoming debate between Carter and Ford. But the experimental group received, in addition, the following message at the end of the first wave interview:

> One more thing—as you may know, there's a televised debate between the presidential candidates this Thursday night (tonight) at 9:30 p.m., and we'd really appreciate it if you could watch the debate because we'd like to call you back in a week or so and ask you what you thought about the candidates and the issues.

To check whether our manipulation had succeeded in raising the level of debate watching, as well as other aspects of involvement with it, we reinterviewed a little over half of both the experimental-panel respondents (n = 136) and the panel controls (n = 138) shortly after the first debate (and before the second one), along with the 138 additional subjects who provided the test for repeated interviewing effects.

Reinforcement of the Design

Because of some uncertainty about the potency of the original manipulation, we decided to reinforce it just before the final debate. We did this by having the interviewers call each of the experimental households to deliver this simple message to any "responsible" adult who answered the telephone—that is, not necessarily the original respondent:

> Hello, this is _____ calling from the University of Cincinnati's Political Science Department. This week we're just calling to encourage everyone to watch the final presidential debate this Friday night (tonight) at 9:30 p.m. We hope that you and your family get a chance to watch it.

We also checked on the success of this manipulation by asking respondents in the postelection wave whether they remembered if they or anyone else in their household had received a call just prior to the final presidential debate, encouraging them to watch it, and also whether it was they that got the call or someone else. We will describe the outcome of this variation along with the rest of the results below.

FINDINGS

Increasing Debate Watching

Did our experiment make a difference? Yes it did, initially, though there are some serious questions as to whether the effects we created persisted over time. Table 10.1 summarizes a multiple regression analysis of the experimental manipulation's impact on watching the first debate and the effects of other variables expected to exert a causal influence: the respondent's base-line involvement with the campaign and the sociodemographic factors of age, sex, and education.*

---

*We constructed the involvement index from responses to four items in the base-line wave: (1) the standard Michigan Survey Research Center's question about the respond-

TABLE 10.1

Multiple Regression Analysis of the Effects of the Experimental Treatment on Watching the First Debate, Controlling for Campaign Involvement and Demographic Covariates

Variable	r	R	Partial Regression Coefficients b	Beta
Age	-.18	.18	-.005	-.201[b]
Education	-.16	.29	-.039	-.161[a]
Campaign involvement	.27	.34	.028	.172[b]
Experimental treatment	.17	.37	.141	.149[a]

[a] $p < .05$.
[b] $p < .01$.
Source: Compiled by the authors.

The beta-weight for the treatment in Table 10.1 tells us that our relatively simple "verbal" manipulation had a significant impact on whether respondents watched the first debate. The results also look good when expressed in simple percentages: 74 percent of the experimental group watched the first debate, compared with 59 percent of the control group. This seems all the more impressive when we consider the ceiling effects on this variable arising not only from complete network saturation but also from the extensive publicity that preceded the first Carter-Ford encounter. The figures in Table 10.1 tell us something else, however: that those most likely to watch the first debate were those who were already interested and involved in the campaign. Nevertheless, we were able to boost debate watching to a significant degree with a fairly mild stimulus.

Further evidence of the effectiveness of our manipulation comes from an analysis of some additional questions we asked about the extent to which the respondents watched the debate—that is, whether they viewed all, most, or part

---

ent's degree of interest in following the campaign, (2) the Center's item measuring concern about the outcome of the election, (3) a question on how often the respondents read newspaper stories about the campaign, and (4) an item asking how likely they thought it was that they would vote on election day. We converted the response to each of these items to a Z-score and then summed them into the overall measure of campaign involvement used throughout this analysis.

of it, including whether they continued to watch the end of it after the sound broke down—and about their postdebate behavior: (1) if they discussed it with any of their friends, family, or coworkers, and (2) if they read any follow-up newspaper stories on the debate. We combined responses to these questions into an overall index of "involvement with the debate" and regressed it on the same set of predictors we used in Table 10.1. This time, however, the analysis was limited to those who had watched the debate, a subgroup already self-selected for a more than average amount of interest in the campaign. In spite of this, we find that the treatment did produce some residual involvement over and above just watching or not watching the debate (see Table 10.2), other factors being statistically controlled.

TABLE 10.2

Multiple Regression Analysis of the Effects of the Experimental Treatment on Degree of Involvement with the First Debate, Controlling for Campaign Involvement and Demographic Covariates

Variable	r	R	Partial Regression Coefficients b	Beta
Campaign involvement	-.36	.36	-.212	-.258*
Age	.20	.39	.039	.223*
Education	.20	.42	.235	.189*
Experimental treatment	-.16	.44	-.630	-.130*

*$p < .01$.
Source: Compiled by the authors.

Impact on Issue Awareness

The important question, of course, is how did all of this translate into informed participation? Getting more people to watch the debates is one thing, but did watching make any difference in their awareness of the issues in the campaign and the positions of the candidates on those issues? We tried to answer these questions, in part, by constructing a set of items in the postelection wave that measured a respondent's knowledge of objective information about four specific issue stands taken by Carter and Ford during the debates, though these issues came up in the general campaign as well. Most of the items we used were deliberately difficult, so as to differentiate the respondents on the dependent variable, a procedure that should be understood from the perspective of constructing a "good test" of political learning (see Chapter 6). For example, we asked: "How about handguns—do you happen to remember which candidate opposed registration of handguns?" This was an issue raised in the fourth debate, and only a small proportion (22 percent) of respondents were able to answer it correctly.* The other three items covered the respondents' awareness of the candidates' positions on: (1) a constitutional amendment to allow voluntary prayer in public schools, (2) the use of U.S. troops in Yugoslavia to counter a Soviet invasion, and (3) a constitutional amendment giving states the right to set up their own standards for abortion. We summed the correct answers to these questions into a five-point index, ranging from 0 to 4, and regressed it on the following predictors: age, sex, education, the experimental treatment, the baseline index of campaign involvement, and an overall index of debate watching. We had created the latter measure from a set of questions in the postelection wave that asked the respondents whether they had specifically watched each of the four debates. This gave us another 5-point scale of involvement, also ranging from 0 to 4. The partial regression coefficients shown in Table 10.3 disentangle the relative contribution of each of these variables.

A first look at these data revealed an interesting dichotomy. On the one hand, the effects of our experimental manipulation had washed out in the overall index of debate watching, not to mention most of the other dependent variables we analyzed later on. On the other, we could see that—with all the important things evidently held constant, especially education and base-line involvement in the campaign—our index of the number of debates watched had accounted for a substantial portion of the variance (see Table 10.3).

The question then arose: could we attribute this effect to watching the debates per se? After all, the respondents could have picked up information about the issue positions of Carter and Ford from a number of other sources, such as the print media or interpersonal contacts. We were fairly confident, though, that we had adequately controlled for the kind of people most likely to do this—namely, the better educated and politically active individuals. Our baseline involvement index had even included a question on how often the respondent read newspaper stories about the campaign, an item that should have tapped such information-seeking habits. One way to test these suspicions, of course, was

---

*In asking these questions we made a special effort to discourage guessing, while at the same time putting the respondent at ease about not knowing the answers. The lead-in statement read as follows: "We'd also like to ask you a few specific questions about issues that Carter and Ford talked about during the campaign. Now we realize a lot of people may not remember many of these things; so feel free to say you 'don't remember'—and don't feel you have to guess. First of all, do you happen to remember—."

TABLE 10.3

Multiple Regression Analysis of the Effects of Debate Watching on Knowledge of Candidates' Issue Positions, Controlling for Campaign Involvement, Experimental Treatment, and Demographic Covariates

			Partial Regression Coefficients	
Variable	r	R	b	Beta
Education	.24	.24	.065	.108[a]
Campaign involvement	-.33	.36	-.064	-.158[b]
Index of debate watching	.44	.48	.281	.352[b]

[a] $p < .05$.
[b] $p < .01$.
Source: Compiled by the authors.

to check whether a specific debate had any consequence at all for learning a specific item of information mentioned in that debate. This was not as direct a measure as asking the respondent where he or she had acquired the information (assuming they could even do this without memory distortions). But if we could at least show that, say, watching the fourth debate was more highly correlated with knowing that Ford opposed registration of handguns than watching the vice-presidential debate or the first and second debates between Carter and Ford, and similarly for the other information questions, then we could make a rough case for assigning some causal responsibility to the debates themselves rather than to some hypothetical or unknown third variable. The beta-coefficients did not have to be very high, or even moderately so, just as long as they were higher for the appropriate predictor debate, all other things being equal.

The results are disappointing, mixed at best. In Table 10.4 we have the correlation and partial regression coefficients for the relationships between watching each of the four presidential debates and knowledge of the candidates' stands on each of four specific issues, controlling for the effects of other relevant predictors. Notice, first, that the best predictor (aside from campaign involvement) for knowing that it was Ford who favored a constitutional amendment to allow voluntary prayer in public schools was not whether you watched the fourth debate, in which the issue was actually raised, but whether you saw the second debate. Watching this debate, which was entirely devoted to foreign

TABLE 10.4

Multiple Regression Analysis of the Effects of Watching Specific Debates on Knowledge of Specific Issue Positions of Candidates, Controlling for Campaign Involvement, Experimental Treatment, and Demographic Covariates

			Partial Regression Coefficients	
Variable	r	R	b	Beta
Voluntary prayer in public schools				
Campaign involvement	-.23	.23	-.075	-.165[b]
Watching second debate	-.19	.26	-.353	-.170[a]
Age	.15	.28	.008	.112[a]
Abortion amendment				
Watching second debate	-.30	.30	-.657	-.236[b]
Education	.21	.34	.099	.148[b]
Watching vice-presidential debate	-.23	.36	-.302	-.111[a]
Experimental treatment	.11	.37	.263	.099[a]
U.S. troops in Yugoslavia				
Watching first debate	-.30	.30	-.559	-.225[b]
Watching fourth debate	.26	.33	-.323	-.144[b]
Age	.16	.35	.007	.109[a]
Handgun registration				
Watching fourth debate	-.37	.37	-.717	-.279[b]
Campaign involvement	-.26	.40	-.066	-.150[b]
Watching vice-presidential debate	-.27	.41	-.278	-.105[a]

[a] $p < .05$.
[b] $p < .01$.
Source: Compiled by the authors.

policy, also emerged as the principal determinant of whether you knew it was Ford who endorsed the idea of an amendment to let each state establish its own standards for abortion, an issue that did not receive mention until the fourth debate, though it had already surfaced in earlier campaign publicity.

The findings for awareness of Carter's remark about not sending U.S. troops into Yugoslavia in the event of a Soviet invasion, during the second debate, look even more confusing. Here it is watching the first and final debates that provides the influencing factor, the second debate being almost totally irrelevant. Only in the case of handgun registration do we find any reasonably direct evidence linking the viewing of a particular debate with a particular piece of information contained in that debate. Of course, we can never definitively establish that it was, in fact, the watching of this debate that causally generated the corresponding knowledge, and not some outside event, such as coverage of this issue in the print media immediately after the debate and during the last week or so of the campaign. Even if we could establish that viewing the fourth debate did have the causal impact on awareness of this issue that we think it did, it is still an exception to the general crazy-quilt pattern we found for the other knowledge items; and, even in this case the variance explained was not substantial. It may be, then, that our index of debate watching was picking up some third variable, that the relationship between watching the debates and issue awareness was, in other words, a spurious consequence of some common "unobserved" factor. But before speculating further about the possible sources of this bewildering pattern of debate effects, we want to describe our findings on the extent to which watching the debates heightened the role of issues in the vote decision.

Issue versus Party Voting

Originally, we had expected the debates to boost the contribution of issues to the voters' calculus relative to the weight of that reliable old predictor: party identification. Watching the debates might not change anyone's decision about whom to vote for—at least not very many, according to the literature (Katz and Feldman 1962)—but, somewhat analogous to the agenda-setting function of the mass media, they might alter a respondent's reason for voting for one candidate or the other, if only as a rationalization of that preference. Therefore, we regressed the respondent's vote on a number of issues questions we had asked of everyone in the postelection wave (for example, abortion, controlling inflation versus reducing unemployment), his or her party identification, and as another indicator of his attachment to the Democrats or Republicans—his vote in the U.S. Senate race for either Howard Metzenbaum or Robert Taft. We ran the analysis for two subgroups separately: (1) those who watched none of the debates or only one of them (the low-exposure group) and (2) those who watched two or more debates (the high-exposure group.* Table 10.5 gives the results of these analyses.

The first finding apparent in these data is that party voting not only still exists but also it may have enjoyed something of a temporary resurgence in the 1976 election (compare *ISR Newsletter* 1977, pp. 4-5). In both subgroups, party identification and the party direction of the Senate vote combined to account for the overwhelming share of the explained variance.† The more

---

*We combined respondents into these two exposure groups because of insufficient cases for calculating R^2-values.

†We are well aware that entering the issue variables, first, into the regression analysis

TABLE 10.5

Multiple Regression Analysis of the Effects of Debate Watching on Issue versus Party Voting for High- and Low-Exposure Groups

Variable	r	R	Partial Regression Coefficients b	Beta
High-exposure group: watched two or more debates (n = 273)				
Party identification	.68	.68	.080	.347[a]
U.S. Senate vote	-.67	.74	-.323	-.340[a]
Unemployment-inflation	.46	.76	.052	.191[a]
Pardon of draft evaders	.42	.77	.037	.106[b]
National defense	-.31	c	c	c
Power of federal government	-.12	c	c	c
Abortion	.04	c	c	c
National health care	.38	c	c	c
Low-exposure group: watched none or one debate (n = 89)				
Party identification	.52	.52	.089	.345[b]
U.S. Senate vote	-.47	.58	-.317	-.318[b]
Unemployment-inflation	.24	.61	.046	.176[a]
Abortion	.21	c	c	c
National health care	.28	c	c	c
National defense	-.01	c	c	c
Pardon of draft evaders	.15	c	c	c
Power of federal government	-.08	c	c	c

[a]$p < .01$.
[b]$p < .05$.
[c]Not statistically significant.
Note: The dependent variable for the regression analysis was vote for Carter or Ford.
Source: Compiled by the authors.

---

would increase their contribution and, correspondingly, decrease the weight of the party factor. In this limited technical sense, the choice is arbitrary. However, we believe it is far more reasonable, causally speaking, to assume that a respondent's party identification is chronologically prior to his or her issue positions, especially those issues specific to the most recent campaign, though there may well be some reciprocal influence between the party and issue factors over time. We would still maintain, though, that the dominant flow in any such reciprocal relation would be from party to issue.

intriguing aspect of these results, though, is the obvious interaction: the party variables made a substantially greater contribution to the vote decisions of those who were more heavily involved in watching the debates ($R^2 = .55$) than of those who watched them very little or not at all ($R^2 = .34$), a finding that clearly goes against the grain of literature that has told us how much more important party identification is to those with little interest in political affairs (compare Campbell et al. 1960; Converse 1962). Whether we can attribute this difference to the debates is another matter. It is always easy to reason after the fact that they did; for example, that they did this by making the party affiliations of Jimmy Carter and Gerald Ford somehow more salient to the viewers, and that this salience was reinforced by repeated watching—thus, the greater party effect among the more exposed. But the mechanism for this transmission of party salience is not too clear, other than the possible effects of repeated mere exposure as a Democrat or Republican making one seem like more of a Democrat or Republican (compare Zajonc 1968).

At the same time, however, it is also fairly evident that those who were more involved with the debates had achieved a greater degree of integration or "consistency" between their positions on various issues and their election day behavior. To take one very conspicuous instance, look at the correlations between one of the central economic issues in the campaign—controlling inflation versus reducing unemployment—and the vote. Among those watching none or just one debate, the correlation is only about .24, meaning that it accounts for just 5 to 6 percent of the total variance; whereas among those who viewed two or more debates, it jumps to .46 and thus explains a little over 20 percent of the variance ($r^2 = .21$), which is not earthshaking, but fairly respectable by most survey data standards. A similar pattern of greater integration between policy attitudes and the vote among moderate to heavy watchers of the debates also holds for the issues of national defense, pardoning of draft evaders, and national health care. Only on the abortion question do we find an apparent reversal, the coefficient being .21 in the low-exposure group, compared with just .04 in the high-exposure group. On the one remaining issue, attitudes toward the power of the federal government, we find almost no difference between them at all. Why the data for these latter two issues should deviate from the general pattern of greater cognitive consistency among the more highly involved respondents is not at all obvious to the authors, though there is some evidence suggesting that one of these issues—whether the federal government is getting too powerful—has lost its discriminatory value for much of the contemporary electorate (Bennett and Oldendick 1977), and thus should not produce any significant differences in attitudinal consistency among the subgroups we have contrasted. The apparent anomaly of the abortion issue, on the other hand, is clearly a stimulus for further research.

Where does all this lead us? For one thing, it led us to ask several questions. What kinds of people are most likely to try to integrate their beliefs about

TABLE 10.6

Multiple Regression Analysis of the Effects of Debate Watching on Awareness of Issue Differences between Carter and Ford, Controlling for Campaign Involvement, the Experimental Treatment, and Demographic Covariates

Variable	r	R	Partial Regression Coefficients b	Beta
Education	-.24	.24	-.036	-.148*
Index of debate watching	-.29	.35	-.073	-.222*

*$p<.01$.
Source: Compiled by the authors.

one issue with another and then with their behavior, or at least care about this sort of thing? Could these people also be the same kind of people who bothered to watch most or all of the debates? And might they also be the same ones who knew the most about the candidates' stands on such things as an amendment to allow voluntary prayer in public schools, or another one—to let the states establish their own standards on abortion? The answer to all these questions is: The same kind of people who have always reaped the greatest profits from these kinds of intellectual forums—the politically active and educated stratum of American society.

The Knowledge-Rich Get Richer

Before drawing any conclusions, we should mention one other analysis of issue awareness that we carried out, using a different kind of measure. In the final wave of interviewing, we also queried the respondents on what they thought was the "most important difference" between Ford and Carter on the issues in the campaign. If they cited any policy issue or made some kind of general ideological reference (for example, Ford's policies are too conservative), we counted them as issue-aware. We then regressed this variable on the same set of predictors used earlier and turned up the findings summarized in Table 10.6. Again, we find variables like education and debate watching to be the most powerful determinants of political awareness. But we have already made the case that it is difficult to attribute any causal significance to the debates per se, at least not in isolation. So we must ask whether the correlations we have uncovered between debate watching and issue awareness to this point are not the

TABLE 10.7

Multiple Regression Analysis of the Effects of Campaign Involvement on Debate Watching, Controlling for Demographic Covariates

Variable	r	R	b	Beta
			\multicolumn{2}{c}{Partial Regression Coefficients}	
Campaign involvement	-.38	.38	.156	.305*
Education	.22	.39	.121	.163*
Age	.13	.41	.011	.136*

*$p<.01$.
Source: Compiled by the authors.

TABLE 10.8

Multiple Regression Analysis of the Effects of Education, Age, and Sex on Campaign Involvement

Variable	r	R	b	Beta
Education	-.32	.32	-.644	-.434*
Age	-.17	.44	-.052	-.321*

*$p<.01$.
Source: Compiled by the authors.

spurious consequence of some third (unmeasured) factor derived from the joint influence of education and prior political involvement. For we also know that the people most likely to have watched the debates were more politically involved in the first place (see Tables 10.1 and 10.7) and that the best predictor of this involvement was education (Table 10.8), though age also makes a significant contribution. Furthermore, there are other studies of the debates, of which we are now aware (Abramowitz 1977; Chapter 6 in this volume), that suggest that respondents who were initially more knowledgeable got even more information out of the debates when they watched them than their less knowledgeable counterparts—in other words, that the knowledge-rich got richer, while the knowledge-poor gained little, if anything. Even if we were able to demonstrate that watching the debates had an unambiguous causal influence on political learning, we would still be forced toward a knowledge-rich-get-richer conclusion, since the average levels of knowledge among groups that initially varied in education and political involvement would be expected to diverge over the course of the campaign because of their differential attention to the debates, something we have already doumented.

A Uses-and Gratifications Hypothesis

The interesting theoretical question, though, is why the more involved respondents tend to get more out of these kinds of forums. In other words, what is the intervening mechanism that links education and political motivation, on the one hand, with both greater debate watching and issue learning, on the other? The most plausible one, and one that communication researchers have given special emphasis in recent years, is the use to which the respondent is putting a medium, or the gratification he receives from it (Katz, Blumler, and Gurevitch 1974; McLeod and Becker 1974). Research by McCombs and Mullins (1973), for instance, indicates that a major effect of a college education is to alter a person's pattern of media use, leading to the formation of media-scanning and information-seeking habits that heighten their interest in politics and that, in turn, stimulate further seeking of political information (Hyman, Wright, and Reed 1975; Robinson 1971). Thus, because of the greater personal relevance of politics to the more educated and involved respondents and, perhaps, because of their greater need to at least appear to be well-informed, they used the debates primarily to seek issue information, if only to confirm their candidate preference, whereas the less involved respondents used the debates, if and when they watched them, largely to satisfy entertainment needs—for example, to watch a "good fight" or "contest." The latter motivation pattern might account for much of the popular concern in the press and the general public about "who won" the debates. We did not measure these psychological variables directly, but we do know from previous research that there are wide individual differences in information-seeking patterns (Atkin 1972; Blumer and McQuail 1969; Chaffee and McLeod 1973; McCombs and Mullins 1973), and we would hypothesize that such differences might well explain a significant portion of the data we have reported here.

Methodological Factors

So far, no mention has been made of two potentially contaminating factors: multiple interviews and mortality, or attrition. We can confidently report that no significant effects of multiple interviews have been observed.

Neither the control group interviewed just after the first debate nor the one interviewed following the election was any less likely to have watched the debates or to have learned issue information than their more frequently interviewed counterparts in the panel condition. Actually, control respondents interviewed in the second wave (after the first debate) were somewhat more likely to have reported watching the first debate than the control group respondents in the panel condition, though not as likely as those in the experimental subgroup. All this, of course, does not rule out other possible effects of repeated interviewing on other variables in the study—for example, voting (Kraus and McConahay 1973; Yalch 1976) and just those analyzed herein.

The selective effects of panel attrition, however, do not yield as readily to experimental or statistical control. As we indicated earlier, the original panel consisted of 480 respondents. In the third and final wave we were able to reinterview 422 (88 percent) of these people, losing the rest to refusals (5.6 percent), disconnected numbers (2.3 percent), and other complications—for example, respondents moving without forwarding numbers or addresses, numerous "no answers." What matters most, though, is how they differed from those who remained in the panel. As expected, those we lost were significantly less interested and involved in the campaign in the first place ($p < .05$); they were also significantly more likely to have been Carter supporters ($p < .05$), somewhat younger ($p < .10$), and less educated ($p < .01$). How might these variations affect our findings? If anything, they increase our confidence since their likely impact would be to attenuate the magnitude of the relationships we have uncovered. In other words, most of the effects we have reported for age, education, campaign involvement, and debate watching are based on a subgroup of the panel that is significantly more homogeneous than the panel as a whole. Had we been able to reinterview everyone, we would expect even stronger associations, due to the greater variance in our measures.

What about the reminder call to respondents just prior to the fourth debate? Stated simply, it made no difference at all. Those respondents in households not getting a call were just as likely to watch the final debate as those that did get one. The lack of impact probably resulted from the patent weakness of the manipulation rather than any resistance associated with respondent characteristics—only 56 percent of the respondents in the experimental condition recalled receiving any such phone call, and, of these, not all (84.6 percent) were taken by the respondent directly. Changing or maintaining respondent behavior, then, obviously requires more than just a gentle reminder.

CONCLUSIONS AND IMPLICATIONS

The findings, which we have just started to unravel here, plus similar ones reported by other researchers, cause us to wonder whether we should even have presidential debates in the future. For if we know that the likely outcome of holding these "Meet the Press" sessions will be to deepen the ever-increasing stratification of public affairs knowledge that Tichenor, Donohue, and Olien (1970) have reported, then we must ask ourselves whether we are willing to accept the consequences of this political-informational division of labor in a democratic society such as ours—one that is, at least in principle, committed more and more to maximizing the participation of its citizens in the political process through devices like election day registration. Some might argue, though, that we should not fault the debates, that they really were not debates after all— just glorified press conferences—and that what we should do is spruce up the format, making them more lively exchanges along the lines of the point-counterpoint encounter on CBS' "Sixty Minutes" between Shana Alexander and Jack Kilpatrick. But would this really make much of a difference? We would argue that, as America and the world move toward the next century, politics and the public policy issues we will face will become much more complex than they are today, and that only those who have been prepared by a fortunate combination of interest and training will have the contextual knowledge and motivation to deal with these complexities. No one, for example, who has followed the debate over the Carter administration's proposals on energy policy could entertain the thought that the average voter can comprehend much of what has been going on, with the exception of impressions like "gasoline taxes are going up" or "more taxes coming on big cars." In fact, he or she probably has given the matter very little attention, as witnessed by the still relatively small proportion of the public that considers the energy problem a serious one (Gallup 1977)— and this despite massive publicity on the issue over the last year or so.

What we are saying, then, is that there are some very definite limits to what we can presently do to raise the rationality of electoral behavior through devices like the presidential debates. Unless we can do something in the meantime about the basic intellectual capacities or media-use patterns of the bulk of the electorate—through some type of continuing political education program that fully exploits the potential of the mass electronic media—or unless we are willing to create a format for the debates that mimics the political commercials that Patterson and McClure (1976) suggest are effective in reaching the less involved segments of the electorate (also see Mendelsohn and O'Keefe, 1976)—an alternative that we do not believe anyone would seriously entertain—we must accept the responsibility for contributing to a growing information gap between the political haves and have-nots in the emerging postindustrial society.

11

SUMMARY AND CONCLUSION

Perhaps the strongest aspect of 1976 debate research is its diversity. The same events, looked at by communication researchers, political scientists, and social psychologists, yield to multiple perspectives and multiple analytical techniques. But, not surprisingly, it is difficult now to infer the state of knowledge with respect to the 1976 debates. Who won? What did viewers learn from debates? Did exposure influence votes? Did candidates' images change? All these, indeed, are questions worth asking—but simple answers are not forthcoming, and are not tremendously satisfying when they do arrive.

Far more instructive is to inquire after the state of social scientific knowledge in the wake of 1976 debate research. Here we are informed again that the perspectives taken determine, for practical purposes, the results of research. Carter, in the opening chapter, reminds us of the pitfalls of confining ourselves to the "rationalist" research paradigm. Some voters under some circumstances do seek information about the policy positions of the candidates to make informed decisions; they are not "fools," as V. O. Key (1966) put it. But voters and candidates alike have additional needs—needs for knowing who is ahead or who is behind and needs for feedback on past commitments, as well as the opportunity to construct a political environment that includes none of the available choices. Recognition of this broader paradigm, however reluctantly, requires a radical revision of our whole way of conceptualizing political campaigns, and may lead to abandoning many of the standard "rationalist" research methods (Phillips 1973) that most of us depend upon. The preoccupation with the rationality of electoral behavior for many of us may thus say more about our current state of theoretical development than it does about the nature and meaning of the presidential debates.

There are those who would dissent from this view, including Robert G. Meadow and Marilyn Jackson-Beeck, who, despite reservations about the performance of the candidates in the 1976 debates and the failure of the print media to cover them accurately, nevethess support the idea that debates have unusual potential for clarifying the choices available to the voter relative to the important issues of the day. And if some of those issues seem to have endured, despite the social turmoil of the past 10 to 15 years, so much the better. That in itself implies a certain predictable logic to American politics. Further, if and when we have another round of presidential debates, and we discover the issues have changed or evolved, that, too, will be a welcome occurrence, because it will add another data point to the content analysis of trends in presidential campaign issues they have begun. Issues, these researchers have shown us, can and should be studied dynamically, and they have provided us with useful suggestions about how to extend their methodological strategy.

The need for an ongoing assessment of the relationship between the content of the mass media and the response of the electorate to that content surfaces again as we recall the research designs used in this volume. Of these, the long-term panel study by Graber, which began before the first primary in January of 1976, represents one kind of methodological strategy that we believe is necessary to adequately deal with some of the research problems continually encountered in political communication. Based on a small sample of voters, she has again taught us about the value of base-line measures of the critical variables that we expect will interact with or be altered by campaign events (like presidential debates); about the drawbacks of identically worded but semantically nonequivalent survey questions; and about the familiar but often forgotten lessons of pretest sensitization. Even more important, she has forced us to reevaluate the term "political learning," thereby making it more difficult to attribute differences in voters' comprehension of issues and candidate positions of those issues to debate exposure.

The chapters by Hagner and Rieselbach, Becker, Nimmo, Bishop, and their associates, informed us of the debates' cognitive and behavior effects: whether they accomplished their intended purpose of increasing the voters' awareness of the issues and the candidates' stands on the issues (Becker et al. say "yes"; Bishop, Oldendick, and Tuchfarber say "sometimes"); whether they altered basic candidate images (Nimmo, Mansfield, and Curry say "no"); and whether they reinforced or converted partisan predispositions (Hagner and Rieselbach conclude the former).

From the Langs and Steeper, we learn again of mass media's potential to shape not only people's perceptions of the candidates and the debates (for example, "who won") but also actual voting intentions. Thus, it seems that media influence is great, but overlooked. Inadvertently, perhaps researchers looked in the wrong place, or rather too much in one place—directly at messages—whereas more potent media effects derive from the larger communications context. Audiences, in other words, often need more than just exposure to debate to produce changes in cognitions or behavior. For many viewers, debates must be interpreted by others—including mass media—before they become fully meaningful.

In the case of Gerald Ford's intended or unintended remark about the absence of Soviet domination in Eastern Europe during the second debate, we see how powerful the "umpiring" role of print and broadcast journalists can be in calling attention to an apparent "infraction," one that evidently escaped most debate viewers until they were told about it and one that seemed to create massive shifts in perceptions and voting intentions. Similarly, the Langs illustrate the difference media interpretation can make. Other debate studies we have encountered in the course of our work (Levine 1976; Sloan 1977) have produced similar results on the extramediating function of the communications context, leading us to believe that this is a significant, but too often neglected, aspect of political communication. These studies, of course, do not imply that direct effects are nonexistent; instead, they suggest that effects occur in a total communication environment.

The implication of these findings for the design of future investigations of campaign debates and other forms of political communication is especially strong. Now that we realize how much reaction to televised events like presidential debates varies with the passage of time, it is apparent that the standard one-shot posttest wave of panel studies should be discarded. Instead, pretested respondents might be reinterviewed in randomized subgroups over a specified interval, beginning immediately after a debate and continuing perhaps for a week. Steeper's continuous monitoring of a small sample's reactions is another innovative design upon which, as technology emerges, we can elaborate.

Together with Graber's recommendations for minimizing pretest sensitization effects, by administering base-line measures at least 60 days in advance of the natural or experimental event, we can imagine a highly complex and costly research strategy for studying political communication. But that may be exactly what is required if we are ever going to come to terms with what is referred to as the "communication process" or the "electoral process." We have learned that the one-shot, cross-sectional survey is an inferior design for analyzing dynamic phenomena; the abundance of quasi-experimental panel designs (and even a few true experimental ones) we have witnessed in studies of the 1976 debates is ample testimony to the coming of age of Campbell and Stanley (1963) in social research. But even the most well-designed of these bear a kinship to cross-sectional surveys of old: each wave is a one-shot affair, telling us how the members of the panel reacted to an event at only one time point.

In the future we also will have to unravel how the issues and themes that emerge in any given debate or set of debates have evolved in the interim—that is, between campaigns—and within the campaign itself, beginning with the early primaries, proceeding through the nominating conventions, and including the debates themselves. The value of this more or less continuous content analysis of public policy issues in the national media could be enhanced materially by linking it with the cognitive and behavioral reactions of respondents empaneled in permanent or quasi-permanent national surveys such as the biennial election studies conducted by the Center for Political Studies at the University of Michigan. Perhaps this appears as an impractical venture in social science research. But the alternative—more and more piecemeal stabs at the same problem every four years (or less often) by numerous investigators working independently or nearly so, and many of them duplicating each other's work in whole or in part—is equally impractical and, over the long run, foolish. It may be a good thing from the standpoint of traditional conceptions of the "critical scientific community," and it will no doubt continue; but it perpetuates a needless sort of individualistic anarchy in social research that may not be advancing the disciplines at all. For this reason, let us consider pooling intellectual, institutional, and financial resources—as the networks do debate coverage. A workable approach might be to build upon the American national election studies already available through the Inter-University Consortium for Political and Social Research at the University of Michigan, now funded on a quasi-permanent basis by the National Science Foundation. The strategy would be to seek joint funding from other sources to add the continuous monitoring of sociopolitical content in the mass media to respondents' data files for the election studies of 1978, 1980, and 1982 and to expand these cross-sectional surveys into the multiwave panel designs we envision.

All of this would, of course, require sacrificing some individualism in research. But if we are serious about upgrading the quality of research on what we recognize as an exceedingly complex set of problems, then there are few, if any, satisfactory alternatives. At least we can be aware (at no cost) that rushing studies into the field the next time presidential debates are held, largely or only because they are there, will produce little new knowledge. The concerted attack on the problem of understanding the impact of events like the 1976 presidential debates, and political communication in general—which many of us feel is necessary, and to which we periodically pay a certain amount of homage in the conclusions of articles, books, and papers—is clearly in order. And a good beginning, as Doris Graber suggested at the Annenberg Research Conference on Presidential Debates, 1960 and 1976, would be to organize predebate or pre-election conferences to set the research agenda.

POLICY IMPLICATIONS

Some of our contributors have hinted in subtle and not so subtle ways that perhaps we should consider institutionalizing presidential debates—though others are not so eager, since they fear that this might also result in institutionalizing political discrimination against independents and minor party movements and, wittingly or unwittingly, increase even further the growing influence of television in U.S. public affairs. Still others are not so convinced they would make that much of a difference, at least not as they are presently constituted. Jackson-Beeck and Meadow (1977), for instance, have drawn our attention to the wide discrepancies that may exist between what the public regards as significant policy concerns, as assessed in national surveys—the public's policy agenda—and what journalists choose to emphasize, either as questioners of the candidates during debates or as reporters of these affairs—what might be called the media's agenda. And each of these policy agendas may differ, in turn, from what the candidates themselves decide to focus on in answering or evading the questions posed to them by the media representatives—that is, the candidates' agenda.

One way, then, in which 1976 debate research suggests how future debates could be made more responsive to the public's policy priorities would be to organize the topics of the debates around the concerns expressed by the electorate in recent public opinion surveys, such as those conducted by the Gallup and Harris organizations. An even better way of bringing the concerns of citizens to bear on the candidates would be ask a large representative sample of the public what questions they would specifically like to ask each candidate in the forthcoming debates. Granted there would be respondents who would have difficulty in formulating questions, and other who would ask things that would not seem appropriate. But a great number of respondents would be able to come up with challenging questions, some of which, while overlapping, would surely not occur to media correspondents with their own personal agendas and their probably unrepresentative perceptions of the public's policy interest, and others that the candidates themselves would rather not have raised at all—for example, questions about unkept promises. This more direct linkage between the public and the candidates, if handled properly and adequately publicized, could generate a good deal of interest in the debates and, as a result, motivate the informed participation in American elections that debates are intended to promote.

Another variation on this theme would be to adapt the national call-in, which President Carter has used, to the debate format. For example, a half hour of the debate time could be set aside for citizens to interview the candidates directly—screened, of course, for the obscene and the ridiculous; another half hour for questions elicited from respondents in a national survey and reduced to a manageable number; and the final half hour for questions constructed by the media representatives. Such a combination, while fraught with unknowns, could do much to heighten the public's sense of participation in the political process and perhaps alleviate many of the overt symptoms of alienation expressed in the growing mistrust of government, politicians, and other public institutions.

Still another possibility would be to experiment, as Carter (Chapter 1) has proposed, with different kinds of debates: (1) one type, to be used when one of the candidates is an incumbent, focusing on policy issues; (2) another, specifically for the primaries, deemphasizing issues in favor of examining the candidates' leadership abilities and previous performance in public affairs; and (3) an even more innovative encounter, before the primaries, involving independents and minor party candidates in a discussion of the accomplishments of the major parties and the incumbent administration, thus removing some of the unfortunate vestiges of nonmajor party discrimination in previous presidential debates. Serious consideration should be given as well to revising the format of the debates—for example, allowing the candidates to question each other directly and to rebut each other's remarks instantaneously, or nearly so. The debate moderator and questioners, moreover, could do much to encourage candidates to stick to the questions that are asked, as was done in the vice-presidential debate between Robert Dole and Walter Mondale (see Appendix E). In all these ways, the debates could be made a more attractive and effective political institution.

Finally, the notion that a tax write-off might be used to finance future presidential debates merits special attention. Along with Richard Carter's related idea of giving citizens the opportunity to use their write-off for choosing among campaign institutions that they are willing to support—for example, primaries, nominating conventions—it would provide a partial evaluation of how well these institutions are performing in meeting the needs of the electorate. Similarly, we could apply this device to explore public support for other innovations, such as the political documentaries suggested by Carter and the long-discussed proposals for regional or national primaries.

These suggestions, of course, are only a few of the alternatives available to debate organizers and sponsors. But they represent an attempt to structure future debates—if these are held—in a way conducive to meeting the needs of candidates and citizens. After all, the promise of the debates, at least in 1976, was to promote "a wider and better informed participation by the American people in the election in November." Be they reconstituted or revitalized or ritualized, presidential debates oriented to the needs of voters may indeed improve the quality of citizen participation in the electoral process.

PART IV

TRANSCRIPTS OF THE 1976 PRESIDENTIAL AND VICE-PRESIDENTIAL DEBATES

12

ASCERTAINMENT AND ANALYSIS OF DEBATE CONTENT

Marilyn Jackson-Beeck and Robert G. Meadow

INTRODUCTION

For the millions of viewers and listeners in the broadcast audience, the 1976 presidential and vice-presidential debates were unusual visual and aural interludes in the quadrennial election ritual. They were fleeting and transient events, if memorable. But for historians, political scientists, rhetoricians, journalists, and researchers from a host of disciplines, debates remain important events to be preserved and studied now and for years to come. Fortunately, the technology is available to preserve these events in the form that audiences witnessed them. Videotape technology allows for high-quality reproduction; indeed, even for researchers who failed to record the debates as they occurred, the Television News Archives at Vanderbilt University provides tapes of these (and other) televised news events to interested researchers.

However, debate videotapes serve primarily to document election campaigns only in a historical sense. They are too rich with data to be of practical use to most researchers. They are akin to questionnaire responses or interview data, which until categorized are of little use. For those concerned with kinesic content, of course, videotapes are necessary. But for those interested mainly in verbal content, videotapes fail to provide the hard copy needed for systematic manual or computer content analysis. Consequently, in this appendix, we provide correct and authenticated debate transcripts for present researchers and future historians.

Not without reason, there are those who would argue against transcription of the 1976 presidential debates. We lose the full richness of interaction, the specific location of the event in time and space, and some of the context necessary for understanding. But it seems to us that the alternative, which is not to be able to analyze debate content in an accurate and systematic way, is unreasonable in light of social-scientific and policy-related research needs. Unless we know what was said it is difficult to anticipate or validate apparent effects; and when we know what was and was not said, we have a basis for criticism and informed review.

Accurate accounting of just what was said in debates is needed for practical analysis of manifest, verbal content. For this purpose, the New York *Times* transcripts of the debates might seem to suffice. But these presumably complete and accurate documents are glossed and subject to error. The debates as they appear in the New York *Times*—the newspaper of record—are far more decorous than they were in actuality. In the first debate alone, candidates, questioners, and moderator interrupted one another five times. In the *Times*, these interruptions are not shown, so it seems that candidates and questioners politely waited their turn.

Numerous errors flaw each *Times* transcript. For example, in the first debate, Jimmy Carter spoke of a program with the acronym "DISC," which the *Times* reports variously as "this" and "gifts." In the vice-presidential debate, Senator Dole called Senator Mondale "probably the most liberal senator," while the *Times* reports him saying Mondale was "one of the most liberal senators." In the same debate, it was reported that peace was "important to me and to some others who may be listening" (rather than "important to me and to mothers who may be listening"). Also, a reference to the National Security Council is incorrectly transcribed as a reference to the National Community Council.

Worse than the *Times*' occasional errors of omission and commission, the newspaper transcripts make the candidates appear far more fluent and less hesitant than they were. Throughout, they stuttered, stammered, hemmed, hawed, used vocalized pauses, such as um— and uh—, and repeated themselves. For example, Carter, in the first debate, declared: "And, and the whole uh— subject of crime is one that concerns our people very much, and I believe that the fairness of it is, is what, uh— is, is a major problem that addresses our, our leader, and this is something that hasn't been addressed adequately by, by this administration." In the newspaper, this appeared as a flawless sentence. So it turns out that the newspaper transcripts are newspaper stories featuring or manufacturing high points through the use of breakers, and including a good smattering of inaccuracy. Thus, for a variety of reasons, the *Times* transcripts are inadequate for scientific purposes (other than studies of the newspaper reporting process), and in the course of our own research we were compelled to generate new transcripts.

The transcripts that follow represent a consensus between the two authors of this appendix; they are the product of a painstaking effort to reconstruct exactly what was said in the 1976 debate series. Although there were no expletives for us to delete, in the process of producing the debate transcripts we came to find a measure of sympathy for RoseMary Woods and her assistants assigned to transcribe the Watergate tapes. It is sometimes truly difficult to discern what was said—even in the absence of partisan interest or personal loyalties, and even using studio-quality videotapes.

PREPARING THE TRANSCRIPTS

There were three basic steps in production of the 1976 debate transcripts:

1. First-run correction of the *Times* transcripts, alternately by researcher, through use of debate videotapes,
2. Joint review of the corrected transcripts by reference to debate videotapes,
3. Re-review of the typed, corrected transcripts by both researchers, again referencing the debate videotapes.

At each stage, a good deal of time was spent playing and replaying the videotapes segment by segment, until each researcher was satisfied with punctuation and the written rendition of spoken words and sounds. Videotapes, rather than audiotapes, were essential because we often found it helpful to "see" what was said, when the candidates and questioners slurred their words or spoke inaudibly and inarticulately. (Conversely, we developed an ability to "hear" what the candidates looked like, but this information is not shared.) The New York *Times*' unknown transcriber(s), of course, provided independent opinion on the events transpiring.

Usually it was not at all difficult to arrive at an accurate description of debate content; fatigue was the greatest problem. However, we found ourselves often frustrated by the poverty of the common usage alphabet, as we encountered indescribable sounds. These were interesting noises, and close to classification as stutters or vocalized pauses, but in good conscience we could not give them the full rating befitting a bonafide utterance. Also, we were disappointed to find no adequate verbal translation of lip-licks, chuckles, sighs, and wavers. These, too, occurred with some frequency but are not included in the transcripts.

"Uh—," it should be noted, functions as a sign of general incoherency. It may encompass a long or short enunciation, and it subsumes a variety of subtle schwa-type vowel sounds. Similarly, there is a departure from the reality of what was said and what we have transcribed, in the case of standard mispronunciations. An outstanding example of this occurs in the use of the titles "Governor" and "Mr. President." To be entirely accurate, the former often would be written "Gov'nor," and the latter "Mr. Pres'dent." But we saw no need to render all the sounds (or lack of sounds) occurring within the debates; rather, our interest was in words, nonwords, and generally describable utterances. False starts and stutters, for example, are clearly indicated in the transcripts.

We had not the phoneticist's interests in the debates, nor the rhetorician's. Instead, like the New York *Times*, we ignored various pronunciations of the same words (that is, regionalisms), and we did not indicate differential stress, loudness, tone, or absolute speed. However, we did note when unorthodox contractions were particularly clear (for example, "gonna" instead of "going to"). Indirectly, by our punctuation, we did indicate pauses and inflection.

With regard to our use of punctuation, it should be noted that functionality is the rule, not grammatical logic. A period indicates a definitive pause and usually, but not always, a new, different, or additional declaration. A dash generally describes a strong or disjointed disclaimer or qualification occurring in midclause, -phrase, -declaration, or -inquiry, and serves to delimit consecutive series of speech parts, phrases, clauses, declarations, or inquiries. The use of question marks is reserved strictly for interrogation, as in asking a legitimate question or requesting (not demanding) action or response.

RESEARCH USES OF THE TRANSCRIPTS

Despite the fact that our transcripts are limited to wordwise renditions of what was said, it should be clear that the use of the appended transcripts need not be restricted to analysis only of "manifest" verbal content. Indeed, we would encourage further exploration of a variety of research questions, for political communications such as debates are analyzed too often only as manifest content. The accompanying imagery, although inspired by the same

TABLE 12.1

Candidates' Use of Imagery in the First 1976 Debate

	Carter		Ford	
	Number	Percent	Number	Percent
Sports	12	7	7	5
Weather	0	0	0	0
Sex, love	5	3	7	5
Food, eating	4	2	7	5
War, violence	9	5	5	4
Health	13	7	2	2
Body parts, functions	31	17	35	28
Weights, measures	23	13	20	16
Destiny	4	2	1	1
Travel	29	16	14	11
Elements	1	1	1	1
Religion	4	2	2	2
Machines, nonhumans	28	16	12	9
Construction, shelter	15	8	14	11
Total	178	99*	127	100

*Numbers may not total 100 because of rounding.
Source: Compiled by the authors.

conscious message selection process, rarely attracts attention. Presumably, imagery carries less meaning because it is abstract. But just the opposite is arguable—that imagery conveys more meaning than manifest content, by virtue of greater generality. Verbal incoherency, similarly, is not well researched, because it is presumed to be unintentional, and therefore meaningless. But incoherency, particularly in conjunction with analysis of issues or politicians, seems quite informative. It may indicate uncertainty about policies as important to know as candidates' issue stands per se. So it seems as useful to look for verbal composure as for issue position; this is part and parcel of a candidate's bearing or image upon which other success may rest. Tables 12.1-12.3 address these dimensions of debate content, by way of illustration.

For example, Table 12.1 suggests a discrepancy between popularly conceived or manufactured candidate stereotypes and the candidates' actual conduct in debate. During the first 1976 debate, Ford, the former football player, made relatively few references to sports, while Carter seldom referred to religion. Both candidates relied most on body parts and functions ("handle the country," "touches human beings," "hands of the taxpayer") and weights, measures, and burdens ("heavier tax burden," "responsibility on my shoulders," "pressure on the president"). They also relied on image of travel and transport ("a president can't deliver," "come to the Oval Office," "dead-end jobs"). Additionally, Carter invoked images of machines ("tapping our people," "breakdown

TABLE 12.2

Time Frames Referenced in the First 1976 Debate

	Number	Percent
Past		
Generalized	6	7
Recent (0-5 years)	29	33
Distant (5 or more years previous)	12	14
Present	26	30
Future		
Generalized	5	6
Near (0-5 years)	8	9
Distant (5 or more years hence)	2	2
Total	88	101*

*Numbers do not total 100 because of rounding.
Source: Compiled by the authors.

in leadership"), while Ford used references to construction and shelter ("build America," "working on the economy").

A simple analysis of the time frames within which candidates discussed political issues (as defined in Chapter 3) further illustrates the uses to which image-related data can be put. As in Table 12.2, participants in the first 1976 presidential debate dwelt mostly on the present (30 percent) and on the events of the past few years (33 percent), despite the reasonable expectation that discussion in a campaign context would center on the future—plans to be executed once in office, improvements to be made, and so forth. Partly, this may be a function of Ford's incumbency; partly it must reflect Carter's concern with the crises of the near past.

As a third dimension of debate content, and with so much media attention devoted to candidate style rather than substance of debates, an objective measure of some aspects of style is useful, as in Table 12.3.

This analysis of semimanifest content helps to reconstitute the emotional component behind candidates' debate performance. Using nonfluency data as a measure of anxiety or stress, there is evidence to support the popular view that Carter was nervous at the start of the first debate but calmed down as he progressed. During the first five coded issue sequences, Carter slipped a remarkable 113 times (84 nonwords and 29 repeats, compared with 26 nonwords and 2 repeats for Ford); however he recovered in his last five sequences to approximate Ford's beginning and ending error rate.

To repeat, these data present findings only from the first 1976 debate, and are meant to be illustrative. Researchers might well consider the political issues raised, completeness of candidates' arguments, relevance of debate discussion to public concerns, responsiveness of candidates to each other and to questioners, logic and illogic, candidates' political philosophy or orientation—to name just a

TABLE 12.3

Candidates' Nonfluencies in the First 1976 Debate

	Carter		Ford	
Issue Sequence	Nonwords	Repeats	Nonwords	Repeats
1	35	7	4	0
2	11	4	9	0
3	16	7	2	0
4	11	6	6	2
5	11	5	5	0
6	0	0	4	0
7	2	0	3	0
8	12	7	10	1
9	10	14	5	0
10	12	12	11	0
11	15	5	4	0
12	16	5	2	1
13	1	2	11	1
14	15	3	4	1
15	18	4	0	1
16	9	4	1	0
17	23	10	5	1
18	8	1	9	0
19	15	2	3	0
20	1	1	5	0
21	12	2	8	0
22	5	2	10	0
23	2	1	1	0
24	2	0		
Total	262	104	122	8
Percent total words	4.3	1.7	2.4	.2
$\bar{x}$	10.9	4.3	5.3	.3
sdv	8.0	3.7	3.3	.6

Source: Compiled by the authors.

few areas inviting exploration (though appropriate analyses, of course, depend on the research questions presented).

We realize that our transcripts inevitably will fail to meet all research needs. But to those who find them useful and relevant, we offer the following pages.

Appendix A

Participants and Procedures for the 1960 Presidential Debates

Debate	Date; City, State; Sponsoring Network; Site; Time; Length; Question Areas	Panelists	Format*
First	9/26/60; Chicago, Ill.; CBS; TV#1, WBBM-TV; 9:30 p.m., EST; 60 minutes; Domestic issues	Moderator: Howard K. Smith, CBS; Robert Fleming, ABC; Stuart Novins, CBS; Sander Vanocur, NBC; Charles Warren, MBS	Opening statements of eight minutes; questions and answers; closing statements of three minutes Warren, MBS
Second	10/7/60; Washington, D.C.; NBC; Studio A, WRC-TV; 7:30 p.m., EDST; 60 minutes; Unlimited	Moderator: Frank McGee, NBC; Edward P. Morgan, ABC; Paul Niven, CBS; Alvin Spivak, UPI; Hal Levy, *Newsday*	No formal statements; two and one-half minutes to answer questions; one and one-half minutes for rebuttal comment by other candidate
Third	10/13/60; New York and Los Angeles (because of scheduling difficulties, Kennedy appeared from New York and Nixon and the panel from two different studios in Los Angeles); ABC; TV#1, ABC, New York/Studio A, Studio B, ABC, Los Angeles; 7:30 p.m., EDST; 60 minutes; Unlimited	Moderator: William Shadel, ABC; Roscoe Drummond, New York *Herald Tribune*; Frank McGee, NBC; Charles Von Fremd, CBS; Douglas Cater, *The Reporter*	No formal statements; two and one-half minutes to answer; one and one-half minutes to comment
Fourth	10/21/60; New York; ABC; TV#1, ABC; 10:00 p.m., EDST; 60 minutes; Foreign policy	Moderator: Quincy Howe, ABC; John Edwards, ABC; Walter Cronkite, CBS; Frank Singiser, MBS; John Chancellor, NBC	Eight-minute opening statements; questions and answers; comment; closing statement

*Announced at outset; revised to fit available time. *Source:* Compiled by the authors.

Appendix B

Participants and Procedures for the 1976 Presidential and Vice-Presidential Debates

Debate	Date; City, State; Site; Time; Length; Question Areas	Panelists	Format*
First	Thursday, 9/23		
First presidential	Thursday, 9/23/76; Philadelphia, Pa.; Walnut Street Theater; 9:30 p.m., EDT; 90 minutes; Domestic policy, economic issues	Moderator: Edwin Newman, NBC Elizabeth Drew, *New Yorker*; James Gannon, *Wall Street Journal*; Frank Reynolds, ABC	Question-answer, up to three minutes; follow-up question (optional), up to two minutes to answer; comment by opposing candidate, up to two minutes; closing statements, up to three minutes for each candidate; questions alternated
Second presidential	Wednesday, 10/6/76; San Francisco, Calif.; Palace of Fine Arts; 9:30 p.m., EDT; 90 minutes; Foreign policy and national defense	Moderator: Pauline Frederick, National Public Radio; Max Frankel, New York *Times*, Henry Trewhitt, Baltimore *Sun*; Richard Valeriani, NBC	Question-answer, up to three minutes; follow-up question (optional), response by opponent up to two minutes; closing statements, up to three minutes for each candidate; questions alternated
Vice-presidential	Friday, 10/15/76; Houston, Tex.; Alley Theatre; 9:30 p.m., EDT; 75 minutes; One-third foreign issues; one-third domestic issues; one-third open to questions on any subject.	Moderator: Jim Hoge, Chicago *Sun-Times*; Marilyn Berger, NBC; Hal Bruno, *Newsweek*; Walter Mears, Associated Press	Opening statement, up to two minutes for each candidate; question-answer, up to two and one-half minutes; first candidate, one minute; closing statements, up to three minutes each candidate; no follow-up questions; questions alternated
Third presidential	Friday, 10/22/76; Williamsburg, Va.; Phi Beta Kappa Hall; 9:30 p.m., EDT; 90 minutes; Open to questions on all issues	Moderator: Barbara Walters, ABC; Joseph Kraft, syndicated columnist; Jack Nelson, Los Angeles *Times*; Robert Maynard, Washington *Post*	Question-answer, up to two and one-half minutes; follow-up question (optional), comment by opposing candidate up to two minutes; closing statements, up to three minutes for each candidate; questions alternated

*Announced at outset; revised to fit available time.   *Source:* Compiled by the authors.

Appendix C

The First Presidential Debate:
September 23, 1976, Philadelphia

Newman

Good evening. I'm Edwin Newman, moderator of this first debate of the 1976 campaign between Gerald R. Ford of Michigan, Republican candidate for president, and Jimmy Carter of Georgia, Democratic candidate for president. We thank you, President Ford, and we thank you, Governor Carter, for being with us tonight. There are to be three debates between the presidential candidates and one between the vice-presidential candidates. All are being arranged by the League of Women Voters' Education Fund. Tonight's debate, the first between presidential candidates in sixteen years, and the first ever in which an incumbent president has participated, is taking place before an audience in the Walnut Street Theater in Philadelphia, just three blocks from Independence Hall. The television audience may reach a hundred million in the United States and many millions overseas. Tonight's debate focuses on domestic issues and economic policy. Questions will be put by Frank Reynolds of ABC News, James Gannon of the *Wall Street Journal*, and Elizabeth Drew of the *New Yorker* magazine. Under the agreed rules, the first question will go to Governor Carter. That was decided by the toss of a coin. He will have up to three minutes to answer. One follow-up question will be permitted with up to two minutes to reply. President Ford will then have two minutes to respond. The next question will go to President Ford with the same time arrangements, and questions will continue to be alternated between the candidates. Each man will make a three-minute statement at the end, Governor Carter to go first. President Ford and Governor Carter do not have any notes or prepared remarks with them this evening. Mr. Reynolds, your question for Governor Carter.

Reynolds

Mr. President, Governor Carter. Governor, in an interview with the Associated Press last week, you said you believed these debates would alleviate a lot of concern that some voters have about you. Well, one of those concerns, not an uncommon one about uh– candidates in any year, is that many voters say they don't really know where you stand. Now, you have made jobs your number one priority and you have said you are committed to a drastic reduction in unemployment. Can you say now, Governor, in specific terms, what your first step would be next January if you are elected, to achieve that?

Carter

Yes. First of all is to recognize a tremendous economic strength in this country, and to set the putting to, back to work of our people as a top priority. This is uh— an effort that ought to be done primarily by strong leadership in the White House, the inspiration of our people, the tapping of uh— business, agriculture, industry, labor, and government at all levels to work on this uh— project. We'll never have uh— an end to the inflationary spiral, and we'll never have a balanced budget until we get our people back to work. There are several things that can be done specifically that are not now being done. First of all, to channel research and development funds into areas that will provide uh— large numbers of jobs. Secondly, we need to have a commitment in the uh— the private sector uh— to cooperate with government in matters like housing. Here, a very small investment of taxpayers' money in the housing field can bring large numbers of extra jobs and the guarantee of mortgage loans and the uh— putting forward of uh— two-oh-two programs for housing for older people and so forth to cut down the roughly twenty percent unemployment that now exists in the, in the construction industry. Another thing is to deal with our uh— needs in the central cities, where the unemployment rate is extremely high, sometimes among minority groups, or those who don't speak English, or who are black, or young people or forty percent unemployment. Here a C.C.C.-type program would be appropriate to channel money into the uh— hu— cha — in— into the sharing with private sector and also local and state governments to employ young people who are now out of work. Another very important a— aspect of our uh— economy would be to increase production in every way possible uh— to hold down uh— taxes on individuals, and to uh— shift the tax burdens onto those who have avoided paying taxes in the past. These uh— kinds of specific things, uh— none of which are being done now, would be a great help in, in reducing uh— unemployment. There is uh— an additional factor that needs to be done and covered very, very succinctly, and that is to make sure that we have a good relationship between management—business on the one hand—and labor on the other. In a lot of uh— places where uh— unemployment is very high, we might channel specific uh— targeted job in— job uh—opportunities by paying part of the salary of unemployed people, uh— and also sharing with uh— local governments the uh— payment of salaries which would uh— let us cut down the unemployment rate much lower, before we hit the inflationary level. But I believe that by the end of the first four years of uh— of the next term, we could have the unemployment rate down to three percent, adult unemployment, which is about uh— four to four and a half percent overall, a controlled inflation rate, and have uh— a balanced growth of about uh— four to six percent—around five percent—which would give us a balanced budget.

Reynolds

Governor uh— in the event you are successful and you do achieve a drastic drop . . .

[Interruption 1]

Carter

Yes.

Reynolds

in unemployment, that is likely to create additional pressure on prices, how willing are you to consider an incomes policy? In other words, wage and price controls?

Appendix C

Carter

Well, we now have such a, a low utilization of uh— our productive capacity uh— about seventy-three percent—I think it's about the lowest since the Great Depression years—and such a high unemployment rate now, uh— seven point nine percent that uh— we have a long way to go in getting people to work before we have the inflationary pressures. And I think this would uh— would be uh— easy to accomplish, to get jobs down, without having the strong in— inflationary pressures that, that would be necessary. I would not favor the uh— payment of uh— of a given fixed income to people unless they are not able to work. But with tax incentives for the low–income groups, we could build up their uh— income levels uh— above the poverty level and not uh— make welfare more uh— profitable than, than work.

Newman

Mr. President, your response?

Ford

I don't believe that uh— Mr. Carter's been any more specific in this case than he has been on many other instances. I notice particularly that he didn't endorse the Humphrey-Hawkins bill which he has on occasions, and which is included as a part of the Democratic platform. That legislation uh— allegedly would help our unemployment, but uh— we all know that it would have controlled our economy. It would have added uh— ten to thirty billion dollars each year in additional expenditures by the federal government. It would have called for export controls on agricultural products. In my judgment the best way to get jobs is to uh— expand the private sector, where f— five out of six jobs today exist in our economy. We can do that by reducing federal taxes as I proposed uh— 'bout a year ago when I called for a tax reduction of twenty-eight billion dollars, three-quarters of it to go to private uh— taxpayers and uh— one-quarter to the business sector. We could add to jobs in the major metropolitan areas by a proposal that I recommended that would give tax incentives to business to move into the inner city, and to expand or to build new plants so that they would take a plant or expand a plant where people are and people are currently unemployed. We could uh— also uh— help our youth with some of the proposals that uh— would give to young people an opportunity to work and learn at the same time, just like we give money to young people who are going to college. Those are the kind of specifics that I think we have to discuss on these uh— debates, and these are the kind of programs that I'll talk about on my time.

Newman

Mr. Gannon, your question to President Ford?

Gannon

Mr. President, I would like to continue for a moment on this uh— question of taxes which you have just raised. You have said that you favor more tax cuts for middle–income Americans—even those earning up to thirty thousand dollars a year. That presumably would cost the Treasury quite a bit of money in lost revenue. In view of the very large budget deficits that you have accumulated and that are still in prospect, how is it possible to promise further tax cuts and to reach your goal of balancing the budget?

Ford

At the time, Mr. Gannon, that I made the recommendation for a twenty-eight billion dollar tax cut—three–quarters of it to go to individual taxpayers and twenty-five percent to American business—I said at the same time, that we had to hold the lid on federal spending, that for every dollar of a tax reduction we had to have an equal reduction in federal expenditures —a one-for-one proposition—and I recommended that to the Congress with a budget ceiling of three hundred and ninety-five billion dollars, and that would have permitted us to have a twenty eight billion dollar tax reduction. In my tax reduction program for middle-income taxpayers, I recommended that the Congress increase personal exemptions from seven hundred and fifty dollars per person, to one thousand dollars per person. That would mean, of course, that for a family of four, that that family would have a thousand dollars more personal exemption, money that they could spend for their own purposes, money that the government wouldn't have to spend. But if we keep the lid on federal spending, which I think we can, with the help of the Congress, we can justify fully a twenty-eight billion dollar tax reduction. In the budget that I submitted to the Congress in January of this year I r– recommended a fifty percent cutback in the rate of growth of federal spending. For the last ten years, the budget of the United States has grown from uh– about eleven percent per year. We can't afford that kind of growth in federal spending. And in the budget that I recommended we cut it in half, a growth rate of five to five-and-a-half percent. With that kind of limitation on federal spending, we can fully justify the tax reductions that I have proposed. And it seems to me with the stimulant of more money in the hands of the taxpayer, and with more money in the hands of business, to expand, to modernize, to provide more jobs, our economy will be stimulated so that we'll get more revenue, and we'll have a more prosperous economy.

Gannon

Mr. President, to follow up a moment. Uh– the Congress has passed a tax bill which is before you now which did not meet exactly the uh– sort of outline that you requested. What is your intention on that bill, uh– since it doesn't meet your, your requirements? Do you plan to v– sign that bill?

Ford

That tax bill does not entirely meet the criteria that I established. I think the Congress should have uh– added another ten billion dollar reduction in personal income taxes, including the increase of personal exemptions from seven hundred and fifty to a thousand dollars. And Congress could have done that if the budget committees of the Congress, and the Congress as a whole had not increased the spending that I recommended in the budget. I'm sure you know that in the resolutions passed by the Congress, they have added about seventeen billion dollars in more spending, by the Congress, over the budget that I recommended. So I would prefer in that tax bill to have an additional tax cut, and a further limitation on federal spending. Now this tax bill—that hasn't reached the White House yet but is expected in a day or two—it's about fifteen hundred pages. It has some good provisions in it. It has uh– left out some that I have recommended, unfortunately. On the other hand uh– when you have a bill of that magnitude with th– tho– those many provisions, a president has to sit and decide if there's more good than bad, and from the a– analysis that I've made so far, it seems to me that the tax bill does uh– justify my signature and my approval.

Appendix C 217

Newman

Governor Carter, your response.

Carter

Well, Mr. Ford is, is uh– changing uh– considerably his p– previous philosophy. The present tax structure is a disgrace to this country, it's just a welfare program for the rich. As a matter of fact, uh– twenty-five percent of the total tax deductions go for only one percent of the richest people in this country. And over fifty percent of the tax uh– credits go for the fourteen percent of the richest people in this country. When Mr. Ford first became president in Octo– August of 1974, the first thing he did in, in October, was to ask for a four point seven billion dollar increase in taxes on our people in the midst of the heaviest recession since uh– since the Great Depression of 19– uh– of the 1940s. In uh– January of 1975, he asked for a tax change, a five point six billion dollar increase on low-- and middle-income private individuals, a six and a half billion dollar decrease on the corporations and the special interests. And uh– December of uh– 1975, he vetoed the roughly eighteen to twenty du– billion dollar uh– tax reduction bill that had been passed by the Congress, and then he came back later on in January of this year and he did advocate a ten billion dollar tax reduction, but it would be offset by a six billion dollar increase, this coming January, in deductions for Social Security payments and for unemployment compensation. The whole philosophy of the Republican party, including uh– my opponent, has been t– to pile on taxes on low-income people to take 'em off on the corporations. As a matter of fact, in, sin– since the late sixties when Mr. Nixon took office, we've had a reduction in uh– in the percentage of taxes paid by corporations from thirty percent down to about twenty percent. We've had an increase in taxes paid by individuals, payroll taxes from fourteen percent up to twenty percent. And this is what the Republicans have done to us. And this is why tax reform is so important.

Newman

Mrs. Drew, your question to Governor Carter?

Drew

Uh– Governor Carter you've proposed a number of new or enlarged programs, including jobs, and health, welfare reform, child care, aid to education, aid to cities, changes in Social Security, and housing subsidies. You've also said that you want to balance the budget by the end of your first term. Now you haven't put a price tag on those programs, but even if we price them conservatively, and we count for full employment by the end of your first term and we count for the economic growth that would occur during that period, there still isn't enough money to pay for those programs and balance the budget by any con– any estimates that I've been able to see. So, in that case, what would give?

Carter

Well, as a matter of fact there is. If we assume the uh– a, a rate of growth of our economy equivalent to what it was during President Johnson, President Kennedy, even before the, the, the uh– Wa– Viet–nese–namese War, and if we assume that at the end of the four-year period we can cut our unemployment rate down to four to four-and-a-half percent, under those circumstances, even assuming no elimination of unnecessary programs and assuming an increase in the at– in the allotment of money to finance programs increasing as the inflation rate does, my economic projections, I think confirmed by the House uh— and the Senate committees, have been with the sixty billion dollar extra amount of money that can be spent in fiscal year '81, which will be the last year of this next term. Within that sixty billion dollars' increase there would be fit the programs that I promised the American people. I might say, too, that, that if we see that these goals cannot be reached—and I believe they're reasonable goals—then I would cut back on the rate of implemen— implementation of new programs in order to accommodate a balanced budget by fiscal year '81, which is the last year of the next term. I believe that we ought to have a balanced budget during normal economic circumstances. And uh— these projections have been very carefully made. I stand behind them. And if they should be in error slightly on the down side, then I'll phase in the programs that we've uh— advocated more slowly.

Drew

Governor um— according to the budget committees of the Congress th— th— that you referred to, if we get to full employment—what they project at a four percent unemployment— and, as you say, even allowing for the inflation in the programs, there would not be anything more than a surplus of five billion dollars by the end of nine— by 1981. And, conservative estimates of your programs would be that they'd be about eighty-five to a hundred billion dollars. So how, how, do you say that you're going to be able to do these things and balance the budget?

Carter

Well, the, the assumption that, that you uh— have described as different is in the rate of growth of our economy.

[Interruption 2]

Drew

No. They took that into account in those figures.

Carter

I believe that it's accurate to say that, that, that the committees to whom you refer, with the employment rate that you uh— state and with a five to five-and-a-half percent growth rate in our economy, that the uh— projections would be a uh— a sixty billion dollar increase in the amount of money that we have to spend in 1981 compared to now. And uh— with that, uh— in that framework would be fit the, any improvements in the programs. Now this does not include uh— any uh— addi— uh— extra control over uh— unnecessary spending, the weeding out of obsolete or obsolescent programs. Uh— we'll have uh— a safety version built in with complete reorganization of the executive branch of government, which I am pledged to do. The present bureaucratic structure of the, of the federal government is a mess. And if I'm elected president that's going to be a top priority of mine to completely revise the structure of the federal government, to make it economical, efficient, purposeful, and manageable for a change. And also, I'm going to institute zero-base budgeting which I used four years in Georgia, which uh— assesses every program every year, and eliminates those programs that are obsolete or obsolescent. But with these projections, we will have a balanced budget by fiscal year 1981, if I'm elected president, keep my promises to the American people. And it's just predicated on very modest, but I think accurate, projections of employment increases, and uh— a growth in our national economy equal to uh— what was experienced under Kennedy, Johnson, before the Vietnam War.

Appendix C

Newman

President Ford?

Ford

If it is uh– true that there will be a sixty billion dollar surplus by fiscal year 1981, rather than spend that money for all the new programs that Governor Carter recommends and endorses, and which are included in the Democratic platform, I think the American taxpayer ought to get an additional tax break, a tax reduction of that magnitude. I feel that the taxpayers are the ones that need the relief. I don't think we should add additional programs of the magnitude that Governor Carter talks about. It seems to me that our tax structure, today, has rates that are too high. But I am uh– very glad to point out that since 1969, during a Republican administration, we have had ten million people taken off of the tax rolls at the lower end of the taxpayer area. And at the same time, assuming that I sign the tax bill that was mentioned by Mr. Gannon, we will in the last two tax bills have increased the minimum tax on all wealthy taxpayers. And I believe that by eliminating ten million taxpayers in the last uh– eight years, and by putting a heavier tax burden on those in the higher tax brackets, plus the other actions that have been taken uh– we can give taxpayers adequate tax relief. Now it seems to me that uh– as we look at the recommendations of the budget committees and our own projections, there isn't going to be any sixty billion dollar dividend. I've heard of those dividends in the past. It always happens. We expected one at the time of the Vietnam War. But it was used up before we ever ended the war and taxpayers never got the adequate relief they deserved.

Newman

Mr. Reynolds?

Reynolds

Mr. President, when you came into office you spoke very eloquently of the need for a time for healing, and very early in your administration you went out to Chicago and you announced, you proposed a program of uh– case-by-case pardons for draft resisters, to restore them to full citizenship. Some fourteen thousand young men took advantage of your offer, but another ninety thousand did not. In granting the pardon to former President Nixon, sir, part of your rationale was to put Watergate behind us, to–if I may quote you again–truly end our long national nightmare. Why does not the same rationale apply now, today, in our bicentennial year, to the young men who resisted in Vietnam, and many of them still in exile abroad?

Ford

The amnesty program that I recommended, in Chicago in September of 1974, would give to all draft evaders and uh– military deserters the opportunity to earn their uh– good record back. About fourteen to fifteen thousand did take advantage of that program. We gave them ample time. I am against a, an across-the-board pardon of draft evaders or military deserters. Now in the case of Mr. Nixon, the reason that the pardon was given, was that when I took office this country was in a very, very divided condition. There was hatred, there was divisiveness uh– people had lost faith in their government in many, many respects. Mr. Nixon resigned, and I became president. It seemed to me that if I was to uh– adequately and effectively handle the problems of high inflation, a growing recession, the uh– involvement of the United States still in Vietnam, that I had to give a hundred percent of my time to those two major problems. Mr. Nixon resigned. That is disgrace. The first president out of thirty-eight that ever resigned from public office under pressure. So when you look at the penalty that he paid, and when you analyze the requirements that I had, to spend all of my time working on the economy, which was in trouble, that I inherited, working on our problems in Southeast Asia, which were still plaguing us, it seemed to me that Mr. Nixon had been penalized enough by his resignation, in disgrace, and the need and necessity for me to concentrate on the problems of the country, fully justified the action that I took.

Reynolds

Oh, I take it then, sir, that you do not believe that uh— it is—that you are going to reconsider and uh— think about those ninety thousand who are still abroad? Uh— have they not been penalized enough—many of them been there for years?

Ford

Well, Mr. Carter has uh— indicated that uh— he would give a blanket pardon to all uh— draft evaders. I do not agree with that point of view. I gave, in September of 1974, an opportunity for all draft evaders, all deserters, to come in voluntarily, clear their records by earning an opportunity to restore their good citizenship. I think we gave them a good opportunity— we're—I don't think we should go any further.

Newman

Governor Carter?

Carter

Well, I think it's uh— very difficult for President Ford to uh— explain the difference between the pardon of President Nixon and, and uh— his attitude toward those who violated the draft laws. As a matter of fact, now, I, I don't advocate amnesty. I advocate pardon. There's a difference, in my opinion, uh— and in accordance with the ruling of the Supreme Court and accordance with the definition in the dictionary. Amnesty means that, that you uh— what, that what you did was right. Pardon means that, what you did, whether it's right or wrong you're forgiven for it. And I do advocate a pardon for, for draft evaders. I think it's accurate to say that in, uh— two years ago when Mr. Nix— Mr. Ford put in this uh— amnesty that three times as many deserters were uh— excused as were, as were the uh— the ones who evaded the draft. But, I think that now is the time to heal our country after the Vietnam War, and I think that what the people are concerned about is not the uh— pardon or the amnesty of uh— those who evaded the draft but, but whether or not our crime system is, is fair. We've got a, a short distinction drawn between white-collar crime. The, the, the big shots who are rich, who are influential, uh— very seldom go to jail. Those who are poor and, and who have uh— no influence uh— quite often are the ones who are punished. And, and the whole uh— subject of crime is one that concerns our people very much, and I believe that the fairness of it is, is what, uh— is, is a major problem that addresses our, our leader, and this is something that hasn't been addressed adequately by, by this administration. But I, I hope to have a complete uh— responsibility on my shoulders to help bring about a, a fair uh— criminal justice system and also to, to bring about uh— a— an end to the, to the divis— divisiveness that has occurred in our country uh— as a result of the Vietnam War.

Appendix C 　　　　　　　　　　　　　　　　　　　　　　　　　　　　　　　　　　*221*

Newman

Mr. Gannon?

Gannon

Governor Carter, you have promised a sweeping overhaul of the federal government, including a reduction in the number of government agencies. You say it would go down about two hundred from some nineteen hundred. That sounds, indeed like a very deep cut in the federal government. But isn't it a fact that you're not really talking about fewer federal employees or less government spending, but rather that you are talking about reshaping the federal government, not making it smaller?

Carter

Well, I've been through this before, Mr. Gannon, as the governor of Georgia. When I took over we had a, a bureaucratic mess, like we have in Washington now. And we had three hundred agencies, departments, bureaus, commissions, uh– some uh– fully budgeted, some not, but all having responsibility to carry out that was in conflict. And we cut those three hundred uh– agencies and so forth down substantially. We eliminated two hundred and seventy-eight of them. We set up a simple structure of government that could be administered fairly and it was a, a tremendous success. It hasn't been undone since I was there. It resulted also in an ability, to reshape our court system, our prison system, our education system, our mental health programs and, and a clear assignment of responsibility and, and authority and also to have uh– our people once again understand and control our government. I intend to do the same thing if I'm elected president. Wh– when I get to Washington, coming in as an outsider, one of the major responsibilities that, that I will have on my shoulder is a complete reorganization of the s– of the executive branch of government. We now have uh– a greatly expanded White House staff. When Mr. Nixon went in office, for instance, we had three-and-a-half million dollars spent on, on the White House and its staff, that has escalated now to sixteen-and-a-half million dollars in the last uh– Republican administration. This needs to be changed. We need to put the responsibilities back on the cabinet members. We also need to have a great reduction in agencies and programs. For instance, we now have uh– in the health area, three hundred and two different programs administered by eleven major departments and agencies, sixty other advisory commissions responsible for this. Medicaid's in one agency, Medicare's in a different one. The, the check on the quality of health care's in a different one. None of them are responsible for health care itself. This makes it almost impossible for us to have a good health program. We have uh– just advocated uh– this past week a, a, a consolidation of the responsibilities for energy. Our country now has no comprehensive energy program or policy. We have twenty different agencies in the federal government responsible for the production, the regulation, the uh– information about energy, the conservation of energy, spread all over government. This is a, a gross waste of money. So tough, competent management of government, giving us a simple, efficient, purposeful, and manageable government would be a great step forward, and if I'm elected–and I intend to be–then it's gonna be done.

Gannon

Well, I'd like to, to press my question on the number of federal employees, whether you would really plan to reduce the overall s– uh– number, or, or merely put them in different departments and relabel them. Uh– in your energy plan uh– you consolidate a number of a– agencies into one, or you would, but uh– does that really change the overall?

Carter

I can't say for sure that we would have fewer federal employees when I go out of office than when I come in. It took me about three years to completely reorganize the Georgia government. The last year I was in office, uh– our budget was, was actually less than it was a year before, uh– which showed a great improvement. Also we had a uh– a two percent increase in the number of employees the last year. But it was a tremendous shift from administrative jobs into the delivery of services. For instance, we uh– completely revised our prison system. We established eighty-four new mental health treatment centers. And we shifted people out of administrative jobs into the field to deliver better services. The same thing will be done uh– at the federal government level. I, I accomplished this w– with substantial reductions in employees in some departments. For instance, in the Transportation Department uh– we had uh– we cut back about twenty-five percent of the total number of employees. In giving our people better mental health care, we increased the number of employees. But the efficiency of it, the simplicity of it, the uh– ability of people to understand their own government and control it was a, was the uh– substantial benefit derived from complete reorganization. We uh– have got to do this at the federal government level. If we don't, the bureaucratic mess is going to continue. There's no way for our people now to understand what their government is. There's no way to get the answer to a question. When you come to Washington to try to–as a governor–to try to begin a new program for your people, like uh– the treatment of drug addicts, I found there were thirteen different federal agencies that I had to go to, to manage the uh– drug treatment program. In the Georgia government, we only had one agency responsible for drug treatment. This is the kind of change that would be made. And uh– it would be of, of tremendous benefit in long-range planning, in tight budgeting, uh– saving the taxpayers' money, making the government more efficient, cutting down on bureaucratic waste, having a clear delineation of authority and responsibility of employees, and giving our people a better chance to understand and control their government.

Newman

President Ford?

Ford

I think the record should show, Mr. Newman, that uh– the Bureau of Census–we checked it just yesterday–indicates that uh– in the four years that uh– Governor Carter was governor of the state of Georgia, uh– expenditures by the government went up over fifty percent. Uh– employees of the government in Georgia during his term of office went up over twenty-five percent, and the figures also show that the uh– uh– bonded indebtedness of the state of Georgia during his governorship went up over twenty percent. And there was some very interesting testimony given by uh– Governor Carter's successor, Governor Busbee, before a Senate committee a few uh– months ago on how he found the Medicaid program, when he came into office following uh– Governor Carter. He testified, and these are his words– the present governor of Georgia– he says he found the Medicaid program in Georgia in shambles. Now let me talk about what we've done in the White House, as far as federal employees are concerned. The first order that I issued, after I became president, was to cut or eliminate the prospective forty thousand increase in federal employees that had been scheduled by my predecessor. And in the term that I've been president–some two years–we have reduced federal employment by eleven thousand. In the White House staff itself, when I became president, we had roughly five hundred and forty employees. We now have about four hundred and eighty-five employees, so we've made a rather significant reduction in the number

Appendix C

of employees on the White House staff working for the president. So I think our record of cutting back employees, plus the uh– failure on the part of the Governor's program to actually save employment in Georgia, shows which is the better plan.

Newman

Mrs. Drew?

Drew

Uh– Mr. President, at Vail, after the Republican convention, you announced that you would now emphasize five new areas, among those were jobs and housing and health and improved recreational facilities for Americans. And you also added crime. You also s– mentioned education. For two years you've been telling us that we couldn't do very much in these areas because we couldn't afford it, and in fact we do have a fifty billion dollar deficit now. In rebuttal to Governor Carter a little bit earlier, you said that if there were to be any surplus in the next few years you thought it should be turned back to the people in the form of tax relief. So how are you going to pay for any new initiatives in these areas you announced at Vail you were going to now stress?

Ford

Well, in the uh– last two years, as I indicated before, we had a very tough time. We were faced with uh– heavy inflation, over twelve percent, we were faced with substantial unemployment. But in the last uh– twenty-four months we've turned the economy around and we've brought inflation down to under six percent and we have reduced the uh– well, we have added e– employment of about four million in the last seventeen months to the point where we have eighty-eight million people working in America today, the most in the history of the country. The net result is, we are going to have some improvement in our receipts. And I think we'll have some decrease in our disbursements. We expect to have a lower deficit in fiscal year 1978. We feel that with this improvement in the economy, we feel with more reciepts and fewer disbursements, we can in a moderate way, increase, as I recommended, over the next ten years a n– new parks program that would cost a billion-and-a-half dollars, doubling our national park system. We have recommended that in the ho– housing program, we can reduce down-payments and moderate monthly payments. But that doesn't cost any more as far as the federal Treasury is concerned. We believe that we can uh– do a better job in the area of crime, but that requires uh– tougher sentencing, mandatory, certain prison sentences for those who violate our criminal laws. We ruh–believe that uh– you can revise the federal criminal code which has not been revised in a good many years. That doesn't cost any more money. We believe that you can uh– do something more effectively, with a moderate increase in money, in the drug abuse program. We feel that uh– in education, we can have a slight increase–not a major increase. It's my understanding that Governor Carter has indicated that uh– he approves of a thirty billion dollar uh– expenditure by the federal government as far as education is concerned. The present time we're spending roughly three billion five hundred million dollars. I don't know where that money would come from. But as we look at the quality-of-life programs–jobs, health, education, crime, recreation–we've uh– feel that as we move forward with a healthier economy, we can absorb this small necessary cost that will be required.

Drew

But sir, in the next few years would you try to reduce the deficit, would you spend money for these programs that you have just outlined, or would you as you said earlier, return whatever surplus you got to the people in the form of tax relief?

Ford

We feel that uh— with the programs that I have recommended, the additional ten billion dollar tax cut, with the moderate increases in the quality-of-life area, we can still have a balanced budget which I will submit, to the Congress, in January of 1978. We won't uh— one year or two years longer, as Governor Carter uh— indicates. As the economy improves—and it is improving—our gross national product this year will average about six percent increase over last year. We will have a lower rate of inflation for the uh— calendar year this year of something slightly under six percent. Employment will be up, revenues will be up—we'll keep the lid on some of these programs that we can hold down as we have a little extra money to spend for those quality-of-life programs which I think are needed and necessary. Now I, I cannot, and would not, endorse the kind of programs that uh— Governor Carter recommends. He endorses the Democratic uh— platform, which as I read it, calls for approximately sixty additional programs. We estimate that those programs would add a hundred billion dollars minimum, and probably two hundred billion dollars uh— maximum each year to the federal budget. Those programs you cannot afford and give tax relief. We feel that you can hold the line and restrain federal spending, give a tax reduction and still have a balanced budget by 1978.

Newman

Governor Carter?

Carter

Well, Mr. Ford takes the uh— same attitude that the Republicans always take. In the last three months before an election, they're always for the programs that they fight the other three-and-a-half years. Uh— I remember when uh— Herbert Hoover was against uh— jobs for people, I remember when Alf Landon was against Social Security, and uh— later President Nixon sixteen years ago was telling the public that John Kennedy's proposals would bankrupt the country and would double the cost. The best thing to do is look at the record uh— of Mr. Ford's administration and, and Mr. Nixon's before his. Uh— we had last year a sixty-five billion dollar deficit, the largest deficit in the history of our country—more of a deficit spending than we had in the entire eight-year period under President Johnson and President Kennedy. We've got five hundred thousand more Americans out of jobs today, than were out of work three months ago. And since Mr. Ford's been in office two years, we've had a fifty percent increase in unemployment from five million people out of work to two-and-a-half million more people out of work and a total of seven-and-a-half million. We'v also got uh— a comparison between himself and Mr. Nixon. He's got four times the size of the deficits that Mr. Nixon even had himself. This uh— talking about more people at work uh— is distorted because with a fourteen percent increase in the cost of living, in the last uh— two years, it means that, that women and young people have had to go to work when they didn't want to because their fathers couldn't make enough to pay the increased cost of uh— of food and uh— housing and clothing. We have uh— in this last uh— two years, alone, a hundred and twenty billion dollars total deficits under President Ford, and uh— at the same time we've had in the last eight years, a, a doubling in the number of bankruptcies for small business.

Appendix C

We've had a negative growth in our, in our national economy, measured in real dollars. The take-home pay of a worker in this country is actually less now than it was in 1968, measured in real dollars. This is the kind of record that's there and talk about the future and a drastic change or conversion on the part of Mr. Ford at this last minute is one that just doesn't go.

Newman

Mr. Reynolds?

Reynolds

Governor Carter, I'd like to turn to uh– what we used to call the energy crisis. Yesterday, a British uh– government commission on air pollution, but one headed by a nuclear physicist, recommended that any further expansion of nuclear energy be delayed in Britain as long as possible. Now this is a subject that is quite controversial among our own people and there seems to be a clear difference between you and the President on the use of nuclear power plants, which you say you would use as a last priority. Why, sir? Are they unsafe?

Carter

Well, among my other other experiences in the past I, I've been a nuclear engineer, and did graduate work in this field. I think I know the, the uh– capabilities and limitations of atomic power. But the energy uh– policy of our nation is one that uh– has not yet been established under this administration. I think almost every other developed nation in the world has an energy policy except us. We have seen uh– the Federal Energy Agency established, for instance. Uh– in the crisis of 1973, it was supposed to be a temporary agency, uh– now it's permanent, it's enormous, it's growing every day. I think the *Wall Street Journal* uh– reported not too long ago they have a hundred and twelve public relations experts working for the Federal Energy Agency to try to justify to the American people its own existence. We've got to have a, a firm way to handle the energy question. The reorganization proposal that I put forward is one uh– first step. In addition to that, we need to have a, a realization that we've got a– about thirty-five years' worth of oil left in the whole world. We're gonna run out of oil. When Mr. Nixon made his famous uh– speech on Operation Independence, we were importing about thirty-five percent of our oil. Now we've increased that amount twenty-five percent. We now import about forty-four percent of our oil. We need to shift from oil to coal. We need to concentrate our research and development effort on uh– coal burning and extraction, that's safe for miners, that also is clean burning. We need to shift very strongly toward solar energy and have strict conservation measures. And then as a last resort only, continue to use atomic power. I would certainly uh– not cut out atomic power altogether, we can't afford to give up that opportunity until later. But to the extent that we continue to use atomic power, I would be responsible, as president, to make sure that the safety precautions were initiated and maintained. For instance, some that have been forgotten. We need to have the reactor core below ground level. The entire power plant that uses atomic uh– power tightly sealed and a heavy, heavy vacuum maintained. There ought to be a standardized design. There ought to be a full-time uh– atomic energy specialist, independent of the power company in the control room full-time, twenty-four hours a day, to shut down a plant if an abnormality develops. These kinds of uh– procedures, along with evacuation procedures, adequate insurance, ought to be initiated. So, shift from oil to coal, emphasize research and development on coal use and also on solar power, strict conservation measures, not yield every time that the special interest group put pressure on the president, like uh– this administration has done, and use atomic energy only as a last resort with the strictest possible safety precautions. That's the best overall energy policy in the brief time we have to discuss it.

Reynolds

Well, Governor, on that same subject, would you require mandatory conservation efforts to try to conserve fuel?

Carter

Yes, I would. Some of the things that can be done about this is a change in the rate structure of electric power companies. We uh– now encourage people to waste electricity, and uh– by giving uh– the, the lowest rates to the biggest users. We don't do anything to cut down on peak–load requirements. We don't have an adequate requirement for the insulation of homes, for the efficiency of automobiles, and whenever the uh– automobile manufacturers come forward and say they can't meet the uh– limits that the Congress has put forward, this Republican administration has delayed the implementation dates. In addition to that, we ought to have a, a shift to the use of coal, particularly in the Appalachian regions, where the coal is located, uh– a lot of uh– very high quality low-carbon coal, uh– I mean low-sulfur coal, is there, it's where our employment is needed. Uh– this would, would help a great deal. So, mandatory conservation measures, yes. Encouragement by the president for people to uh– voluntarily conserve, yes. And also the private sector ought to be encouraged to, to bring forward to the public the benefits from efficiency. One bank in uh– Washington f– for instance, gives lower interest loans for people who adequately insulate their homes or who buy efficient automobiles. And some major uh– uh– manufacturing companies, like Dow Chemical, have through uh– very effective efficiency mechanisms, cut down the use of energy by uh– as much as forty percent with the same out-product. These kind of things uh– ought to be done. Uh– they ought to be encouraged and supported, and even required uh– by the government, yes.

Newman

President Ford?

Ford

Governor Carter skims over a very serious and a very broad subject. In January of uh– 1975 I submitted to the Congress and to the American people the first comprehensive energy program recommended by any president. It called for an increase in the production of energy in the United States. It called for uh– conservation measures so that we would save the energy that we have. If you're going to increase domestic oil and gas production–and we have to– you have to give to those producers an opportunity to uh– develop their land or their wells. I recommended to the Congress that we should increase coal production in this country from six hundred million tons a year to twe– um– a, billion two hundred million tons by 1985. In order to do that we have to improve our extraction of coal from the m– ground, we have to improve our utilization of coal–make it more efficient, make it cleaner. In addition we uh– have to expand our research and development. In my program for energy independence, we have increased for example, solar energy research from about eighty-four million dollars a year to about a hundred and twenty million dollars a year. We're going as fast as the experts say we should. In nuclear power we have increased the research and development uh– under the Energy Research and Development Agency uh– very substantially, to insure that our ener– uh– nuclear power plants are safer, that they are more efficient, and that we

Appendix C

have adequate safeguards. I think you have to have greater oil and gas production, more coal production, more nuclear production, and in addition you have to have energy conservation.

Newman

Mr. Gannon?

Gannon

Mr. President, I'd like to return for a moment to this problem of unemployment. You have vetoed or threatened to veto number of jobs bills passed or uh– in development in the Democratic Congress–Democratic-controlled Congress. Yet at the same time the government is paying out uh– I think it is seventeen billion, perhaps twenty billion dollars a year in unemployment compensation, caused by the high unemployment. Why do you think it is better to pay out unemployment compensation to idle people than to put them to work in public service jobs?

Ford

The bills that I've vetoed, the one for an additional six billion dollars, was not a bill that would have solved our unemployment problems. Even the proponents of it admitted that no more than four hundred thousand jobs would be uh– made available. Our analysis indicates that something in the magnitude of about a hundred and fifty to two hundred thousand jobs would uh– be made available. Each one of those jobs would have cost the taxpayer twenty-five thousand dollars. In addition, the jobs would not be available right now. They would not have materialized for about nine to eighteen months. The immediate problem we have is to stimulate our economy now so that we can get rid of unemployment. What we have done is to hold the lid on spending in an effort to reduce the rate of inflation. And we have proven, I think very conclusively, that you can reduce the rate of inflation and increase jobs. For example, as I have said, we have added some four million jobs in the last seventeen months. We have now employed eighty-eight million people in America, the largest number in the history of the United States. We've added five hundred thousand jobs in the last two months. Inflation is the quickest way to destroy jobs. And by holding the lid on federal spending, we have been able to do an, a good job an affirmative job in inflation and as a result have added to the jobs in this country. I think it's uh– also appropriate to point out that through our tax policies we have stimulated uh– added employment throughout the country, the investment tax credit, the tax incentives for expansion and modernization of our industrial capacity. It's my, my opinion that the private sector, where five out of the six jobs are, where you have permanent jobs, with the opportunity for advancement, is a better place than make-work jobs under the program recommended by the Congress.

Gannon

Just to follow up, Mr. President. The, the Congress has just passed a three point seven billion dollar appropriation bill, which would provide money for the public works jobs program that you earlier tried to kill by your veto of the authorization legislation. In light of the fact that uh– unemployment again is rising–or has in the past three months–I wonder if you have rethought that question at all? Whether you would consider uh– allowing this program to be funded, or will you veto that money bill?

Ford

Well, that bill has not yet come down to the Oval Office, so I am not in a position to make any judgment on it tonight. But that is an extra four billion dollars that would uh— add to the deficit, which would add to the inflationary pressures, which would help to destroy jobs in the private sector, not make jobs, where the jobs really are. These make-work, temporary jobs, dead-end as they are, are not the kind of jobs that we want for our people. I think it's interesting to point out that uh— in the uh— two years that I've been president, I've vetoed fifty-six bills. Congress has sustained forty-two vetoes. As a result, we have saved over nine billion dollars in federal expenditures. And the Congress by overriding the bills that I did veto, the Congress has added some thirteen billion dollars to the federal expenditures and to the federal deficit. Now, Governor Carter complains about the deficits that um— uh— this administration has had, and yet he condemns the vetoes that I have made that has, that have saved the taxpayer nine billion dollars and could have saved an additional thirteen billion dollar. Now he can't have it both ways. And therefore, it seems to me that we should hold the lid, as we have, to the best of our ability, so we can stimulate the private economy and get the jobs where the jobs are—five out of six—in this economy.

Newman

Governor Carter?

Carter

Well, Mr. Ford doesn't seem to put into perspective the fact that when, when uh— five hundred thousand more people are out of work than there were three months ago, while we have two-and-a-half million more people out of work than were when he took office, that this touches human beings. I was in uh— a city in uh— Pennsylvania not too long, near here, and uh— there were about four or five thousand people in the audience, it was on a, on the train trip. And I said how many uh— adults here are out of work. About a thousand raised their hands. Mr. Ford uh— actually has fewer people now in the private sector in nonfarm jobs than when he took office. And still he talks about uh— success. Uh— seven point nine percent unemployment is a terrible tragedy in this country. He says he's learned how to match unemployment with inflation. That's right. We've got the highest inflation we've had in twenty-five years right now, except under this administration, and that was fifty years ago. And we've got uh— the highest unemployment we've had uh— under Mr. Ford's administration, since the Great Depression. This affects human beings. And, and his insensitivity in providing those people a chance to work has made this a welfare administration, and not a work administration. He hasn't saved nine billion dollars with his vetoes. There's only been a, a net saving of four billion dollars. And the cost in unemployment compensation, welfare compensation, and lost revenues has increased twenty-three billion dollars in the last two years. This is a, a typical attitude that really causes havoc in people's lives, and then it's covered over by saying that our country is naturally got a six percent unemployment rate or a seven percent unemployment rate and a six percent inflation. It's a travesty. It shows a lack of leadership. And we've never had a president since the War Between the States that vetoed more bills. Mr. Ford has vetoed four times as many bills as Mr. Nixon per year. And eleven of them have been overridden. One of his bills that was overridden, he only got one vote in the Senate, and seven votes in the House, from Republicans.

Appendix C 229

[Interruption 3]

Newman

Governor Carter . . .

Carter

So this shows a breakdown in leadership.

Newman

Under the rules, I must stop you there. Mrs. Drew?

Drew

Governor Carter, I'd like to come back to the subject of taxes. You have said that you want to cut taxes for the middle- and lower-income groups.

[Interruption 4]

Carter

Right.

Drew

But unless you're willing to do such things as reduce the itemized deductions for charitable contributions or home mortgage payments, or interest, or taxes, or capital gains, you can't really raise sufficient revenue to provide an overall tax cut of any size. So how are you going to provide that tax relief that you're talking about?

Carter

Now we have uh— such a grossly unbalanced tax system—as I said earlier, that it is a disgrace—o— of all the tax uh— benefits now, twenty-five percent of them go to the one percent of the richest people in this country. Over fifty percent—fifty-three to be exact—percent of the tax benefits go to the fourteen percent richest people in this country, and we've had a fifty percent increase in payroll deductions since Mr. Nixon went in office eight years ago. Mr. Ford has, has advocated since he's been in office, over five billion dollars in reductions for corporations, special interest groups, and the very, very wealthy who derive their income not from labor, but from investments. That's got to be changed. A few things that can be done. We have now a deferral system so that the multinational corporations who invest overseas, if they make a million dollars in profits overseas, they don't have to pay any of their taxes unless they bring their money back into this country. When they don't pay their taxes, the average American pays the taxes for them. Not only that, but it robs this country of jobs, because instead of coming back with that million dollars and creating a shoe factory, say in New Hampshire or Vermont, if the company takes the money down to Italy and bus— builds a shoe factory, they don't have to pay any taxes on the money. Another thing is a system called DISC, which was originally designed, proposed by Mr. Nixon, to encourage exports. This permits a company to create a, a dummy corporation, to export their products and then not to pay the full amount of taxes on them. This costs our, our government about uh— one point four billion dollars a year, and when those rich corporations, don't pay that tax, the average American taxpayer pays it for 'em. Another one that's uh— that's very important, is the uh— is the business deductions, uh— jet airplanes, uh— first-class travel, the fifty dollar martini lunch. Uh— the average working person can't uh— can't take advantage of that, but the, the wealthier people uh— can. Uh— another system is where a, a, a dentist can invest money in, say, raising cattle and uh— can put in a hundred thousand dollars of his own money, borrow nine hundred thousand dollars, nine hundred mi— thousand dollars—that makes a million—and mark of a great amount of uh— of loss uh— through that procedure. Uh— there was one example, for instance, where uh— somebody uh— produced pornographic movies. They put in thirty thousand dollars of their own money, and got a hundred and twenty thousand dollars in tax savings. Well, these special kinds of programs have, have robbed the average taxpayer and have benefited those who are powerful and who can employ lobbyists and who can have the C.P.A.s and the lawyers to help them benefit from the roughly uh— eight thousand pages of the tax code. The average uh— American person can't do it. You can't hire a lobbyist uh— out of uh— unemployment compensation checks.

Drew

Uh— Governor, to follow up on your answer. Um— in order for any kind of tax relief to really be felt by the middle- and lower-income people . . .

[Interruption 5]

Carter

Yes.

Drew

you need about, according to Congressional committees on this, you need about ten billion dollars. Now you listed some things, the uh— deferral on foreign income as estimated that would save about five hundred million dollars. DISC, you said, was one point four billion. Uh— the estimate at the outside, if you eliminated all tax shelters, is five billion. Wh— so where else would you raise the revenue to provide this tax relief? Would you, in fact, do away with all business deductions, and what other kinds of preferences would you do away with?

Carter

No, I wouldn't do away with all uh— business deductions. I think that would be a, a very serious mistake. But uh— i— if you could just do away with the ones that are unfair, you could lower taxes for everyone. I would never do anything that would increase the taxes for those who work for a living, or who are presently required to list all their income. What I want to do is not to raise taxes, but to eliminate loopholes. And this is uh— the point of my first statistics that I gave you, that th— the present tax benefits that have been carved out over a long period of years—fifty years—by sharp tax lawyers and by lobbyists have benefited just the rich. Uh— these programs that I described to you earlier—the tax deferrals for overseas, the DISC, and the tax shelters—uh— they only apply to people in the fifty thousand dollar-a-year bracket or up, and I think this is the best way to approach it. It's to make sure that everybody pays uh— taxes on the income that they earn, and make sure that you take whatever savings there is from the higher income levels and give it to the lower- and middle-income families.

Appendix C 231

Newman

President Ford?

Ford

Governor Carter's answer tonight does not coincide with the answer that he gave in an interview to the Associated Press a week or so ago. In that interview uh— Governor Carter indicated that uh— he would raise the taxes on those in the medium- or middle-income brackets or higher. Now if you uh— take the medium- or middle-income taxpayer—that's about fourteen thousand dollars per person. Uh— Governor Carter has indicated, publicly, in an interview, that he would increase the taxes on about fifty percent of the working people of this country. I think uh— the way to get tax equity in this country, is to give tax relief to the middle-income people, who have an income from roughly eight thousand dollars up to twenty-five or thirty thousand dollars. They have been shortchanged as we have taken ten million taxpayers off the tax rolls in the last eight years and as we have uh— added to the minimum tax uh— provision, to make all people pay more taxes. I believe in tax equity for the middle-income taxpayer, increasing the personal exemption. Mr. Carter wants to increase taxes for roughly half of the taxpayers of this country. Now, the Governor has also played a little fast and loose with the facts about vetoes. The records show that President Roosevelt vetoed on an average of fifty-five bills a year. President Truman vetoed, on the average, while he was president, about thirty-eight bills a year. I understand that Governor Carter when he was Governor of Georgia vetoed between thirty-five and forty bills a year. My average in two years is twenty-six. But in the process of that we have saved uh— nine billion dollars. And one final comment, uh— Governor Carter talks about the tax bills and all of the inequities that exist in the present law. I must remind him, the Democrats have controlled the Congress for the last twenty-two years, and they wrote all the tax bills.

Newman

Mr. Reynolds?

Reynolds

I suspect that uh— we could continue on this tax argument for some time, but I'd like to move on to another area. Mr. President, uh— everybody seems to be running against Washington this year. And I'd like to raise two coincidental events, then ask you whether you think perhaps this may have a bearing on the attitude throughout the country. The House Ethics Committee has just now ended its investigation of Daniel Schorr, after several months and many thousands of dollars, trying to find out how he obtained and caused to be published a report of the Congress that probably is the property of the American people. At the same time, the Senate Select Committee on Standards and Conduct has voted not really to begin an investigation of a United States senator, because of allegations against him, that he may have been receiving corporate funds illegally over a period of years. Do you suppose, sir, that events like this contribute to the feeling in the country that maybe there's something wrong in Washington, and I don't mean just in the executive branch but throughout the, the whole government?

Ford

There is a considerable anti-Washington feeling throughout the country. But I think the feeling is misplaced. In the last two years, we have restored integrity in the White House, and we've set high standards in the executive branch of the government. The anti-Washington feeling, in my opinion, ought to be focused on the Congress of the United States. For example, this Congress, very shortly, will spend a billion dollars a year for its housekeeping, its salaries, its expenses, and the like. It—the next Congress will probably be the first billon-dollar Congress in the history of the United States. I don't think the American people are getting their money's worth from the majority party that run this Congress. We, in addition, see that uh— in the last uh— four years, the number of employees hired by the Congress has gone up substantial uh— much more than uh— the gross national product, much more than any other increase throughout our society. Congress is hiring people by the droves, and the cost as a result has gone up, and I don't see any improvement in the performance of the Congress under the present leadership. So it seems to me instead of the anti-Washington feeling being aimed at everybody in Washington, it seems to me that the focus should be where the problem is, which is the Congress of the United States, and particularly the majority in the Congress. They spend too much money on themselves, they have too many employees, there's some question about their morality. It seems to me that in this election, the focus should not be on the executive branch, but the corrections should come as the voters vote for their members of the House of Representatives or for their United States senator. That's where the problem is, and I hope there will be some corrective action taken, so we can get some new leadership in the Congress of the United States.

Reynolds

Mr. President, if I may follow up uh— I think you've made it plain that you take a dim view of the uh— majority in the Congress. Isn't it quite likely, sir, that you will have a Democratic Congress in the next session, if you are elected president. And hasn't the country uh— a right to ask whether you can get along with that Congress, or whether we'll have continued confrontation?

Ford

Well, it seems to me that uh— we have a chance—the Republicans—to get a majority in the House of Representatives. We will make some gains in the United States Senate. So there will be different ratios in the House, as well as in the Senate, and as president I will be able to uh— work with that Congress. But let me take the other side of the coin, if I might. Supposing we had had a Democratic Congress for the last two years and we had had uh— Governor Carter as president. He has, in effect, said that he would agree with all of—uh— he would disapprove of the vetoes that I have made, and would have added significantly to expenditures and the deficit in the federal government. I think it would be contrary to one of the basic concepts in our system of government—a system of checks and balances. We have a Democratic Congress today, and fortunately we've had a Republican president to check their excesses with my vetoes. If we have a Democratic Congress next year, and a president who wants to spend an additional one hundred billion dollars a year, or maybe two hundred billion dollars a year, with more programs, we will have uh— in my judgment, greater deficits with more spending, more dangers of inflation. I think the American people want a Republican president to check on any excesses that come out of the next Congress, if it is a Democratic Congress.

Newman

Governor Carter?

Appendix C

Carter

Well, it's not a matter of uh— Republican and Democrat, it's a matter of leadership or no leadership. Uh— President Eisenhower worked with the Democratic Congress very well. Even President Nixon, because he was a strong leader at least, worked with a Democratic Congress very well. Uh— Mr. Ford has vetoed, as I said earlier, four times as many bills per year as Mr. Nixon. Mr. Ford quite often puts forward a program just as a public relations stunt, and never tries to put it through the Congress by working with the Congress. I think under President Fo— uh— Nixon and Eisenhower they passed about sixty to seventy-five percent of their legislation. This year Mr. Ford will not pass more than twenty-six percent of all the legislative proposals he puts forward. This is government by stalemate, and we've seen almost a complete breakdown in the proper relationship between the president who represents this country, and the Congress who collectively also represent this country. We've had uh— Republican presidents before, who've tried to run against the Democratic uh— Congress and I don't think it's uh— the Congress is Mr. Ford's opponent, but if uh— if, if he insists that uh— that I be responsible for the Democratic Congress of which I am, have not been a part, then I think it's only fair that he be responsible for the Nixon Administration in its t— entirety, of which he was a part. That, I think, is a good balance. But the point is that, that a president ought to lead this country. Mr. Ford, so far as I know, except for avoiding another Watergate, has not accomplished one single major program for this country. And, there's been a constant squabbling between the president and the Congress and that's not the way this country ought to be run. I might go back to one other thing. Mr. Ford has uh— misquoted an A.P. uh— news story that was in error to begin with. That uh— story reported several times that I would lower taxes for low- and middle-income families and uh— that correction was delivered to the White House and I am sure that the President knows about this uh— correction, but he still insists uh— on repeating an erroneous statement.

Newman

President Ford, Governor Carter, we no longer have enough time for two complete sequences of questions. We have only about six minutes left for questions and answers. For that reason we will drop the follow-up questions at this point but each candidate will still be able to respond to the other's answers. Uh— to the extent that you can, gentlemen, please keep your remarks brief. Mr Gannon?

Gannon

Governor Carter, one uh— important uh— part of the government's uh— economic policy uh— apparatus that we haven't talked about is the Federal Reserve Board. I'd like to ask you something about what you've said and that is that uh— you believe that a president ought to have a chairman of the Federal Reserve Board whose views are compatible with his own. Based on the record of the last few years, would you say that your views are compatible with those of Chairman Arthur Burns. And if not, would you seek his resignation if you are elected?

Carter

What I have said is, that the president ought to have a chance to appoint the chairman of the Federal Reserve Board to have a coterminous uh— term, in other words, both of 'em serve the same four, four years. The Congress can modify the supply of money by modifying the income tax uh- laws. The president can modify the uh- economic structure of our country by published statements and general attitudes in the budget that he proposes. The Federal Reserve has a, an independent status that ought to be preserved. I think that Mr. uh— Burns did take a typical erroneous Republican attitude, in the 1973 year when inflation was so high. They assumed that the uh— inflation rate was because of excessive demand and uh— therefore put into effect tight constraint on the economy, very high interest rates, which is typical also of the Republican administration, uh— tried to increase the uh— the tax uh— payments by individuals, cut the tax payments by corporations. I would have uh— done it opposite. I think the uh— problem should have been addressed by increasing productivity, by having uh— put, put people back to work, so they could purchase more goods, lower income taxes on individuals, perhaps raise them, if necessary, on corporations in comparison. But uh— Mr. Burns uh— in that respect made a very serious mistake. I would not want to destroy the, the independence of the uh— Federal Reserve uh— Board. But I do think we ought to have a cohesive economic policy with at, at least the chairman of the Federal Reserve Board and the president's terms being uh— the same, and letting the Congress, of course, be the third uh— entity with uh— with independence, subject only to the president's veto.

Newman

President Ford, your response.

Ford

The chairman of the Federal Reserve Board should be independent. Fortunately he has been during Democratic as well as Republican administrations. As a result, in the last uh— two years uh— we have had a responsible monetary policy. Uh— the Federal Reserve Board indicated that the supply of money would be held between four to four and a half and seven and seven and a half. They have done a good job in i— integrating the money supply with the uh— fiscal policy of the uh— executive and legislative branches of the government. It would be catastrophic if the chairman of the Federal Reserve Board became the tool of the political uh— party that was in power. It's important for our future uh— eh— economic security that that job be nonpolitical and uh— separate from the executive and the legislative branches.

Newman

Mrs. Drew?

Drew

Um— Mr. President, the real problem with the F.B.I., in fact all of the intelligence agencies, is there no real laws governing them. Such laws as there are tend to be vague and open-ended. Now, you have issued some executive orders, but we've learned that leaving these agencies to executive discretion and direction can get them and, in fact, the country, in a great deal of trouble. One president may be a decent man, the next one might not be. So would, what do you think about trying to write in some more protection by getting some laws governing these agencies?

Ford

You are familiar, of course, with the fact that I am the first president in thirty years, who has reorganized the intelligence agencies in the federal government: the C.I.A., the Defense Intelligence Agency, the National Security Agency, and the others. We've done that by executive order. Uh— and I think uh— we've tightened it up, we've uh— straightened out their problems that developed over the last few years. It doesn't seem to me that it's needed or

Appendix C 235

necessary to have legislation in this particular regard. Uh— I have recommended to the Congress, however—I'm sure you're familiar with this—legislation that would uh— make it uh— very uh— proper, and uh— in the right way, that the Attorney General could go in and get the right for wiretapping under security cases. This was an effort that was made by the Attorney General and myself, working with the Congress. But even in this area, where I think new legislation would be justified, uh— the Congress has not responded. So I feel in that case, as well as in the reorganization of the intelligence agencies, as I've done, we have to do it by executive order, and I'm glad that we have a good director in George Bush, we have good executive orders, and the C.I.A. and the D.I.A. and NASA uh— ah— N.S.A. are now doing a good job under proper supervision.

Newman

Governor Carter?

Carter

Well, one of the very serious things that's happened in our government in recent years, and has continued uh— up until now, is a breakdown in the trust among our people in the . . .

[Interruption 6]

Newman

. . .uh— during Governor Carter's response to what would have been, and what was, the last question put to the candidates. That question went to President Ford. It dealt with the control of government intelligence agencies. Uh— Governor Carter was making his response and had very nearly finished it. Uh— he will conclude that response now, after which uh— President Ford and Governor Carter will make their closing statements. Governor?

Carter

There has been too much government secrecy and not uf— not enough respect for the personal privacy of American citizens.

Newman

It is now time for the closing statements, which are to be up to four minutes long. Governor Carter, by the same toss of the coin that directed the first question to you, you are to go first now.

Carter

Well, tonight we've had a chance to talk a lot about the past. But I think it's time to talk about the future. Our nation in the last eight years has been divided as never before. It's a time for unity. It's a time to draw ourselves together. To have a president and a congress that can work together, with mutual respect, for a change, cooperating for a change, in the open for a change. So the people can understand their own government. It's time for government, industry, and labor, manufacturing, agriculture, education, other entities in our society to cooperate. And it's a time for government to understand and to cooperate with our people. For a long time our American citizens have been excluded, sometimes misled, sometimes have been lied to. This is uh— not compatible with the purpose of our nation. I believe in our country. It needs to be competent. The government needs to be well-managed, efficient, economical. We need to have a government that's sensitive to our people's needs, to those who are poor, who don't have adequate health care, who have been cheated too long with our tax programs, who've been out of jobs, whose families have been torn apart. And we need to restore the faith and the trust of the American people in their own government. In addition to that, we've suffered because we haven't had leadership in this administration. We've got a government of stalemate. We've lost the vision of what our country can and oughta be. This is not the America that we've known in the past. It's not the America that we have to have in the future. I don't claim to know all the answers. But I've got confidence in my country. Our economic strength is still there. Our system of government—in spite of Vietnam, Cambodia, C.I.A., Watergate—is still the best system of government on earth. And the greatest resource of all, are the two hundred and fifteen million Americans, who still have within us the strength, the character, the intelligence, the experience, the patriotism, the idealism, the compassion, the sense of brotherhood, on which we can rely in the future, to restore the greatness to our country. We ought not to be excluded from our government any more. We need a president who can go in, who derives his strength from the people. I owe the special interests nothing. I owe everything to you, the people of this country. And I believe that we can bind our wounds. I believe that we can work together. And I believe that wif— we can tap the tremendous untapped reservoir of innate strength in this country, that we can once again have a government as good as our people, and let the world know what we still know and hope for—that we still live in the greatest, and the strongest, and the best country on earth.

Newman

President Ford?

Ford

On November second all of you will make a very, very important decision. One of the major issues in this campaign is trust. A president should never promise more than he can deliver, and a president should always deliver everything that he's promised. A president can't be all things to all people. A president should be the same thing to all people. Another issue in this campaign. Governor Carter has endorsed the Democratic platform, which calls for more spending, bigger deficits, more inflation, or more taxes. Governor Carter has embraced the record of the present Congress, dominated by his political party. It calls for more of the same. Governor Carter in his acceptance speech called for more and more programs, which means more and more government. I think the real issue in this campaign, and that which you must decide on November second, is whether you should vote for his promises or my performance in two years in the White House. On the Fourth of July, we had a wonderful two hundredth birthday for our great country. It was a wo— superb occasion. It was a glorious day. In the first century of our nation's history our forefathers gave us the finest form of government in the history of mankind. In the second century of our nation's history, our forefathers developed the most productive industrial nation in the history of the globe. Our third century should be the century of individual freedom for all our two hundred and fifteen million Americans today, and all that join us. In the last few years government has gotten bigger and bigger. Industry has gotten larger and larger, labor unions have gotten bigger and bigger, and our children have been the victims of mass education. We must make this next century, the century of the individual. We should never forget that a government big enough to give us everything we want, is a government big enough to take from us everything we have. The individual worker in the plants throughout the United States, should not be a small cog in a big machine. The member of the labor union must have his rights strengthened and broadened, and our children in their education should have an opportunity to improve themselves based on their talents and their abilities. My mother and father, during the Depression, worked very hard to give me an opportunity to do better in our great country. Your mothers and fathers did the same thing for you and others. Betty and I have worked very hard to give our children a brighter future in the United States, our beloved country. You and others in this great country have worked hard and done a great deal to give your children and your grandchildren the blessings of a better America. I believe we can all work together, to make the individuals in the future have more, and all of us working together can build a better America.

Newman

Thank you, President Ford. Thank you, Governor Carter. Our thanks also to the questioners and to the audience in this theater. Uh— we much regret the technical failure that caused a twenty-eight minute delay in the broadcast of the debate. We believe, however, that everyone will agree that it did not detract from the effectiveness of the debate or from its fairness. The next presidential debate is to take place on Wednesday, October sixth in San Francisco at nine-thirty p.m. eastern daylight time. The topics are to be foreign and defense issues. As with all three debates between the presidential candidates and the one between the vice-presidential candidates, it is being arranged by the League of Women Voters' Education Fund in the hope of promoting a wider and better-informed participation by the American people in the election in November. Now, from the Walnut Street Theater in Philadelphia, good night.

Appendix D

The Second Presidential Debate: October 6, 1976, San Francisco

Frederick

Good evening. I'm Pauline Frederick of N.P.R., moderator of this second of the historic debates of the 1976 campaign between Gerald R. Ford of Michigan, Republican candidate for president, and Jimmy Carter of Georgia, Democratic candidate for president. Thank you President Ford, and thank you Governor Carter, for being with us tonight. This debate takes place before an audience in the Palace of Fine Arts Theater in San Francisco. An estimated one hundred million Americans are watching on television as well. San Francisco was the site of the signing of the United Nations Charter, thirty-one years ago. Thus, it is an appropriate place to hold this debate, the subject of which is foreign and defense issues. The questioners tonight are Max Frankel, associate editor of the New York *Times*, Henry L. Trewhitt, diplomatic correspondent of the Baltimore *Sun*, and Richard Valeriani, diplomatic correspondent of NBC News. The ground rules tonight are basically the same as they were for the first debate two weeks ago. The questions will be alternated between candidates. By the toss of a coin, Governor Carter will take the first question. Each question sequence will be as follows. The question will be asked and the candidate will have up to three minutes to answer. His opponent will have up to two minutes to respond. And prior to the response, the questioner may ask a follow-up question to clarify the candidate's answer when necessary, with up to two minutes to reply. Each candidate will have three minutes for a closing statement at the end. President Ford and Governor Carter do not have notes or prepared remarks with them this evening, but they may take notes during the debate and refer to them. Mr. Frankel, you have the first question for Governor Carter.

Frankel

Governor, since the Democrats last ran our foreign policy, including many of the men who are advising you, country has been relieved of the Vietnam agony, and the military draft, we've started arms control negotiations with the Russians, we've opened relations with China, we've arranged the disengagement in the Middle East, we've regained influence with the Arabs without deserting Israel, now maybe, we've even begun a process of peaceful change in Africa. Now you've objected in this campaign to the style with which much of this was done, and you've mentioned some other things that, that you think ought to have been done. But do you really have a quarrel with this Republican record? Would you not have done any of those things?

Appendix D   *239*

Carter

Well I think this Republican administration has been almost all style and spectacular and not substance. We've uh— got a chance tonight to talk about, first of all, leadership, the character of our country, and a vision of the future. In every one of these instances, the Ford administration has failed, and I hope tonight that I and Mr. Ford will have a chance to discuss the reason for those failures. Our country is not strong any more, we're not respected any more. We can only be strong overseas if we're strong at home. And, when I become president we'll not only be strong in those areas but also in defense—a defense capability second to none. We've lost in our foreign policy, the character of the American people. We've uh— ignored or excluded the American people and the Congress from participation in the shaping of our foreign policy, it's been one of secrecy and exclusion. In addition to that we've had a chance to become now—contrary to our longstanding beliefs and principles—the arms merchant of the whole world. We've tried to buy success from our enemies, and at the same time we've excluded from the process, the normal friendship of our allies. In addition to that, we've become fearful to compete with the Soviet Union on an equal basis. We talk about detente. The Soviet Union knows what they want in detente, and they've been getting it. We have not known what we've wanted, and we've been outtraded in almost every instance. The other point I want to make is about our defense. We've got to be a nation blessed with a defense capability that's efficient, tough, capable, well organized, narrowly focused, fighting capability. The ability to fight if necessary, is the best way to avoid the chance for, or the requirement to fight. And the last point I want to make is this. Mr. Ford, Mr. Kissinger have uh— continued on with the policies and failures of Richard Nixon. Even the Republican platform has criticized the lack of leadership in Mr. Ford, and they've criticized the foreign policy of this administration. This is one instance where I agree with, with the Republican platform. I might say this in closing, and that is that as far as foreign policy goes, Mr. Kissinger has been the president of this country. Mr. Ford has shown an absence of leadership, and an absence of a grasp of what this country is and what it ought to be. That's got to be changed. And that is one of the major issues in this uh— campaign of eh— 1976.

Frederick

President Ford, would you like to respond?

Ford

Governor Carter again is talking in broad generalities. Let me take just one question that he raises, the military strength and capability of the United States. Governor Carter in November of 1975 indicated that he wanted to cut the defense budget by fifteen billion dollars. A few months later, he said he wanted to cut the defense budget by eight or nine billion dollars. And more recently, he talks about cutting the defense budget by five to seven billion dollars. There is no way you can be strong militarily and have those kind of reductions in our military uh— appropriations. Now let me just tell you a little story. About uh— late October of 1975, I asked the then Secretary of Defense, Mr. Schlesinger, to tell me what had to be done if we were going to reduce the defense budget by uh— three to five billion dollars. A few days later Mr. Schlesinger came back and said if we cut the defense budget by three to five billion dollars, we will have to cut military personnel by two hundred and fifty thousand, civilian personnel by a hundred thousand, jobs in America by a hundred thousand. We would have to stretch out our aircraft procurement. We would have to reduce our naval construction program. We would have to reduce the uh— research and development for the Army, the Navy, the Air Force and Marines, by eight percent. We would have to close twenty military bases in the United States immediately. That's the kind of a defense program that uh— Mr. Carter wants. Let me tell you this straight from the shoulder. You don't negotiate with Mr. Brezhnev from weakness, and the kind of a defense program that Mr. Carter wants will mean a weaker defense and a poorer negotiating position.

Frederick

Mr. Trewhitt, a question for President Ford.

Trewhitt

Mr. President, my question really is the other side of the coin from Mr. Frankel's. For a generation the United States has had a foreign policy based on containment of communism. Yet we have lost the first war in Vietnam, we lost a shoving match in Angola. Uh— Communists threatened to come to power by peaceful means in Italy and relations generally have cooled with the Soviet Union in the last few months. So las— let me ask you first—what do you do about such cases as Italy? And secondly, does this general drift mean that we're moving back toward something like an old cor— cold war relationship with the Soviet Union?

Ford

I don't believe we should move to a cold war relationship. I think it's in the best interest of the United States, and n— the world as a whole, that the United States negotiate rather than go back to the cold war relationship with the Soviet Union. I don't uh— look at the picture as bleakly as you have indicated in your question, Mr. Trewhitt. I believe that the United States has had many successes in recent years, in recent months, as far as the Communist movement is concerned. We have been successful in Portugal, where a year ago it looked like there was a very great possibility that the uh— Communists would take over in Portugal. It didn't happen. We have a democracy in Portugal today. A few uh— months ago—or I should say maybe two years ago—the Soviet Union looked like they had continued strength in the Middle East. Today, according to Prime Minister Rabin, the Soviet Union is weaker in the Middle East than they have been in many, many years. The facts are, there the Soviet Union relationship with Egypt is uh— at a low level. The Soviet Union relationship with Syria is at a very low point. The United States today, according to Prime Minister Rabin of Israel, is a— at a peak in its uh— influence and power in the Middle East. But let's turn for a minute to the uh— southern African operations that are now going on. The United States of America took the initiative in southern Africa. We wanted to end the bloodshed in southern Africa. We wanted to have the right of self-determination in southern Africa. We wanted to have majority rule with the full protection of the rights of the minority. We wanted to preserve human dignity in southern Africa. We have taken the initiative, and in southern Africa today, the United States is trusted by the black front-line nations and black Africa. The United States is trusted by the other elements in southern Africa. The United States foreign policy under this administration has been one of progress and success. And I believe that instead of talking about Soviet progress, we can talk about American successes. And may I make an observation, part of the question you asked, Mr. Trewhitt? I don't believe that it's in the best interest of the United States and the NATO nations to have a Communist government in NATO. Mr. Carter has indicated he would look with sympathy to a Communist government in NATO. I think that would destroy the integrity and the strength of NATO, and I am totally opposed to it.

Appendix D

Carter

Uh— Mr. Ford unfortunately has just made a statement that's not true. I have never advocated a Communist government for Italy. That would obviously be a ridiculous thing for anyone to do who wanted to be president of this country. I think that this is uh— an instance of uh— deliberate distortion, and this is occurred, also in the question about defense. As a matter of fact uh— I've never advocated any cut of fifteen billion dollars in our defense budget. As a matter of fact, Mr. Ford has made a political football out of the defense budget. About a year ago he cut the Pentagon budget six point eight billion dollars. After he fired James Schlesinger, the political heat got so great that he added back about three billion dollars. When Ronald Reagan won the Texas primary election, Mr. Ford added back another one and half billion dollars. Immediately before the Kansas City convention, he added back another one point eight billion dollars in the defense budget. And his own uh— Office of Management and Budget testified that he had a three billion dollar cut insurance added to the defense debudget, defense budget under the pressure from the Pentagon. Obviously, this is another indication of trying to use the defense budget for political purposes, which he's trying to do tonight. Now we've went into South Africa late, after Great Britain, Rhodesia, the black nations had been trying to solve this problem for many, many years. We didn't go in until right before the election, similar to what was taking place in 1972, when Mr. Kissinger announced peace is at hand, just before the election at that time. And uh— we have weakened our position in NATO because the other countries in Europe supported the demo— democratic forces in Portugal long before we did, we stuck to the Portugal dictatorships much longer than other democracies did in this world.

Frederick

Mr. Valeriani, a question for Governor Carter.

Valeriani

Governor Carter, much of what the United States does abroad is done in the name of the national interest. What is your concept of the national interest? What should the role of the United States in the world be? And in that connection, considering your limited experience in foreign affairs, and the fact that you take some pride in being a Washington outsider, don't you think it would be appropriate for you to tell the American voters, before the election, the people that you would like to have in key positions, such as Secretary of State, Secretary of Defense, national security affairs adviser at the White House?

Carter

Well, I'm not gonna name my Cabinet before I get elected. I've got a little ways to go before I start doing that. But I have uh— an adequate background, I believe. I am a graduate of the U.S. Naval Academy, our first military graduate since uh— Eisenhower. I've served as governor of Georgia, and have traveled extensively in foreign countries in South America, Central America, Europe, the Middle East, and in Japan. I've traveled the last twenty-one months among the people of this country. I've talked to them and I've listened. And I've seen at first hand, in a very vivid way, the deep hurt that's come to this country, in the aftermath of Vietnam and Cambodia and Chile and Pakistan, and Angola and Watergate, C.I.A. revelations; What we were formerly so proud of, the strength of our country, its uh— moral integrity, the representation in foreign affairs of what our people or what our Constitution stands for—has been gone. And in the secrecy that has surrounded our foreign policy in the last few years, uh— the American people, the Congress have been excluded. I believe I know what this country ought to be. I've uh– been one who's loved my nation as many Americans do, and I believe that there's no limit placed on what we can be in the future, if we can harness the tremendous resources, militarily, economically, and the stature of our people, the meaning of our Constitution, in the future. Every time we've made a serious mistake in foreign affairs, it's been because the American people have been excluded from the process. If we can just tap the intelligence and ability, the sound common sense, and the good judgment of the American people, we can once again have a foreign policy that will make us proud instead of ashamed. And I'm not going to exclude the American people from that process in the future, as Mr. Ford and Kissinger have done. This is what it takes to have a sound foreign policy–strong at home, strong defense, permanent commitments–not betray the principles of our country and involve the American people and the Congress in the shaping of our foreign policy. Every time Mr. Ford speaks, from a position of secrecy in negotiations and seca– ec– in secret treaties that have been uh– pursued and achieved in supporting dictatorships, in ignoring human rights, we are weak, and the rest of the world knows it. So these are the ways that we can restore the strength of our country, and they don't require long experience in foreign policy, nobody has that except a president who's served a long time or a secretary of state. But my background, my experience, my knowledge of the people of this country, my commitment to our principles that don't change–those are the best bases to correct the horrible mistakes of this administration, and restore our own country to a position of leadership in the world.

Valeriani

How specifically, uh– Governor, are you going to bring the American people into the decision-making process uh– in foreign policy? What does that mean?

Carter

First of all, I would quit conducting the decision-making process in secret, as has been a characteristic of Mr. Kissinger and Mr. Ford. In many instances we've made agreements, like in Vietnam un– that have uh– been revealed later on to our uh– embarrassment. Recently Ian Smith, the uh– president of uh– Rhodesia, announced that he had unequivocal commitments from Mr. Kissinger that he could not reveal. The American people don't know what those commitments are. We've seen uh– in the past a destruction of elected governments, like in Chile, and the strong support of military dictatorship there. These kinds of things have hurt us very much. I would restore the concept of the fireside chat, which was an integral part of the administration of Franklin Roosevelt. And I would also restore the involvement of the Congress. When Harry Truman was president, he was not afraid to have a strong secretary of defense. Dean Acheson, George Marshall were strong Secretaries of uh– State 'scuse me– State. But he also made sure that there was a bipartisan support. The members of Congress, Arthur Vandenburg, Walter George, were part of the process, and before our nation made a secret agreement, or before we made a bluffing statement, we were sure that we had the backing not only of the president and the Secretary of State, but also the Congress and the people. This is a responsibility to the president, and I think it's very damaging to our country for Mr. Ford to have turned over this responsibility to the Secretary of State.

Frederick

President Ford, do you have a response?

Appendix D

Ford

Governor Carter again contradicts himself. He complains about secrecy, and yet he is quoted as saying that in the attempt to find a solution in the Middle East, that he would hold unpublicized meetings with the Soviet Union, I presume for the purpose of an imposing a settlement on Israel and the Arab nations. But let me talk just a minute about what we've done to avoid secrecy in the Ford administration. After the United States took the initiative in working with Israel and with Egypt, and achieving the Sinai Two agreement—and I'm proud to say that not a single Egyptian or Israeli soldier has lost his life since the signing of the Sinai agreement. But at the time that uh— I submitted the Sinai agreement to the Congress of the United States, I submitted every single document that was applicable to the Sinai Two agreement. It was the most complete documentation by any president of any agreement signed by a president on behalf of the United States. Now as far as meeting with the Congress is concerned, during the twenty-four months that I've been the President of the United States, I have averaged better than one meeting a month with responsible groups or committees of the Congress—both House and Senate. The Secretary of State has appeared in the several years that he's been the Secretary, before eighty different uh— committee hearings in the House and in the Senate. The Secretary of State has made better than fifty speeches, all over the United States explaining American foreign policy. I have made myself, at least ten uh— speeches in various parts of the country, where I have discussed with the American people defense and foreign policy.

Frederick

Mr. Frankel, a question for President Ford.

Frankel

Mr. President, I'd like to explore a little more deeply our relationship with the Russians. They used to brag back in Khrushchev's day that because of their greater p— patience and because of our greed for, for business deals, that they would sooner or later get the better of us. Is it possible that despite some setbacks in the Middle East, they've proved their point? Our allies in France and Italy are now flirting with communism. We've recognized a permanent communist regime in East Germany. We've virtually signed in Helsinki an agreement that the Russians have dominance in Eastern Europe. We've bailed out Soviet agriculture with our huge grain sales. We've given them large loans, access to our best technology and if the Senate hadn't interfered with the Jackson Amendment, maybe you would have given them even larger loans. Is that what you call a two-way street of traffic in Europe?

Ford

I believe that we have uh— negotiated with the Soviet Union since I've been president from a position of strength. And let me cite several examples. Shortly after I became president in uh— December of 1974, I met with uh— General Secretary Brezhnev in Vladivostok, and we agreed to a mutual cap on the ballistic missile launchers, at a ceiling of twenty-four hundred, which means that the Soviet Union, if that becomes a permanent agreement, will have to make a reduction in their launchers that they now have or plan to have. I negotiated at Vladivostok with uh— Mr. Brezhnev, a limitation on the MIRVing of their uh— ballistic missiles at a figure of thirteen twenty, which is the first time that any president has achieved a cap either on launchers or on MIRVs. It seems to me that we can go from there to uh— the uh— grain sales. The grain sales have been a benefit to American agriculture. We have achieved a five and three-quarter-year uh— sale of a minimum of six million metric tons, which means that they have already bought about four million metric tons this year, and are bound to buy another two million metric tons to take the grain and corn and wheat that the American farmers have produced, in order to uh— have full production, and these grain sales to the Soviet Union have helped us tremendously in meeting the costs of the additional oil and the oil that we have bought from overseas. If we turn to Helsinki—I'm glad you raised it, Mr. uh— Frankel. In the case of Helsinki, thirty-five nations signed an agreement, including the Secretary of State for the Vatican. I can't under any circumstances believe that the—His Holiness the Pope—would agree, by signing that agreement, that the thirty-five nations have turned over to the Warsaw Pact nations the domination of uh— Eastern Europe. It just isn't true. And if Mr. Carter alleges that His Holiness by signing that has done it, he is totally inaccurate. Now what has been accomplished by the Helsinki agreement? Number one, we have an agreement where they notify us and we notify them of any uh— military maneuvers that are to be undertaken. They have done it, in both cases where they've done so. There is no Soviet domination of Eastern Europe and there never will be under a Ford administration.

Frankel

Uh— I

[Interruption 1]

Frederick

Mr. Carter.

Frankel

I'm sorry, I wan— could I just fol— did I understand you to say sir, that the Russians are not using Eastern Europe as their own sphere of influence in occupying mo— most of the countries there and in s— making sure with their troops that it's a, that it's a Communist zone, whereas on our side of the line, the Italians and the French are still flirting with the possibility . . .

[Interruption 2]

Ford

I don't believe

[Interruption 3]

Frankel

of communism.

Ford

uh— Mr. Frankel, that uh— the Yugoslavians consider themselves dominated by the Soviet Union. I don't believe that the Rumanians consider themselves dominated by the Soviet Union. I don't believe that the Poles consider themselves dominated by the Soviet Union. Each of those countries is independent, autonomous, it has its own territorial integrity, and the United States does not concede that those countries are under the domination of the

Appendix D

Soviet Union. As a matter of fact, I visited Poland, uh— Yugoslavia, and Rumania, to make certain that the people of those countries understood that the President of the United States and the people of the United States are dedicated to their independence, their autonomy, and their freedom.

Frederick

Governor Carter, have you a response?

Carter

Ha. Well in the first place, I'm not criticizing His Holiness the Pope. I was talking about Mr. Ford. The uh— fact is that secrecy has surrounded the decisions made by the Ford administration. In the case of uh— the Helsinki agreement, it may have been a good agreement at the beginning, but we have failed to enforce the so-called Basket Three part, which insures the right of people to migrate, to join their families, to be free, to speak out. The Soviet Union is still jamming Radio F— Free Europe—Radio uh— uh— Radio Free Europe is being jammed. We've also seen a very serious uh— problem with the so-called Sonnenfeldt document—which apparently Mr. Ford has just endorsed—which said that there's an organic linkage between the Eastern European countries and the Soviet Union. And I would like to see Mr. Ford convince the Polish-Americans and the Czech-Americans and the Hungarian-Americans in this country, that those countries don't live under the domination and supervision of the Soviet Union behind the Iron Curt— uh— Curtain. We also have seen Mr. Ford exclude himself from access to the public. He hasn't had a tough, cross-examination-type press conference in over thirty days. One press conference he had without sound. He's often shown a weakness in yielding to pressure. The Soviet Union for instance, put pressure on Mr. Ford, and he refused to see a symbol of human freedom recognized around the world, Aleksandr Solzhenitsyn. The Arabs have put pressure on Mr. Ford and he's yielded, and has permitted a boycott by the Arab countries, of American businesses who trade with Israel, or who have American Jews owning or taking part in the management of American comp— contri— companies. His own Secretary of Commerce had to be subpoenaed by the Congress, to reveal the names of businesses who were subject to this boycott. They didn't volunteer the information. He had to be subpoenaed. And the last thing I'd like to say is this. This grain deal, with the Soviet Union in '72 was terrible, and Mr. Ford made up for it with three embargoes, one against our own ally in Japan. That's not the way to run our foreign policy, including international trade.

Frederick

Mr. Trewhitt, a question for Governor Carter.

Trewhitt

Governor, I'd like to pick up on that point, actually, and on your appeal for a greater measure of American idealism in foreign affairs. Foreign affairs come home to the American public pretty much in such issues as oil embargoes and grain sales, that sort of thing. Would you be willing to, to risk an oil embargo, in order to promote human rights in Iran, Saudi Arabia, withhold arms from Saudi Arabia for the same purpose? Um— wha—war— I think you, matter of fact you've m— perhaps answered this final part, but would you withhold grain from the Soviet Union, in order to promote ci— civil rights in the, in the Soviet Union?

Carter

I would never single out food as a trade embargo item, if I ever decided to impose an embargo because of a crisis in international relationships, it would include all shipments of all equipment. For instance, if the Arab countries ever again declare an embargo against our nation on oil, I would consider that not a military but an economic declaration of war, and I would respond instantly and in kind. I would not ship that Arab country anything—no weapons, no spare parts for weapons, no oil-drilling rigs, no oilpipe, no nothing. I wouldn't single out just food. Another thing I'd like to say is this. In our international trade, as I said in my op— opening statement, we have become the arms merchant of the world. When this Republican administration came into office, we were shipping about one billion dollars worth of arms overseas, now ten to twelve billion dollars worth of arms overseas, to countries that quite often use these weapons to fight each other. The shift in emphasis has been very disturbing to me, speaking about the Middle East. Under the last Democratic administration, sixty percent of all weapons that went into the Middle East were for Israel. Nowadays, seventy-five percent were for Israel before. Now sixty percent go to the Arab countries, and this does not include Iran. If you include Iran, our present shipment of weapons to the Middle East, only twenty percent goes to Israel. This is a deviation from idealism, it's a deviation from a commitment to our major ally in the Middle East, which is Israel, it's a yielding to economic pressure on the part of the Arabs, on the oil issue, and it's also a tremendous indication that under the Ford administration, we have not addressed the energy policy adequately. We still have no comprehensive energy policy in this country. And it's an overall sign of weakness. When we're weak at home e— economically, high unemployment, high inflation, a confused government, a wasteful defense establishment, this encourages the kind of pressure that's been put on us successfully. It would have been inconceivable ten, fifteen years, ago for us to be brought to our knees with an Arab oil embargo. But it was done three years ago, and they're still putting pressure on us from the Arab countries, to our discredit around the world. These are the weaknesses that I see, and I believe it's not just a matter of idealism, it's a matter of being tough. It's a matter of being strong, it's a matter of being consistent. Our priorities ought to be first of all to meet our own military needs, secondly to meet the needs of our allies and friends, and only then should we ship military equipment to foreign countries. As a matter of fact, Iran is gonna get eighty F-14s before we even meet our own Air Force orders for F-14s. And the shipment of Spruance-class destroyers to Iran, are much more highly sophisticated than the Spruance-class destroyers that are present being delivered to our own Navy. This is ridiculous, and it ought to be changed.

Trewhitt

Governor, let me pursue that if I may. If I understand you correctly you would in fact, to use my examples, withhold arms from Iran and Saudi Arabia even if the risk was an oil embargo and if they should be securing those arms from somewhere else, and then if the embargo came, then you would respond in kind. Do I have it correctly?

Carter

If Iran is not an Arab country, as you know ...

[Interruption 4]

Trewhitt

I know.

Appendix D 247

Carter

it is a Moslem country. But if Saudi Arabia should declare an oil embargo against us, then I would consider that an economic declaration of war. And I would make sure that the uh– Saudis understood this ahead of time, so there would be no doubt in their mind. I think under those circumstances, they would refrain from pushing us to our knees as they did in 1973 with their previous oil embargo.

Frederick

President Ford.

Ford

Governor Carter um– apparently doesn't realize that since I've been president, we have sold to the Israelis over four billion dollars in military hardware. We have made available to the Israelis over forty-five percent of the total economic and military aid since the establishment of Israel twenty-seven years ago. So the Ford administration has done a good job in helping our good ally Israel, and we're dedicated to the survival and security of Israel. I believe that Governor Carter doesn't realize the need and necessity for arms sales to Iran. He indicates he would not make those. Iran is bordered very extensively by the Soviet Union. Iran has Iraq as one of its neighbors. The Soviet Union and the communist-dominated government of Iraq are neighbors of Iran, and Iran is an ally of the United States. It's my strong feeling that we ought to sell arms to Iran for its own national security, and as an ally, a strong ally of the United States. The history of our relationship with Iran goes back to the days of President Truman, when he decided that it was vitally necessary for our own security as well as that of Iran, that we should help that country. And Iran has been a good ally. In 1973, when there was an oil embargo, Iran did not participate. Iran continued to sell oil to the United States. I believe that it's in our interest, and in the interest of Israel and Iran and Saudi Arabia, for the United States to sell arms to those countries. It's for their security as well as ours.

Frederick

Mr. Valeriani, a question for President Ford.

Valeriani

Mr. President, the policy of your administration is to normalize relations with mainland China. And that means establishing at some point full diplomatic relations, and obviously doing something about the mutual defense treaty with Taiwan. If you are elected, will you move to establish full diplomatic relations with Peking, and will you abrogate the mutual defense treaty with Taiwan? And, as a corollary, would you provide mainland China with military equipment, if the Chinese were to ask for it?

Ford

Our relationship with the People's Republic of China is based upon the Shanghai Communique of 1972, and that communique calls for the normalization of relations between the United States and the People's Republic. It doesn't set a time schedule. It doesn't uh– make a determination as to how uh– that relationship should be achieved, in relationship to our current uh– diplomatic recognition and obligations to the Taiwanese government. The Shanghai Communique does say that the eh– differences between the People's Republic on the one hand and Taiwan on the other, shall be settled by peaceful means. The net result is, this administration, and during my time as the president for the next four years, we will continue to move for normalization of relations in the traditional sense, and we will insist that the disputes between Taiwan and the People's Republic be settled peacefully, as was agreed in the Shanghai Communique of 1972. The Ford administration will not let down, will not eliminate or forget our obligation to the people of Taiwan. We feel that there must be a continued obligation to the people, the some nineteen or twenty million people in Taiwan. And as we move during the next four years, those will be the policies of this administration.

Valeriani

And sir, the military equipment for the mainland Chinese?

Ford

There is no policy of this government to give to the People's Republic, or to sell to the People's Republic of China, military equipment. I do not believe that we, the United States, should sell, give, or otherwise transfer, military hardware to the People's Republic of China, or any other Communist nation, such as the Soviet Union, and the like.

Frederick

Governor Carter.

Carter

Well I'd like to go back just one moment to the previous question, where uh— Mr. Ford, I think, confused the issue by trying to say that we are shipping Israel forty percent of our aid. As a matter of fact, during this current year, uh— we are shipping Iran, or have contracted to ship to Iran, about seven and a half billion dollars worth of arms, and also to Saudi Arabia, about seven and a half billion dollars worth of arms. Also in 1975, we almost brought Israel to their knees, after the uh— Yom Kippur War, by the r— so-called reassessment of our relationship to Israel. We in effect tried to make Israel the scapegoat for the problems in the Middle East, and this weakened our relationships with Israel a great deal and put a cloud on the total commitment that our people feel toward the Israelis. There ought to be a clear, unequivocal commitment without change, to Israel. In the Far East, I think we need to continue to be uh— strong, and uh— I would certainly uh— pursue the uh— normalization of uh— relationships with the People's Republic of China. We opened up a great opportunity in 1972, which has pretty well been frittered aray, frit— frittered away under Mr. Ford, that ought to be a constant uh— in connection toward uh— toward friendship, but I would never let that friendship with the People's Republic of China stand in the way of the preservation of the independence and freedom of the people on Taiwan.

Frederick

Mr. Frankel, a question for Governor Carter.

Frankel

Governor, we always seem in our elections, and maybe in between too, to argue about uh— who can be tougher, in the world. Give or take a, a few billion dollars, give or take one weapons systems, our leading politicians, and I think you two gentlemen, seem to settle

Appendix D 249

roughly on the same strategy in the world, at roughly the same Pentagon budget cost. How bad do things have to get in our own economy, or how much backwardness and hunger would it take in the world to persuade you that our national security, and our survival, required very drastic cutbacks in arms spending and dramatic new efforts in other directions?

Carter

Well, always in the past we've had an ability to have a strong defense and also have, to have a strong uh– domestic economy, and also to be strong in our reputation and influence within the community of nations. These uh– characteristics of our country have been endangered under Mr. Ford. We are no longer respected, in a showdown vote in the United Nations or in, in any other international council, we're lucky to get twenty percent of the other nations to vote with us. Our allies feel that we've neglected them. The so-called Nixon shocks against Japan have weakened our relationships there. Under this administration we've also had an inclination to s– keep separate the European countries, thinking that if they are separate, then we can dominate them and proceed with our secret, Lone Ranger-type diplomatic efforts. I would uh– also like to point out that we, in this country, have let our economy go down the drain. The worst inflation since the Great Depression. The highest unemployment of any developed nation of the world. We have a higher unemployment rate in this country than Great Britain, than West Germany. Our unemployment rate is twice as high as it is in Italy, is three or four times as high as it is, as it is, in Japan. And that terrible circumstance in this country is exported overseas. We comprise about thirty percent of eh– world's economic trade power influence. And when we're weak at home–weaker than all our allies– that weakness weakens the whole free world. So strong economy is very important. Another thing that we need to do is to reestablish the good relationships that we ought to have between the United States and our natural allies and friends. They've have felt neglected. And using that base of strength, and using the idealism, the honesty, the predictability, the commitment, the integrity, of our own country, that's where our strength lies. And that would permit us to deal with the developing nations in a position of strength. Under this administration we've had a continuation of the so-called balance-of-power politics, where everything is looked on as a struggle between us on the one side, the Soviet Union on the other. Our allies, the smaller countries get trampled in the rush. What we need is to try to seek individualized bilateral relationships with countries regardless of their size, and to establish world-order politics, which means that we want to preserve peace through strength. We also want to revert back to the stature and the respect that our country had in previous administrations. Now, I can't say when this can come. But I can guarantee it will not come if Gerald Ford is reelected and this present policy is continued. It will come if I'm elected.

Frankel

If I hear you right, sir, you're saying guns and butter both, but President Johnson also had trouble uh– keeping up both Vietnam and his domestic programs. I was really asking, when do the, the needs of the cities and our own needs and those of other backward and, and even more needy countries and societies around the world take precedence over some of our military spending. Ever?

Carter

Well let me say very quickly that under President Johnson, in spite of the massive investment in the Vietnam War, he turned over a balanced budget to Mr. Nixon. The unemployment rate was less than four percent. The inflation rate under Kennedy and Johnson was about two percent–one-third what is under this administration. So we did have at that time with good management, the ability to do both. I don't think anybody can say that Johnson and Kennedy neglected the poor and the destitute people in this country or around the world. But I can say this. The number one responsibility of any president, above all else, is to guarantee the security of our nation, an ability to be free of the threat of attack, or blackmail, and to carry out our obligations to our allies and friends, and to carry out a legitimate foreign policy. They must go hand in hand, but the security of this nation has got to come first.

Frederick

President Ford?

Ford

Let me say very categorically, you cannot maintain the security and the strength of the United States with the kind of defense budget cuts that Governor Carter has indicated. In 1975, he wanted to cut the budget fifteen billion dollars. He's now down to a figure of five to seven billion dollars. Reductions of that kind will not permit the United States to be strong enough to deter aggression and maintain the peace. Governor Carter apparently doesn't know the facts. As soon as I became president, I initiated meetings with the NATO heads of state and met with them in Brussels to discuss how we could improve the re— defense relationship in Western Europe. In uh— November of 1975, I met with the leaders of the five industrial nations in France, for the purpose of seeing what we could do acting together, to meet the problems of uh— the coming recession. In Puerto Rico this year, I met with six of the leading industrial nations' heads of state, to meet the problem of inflation so we would be able to solve it before it got out of hand. I have met with the heads of government bilaterally, as well as multilaterally. Our relations with Japan have never been better. I was the first United States president to visit Japan, and we uh— had the emperor of Japan here this us— past year, and the net result is, Japan and the United States are working more closely together now than at any time in the history of our relationship. You can go around the world—and let me take Israel for example. Just recently, President Rabin said that our relations were never better.

Frederick

Mr. Trewhitt, a question for President Ford.

Trewhitt

Mr. President, uh— you referred earlier to your meeting with Mr. Brezhnev at Vladivostok in 1974. At y— you agreed on that occasion to try to achieve another strategic arms limitation—SALT—agreement uh— within the year. Uh— nothing happened in 1975, or not very much publicly at least. And those talks are still dragging and eh— things got quieter as the current season approached. Is there, is there a bit of politics involved there, perhaps on both sides? Or perhaps more important, are interim weapons developments—and I'm thinking of such things as the cruise missile and the Soviet SS-20 intermediate-range rocket—making SALT irrelevant, by-passing the SALT negotiations?

Ford

First we have to understand that SALT One expire October third, 1977. Uh— Mr. Brezhnev and I met in Vladivostok in December of 1974 for the purpose of trying to take the initial step so we could have a SALT Two agreement that would go to 1985. As I indicated earlier, we did agree on a twenty-four hundred limitation on um— uh— launchers of ballistic missiles. Uh— that would mean a cutback in the Soviet program, it would not interfere with our

Appendix D 251

own program. At the same time we put a limitation of thirteen hundred and twenty on MIRVs. Our technicians have been working since that time in Geneva, trying to put into technical language a, an agreement that can be verified by both parties. In the meantime, there has developed, the problem of the Soviet Backfire, their high-performance aircraft which they say is not a long-range aircraft and which some of our people say is a intercontinental aircraft. In the interim there has been the development on our part primarily, the cruise missiles, cruise missiles that could be launched from land-based mobile installations, cruise missiles that could be lanched uh— launched from high-performance aircraft, like the B-52s or the B-1s, which I hope we proceed with, cruise missiles which could be launched from either surface or submarine uh— naval vessels. Those gray-area weapons systems are creating some problems in uh— the agreement for a SALT Two negotiation. But I can say that I am dedicated to proceeding, and I met just last week with the foreign minister of the Soviet Union, and he indicated to me that uh— the Soviet Union was interested in narrowing the differences and making a realistic and a sound compromise. I hope and trust in the best interest of both countries, and in the best interest of all people throughout this globe, that the Soviet Union and the United States can make a mutually beneficial agreement. Because if we do not, and SALT One expires on October three, 1977, you will unleash again an all-out nuclear arms race with the potential of a nuclear holocaust of unbelievable dimensions. So it's the obligation of the president to do just that, and I intend to do so.

Trewhitt

Mr. President, let me follow that up by—I'll submit that the cruise missile adds a, a whole new dimension to the, to the arms competition—and uh— then cite a statement by your office to the Arms Control Association a few days ago in which you said that the cruise missile might eventually be included in a comprehensive arms limitation agreement but that in the meantime, it was an essential part of the American strategic arsenal. Now, eh— may I assume from that, that you're tending to exclude the cruise missile from the next SALT agreement, or is it still negotiable in that context?

Ford

I believe that the cruise missiles which we are now developing in research and development across the spectrum from air, from the sea, or from the land, uh— can be uh— included within a SALT Two agreement. They are a new weapons system that has a great potential, both conventional and nuclear-armed. At the same time, we have to make certain that the Soviet Union's Backfire, which they claim is not an intercontinental aircraft and which some of our people contend is, must also be included if we are to get the kind of an agreement which is in the best interests of both countries. And I really believe, that i— it's far better for us and for the Soviet Union, and more importantly for the people around the world, that these two superpowers find an answer for a SALT Two agreement before October three, 1977. I think goodwill on both parts, hard bargaining by both parties, and a reasonable compromise will be in the best interest of all parties.

Frederick

Governor Carter?

Carter

Well, Mr. Ford acts like he's uh— running for president for the first time. He's been in office two years, and there has been absolutely no progress made toward a new SALT agreement. He has learned the date of the expiration of SALT One apparently. We've seen, in this world, a development of a tremendous threat to us. As a nuclear engineer myself, I know the limitations and capabilities of atomic power. I also kno— ne— know that as far as the human beings on this earth are concerned, that the nonproliferation of atomic weapons is number one. Only the last few days with the election approaching, has Mr. Ford taken any interest in a nonproliferation movement. I advocated last May in a speech at the United Nations that we move immediately as a nation, to declare a complete moratorium on the testing of all nuclear devices, both weapons and peaceful devices, that we not ship any more atomic fuel to a country that refuses to comply with strict controls over the waste, which can be reprocessed into explosives. I've also advocated that we stop the sale by Germany and France of rese— reprocessing plants for Pakistan and Brazil. Mr. Ford hasn't moved on this. We also need to provide an adequate supply of enriched uranium. Mr. Ford again, under pressure from the atomic energy lobby, has insisted that this reprocessing or rather reen— enrichment, be done by private industry, and not by the existing uh— government uh— plants. This kind of confusion and absence of leadership has let us drift now for two years, with a constantly increasing threat of atomic weapons throughout the world. We now have five nations that have atomic bombs that we know about. If we continue under Mr. Ford's policy by 1985 or '90, we'll have twenty nations that have the capability of exploding atomic weapons. This has got to be stopped. That is one of the major challenges and major undertakings that I will assume, as the next president.

Frederick

Mr. Valeriani, a question for Governor Carter.

Valeriani

Governor Carter, earlier tonight you said America is not strong any more, America is not respected any more. And I feel that I must ask you, do you really believe that the United States is not the strongest country in the world, do you really believe that the United States is not the most respected country in the world, or is that just campaign rhetoric?

Carter

No, it's not just campaign rhetoric. I think that militarily, we are strong as any nation on earth. I think we gotta stay that way, and continue to increase our capabilities to meet any potential threat. But as far as strength derived from commitment to principles, as far as strength derived from the unity within our country, as far as strength derived from the people, the Congress, the Secretary of State, the president, sharing in the evolution and carrying-out of a foreign policy, as far as strength derived from the respect of our own allies and friends, there's assurance that we will be staunch in our commitment, that we will not deviate, and that we'll give them adequate attention. As far as, as strength derived from doing what's right, caring for the poor, providing food, becoming the breadbasket of the world instead of the arms merchant of the world—in those respects, we're not strong. Also, we'll never be strong again overseas, unless we're strong at home. And with our economy in such terrible disarray and getting worse by the month, we've got five hundred thousand more Americans unemployed today than we had three months ago, we've got two and a half million more Americans out of work now than we had when Mr. Ford took office. This kind of deterioration in our economic strength is bound to weaken us around the world. And we not only have uh— problems at home, but we export those problems overseas. So as far as the respect of our own people toward our own government, as far as participation in the shaping of uh— concepts and commitments, as far as the trust of our country among the nations of the world, as far as dependence of our country in meeting the needs and obligations that we've expressed to our allies, as far as the respect of our country, even among our potential adversaries, we are weak. Potentially we're strong. Under this administration, that strength has not been realized.

Appendix D 253

Frederick

President Ford.

Ford

Governor Carter uh— brags about the unemployment during Democratic administrations and condemns the unemployment at the present time. I must remind him that we're at peace and during the period that he brags about unemployment being low, the United States was at war. Now let me correct one other comment that uh— Governor Carter has made. I have recommended to the Congress that we develop the uranium enrichment plant at Portsmouth Ohio, which is a publicly owned go— U.S. government facility, and have indicated that the private program which would follow on in Alabama is one that may or may not uh— be constructed. But I am committed to the one at Portsmouth Ohio. The Governor also talks about morality in foreign policy. The foreign policy of the United States meets the highest standards of morality. What is more moral than peace, and the United States is at peace today. What is more moral in foreign policy than for the administration to take the lead in the World Food Conference in Rome in 1974, when the United States committed six million metric tons of food, over sixty percent of the food committed for the disadvantaged and underdeveloped nations of the world? The Ford administration wants to eradicate hunger and disease in our underdeveloped countries throughout the world. What is more moral than for the United States under the Ford administration to take the lead in southern Africa, in the Middle East? Those are initiatives in foreign policy which are of the highest moral standard, and that is indicative of the foreign policy of this country.

Frederick

Mr. Frankel, a question for President Ford.

Frankel

Mr. President, can we stick with morality? Uh— for a lot of people seems to cover a buncha sins. Um— Mr. Nixon and Mr. Kissinger used to tell us that instead of morality we had to worry in the c— world about living with and letting live all kindsa governments that we really didn't like. North and South Korean dictators, Chilean fascists, uh— Chinese Communists, Iranian emperors and so on. They said the only way to get by in a wicked world was to treat others on the basis of how they treated us, and not how they treated their own people. But more recently uh— we seem to have taken a different tack. Uh— we've seem to decided that uh— th— it is part of our business to tell the Rhodesians, for instance, that the way they're treating their own black people is wrong and they've got change their government, and we put pressure on them. We were rather liberal in our advice to the Italians as to how to vote. Um— is this a new Ford foreign policy in the making? Can we expect that you are now going to turn to South Africa and f— force them to change their government to intervene in similar ways to end the bloodshed as you called it, say, in Chile or Chilean prisons, and to throw our weight around for the, for the values that w— that we hold dear in the world?

Ford

I believe that uh— our foreign policy must express the highest standards of morality. And the initiatives that we took in southern Africa are the best examples of what this administration is doing and will continue to do in the next four years. If the United States had not moved when we did in southern Africa, there's no doubt there would have have been an acceleration of bloodshed in that tragic part of the world. If we had not taken our initiative, it's very, very possible that uh— the government of Rhodesia would·have been overrun, and that uh— the Soviet Union and the Cubans would have dominated uh— southern Africa. So the United States, seeking to preserve the principle of self-determination, to eliminate the possibility of bloodshed, to protect the rights of the minority as we insisted upon the rights of the majority, uh— I believe followed the good conscience of the American people in foreign policy, and I believe that we have used our skill. Secretary of State Kissinger had done a superb job in working with the black African nations, the so-called front-line nations. He has done a superb job in getting the Prime Minister of South Africa, Mr. Vorster, to agree that the time had come for a solution to the problem of Rhodesia. Secretary Kissinger in his meeting with uh— Prime Minister Smith of Rhodesia, was able to convince him that it was in the best interests of whites as well as blacks in Rhodesia to find an answer for a transitional government and then a majority government. This is a perfect example of the kind of leadership that the United States, under this administration, has taken. And I can assure you that this administration will follow that high moral principle in our future efforts in foreign policy, including our efforts in the Middle East, where it is vitally important because the Middle East is the crossroads of the world. There have been more disputes in its un— area where there's more volatility than any other place in the world. But because Arab nations and the Israelis trust the United States, we were able to take the lead in the Sinai Two agreement. And I can assure you that the United States will have the leadership role in moving toward a comprehensive settlement of the Middle Eastern problems, I hope and trust as soon as possible. And we will do it with the highest moral principles.

Frankel

Mr. President, just clarify one point. There are lots of majorities in the world that feel they're being pushed around by minority governments, and are you saying they can now expect to look to us for not just good cheer but throwing our weight on their side, in South Africa or on Taiwan, or in Chile uh— to help change their governments, as in Rhodesia?

Ford

I would hope that as we move to one area of the world from another—and the United States must not spread itself too thinly—that was one of the problems that helped to create the circumstances in Vietnam—but as we as a nation found that we are asked by the various parties, either one nation against another or individuals within a nation, that the United States will take the leadership and try to resolve the differences. Let me take uh— uh— South Korea as an example. I have personally told President Park that the United States does not condone the kind of repressive measures that he has taken in that country. But I think in all fairness and equity, we have to recognize the problem that South Korea has. On the north they have North Korea with five hundred thousand well-trained, well-equipped troops. They are supported by the People's Republic of China. They are supported by the Soviet Union. South Korea faces a very delicate situation. Now the United States, in this case, this administration, has recommended a year ago and we have reiterated it again this year, that the United States, South Korea, North Korea and the uh— People's Republic of China sit down at a conference table to resolve the problems of the Korean peninsula. This is a leadership role that the United States under this administration is carrying out, and if we do it, and I think the opportunities and the possibilities are getting better, we will have solved many of the internal domestic problems that exist in South Korea at the present time.

Appendix D 255

Frederick

Governor Carter.

Carter

I notice that Mr. Ford didn't comment on the uh– prisons in Chile. This is an– uh– a typical example, maybe of many others, where this administration overthrew an elected government and helped to establish a military dictatorship. This has not been an ancient history story. Last year under Mr. Ford, of all the Food for Peace that went to South America, eighty-five percent went to the military dictatorship in Chile. Another point I want to make is this. He says we have to move from one area of the world to another. That's one of the problems with this administration's so-called shuttle diplomacy. While the Secretary of State's in one country, there are almost a hundred and fifty others that are wondering what we're going to do next, what will be the next secret agreement. We don't have a comprehensive, understandable foreign policy that deals with world problems or even regional problems. Another thing that concerned me was what Mr. Ford said about unemployment, that insinuating that under Johnson and Kennedy that unemployment could only be held down when this country is at war. Karl Marx said that the free enterprise system in a democracy can only continue to exist when they are at war or preparing for war. Karl Marx was the grandfather of communism. I don't agree with that statement. I hope Mr. Ford doesn't either. He has put pressure on the Congress–and I don't believe Mr. Ford would even deny this–to hold up on nonproliferation legislation until the Congress agreed for an eight billion dollar program for private industry to start producing enriched uranium. And the last thing I want to make is this. He talks about peace, and I'm thankful for peace. We were peaceful when Mr. Ford went into office. But he and Mr. Kissinger and others tried to start a new Vietnam in Angola, and it was only the outcry of the American people, and the Congress, when their secret deal was discovered, that prevented our renewed involvement in that confligaration which was taking place there.

Frederick

Gentlemen, I'm sorry to say we do not have time enough for two complete sequences of questions. We now have only twelve minutes left. Therefore, I would like to ask for shorter questions and shorter answers. And we also will drop the follow-up question. Each candidate may still respond, of course, to the other's answer. Mr. Trewhitt, question for Governor Carter.

Trewhitt

Governor Carter, before this event the most communications I received concerned Panama. Uh– it, would you as president be prepared to sign a treaty which at a fixed date yielded administrative and economic control of the Canal Zone and shared defense, which as I understand it, is the position the United States took in 1974?

Carter

Well here again uh– the Panamanian question is one that's been confused by Mr. Ford. Uh– he had directed his uh– diplomatic relati– uh– rela– uh– representative to yield to the Panamanians, full sovereignty over the Panama Canal Zone at the end of a certain period of time. When Mr. Reagan raised this uh– question in Florida, uh– Mr. Ford not only disavowed his instructions, but he also even dropped parenthetically the use of the word detente. I would never give up complete control or practical control of the Panama Canal Zone, but I would continue to negotiate with the Panamanians. When the original treaty was signed back in the early 1900s, when Theodore Roosevelt was president, Panama retained sovereignty over the Panama Canal Zone. We retained control, as though we had sovereignty. Now I would be willing to go ahead with negotiations. I believe that we could share more fully, responsibilities for the Panama Canal Zone with Panama. I would be willing to continue to raise the payment for shipment of goods through the Panama Canal Zone. I might even be willing to reduce to some degree our military emplacements in the Panama Canal Zone, but I would not relinquish practical control of the Panama Canal Zone any time in the forseeable future.

Frederick

President Ford.

Ford

The United States must and will maintain complete access to the Panama Canal. The United States must maintain a defense capability of the Panama Canal. And the United States will maintain our national security interest in the Panama Canal. The negotiations for the Panama Canal started under President Johnson and have continued up to the present time. I believe those negotiations should continue. But there are certain guidelines that must be followed, and I've just defined them. Let me take just a minute to comment on something that Governor Carter said. On nonnu– on uh– nonpoliferation, in May of 1975, I called for a conference of uh– nuclear suppliers. That conference has met six times. In May of this year, Governor Carter took the first initiative, approximately twelve months after I had taken my initiative a year ago.

Frederick

Mr. Valeriani, a question for President Ford.

Valeriani

Mr. President, the Government Accounting Office has just put out a report suggesting that you shot from the hip in the Mayaguez rescue mission, and that you ignored diplomatic messages saying that a peaceful solution was in prospect. Um– why didn't you do more diplomatically at the time, and a related question, did the White House try to prevent the release of that report?

Ford

The White House did not uh– prevent the release of that report on July twelfth of this year and we gave full permission for the release of that report. I was very disappointed in the fact that the uh– G.A.O. released that report, because I think it interjected political partisan politics at the present time. But let me comment on the report. Somebody who sits in Washington D.C., eighteen months after the Mayaguez incident, can be a very good grandstand quarterback. And let me make another observation. This morning I got a call, from the skipper of the Mayaguez. He was furious because he told me that it was the action of me, President Ford, that saved the lives of the crew of the Mayaguez. And I can assure you, that if we had not taken the strong and forceful action that we did, we would have been uh– criticized very, very uh– severely for sitting back and not moving. Captain Miller is thankful. The crew is thankful. We did the right thing. It seems to me that those who sit in Washington eighteen months after the incident are not the best judges of the decision-making

Appendix D

process that had to be made by the National Security Council and by myself at the time the incident was developing in the Pacific. Let me assure you that we made every possible overture to the People's Republic of China and through them to the Cambodian government. We made uh— diplomatic uh— protests to the Cambodian government through the United Nations. Every possible diplomatic means was utilized. But at the same time, I had a responsibility, and so did the National Security Con— Council, to meet the problem at hand. And we handled it responsibly, and I think Captain Miller's testimony to that effect is the best evidence.

Frederick

Governor Carter.

Carter

Well, I'm reluctant to uh— comment on the recent report. I haven't read it. I think the American people have only one uh— requirement—that the facts about Mayaguez be given to them accurately and completely. Mr. Ford has been there for eighteen months. He had the facts that were released today immediately after the Mayaguez incident. I understand that the report today is accurate. Mr. Ford has said, I believe, that it was accurate, and that the White House made no attempt to block the issuing of that report. I don't know if that's exactly accurate or not. I understand that both the Sec— the uh— Department of State, and the Defense Department have approved the accuracy of today's report, or yesterday's report, and also the National Security Agency. I don't know what was right, or what was wrong, or what was done. The only thing I believe is that whatever the, the knowledge was that Mr. Ford had, should have been given to the American people eighteen months ago, immediately after the Mayaguez uh— incident occurred. This is uh— what the American people want. When something happens that endangers our security, or when something happens that threatens our stature in the world, or when American people are endangered by the actions of a foreign country, uh— just forty uh— sailors on the Mayaguez, we obviously have to move aggressively and quickly to rescue them. But then after the immediate action is taken, I believe the president has an obligation to tell the American people the truth, and not wait eighteen months later for the report to be issued.

Frederick

Gentlemen, at this time we have time for only two very short questions. Mr. Frankel, a question for Governor Carter.

Frankel

Governor Carter, if the price of uh— gaining influence among the Arabs is closing our eyes a little bit to their boycott against Israel, how would you handle that?

Carter

I believe that the boycott of American businesses by the Arab countries because those businesses trade with Israel or because they have American Jews who are owners or directors in the company, is an absolute disgrace. This is the first time that I've eh— remember in the history of our country when we've let a foreign country circumvent or change our Bill of Rights. I'll do everything I can as president, to stop the boycott of American businesses by the Arab countries. It's not a matter of diplomacy or trade, with me. It's a matter of morality. And I don't believe that the Arab countries will pursue it, when we have a strong president who will protect the integrity of our country, the commitment of our Constitution and Bill of Rights, and protect people in this country who happen to be Jews. It may later be Catholics, it may be, later be Baptists who are threatened by some foreign country, but we ought to stand staunch. And I think it's a disgrace that so far Mr. Ford's administration has blocked the passage of legislation that would have revealed by law every instance of the boycott, and it would have prevented the boycott from continuing.

Frederick

President Ford.

Ford

Again Governor Carter is inaccurate. The Arab boycott action was first taken in 1952. And in November of 1975, I was the first president to order the executive branch to take action, affirmative action, through the Department of Commerce and other Cabinet departments, to make certain that no American businessman or business organization should discriminate against Jews because of an Arab boycott. And I might add that uh– my administration–and I'm very proud of it–is the first administration that has taken an antitrust action against companies in this country that have allegedly cooperated with the Arab boycott. Just on Monday of this week, I signed a tax bill that included an amendment that would prevent companies in the United States from taking a tax deduction, if they have in any way whatsoever cooperated with the Arab boycott. And last week when we were trying to get the Export Administration Act through the Congress—necessary legislation— my administration went to Capitol Hill and tried to convince the House and the Senate that we should have an amendment on that legislation which would take strong and effective action against those who uh– participate or cooperate with the Arab uh– boycott. One other point. Because the Congress failed to act, I am going to announce tomorrow that the Department of Commerce will disclose those companies that have uh– participated in the Arab boycott. This is something that we can do, the Congress failed to do it, and we intend to do it.

Frederick

Mr. Trewhitt, a very brief question for President Ford.

Trewhitt

Mr. President, if you get the accounting of missing in action you want from North Vietnam—or from Vietnam, I'm sorry, now—would you then be prepared to reopen negotiations for restoration of relations with that country?

Ford

Let me restate uh– our policy. As long as Vietnam, North Vietnam, does not give us a full and complete accounting of our missing in action, I will never uh– go along with the admission of Vietnam to the United Nations. If they do give us a bona fide, complete uh– accounting of the eight hundred M.I.A.s, then I believe that the United States should begin negotiations for the uh– admission of Vietnam to the United Nations. But not until they have given us the full accounting of our M.I.A.s.

Frederick

Governor Carter.

Appendix D

Carter

One of the most uh– embarrassing uh– failures of the Ford administration, and one that touches specifically on human rights, is his refusal to appoint a presidential commission to go to Vietnam, to go to Laos, to go to Cambodia, and try to trade for the release of information about those who are missing in action in those wars. This is what the families of M.I.A.s want. So far, Mr. Ford has not done it. We've had several fragmentary efforts by members of the Congress and by, by private citizens. Several months ago the Vietnam government said, we are ready to sit down and negotiate for release of information on M.I.A.s. So far, Mr. Ford has not responded. I also would never normalize relationships with Vietnam, nor permit them to join the United Nations until they've taken this action. But that's not enough. We need to have an active and aggressive action on part of the president, leader of this country, to seek out every possible way to get that information which has kept the M.I.A. families in despair and doubt, and Mr. Ford has just not done it.

Frederick

Thank you, Governor Carter. That completes the questioning for this evening. Each candidate now has up to three minutes for a closing statement. It was determined by the toss of a coin that Governor Carter would take the first question, and he now goes first with his closing remarks. Governor Carter.

Carter

The purpose of this debate and the outcome of the election will determine three basic things—leadership, upholding the principles of our country, and proper priorities and commitments for the future. This election will also determine what kind of world we leave our children. Will it be a nightmare world threatened with the proliferation of atomic bombs, not just in five major countries, but dozens of smaller countries that have been permitted to develop atomic weapons because of a failure of our top leadership to stop proliferation? Will we have a world of hunger and, and hatred and will we be living in an armed camp stripped of our friendship and allies, hiding behind a tight defense that's been drawn in around us because we are fearful of the outside world? Will we have a government of secrecy that excludes the American people from participation in making basic decisions and therefore covers up mistakes and makes it possible for our government—our government—to depart from the principles of our Constitution and Bill of Rights? Or will we have a world of peace, with the threat of atomic weapons eliminated, with full trade, with our people at work, inflation controlled, openness in government, our people proud once again, Congress, citizens, president, Secretary of State working in harmony and unity toward a common future? A world where people have enough to eat, and a world where we care about those who don't. Can we become a breadbasket of the world, instead of the arms merchant of the world? I believe we can and we ought to. Now we've been hurt in recent years, in this country, in the aftermath of Vietnam, Cambodia, Chile, Pakistan, Angola, Watergate, C.I.A. We've been hurt. Our people feel that we've lost something precious. That's not necessary. I want to see our nation res– return to a posture and an image and a standard to make us proud once again. I remember the world of NATO and the world of Point Four and the world of the Marshall Plan and the world of the Peace Corps. Why can't we have that once again? We ought to be a beacon for nations who search for peace and who search for freedom, who search for individual liberty, who search for basic human rights. We've haven't been lately. We can be once again. We'll never have that world leadership until we are strong at home, and we can have that strength if we return to the basic principles. It ought not to be a strength of bombast and threats. It ought to be a quiet strength, based on the integrity of our people, the vision of the Constitution, an in– innate strong will and purpose that God's given us in the greatest nation on earth . . .

[Interruption 5]

Frederick

President Ford.

Carter

the United States.

Ford

As we have seen tonight, foreign policy and defense policy are difficult and complex issues. We can debate methods. We can debate one decision or another, but there are two uh— things which cannot be debated—experience and results. In the last two years, I have made policy decisions involving long-range difficulties and policies, and made day-to-day judgments, not only as President of the United States, but as the leader of the free world. What is the result of that leadership? America is strong. America is free. America is respected. Not a single young American today is fighting or dying on any foreign battlefield. America is at peace, with freedom. Thank you, and good night.

Frederick

Thank you, President Ford. Thank you, Governor Carter. I also want to thank our questioners and the audience here this evening. The third and final debate between President Ford and Governor Carter will take place on October the twenty-second at nine-thirty p.m. eastern daylight time on the campus of the College of William and Mary in Williamsburg, Virginia. The subject matter will cover all issues. These debates are sponsored by the League of Women Voters' Education Fund to help voters become better informed on the issues, and to generate greater voter turnout in the November election. Now, from the Palace of Fine Arts Theater in San Francisco, good night.

Appendix E

The Vice-Presidential Debate: October 15, 1976, Houston

Hoge

Good evening. I'm James Hoge, editor of the Chicago *Sun Times* and moderator of this third of the historic debates of the 1976 campaign. Tonight we have the vice-presidential candidates: for the Democrats, Senator Walter Mondale of Minnesota, for the Republicans, Senator Robert Dole of Kansas. Thank you, Senator Mondale and thank you, Senator Dole, for being with us this evening. This debate is taking place before an audience in the Alley Theatre in Houston Texas. It is also being broadcast by radio and television to an audience estimated at some eighty-five million persons in this nation and overseas. As far as we can tell this is the first formal debate ever held between vice-presidential candidates. Their views are important not only because they seek the second-highest office in the land, but because as potential vice-presidents, they must be judged on their capacities to serve as president of the United States. For example, of the last five vice-presidents, three have become president due to death, or resignation, by a chief executive. We will begin this debate tonight with opening statements of up to two minutes by each candidate. By the toss of a coin it was determined that Senator Dole would go first. Senator Dole, your opening statement.

Dole

Thank you very much. Uh– first I wish to thank the League of Women Voters, and this is a great privilege and honor for me. I also want to thank my many friends in Russell Kansas, for that big long telegram I received today. I think tonight may be sort of a fun evening. It's a very important evening, it's a very historic evening. But I've known uh– my counterpart for some time, and we've been friends and we will be friends when this debate is over, and we'll be friends when the election is over and he'll still be in the Senate. And, I think first of all I should make it very clear that I'm most proud to be on the ticket with President Ford. I've known President Ford for sixteen years—sixteen years. It's a long time. He's known me for that long. I know him to be a man of compassion and competence. He has that confidence and he projects that leadership that America needs and that you need, right now. Now I don't know much about uh– Governor Carter. I've tried to find out. I know he's very ambitious. I know he wants to be president. He's been running for three years. But I know he said uh– at least one thing, that he does agree with my opponent, my friend uh– Walter Mondale, probably the most liberal senator in the United States Senate. And that's really

261

what this debate's all about. If by some uh— tragic circumstance one of us should become president of the United States, where do we stand on the issues? I would just say in a very uh— summary way, that I have a great deal of faith in you the American people. I'm concerned about farmers and housewives and young people and professional people, working men and women. I think we can find our solutions working together. My opponent has a record of voting for ever— every inflationary spending program except in defense, when he votes for every cut. And we'll explore that as this debate goes on.

Hoge

Thank you, Senator Dole. Senator Mondale, your opening statement.

Mondale

I believe that most Americans would agree on the problems that this country faces and that the next, and which the next administration must solve. They include the need, once again, for an economy that works. The economy today is in very, very bad shape—the highest unemployment since the Great Depression. Fifty percent higher than when Mr. Ford took office, raging inflation, with the latest uh— wholesale price indexes once again sig— raising the specter of double-digit inflation. The purchasing power of the average American has slipped so much, that it is now the equivalent of the purchasing power in 1965. It is not getting better, it is getting worse. All the leading indicators now point downward, and stock investors are now losing confidence, and over fifty billion dollars of value has disappeared from the stock market in less than a month. We need a government that works, and we need a government that cares, and once again we have to get back to work on education, on health, on housing, on the environment, on energy, and we need a foreign policy that once again reflects the values and the beliefs of the American people. This will take leadership, and we need leadership, too. The Republican administration, the Republican party, has had eight years to solve these problems. All of them have gotten worse. The Republican ticket does not offer new plans for their solution, but is engaged in a frantic effort to defend the past. This nation desperately needs new leadership. The Carter-Mondale ticket would offer a new generation of leadership dedicated to solu— uh— to solving the problems which I have listed, and that is the basis of our appeal.

Hoge

Thank you gentlemen. The subject matter of tonight's debate, like that of the first two presidential debates, covers domestic and economic policies, and foreign and defense issues. The questioners tonight are Hal Bruno, chief political correspondent of *Newsweek* magazine, Marilyn Berger, White House correspondent of NBC News, and Walter Mears, special correspondent for the Associated Press. Questions will be alternated between the two candidates. After a question is asked, the candidate will have up to two and a half minutes to respond. His opponent will then have two and a half minutes to reply to that. The first candidate then may reply to those remarks for up to one minute. I should mention at this point that I will intervene, if a candidate is not addressing the question which has been posed to him. At the conclusion of the questioning, each candidate will be allowed up to three minutes for a closing remark. Senator Mondale and Senator Dole do not have prepared notes or comments with them this evening. However, they may make notes and refer to them during the debate. We now begin with questions on domestic and economic policies. The first question goes to Senator Dole, as was determined by the coin toss. Mr. Bruno, you have the first question.

Appendix E

Bruno

Uh— Senator Dole, presidential candidates uh— always promise that their vice-president will play an important role. But it seldom turns out that way, and they usually wind up uh— as standby equipment, which is the way Vice-President Rockefeller once described the job. What's your view of this office that you're seeking? Has President Ford told you what your role might be, and what would you like it to be?

Dole

Well, I've said as I've traveled around the country in, mostly in jest, that is why you running for vice-president, I said well, it's, it's indoor work and no heavy lifting. But, I've also thought very seriously about it. President Ford has discussed it with me. It's a great opportunity, it's a great responsibility. I can't stand here tonight uh— in Houston Texas, and say that come uh— January, when I'll be in, sworn in as vice-president, that uh— I'm going to do anything in the first hundred days, or even the second hundred days. But I have discussed 't with President Ford. He's indicated two uh— responsibilities that he's going to designate. One will be having some role in increasing our agricultural exports, because we believe, we believe together, that the future of American agriculture lies in its exports. Also, because of my long association with families who had uh— their sons or husbands as missing in action and prisoners of war, he indicated to me last week that I would have a role as his representative, try to get some accounting for the missing in action in Southeast Asia. But beyond that, of course our constitutional duty is to preside over the Senate, and vote in case of a tie. We also serve on the National Security Council, Domestic Council, and whatever other assignments we may have from time to time. I think probably one important aspect that we ought t' talk about, and that's our vision for America. I believe the people viewing tonight, people who are watching us tonight, may well determine the role I play as vice-president. I believe that we're going forward in America, under the leadership of President Ford, and I believe there'll be more and more challenges—positive challenges—for those of us who hold high office, to serve the American people, and that's really what it's all about. Whether we're vice-president, on the city council, member of the legislature, or whatever. Our obligation is to the people. We must have faith in the American people. And I have that faith. What I think the opponents have more faith in bigger government, more controls, and more interference with their everyday lives.

Hoge

Senator Mondale, your response.

Mondale

The problems that our country faces are so great, that a very strong role is required of the vice-president and of all federal officials. I've discussed this matter uh— extensively with Governor Carter, and as vice-president, I would have such a substantial role in both domestic and foreign policy. I would work with the president, for example, in this long overdue effort to basically restructure and reorganize the federal government. Today it's a mess. There's no one in charge. There's great waste, great duplication, and the time has come for a long overdue reorganization. That would be one of the first tasks that I would have, working with the new president. There would be a whole range of duties that I would have working with the president and uh— on problems of economic growth, we've gotta get people back to work, attacking inflation and finally getting a policy to, to keep the dollar worth a dollar, and the other problems that we face here at home. One of the specific suggestions that uh— we are considering now, is that I would head up a task force to deal with the federal aspects of crime in America. Today, the federal function in law enforcement is in disarray. The Drug Enforcement Ad— Administration is totally demoralized. The F.B.I. is also under great difficulty. We need to have a coordinated, effective, and national attack on organized and hard crime, those crimes prohibited by federal law. We need to finally get a national effort that really makes sense, that stops the importation of these death-dealing imported illegal drugs. We need to have a new look at official lawlessness at the federal level, because we've seen too many instances where people in high public office u— uh— violate the law themselves. And one of the things that w— we're considering is establishing an interdepartmental agency under the chairmanship of the vice-president, to finally at long last put some strength behind a national effort to deal with these uh— terrible problems in American life. And may I close by saying that uh— one of the reasons that I believe I am gonna be the vice-president, is one of the reasons that uh— my opponent mentioned, and that is that the present president imposed an embargo on farm exports four times in three years, and they want a change.

Hoge

Senator Dole, do you have a further comment?

Dole

Well, I would just say to my good friend uh— I'm happy that you're going to be responsible uh— for reorganization. I hope you don't pattern it after Governor Carter's efforts in Georgia. They added more bureaucrats to the government in Georgia, the cost of government went up, his Human Resources uh— Committee or whatever it's called was called an organizational nightmare by Governor Buzzy— Busbee, his successor. I understand from Bobby Smith, who's supposed to be the ag expert in the Carter campaign, that you're gonna do away with the Department of Agriculture. That's in essence what he said. You're gonna put it together with a lot of other things. And I know the farmers who may be viewing will be pleased to know that. They should also be pleased to know that uh— Senator Mondale uh— sponsors export licensing proposals in the Congress, which would make it necessary for farmers to get an export license before they could ship their goods overseas. And under his proposal—which is still pending, thank goodness, it hasn't passed or we'd all be in difficulty—we wouldn't be able to ship anything now.

Hoge

Miss Berger, your question to Senator Mondale.

Berger

Senator Mondale, the polls indicate that less than half of those eligible will vote in this coming election. And although you and Senator Dole have both touched on the very important issues that are before the country, many Americans feel that they're being short-changed by a campaign that has descended into a name-calling contest. For example, Governor Carter has said that President Ford has been brainwashed, President Ford says that Carter is slandering America. If the tone of the campaign worries the electorate, does it worry you, Senator Mondale?

Mondale

There are many things that I think have contributed to this phenomenon that I find very, very discouraging and that is the great numbers of Americans do not plan to participate in

Appendix E 265

the electoral process which is so crucial to uh— a sound and effective nation. We can't solve our problems unless everyone helps. There have been so many things that have dispirited the American people, that have fed frustration and despair. We've gone through the worst war in American history, that divided this country perhaps as, as much as it's ever been divided. We then went through the worst political scandal in American history, with the highest officers in government being found guilty or at least charged with guilt in very serious crimes. We then saw evidence that even our own intelligence agencies and law enforcement agencies, charged to enforce the law, had themselves violated the law. And then we've seen a government that is unable to deal with the real problems that the American people face. People need jobs. It's a tragedy every time an able-bodied American is denied the opportunity to make, uh— to work. There are now eight million Americans who can't find work. It's a tragedy when Americans work and find the value of their dollar disappearing. It's a tragedy when children can't get educated, when health care wipes them out, when senior citizens find that the attention and the credit that they're entitled to—through Social Security and Medicaid—is being taken from them. These things have all contributed to a growing feeling in America that government does not respond to solve people's problems, that government lives by one standard and expects Americans to live by another. And because of that we have this large feeling in America, reflected in those surveys, that s— were suggested in your question, that has contributed to this feeling that involvement in politics does not count. And if there's one hope that Governor Carter and I have, if there's one objective that's central above all, is that we can restore the faith in the American people, by simply telling the truth, obeying the law, seeing problems as they really are, attacking the real questions, the real problems that 'fect, affect Americans, and then I think we will see the restoration of public trust.

Hoge

Senator Dole, your response.

Dole

Well, I think it's a very good question. It goes back to the party institutions. Uh— maybe it's uh— an indictment uh— in that sense of uh— those of us who seek office. It goes back to my basic premise, and that's faith in the people. It just seems to me that some of those who lust for power are not really concerned about the people. They say they're concerned about the people, they talk about the people, they never give us uh— their positions, and so I think many Americans are sort of turned off, and they were turned off by the war in Southeast Asia. They were turned off by Watergate. I'll say that word first. They were turned off by Watergate. But we're looking ahead. They were probably turned off by what they saw in the U.S. House of Representatives. They've been turned off by a lot of things they've seen in politics. But I think they've been turned off, too, by promises and promises, and bigger spending programs and more and more inflation. They're looking for leadership. They yearn for leadership, and they found that leadership in President Ford. And Governor Carter talks about taxing the rich. He talks about nearly everyone. He said former President Johnson lied and cheated and distorted the facts. I think that turns a lot of people off. He was quick to apologize to Mrs. Johnson. He insulted Governor Wallace, but he was quick to apologize to Governor Wallace. Someone in the family insulted Billy Graham, but they were quick to apologize to Billy Graham. I think it's time we stopped uh— apologizing and talked, 'stime we started talking to you, the American people. We need your help. We want to restore faith in this system. And I think we can. Let's not promise what we can't deliver. Let's uh— be honest with you, the voter, with you, the taxpayer. It's fine to talk about education, more this, more that, 'n more that. But there are eighty-eight million people working in America that are gonna pay their taxes—the highest number every working in America—some forty percent of the population, the highest in history, working now in America. And we're concerned about the seven point eight percent unemployed. We'll be concerned until that's reduced to four percent or three percent or wherever. But we can't lose sight of the number one enemy, and that number one enemy, enemy is inflation. And I think the American people are coming around. They're beginning to understand that President Ford says what he means and does what he says.

Hoge

Senator Mondale.

Mondale

Well, who really has faith in the people? A candidate like Governor Carter, who campaigns with the people, is out every day meeting and talking with the people, holds news conferences and answers questions of the, of the news media as he has every day for twenty-four months, or a president who is in the White House, not through election but through appointment, who has held only two preannounced news conferences since February? Who trusts the people more—Governor Carter and Senator Mondale, who have disclosed our income tax returns so the American people can look at our private financial affairs and determine wha— how we've conducted our affairs, or President Ford and Senator Dole, who refuse to let the American people see their tax returns? Who trusts the people? A candidate like Governor Carter, who tells the truth, or a president like Mr. Ford, who last week told the American people that he had fought the Arab boycott and sought legislation and sanctions against it when the whole record shows he's procee— proceeded in just the opposite direction?

Hoge

Thank you. Mr. Mears, your question for Senator Dole.

Mears

Senator Dole, prior to your current campaign you sometimes expressed concern about a negative image of the Republican party. You're quoted as having said last spring that we're in the unfortunate position of having a president vetoing bills and getting on the wrong side of people issues. He's vetoed the education bill, the jobs bill, you name it. Are you still concerned about the risk that Republicans will be perceived as opposed to what you call ve— uh— people issues. And do you think that President Ford has exercised the veto too frequently?

Dole

Well, I might say at the outset I haven't always agreed with President Ford and I've voted to override on occasion but not every time, as my counterpart has. I think President Ford uh— and hindsight's very good particularly when you're on the ticket. And my hindsight is, the president's been courageous. And there is a difference. You know, we look at our states and we look at the bills and we decide to sustain or override. The president— and particularly this president, who has the courage—President Ford looks at the nation, he looks at all the American people, and he makes that judgment—should I sign this, can I sign, or must I veto this bill? And so he's vetoed sixty-two bills—I think the sixty-second happened today. And I say that's uh— a courageous act, repeated sixty-two time, because much of that legislation sounded good, some of it was good, but some of it we just couldn't have unless we're gonna fuel the fires of inflation. I don't suggest that every veto uh— I must agree with. But I also suggest that I'm a Republican. I'm proud to be a Republican. We're sometimes perceived, as I've said before, as the antipeople party because we're not for more spending, we're not for more governing, we're for a strong defense, we're for peace in the world. Those aren't very attractive to some people. They want to know how much we're gonna spend for this, and how much we're gonna spend for that. Well Senator Mondale could tell 'em that because he votes for every piece of spending legislation comes down the pike. Unless it's in that area of defense, and then he votes for every budget cut, I think he's voted to cut the budget, in addition to what had already been cut in the Congress some sixteen billion dollars, against the B-1 bomber, which means a lot of jobs, against the C5-A, against the Trident submarine. And the list goes on and on and on and on. I believe the American people want us to be responsible. We've got to make the tough decisions. It's one thing to be in the office of the president, or a senator of the United States, and vote for every spending program, never concern ourselves with inflation or the total cost. But I would only close by saying, that I hope the viewers remember that we have a Democratic Congress, we've had one for twenty-two straight years. And so when anyone stands up to debate this Republican Senator and tries to dump all the responsibility on a Republican President by the name of Gerald Ford, I'd just ask that question—where have you been for twenty-two years?

Hoge

Senator Mondale, your response.

Mondale

Perhaps the most pronounced different that refl— separates the Democratic and the Republican candidates, is reflected in the question that was just asked. There is practically no difference between the two parties in terms of how much they would spend. The Senate Budget Committee estimated that the Republican Platform cost fifty billion dollars, the Democratic Platform cost forty billion dollars. The difference between the Democratic Congressional budget which I supported and the Rep— and the president's budget, was only three billion dollars in deficit, and if you removed the gimmickry in the president's budget, it was exactly the same. The difference is in how we spend those resources. And I am unashamed, of my support for programs to put people back to work. I am unashamed of my support for programs to build housing, so the families of this country can live in decent housing. I'm unashamed of supporting education programs that give our kids a decent education. I'm unashamed of supporting health programs, that give people who get ill a chance to have decent help without being totally wiped out. And I'm unashamed of supporting programs such as Medicare. My opponent voted against Medicare. Can you imagine, voting against program, as did the president, that would provide help for senior citizens, after they're past their earning years, so that they could have decent health care, without being wiped out? Now where do the Republicans want to spend their money? Well I'll tell you. First of all this year they're spending fifty-five billion dollars in the cost of the recession that they created. We didn't give them this recession. We had full employment when they took over. Mr. Ford in just two years has increased unemployment by two and a half million Americans. They haven't solved inflation and the, and in— instead of trying to deal with the problem of unemployment, instead of that, they propose a twenty billion dollar tax cut for wealthy corporations despite the fact that just yesterday, a newspaper carried a story that ten major corporations made massive amounts of money and didn't owe a dime in federal taxes. Ford Motor Corporation earned eight hundred million dollars and didn't owe a dime to the federal government, in fact got a hundred and eighty million dollars back. So between those tax cuts, and between the massive costs of unemployment, they spend much more than we would. But what do they get for it? We want to see money spent to help problems that people really face in their lives.

Hoge

Senator Dole.

Dole

Well, we're all for those programs uh— Fritz, uh— we just won't believe in excesses. I think in retrospect uh— the elder care program that I voted for instead of Medicare, is probably a better program because Medicare, everybody gets the benefits, whether you're in need or not, once you reach age sixty-five. Now they're having a lot of problems with Medicare. I'm glad you mentioned Ford Motor Company not paying taxes. Again, the Democrats control the committee. I'm on the committee. Senator Mondale's on the Finance Committee. Henry Ford happens to be supporting Governor Carter, maybe that's why. Governor Carter did have a little meeting with him at the 21 Club, and had some small businessmen there, and said don't worry about taxes, I won't do anything for at least a year. That's after he said the tax system was a disgrace. We have peace in this country today. That's important to me and important to mothers who may be listening. They talk about their full employment, when we took over. That's because they had a full-grown war going in Southeast Asia. That's not the way we try to end unemployment in the Republican party.

Hoge

Mr. Bruno, your question to Senator Mondale.

Bruno

Uh— Senator Mondale uh— everyone seems to agree that solving the economic problems of inflation and unemployment has to be given top priority. Uh— you and Governor Carter have a whole shopping list of things that you want to do. After une— after the uh— economic problem, what do you see as the next most urgent and crucial domestic problems? In what order of importance would you go to work on such problems as the decay and bankruptcy of the cities, uh— tax reform, health insurance, uh— help for the poor and the elderly. In short, after the economy, what would be the very specific priorities of a Carter administration?

Mondale

Well you have to work on several problems at once, because they all demand the attention of the American people. One of the key problems would be to try to finally get a health insurance program to deal with the health crisis in America. In just the past two years, health costs in America have risen in the cities by over twenty-five percent. We have to do something about that. There's no hope under the admin— the Republican administration, Mr. Ford said he'd ve— he would veto any legislation if we sent it. We have to do something about housing. We're in a housing depression. Today, nearly twenty percent of the building tradesmen in America are unemployed. We need to put them back to work, to build housing that Americans need. We need to continue to, to build support, as the budget permits, for education. We need t— to get back to work on the problems of senior citizens. Now all of this has to be done prudently, within a budget, and within the constraints that our resources permit. But once we put people back to work, once we end this recession—which we will do— even the president's own estimates indicates that we will have somewhere between sixty and seventy billion dollars of increased revenues on existing tax rates, just from economic growth which we can use to work on these programs. Then we'll have tax reform, and I want to deal with this problem just a moment. Mr. Dole has probably the worst record in favor of loopholes

Appendix E

of any senator in the United States Senate. Mr. Ford has one of the worst records in favor of tax loopholes in the history of the House of Representatives. I have one of the best records of tax reform in the United States Senate. And it, I find it very peculiar, to find two people who spent their Congressional careers trying to block tax reform that permits very wealthy Americans to avoid most of their taxes, to suddenly complain when the Congress hadn't passed the kind of legislation that we're talking about. What we're basically talking about is presidential leadership. We need leadership in the presidency, to help support those of us in the Congress that have been pushing for tax reform. And then we will have it. It is now possible for people of great wealth, by using complete tax fictions, to avoid all or most their taxes. But most Americans listening to me tonight could hire the best tax lawyer in America, and you couldn't save a dime. There are no loopholes for you.

Hoge

Senator Dole, your response.

Dole

Well I think Senator Mondale is a little nervous, but uh– trying to make a loophole, I think, of Governor Carter. I don't know why it comes to me, but uh– uh– I remember his '75 tax return–you've probably seen it, since it's public. His tax liability was fifty-eight thousand dollars. Not many Americans–I don't imagine many of you in the viewing audience uh– had to worry about fifty-eight thousand dollar tax bill. I didn't. But Governor Carter did. Until he took off forty-one thousand dollars. That's called the investment tax credit. He bought some peanut machinery, gonna use it next year. So he took forty-one thousand dollars off his tax and sent the government a check for seventeen thousand dollars. So how much did he pay on his income? Well, he paid about twelve point eight percent. This that same man, the same Governor Carter, who runs around the country talking about tax reform, loopholes, and the rich. I don't know who uh– rates uh– Senator Mondale in the Finance Committee. I don't know how they rated him on the Honeywell Amendment he offered and the I.D.S. Amendment he offered, they never passed, they never got out of the Senate. They're both special-interest amendments. That's all right. Because those were his amendments. I don't know where Governor Carter's corporate returns are and partnership returns, I haven't seen those published anywhere. But I know about his tax reform. But I want to get back to the question, if that's all right. We're talking about the economy. What are we going to do after the economy's taken care of? Well I don't know if t's occurred to me, and I'm certain it hasn't occurred to my counterpart, we might, it's not illegal, to take some of that surplus and apply it to the national debt. We've never done it, but we wouldn't be put in jail if Congress voted to try to retire some of that debt, to take some of the pressure off the American working man and the American working woman. And I get a little tired of Governor Carter's antibusiness attitude. I know they get great support, monetary support, from George Meany. In fact I've been suggesting that George Meany was probably Senator Mondale's makeup man–he may or may not have been, they did a good job–but I think it's time the American people understand that this is in a very serious election, that we've got a tough choice to make. Governor Carter talks about raising everyone's taxes above the median income. He didn't know what the median income was, of course. It's fourteen thousand dollars per American family, that's what it is. So I say take a look, and you'll vote for Ford.

Hoge

Senator Mondale.

Mondale

The question was what would we do to deal with the human problems in America. The first thing we would do is to put people back to work. The most atrocious result of the Republican policy is massive unemployment. It costs us fifty billion dollars this year. Secondly, we will fight inflation. Today, inflation is three times worse than it was under the Democrats. And the latest indexes indicate that it's back on its way up. No effort to fight this at all. We will have tax reform. There's no question about our commitment to tax reform. My record proves it. Governor Carter's uh– positions prove that. We are fully committed to tax reform, and when the Republicans are raising money around the country, they say give us some money to defeat Governor Carter because if he gets elected, there'll be tax reform. And they are right when they say that, because we'll have tax reform and bring relief to the average income earner in this country. They know what Governor Carter is talking about. He's talking about the loopholes that favor Americans usually earning above fifty thousand dollars a year.

Hoge

Thank you, Senator Mondale. We now turn to questions on foreign and defense issues. Miss Berger, you have the first question in this subject area and it is for Senator Dole.

Berger

Senator Dole, President Ford said in an interview this week, that if he's elected he would like to see Henry Kissinger stay on as Secretary of State. This hardly seems to square with the Republican platform which appears to repudiate much of Kissinger's foreign policy. Which way do you go, Senator Dole, with President Ford or with the Republican platform?

Dole

I go with both and stay with Henry. Uh– you know if you look back over history, uh– President Washington had Thomas Jefferson for his Secretary of State, uh– Harry Truman had Dean Acheson for his Secretary of State, both very strong men, both very active men, both very powerful men. Henry Kissinger's a powerful man. And I haven't always agreed with Henny, Henry Kissinger but I, when I start disagreeing with Henry I start looking at what he's done for America, and what he's done for the free world. I think about the breakthrough in China. I think about our increased responsive relations with, with the Soviet Union. I think about winding down the war that we inherited from another Democrat administration in Southeast Asia. I think most recently about his efforts in South Africa, where he's trying to protect the rights of the majority and the rights of the minority. Now we sort of thought that Henry mighta had a role to play in grain embargoes, so we weren't totally happy at that time. We're not happy with embargoes, there'll not be any more embargoes except in extreme circumstances under a Ford-Dole administration. So I agree with the president. Secretary Kissinger has performed yeoman service. Anywhere you look, you find Henry's tracks and they are tracks that are right for America. They are tracks that are right for the free world. And I wonder how many mothers and how many fathers and how many young men and young women who may be viewing tonight, have really stopped to think about what this Republican administration has done. No one's being drafted. No one's going off to war. No one's being shot at. No one's being hospitalized. No one's being buried in America. Not a single shot being fired in anger. And this is a Republican administration. This is a Republican policy. And this policy by and large has been spearheaded by one Henry Kissinger. And we can have our differences. When I looked at the platform–I was on the Platform Committee–I don't see any contradiction in that platform. I've read the morality section. I think it sustains President Ford and sukstain– sustains Secretary Kissinger.

Appendix E

Hoge

Senator Mondale, your response.

Mondale

The real question of the foreign policy of the next administration is the responsibility of the president of the United States. He is the person elected to discharge the responsibility of foreign policy. He is the person that must conduct it and lead this nation's efforts. And that's where I think the key difference between the two parties lie. We want a change. We want new leadership. And above all we want a change of philosophy and direction. America's greatest strength, is to be found in its values and its beliefs. At every time in our pursuit of foreign policy, that we disregard those basic values, of freedom, of democracy, of national independence, we pursue a policy that is not credible, that's not sustainable, either overseas or at home. And let me say what I mean. For example, in Africa, for seven and a half years it was the policy of this administration to support the colonial control of black Africa and support white minority rule in majority black states. That was our explicit policy. And after that failed, and on the eve of this election, suddenly we've turned around, and wanted to be believed as we pursued the policy that we should have pursued in the first place. Failure to follow our beliefs in the first instance, is causing us great trouble in Africa. Look at Greece. During the whole period that the military junta controlled Greek government, this administration cozied up to that military dictatorship, befriended them, did everything they could to support them, but once Greeks restored their own democracy, we turned our back on them and have not assisted them in seeking a just and final settlement on the island of Cyprus. Take the issue of the Middle East. This government of ours is pursuing a policy of permitting the vicious Arab boycott to continue in this country. They have not sought any reform. They are pursuing an arms peddling policy in this world wh– in which we s– sell more arms by double, of all the rest of the world put together. And last year alone, or this year, we're selling and contracting for seven and a half billion dollars of arms for Saudi Arabia, and only a billion four for Israel. We've lost our way, we need a new sense of values, and we intend to restore them.

Hoge

Senator Dole.

Dole

Well I notice in all that discussion you never once d– criticized Secretary Kissinger, I don't recall Senator Mondale ever criticizing Secretary Kissinger. As I think back uh– the Democrat policies at, and their secret agreements at Yalta and Potsdam and how this had the effect of enslaving Eastern Europe, and when I think of uh– the leadership of President Roosevelt–and I think about that every day because of a personal experience in World War Two–I'm kind of thankful we have somebody who's concerned about peace. And whether Senator Mondale likes it or not, or whether Governor Carter likes it or not–and Governor Carter won't tell us who he's gonna put in the Cabinet–he probably doesn't know–I think it's kind of nice to be at peace in the world, to be respected in the world. We've had more respect than we've ever had. Prime Minister Rabin said our relations with Ih– Israel, are aaa– are at a peak, the highest they've been. The same is true of France and West Germany. We have a balanced peace in the Mideast because of our leadership.

Hoge

Mr. Mears, your question to Senator Mondale.

Mears

Senator Mondale *Clears throat*, you and Governor Carter have made an issue of President Ford's statement that there is no Soviet domination of Eastern Europe, a statement the president now says was in error. I'd like to know whether there's any real difference between the two tickets on Eastern Europe, or whether this is simply an effort by the Democrats to attract voters of Eastern European backgrounds. What would a Democratic administration do that the Republicans are not doing to foster freedom in Eastern Europe, and what would a new administration do on the question that the president declined to answer yesterday. If an Eastern European nation attempted to overthrow Soviet domination, should the United States help?

Mondale

Well there are several things that we would do. The first thing we would do was, is to make clear, consistently, what the facts are in Eastern Europe. The comment that the president made, that Eastern Europe was independent and aut— autonomous from Soviet control, is probably one of the most outrageous statements made by a president in recent political history. It's caused great confusion in Europe, Communist newspapers in Poland are praising the president because his statement helped give credibility to Soviet control. I'm glad the president finally apologized for that remark, but it's surprising that it took six days, and several attempts, before we finally received that apology. What we think is needed in our policies with Eastern Europe, is not to deal with Eastern Europe as a bloc, as does this administration, but to deal with each country individually, on its own status directly, and not through the Soviet Union, to continue to identify with their aspirations for national independence, not because we are any, under any illusions about how easy it would be for them to become independent, but because it's important for us to identify as the nation which above all stands for freedom and independence, with the aspirations of all people around the world for those same objectives. Secondly, we would push eh— the, that part of the Helsinki accords known as Basket Three, which requires much opening up, much more opening up, in people-to-people contacts and informational contacts. This administration signed the Helsinki accords, but duh— has done practically nothing to push those agreements which would open up communications between our nation and our peoples and the peoples of Eastern Europe and the Soviet Union. As a matter of fact, it was just the other day, after several weeks delay, before they even finally appointed uh— re— representatives of the administration to the commission looking into the enforcement of that provision. And finally, I think it's important that we honor people from Eastern Europe, who stand as symbols of the human spirit's ability to stand up to police oppression. And I will never understand why this president of the United States refused to even receive and honor Mr. Solzhenitsyn, who perhaps above all people in the human race, stands as a symbol for the ability and the strength of spirit against police oppression.

Hoge

Senator Dole, your response.

Appendix E 273

Dole

Well, I'm glad you mentioned Solzhenitsyn. I checked today with his interpreter and I understand you've never met Mr. Solzhenitsyn uh— neither has Mr. Carter. Now I've had the privilege of meeting uh— uh— Mr. Solzhenitsyn—maybe you've shook his hand somewhere— but uh— I want to move into the Eastern Europe sector. I'm reminded of how the Berlin Wall went up and the, who was in power when it went up. I think we take a hard look at President Ford's record, rather than all the rhetoric that followed uh— a mistake in the last debate about uh— Poland, we'd know very clearly where President Ford not only stands but has stood for twenty-some years. I think one way to let the people in Eastern Europe know of our concern is by trade. As President Ford said, they've never really given up hope. Their government may be dominated, their leaders of that government may be dominated by Soviet Russia, but the hearts and the minds of the Polish people, or the Yugoslavs or Rumanians, or the Czechs, or wherever, have never been dominated. And they're good customers. You know we have a favorable balance of trade with Eastern Europe. I think last year they exported almost a half-billion dollars' worth of goods and material and we sent in about a billion dollars' worth. I just wish Governor Carter had a foreign policy. He doesn't have any, doesn't have any experience. He made some statement about Italy that bothers me because I was in World War Two in Italy. My whole life changed because of my experience in Italy. I know the Italian people. I know they're God-fearing freedom-loving people. I couldn't quite understand what Governor Carter meant in *Playboy Magazine*. I couldn't understand frankly why he was in *Playboy Magazine*—but he was, and we'll give him the bunny vote. But I couldn't understand, what he meant when he said, that we ought to extend a hand of friendship to the Communists in Portugal and governments of France and Italy, because by doing that he simply invites difficulty from Communist leaders in those countries. So I say, oh we're strong, we're firm, President Ford understands, we're still at peace, we still have those same hopes and aspirations of the Eastern Europeans—and that's what it's all about—freedom, peace, no bloodshed.

Hoge

Senator Mondale.

Mondale

Well I regret that uh— Mr. Dole made that statement about Mr. Solzhenitsyn, because it's false. I've repeatedly spoken out in admiration of him. I served on the host committee receiving Mr. Solzhenitsyn in the United States Senate. He's a man that deserved to be honored, and it was a shame to me that the president of the United States, because we were fearful of offending the Soviet Union, failed to accord that high honor to Mr. Solzhenitsyn. I'm also sorry that he's tried to misrepresent Governor Carter's position on the government that should control Portugal and Italy. The governor made it very clear that he hoped the non-Communists would continue control those countries. The biggest thing that we're doing today, that is undermining those forces of democracy, is the disarray of our economy here at home. With our tremendous unemployment, with our tremendous inflation, and the dominance of our economy on the economies of Western Europe, of Japan and Canada, we have contri— contributed to such conditions that it has strengthened the radical forces in those countries. And that's what we need to do to best help the democratic forces of those nations.

Hoge

Thank you, senators. We have reserved time this evening for questions on general subjects. The first question in this area is from Mr. Bruno, and it is for Senator Dole.

Bruno

Eh— Senator Dole, out there in the campaign trail uh— you've been saying that a Carter-Mondale administration would take its orders from George Meany and the A.F. of L.-C.I.O. Yet Mr. Meany was among those who influenced President Ford on the grain embargo, which you personally opposed. Now how do you know that Mr. Meany will influence Governor Carter any more than he already has influenced President Ford, and what if anything, is wrong with labor or business or farmers making their views known in the White House as long as it's done openly and honestly.

Dole

Well I don't have any quarrel, uh— say, first of all, with anybody making their views known. I wish more businessmen would participate in active politics. In fact, I've held up labor as an example, for others to follow because they are very active. I just don't believe that uh— labor leaders, whether it's Leonard Woodcock, or George Meany, or Jerry Wurf, whoever, ought to make a decision for thousands and millions of working men and women, who are concerned about spending, they're concerned about taxes, they're concerned about the gun control that Mondale and Carter favor. They're concerned about abortion. They're concerned about a lot of things. And their labor leader makes the decision, we're gonna support the Carter-Mondale ticket. Now George Meany did exercise some influence on the first embargo. I don't know how much because I wasn't privy to those meetings. He said he did it in the name of the consumer. When he really did it in the name of organized labor, to increase the shipping subsidies at the taxpayers' expense. Working with Mr. Gleason and the Longshoremen's Union they refused to load the ships, and it really put the president in a very difficult spot. 'Cause I think back of all the Democrat Senators who are now talking about embargoes, I can only recall one who spoke out at the time. That was Senator George McGovern. He had no allegiance and owed nothing to Mr. Meany because, as you know, Meany didn't support him in 1972. But all of a sudden the embargoes have cropped up as a great big issue. I know how much strength uh— labor leaders have. I know how much they're out there pushing voter registration. I know how much they, control they have in the Democratic party. And that's their right, to have influence, but not to take over the party. They have great influence on Senator Mondale, always have had. He's got a ninety-five percent labor rating or higher, the most liberal Senar— Senator in the United States Senate, and that's his right, if he wants to be a liberal and spend your money and tax and tax and spend and spend. That's his right. He get, when at first he was appointed as Attorney General, and then appointed to the Senate. Some of us had to run for what we have. But when you have had things given to you, you like to give something else to someone else. You give away your tax money, back to the taxpayers. And I just think that George Meany has every right to have influence, but not domination of a great party like the Democratic party.

Hoge

Senator Mondale.

Appendix E

Mondale

Well there are many things that could be said about that. I might begin first with voting records. Uh– there are many organizations that uh– prepare voting records. I'm pleased to have a very high rating in small business groups, among farmer groups–a much higher rating than my opponent from, the Senator from Kansas–good ratings, high ratings in housing, in health and education. Good ratings from organizations dealing with economic management. And I'm pleased by that. But perhaps one that's most appropriate tonight, is an independent dispassionate organization that represents the views of all Americans–conservative, liberal, moderate, and so on–called the League of Women Voters. For five years the League has prepared the list of the most crucial issues that they believe affects governmental effectiveness, that affects governmental honesty, that affects dealing with America's real problems. And I'm proud of the fact that in each of those five years, the League of Women Voters has rated me one hundred percent in favor of every one of those issues that they on an independent and bipartisan basis, have believed to be the most important to this country. And I note in the same record, that my opponent was wrong half the time. He only was there fifty percent of the time. And I noted that the president of the United States, Mr. Ford, when he was in the Congress, was right only thirty-five percent of the time. And I think that says something about balance. We are in the mainstream of public life. We want to get along with business, we want to get along with farmers, we want to get along with labor. We think a president has to lead everyone. And that's the only way that a president can lead. This president and his running mate think they can get elected by whipping labor on the back. Well labor's got a right to participate in the public life of this country as well as anyone else. Just take the embargo, for example. I was opposed, and said so at the time, of all the embargoes–the four imposed by the Republicans, and the short one imposed by members of the labor movement. I thought it was wrong in both instances. This, this particular ticket here uh– is selects out Mr. Meany as the scapegoat. Well you can't run this country by trying to scapegoat Americans. You have to bring everybody together and have a united country, working together to solve our real problems. And that's another reason why we need Governor Carter.

Hoge

Senator Dole, any further response.

Dole

Well I would say as far as the League of Women Voters uh– concerned, you can look at that two ways–either I was wrong half the time or they were wrong half the time. And, I think, knowing the League of Women Voters, I think I'll take my interpretation. But with reference to uh– and it, ca– they very fine but they tend to be a little bit liberal. Now, George Meany, he wants the right-to-work law repealed in Texas, in my state. Senator Mondale's for the repeal of right-to-work laws. He wants to force you to join a labor union. Seventy-five percent of America's working men and women don't belong to labor unions, but they will if George Meany and Governor Carter and Senator Mondale have their way. They've also got some big Proposition Fourteen out in California, where organizers come on your property three hours a day and organize farmers, unionize farmers. Governor Carter's for that, I assume Senator Mondale's for that. Certainly Cesar Chavez is, and other labor leaders. I just say they oughta have influence, they shouldn't have domination. What about your national security voting record where you get a zero every year, when you talk about our defense.

Hoge

Thank you. Miss Berger, your question to Senator Mondale.

Berger

Senator Mondale, you've criticized Mr. Ford for having defended Richard Nixon—that is, while Mr. Ford was vice-president—and you did see in your own political career that Hubert Humphrey suffered a great deal politically by standing with Lyndon Johnson almost to the end on Vietnam. And now you've acknowledged that you have differences with Governor Carter. You've said that an important mark of national leadership is the ability to put loyalty to principle above loyalty to party, or even to the president of the United States. If push came to shove, would you put principle above loyalty to your running mate, and possibly to the president of the United States? And what issues are important enough to do that?

Mondale

The answer is, yes I would. But I would not have accepted a place as the running mate of Governor Carter, if I thought that was a real possibility. We had a long talk about the problem of independence between the two, the president and the vice-president. And I made it clear to him that I was not interested in serving in a role that was ceremonial, or serving in a role where if I really felt deeply about something, I was prevented from saying so. I did not want to go through that, I did not want to give up my position in the Senate, where I have that right. We agreed that that would be the relationship. And during this campaign on three separate occasions where I have agreed, wi— disagreed with Mr. Carter, I've said so in the course of this campaign. And I think the whole issue of public trust and public faith is bound up very closely with that question. We have had so much politics-as-usual, so much political trimming, that Americans have lost faith in public leadership. For example, in Watergate, when this nation's whole system of liberty was at stake, and the Ervin Committee was established to investigate wrongdoing by the president of the United States, my opponent introduced a resolution to slam the door shut on the Ervin Committee so the people could not see and hear what was going on. And the Sa— night of the Saturday Night Massacre, perhaps the most treacherous moment in the history of American liberty, when the high officers—Richardson and Ruckelshaus—were fired, for enforcing the law, fired by the president of the United States, both Mr. Ford and Mr. Dole stood up and defended Mr. Nixon. And if Mr. Nixon had gotten away with that massacre that night, he would stra— probably still be president of the United States, and we would not have taught that crucial lesson, that not even the highest officials in government can violate the law. Never again can we permit that kind of politics-above-all to dominate this country. Even today this administration is fighting all the Watergate reforms, opposed the appointment of a special prosecutor, opposed the reforms that c— were cried out for adoption following the revelations of the abuse of the C.I.A. and the F.B.I. And with a record like that, and with all of the abuse of public faith and trust that we've been through, surely that too is another reason for a new generation of leadership.

Hoge

Senator Dole.

Appendix E

Dole

Well, Watergate is a Republican problem, and I voted for the Watergate investigation. My opponent was absent, which is, we're all absent sometime, but he's absent more than others. I think also its well to point up that uh– I did introduce a resolution to shut off the public hearings and to get down to business and get Watergate behind us. Democrats didn't want to do that. They were having great fun on T.V. every day, and then for a while they didn't want to find a solution. But I remember Senator Ervin's report, the chairman of the Watergate Committee, and he said in that report, and I was chairman of the Republican party during the Watergate years, and I'm very proud to have been chairman, I've always said that the night Watergate happened was my night off, so can't hook me for that. But Senator Ervin said, had Senator Dole been in charge, there wouldn't have been a Watergate, so I don't want any rub-off from Senator Mondale's statements to want any of you people to believe that he might be suggesting that somehow President Ford or Senator Dole was any way involved in Watergate. We were not. He brings it up all the time, he brings up the pardon all the time, he doesn't bring up the fact that when we tried to extend the investigation of Watergate back into other areas that, that were voted down along straight party lines. That's their right. They control the Senate. He doesn't bring up the fact that uh– when the problems in the House uh– Democrats this year, the speaker appointed three Democrats to investigate the Democrats. Can you imagine the hue and cry in America, had the Republicans done that? Why Mondale would have dropped dead. And that's the way it's been–that's the way it's been. But Watergate's our burden. We're going forward. It's behind us. And Governor Carter can talk about it and Senator Mondale can talk about it, but beyond that, I think we must say as Senator Mondale has–and I don't quarrel with him–that if there comes a time when I'm the vice-president, I can't agree with the president, then I must say so. I think that's fundamental. I think we're both honorable men. I think we both make that judgment. The only mystery to me is how do you know what Governor Cus– Carter stands for? I've been trying to find out for six weeks. He has three positions on everything–that's why they're having three T.V. debates. So I just suggest that uh– maybe in the time remaining, Senator Mondale can tell us, what his running mate stands for. The American people would like to know.

Hoge

Senator Mondale.

Mondale

My candidate stands for jobs for all Americans. He stands for a government that fights inflation. He stands for tax reform, and to take those revenues and reduce taxes for the average American. He stands for a program at long last to solve the hi– ho– health crisis in America. He stands for at long last to get the housing industry back on its feet. He will support programs to give senior citizens a decent break. He will not try as Mr. Ford did, to put a cap on Social Security so senior citizens were robbed of their inflationary adjustments. He will not destroy the housing programs for senior citizens, as this Republican administration has done. Governor Carter stands for leadership. He's gonna take charge. We need someone to lead this country. We haven't had it. Governor Carter will provide that leadership. And Governor Carter will restore to this nation a foreign policy that operates in the public, and on the basis of the beliefs of the American people.

Hoge

Gentlemen, we have about five minutes left for short questions and short answers. Each sequence from now on will consist only of the question, the answer, and the other candidate's response. We'll drop the further response. The first question is from Mr. Mears to Senator Dole.

Mears

Senator Dole, ten days ago when Senator Mondale raised the issues of Watergate and the Nixon pardon, you called it the start of the campaign mudslinging. Two years ago when you were running for the Senate, you said that the pardon was prematurely granted and that it was a m— and that it was a mistake. You were quoted by the Kansas City *Times* as saying, you can't ignore our tradition of equal application of the law. Did you approve of the Nixon pardon when President Ford granted it? You approve of it now, and if the issue was fair game in your 1974 campaign in Kansas, why is it not an appropriate topic now?

Dole

Well, it *Clears throat* i— it is an appropriate topic I guess, but it's not a very good issue any more than the war in Vietnam would be, or World War Two, or World War One, or the war in Korea, all Democrat wars, all in this century. I figured up the other day, if we added up the killed and wounded, in Democrat wars in this century it would be about one point six million Americans, enough to fill the city of Detroit. Now if we want to go back and rake that over and over and over, we can do that. I assume Senator Mondale doesn't want to do that. But it seems to me that the pardon of Richard Nixon is behind us. Watergate's behind us. If we have this vision for American and if we are really concerned about those people out there, and their problems, yes, and their education and their jobs, we ought to be talking about that. Now I know it strikes a responsive chord for some, to kick Richard Nixon around. I don't know how long you can keep that up. How much mileage is there in someone who's been kicked, whose wife suffered a serious stroke, who's been disgraced in office and stepped down from that office, and I think after two years and some months that it's probably a dead issue. But let 'em play that game. That's the only game they know.

Hoge

Senator Mondale.

Mondale

I think uh— Senator Dole has richly earned his reputation as a hatchet man tonight, by implying and stating that World War Two and the Korean War were Democratic wars. Does he really mean to suggest to the American people, that there was a partisan difference over our involvement in the war to fight Nazi Germany? I don't think any reasonable American would accept that. Does he really mean to suggest that it was only partisanship, that got us into the war in Korea? Does he really mean to forget that part of the record, where Mr. Nixon and the Republican party wanted us to get involved earlier in the war in Vietnam, and long after Mr. Nixon and the Republican party promised to finish the war in Vietnam, they kept urging us forward, and that in fact it was the Democratic Congress that passed the law ending the war in Vietnam and preventing a new war in Angola. Now on Watergate, we're not charging and he knows it, his involvement in Watergate. What we're saying is that they defended Mr. Nixon up to the last.

Appendix E

Hoge

Mr. Bruno, your question to Senator Mondale.

Bruno

Senator Mondale, uh— you cited the priorities of a Carter administration. At the same time Governor Carter has promised to balance the federal budget within four years. Now can we take just one of those items that you gave very high priority to that would be very costly, uh— national health insurance? Now realistically, what are the chances of getting this program in a Carter-Mondale administration, or would it have to be postponed until the budget is balanced? Which comes first?

Mondale

Well I think both the presidential budget and our estimates agree, that if we move back to full employment, as we intend to do, and achieve a five and a half percent real growth rate, as we did under Truman, and as we did under Kennedy and Johnson, that within four years, the revenues generated by that growth, without increasing taxes, will pay for the costs of the programs now in place, such as Social Security, pensions and the rest, the ongoing programs that are essential in America—the defense program and the rest—and that we will have a full employment yield of somewhere between seventy and eighty billions of dollars. Some of that can be used for tax relief, and it should be. Some of it should be, however, used for programs that at long last start dealing with the real problems that America faces, such as health care. Now there are many different versions of health care, but we would work closely with Senator Kennedy, with Paul Rogers and ev— and others, to develop a health program. Now there's no question about the difference in spending. The Republicans would spend more than we do during that same period, but they would spend it first by twenty billion dollars in tax relief for wealthy businessmen or wealthy corporations, and secondly by the continuation of these economic policies, that are costing us over fifty billion dollars a year. So the question is not spending, the question is the priorities.

Hoge

Senator Dole.

Dole

Well, I would remind uh— those who may be still tuned in that the Democrats still control the Congress—they did when we started this debate and hour and twenty minutes ago, they still do by two-to-one margins almost, and they're responsible for legislation. I know Senator Long who's chairman of our Finance Committee, will be very pleased to learn what Senator Mondale's gonna do now, with Governor Carter. Now if they're talking about full employment, they're talking about the Humphrey-Hawkins Bill, which they support. We don't know what it costs. Twenty billion dollars? Forty billion dollars? Or more? Another government employment program. I'd like to add up the number of jobs Senator Mondale has cost this country in defense plants, defense jobs, in all his anti-defense votes. It'd be hundreds and hundreds of thousands. And he knows it. He wants bigger welfare programs, bigger giveaway programs. We want to take care of those out of work, we want to take care of those in need. Let's not wreck our business system, let's not wreck our free enterprise system, just to prove a point.

Hoge

Thank you, Senators. That concludes the questioning for this evening. Each candidate now has up to three minutes for a closing statement. By the coin toss, it was determined that Senator Dole would make the first opening statement and take the first question. He now also goes first with his closing statement. Senator Dole.

Dole

Clears throat Well, first I wish to thank the panel for their indulgence and of course all those in the viewing audience who may still be with us. I really hope, and I haven't prepared any final statement in advance, I really hope you were listening, and we were able to tell you who's concerned about the American people, which party has faith in the American people, which party and which candidates want bigger and bigger and bigger government, which candidates want more and more spending, more and more interference. When we added up five of the programs that Governor Carter and Mondale talk about—only five— they really want sixty-some new programs in their platform or expanded programs—they want to create twenty-two new agencies, or expand that many existing agencies. We only added up five programs and the cost is a hundred and three billion dollars, a hundred and three billion. That would cost every taxpayer in America several hundred dollars. They don't care about inflation—the cruelest tax of all. And if you're in your living room watching tonight, and you're making six thousand dollars a year on fixed income, and there's a six percent inflation, that's three hundred and sixty dollars a year—that's thirty dollars a month—that affects everybody in America. And add up your inflation if you let Carter and Mondale have their way. One spending program after another. We're concerned about the poor. We're concerned about the sick. We're concerned about the disabled. We're concerned about those on Social Security. And we have programs for that. We're concerned about housing—Carla Hills announced one today, to reduce the interest payments, from eight and a half to eight percent for F.H.A. and V.A. homes. Governor Carter wants to preclude you from taking off your interest, your mortgage interest, as a tax deduction. He says nobody wants their taxes lowered. Well maybe not, if they're getting a forty-one thousand dollar tax credit as he is. I just say in my final minute, it's a great honor and a privilege to even be standing here—whatever happens November Second—it's an honor and a privilege. It's an honor and a privilege to have known President Ford for sixteen years, sixteen years as I said at the outset. He's a man of unparalleled decency and honesty and courage. He's a man we can be proud of. He's gonna give us that leadership that America needs—all Americans—white; black, Spanish-speaking, rich, poor. Don't be fooled by the words, don't be fooled by the rhetoric, don't be fooled by the promises because somebody has to pay for those promises. Just take a look at the leadership. Take a look at President Ford, and thank President Ford for the fact that we live in peace, and freedom, and your sons and your husbands and your relatives are home and they're safe. It can only happen in America. Thank you.

Hoge

Senator Mondale.

Mondale

Americans are not interested in partisan debating points. They're not interested in how many uh– debate points are scored. That means little, the lives of Americans. What really counts, is whether this country can begin to solve those problems that are overwhelming so many Americans—record unemployment—the highest since the Great Depression, and getting worse. Runaway inflation—three times worse than that under the Democratic party,

Appendix E

deficits that are unbelievable. Just last year, under this administration, we had a deficit larger than all the deficits created in the eight years of the Democratic administration, and under this Republican party, higher deficits than in the previous one hundred and ninety-two years of this government's history. Now we recognize that you have to be prudent, that you have to live within a budget, that you have to deal with the resources that are at hand. There's no dispute on that. The question is how will those resources be used. And we believe that we need a government that works, that's efficient, but we also think we need a government that cares. We've cared too little for people in this country that have gotten sick and can't afford decent health care. We've cared too little for the thousands and thousands of American families that cannot get or afford decent housing. This administration has fought time and time again to cut back support for our senior citizens. They have no energy policy, they have no environmental policy. Those things must change. We believe in a strong defense. We're not going to let this nation's defenses drop. But there's a big difference between waste and strength. And what we've been attacking is waste, because waste does not contribute to strength, it tri– tributes to weakness. There are many problems in the Defense Department that require better management in order to get that increased strength. We need leadership in this country, to do all of those things. For eight years now, the Republicans have controlled government. For eight years they've controlled the White House, and every one of those problems has gotten worse. They are not now proposing new policies and new directions. Tonight you heard what they are doing. They are defending the past. Everything is all right. The problems are not as bad as the statistics or the people believe, and therefore they might go away. That is not enough. This country cries out for new leadership. We need a fresh start. And the Carter-Mondale ticket promises that start. Not because we know all the answers, we know better. Not because we can do everything at once, because we know better than that, but because a good nation requires that we begin the effort.

Hoge

Thank you Senator Mondale, and thank you Senator Dole. I want to thank as well the audience here tonight, and my colleagues who were our questioners. The final debate in this series will be between the presidential candidates Gerald Ford and his challenger Jimmy Carter. It will be held on October twenty-second at nine-thirty p.m. eastern daylight time, on the campus of William and Mary College, in Williamsburg Virginia. The subject matter will cover all issues. The sponsors of these debates is the League of Women Voters' Education Fund, whose purpose is to promote greater participation by a better-informed electorate in the election on November Second. Now, from the Alley Theatre in Houston Texas, good night.

Appendix F

The Third Presidential Debate: October 22, 1976, Williamsburg

Walters

Good evening. I'm Barbara Walters, moderator of the last of the debates of 1976, between Gerald R. Ford, Republican candidate for president, and Jimmy Carter, Democratic candidate for president. Welcome, President Ford, welcome, Governor Carter, and thank you for joining us this evening. This debate takes place before an audience in Phi Beta Kappa Memorial Hall on the campus of the College of William and Mary in historic Williamsburg Virginia. It is particularly appropriate in this bicentennial year, that we meet on these grounds to hear this debate. Two hundred years ago, five William and Mary students met at nearby Raleigh Tavern, to form Phi Beta Kappa, a fraternity designed, they wrote, to search out and dispel the clouds of falsehood by debating without reserve the issues of the day. In that spirit of debate, without reserve, to dispel the clouds of falsehood, gentlemen, let us proceed. The subject matter of this debate is open, covering all issues and topics. Our questioners tonight are Joseph Kraft, syndicated columnist, Robert Maynard, editorial writer for the Washington *Post*, and Jack Nelson, Washington bureau chief of the Los Angeles *Times*. The ground rules tonight are as follows. Questioners will alternate questions between the candidates. The candidate has up to two and a half minutes to answer the question. The other candidate then has up to two minutes to respond. If necessary, a questioner may ask a follow-up question for further clarification, and in that case the candidate has up to two minutes to respond. As was initially agreed to by both candidates, the answers should be responsive to the particular questions. Finally each candidate has up to three minutes for a closing statement. President Ford and Governor Carter do not have prepared notes or comments with them this evening, but they may make notes and refer to them during the debate. It has been determined that President Ford would take the first question in this last debate, and Mr. Kraft you have that first question for President Ford.

Kraft

Mr. President uh— I assume that the Americans all know that these are difficult times and that there's no pie in the sky and that they don't expect something for nothing. Uh— so I'd like to ask you as a first question as you look ahead in the next four years uh— what sacrifices are you gonna call on the American people to make, what price are you gonna ask them to pay uh— to realize your objectives? Uh— let me add, uh— Governor Carter, that if, if you felt uh— that it was appropriate to answer that question in, in your comments, uh— as to what price it would be appropriate for the American pay, people to pay uh— for a Carter administration, I think that would be proper, too. Mr. President.

Appendix F 283

Ford

Well, Mr. Kraft, I believe that the American people in the next four years under a Ford administration, will be called upon to make those necessary sacrifices to preserve the peace which we have, which means of course that uh– we will have to maintain an adequate military capability, which means of course that we will have to add, uh– I think uh– a few billion dollars to our defense appropriations to make certain that we have adequate uh– strategic forces, adequate conventional forces. I think the American people will be called upon to um– uh– be in the forefront in giving leadership to the solution of those problems that must be solved in the Middle East, in southern Africa, and any problems that might arise in the Pacific. The American people will be called upon to tighten their belts a bit in meeting some of the problems that we face domestically. I don't think that uh– America can go on a big spending spree with a whole lot of new programs uh– that would add significantly to the federal budget. I believe that the American people, if given the leadership that I would expect to give, would be willing to give this thrust to preserve the peace, and the necessary uh– restraint at home to hold the lid on spending so that we could, I think, have a long overdue and totally justified tax decrease for the middle-income people. And then with the economy that would be generated from a restraint on spending, and a tax uh– reduction primarily for the middle-income people, then I think the American people would be willing to make those sacrifices for peace and prosperity in the next uh– four years.

Kraft

Can I be a little bit more specific, Mr. Pres . . .

[Interruption 1]

Ford

Surely, surely.

Kraft

ident? Doesn't your policy really imply that we're gonna have to have a pretty high rate of unemployment over a fairly long time, that growth is gonna be fairly slow, and that we're not gonna be able to do le– very much in the next four or five years to meet the basic agenda of our national needs in the cities, in health uh– in transit and a whole lot of other things like that?

[Interruption 2]

Ford

Not at all.

Kraft

Aren't those the real costs?

Ford

No, Mr. Kraft, we're spending very significant amounts of money now–some two hundred billion dollars a year, almost fifty percent of our total federal expenditure uh– by the federal government at the present time for human needs. Now, we will probably have to increase that to some extent. But we don't have to have eh– growth in spending that will blow the lid off and add to the problems of inflation. I believe we can meet the problems within the cities of this country, and still uh– give a tax reduction. I've proposed, as you know, a reduction to increase the personal exemption from seven hundred and fifty to a thousand dollars. With the fiscal program that I have–and if you look at the projection it shows that we will reduce unemployment, that we will continue to win the battle against inflation, and at the same time give the kind of quality of life that I believe is possible in America. Uh– a job, a home for all those that'll work and save for it, uh– safety in the streets, uh– health that is of– health care that is affordable. These things can be done if we have the right vision and the right restraint and the right leadership.

Walters

Thank you. Governor Carter, your response, please.

Carter

Well, I might say first of all that I think in case of the Carter administration the sacrifices would be much less. Mr. Ford's own uh– environmental agency has projected a ten percent unemployment rate by 1978, if he's uh– president. The American people are ready to make sacrifices if they're part of the process, if they know that they will be helping to make decisions and won't be excluded from being an involved party to the national purpose. The major effort that we must put forward is to put our people back to work. And I think that this uh– is one example where uh– a lot of people have selfish, grasping ideas now. I remember 1973 in the depth of the uh– energy crisis, when President Nixon called on the American people to make a sacrifice, to cut down the waste of uh– gasoline, to cut down on the uh– speed of automobiles. There was a, a tremendous surge of patriotism, and I want to make a sacrifice for my country. I think we uh– could call together–with strong leadership in the White House–business, industry and labor, and say let's have voluntary price restraints, let's lay down some guidelines so we don't have continuing inflation. We can also have a, an end to the extremes. We now have one extreme, for instance, of some welfare recipients who by taking advantage of the welfare laws, the housing laws, the uh– medicaid uh– laws, and the uh– food stamp laws make over a ten thousand dollars a year, and uh– they don't have to pay any taxes on it. At the other extreme, uh– just one percent of the richest people in our country, derive twenty-five percent of all the tax benefits. So both those extremes grasp for advantage and the person who has to pay that expense, is the middle-income family who's still working for a living, and they have to pay for the rich who have privilege and for the poor who are not working. But I think that a, a, a balanced approach, with everybody being part of it, and a striving for unselfishness, could help, as it did in 1973, to let people sacrifice for their own country. I know I'm ready for it. I think the American people are, too.

Walters

Thank you. Mr. Maynard, your question to Governor Carter.

Maynard

Governor, by all indications, the voters are so turned off by this election campaign so far, that only half intend to vote. One major reason for this apathetic electorate appears to be the low level at which this campaign has been conducted. It has digressed frequently from important issues into allegations of blunder and brainwashing and fixations on lust and *Play-*

Appendix F 285

boy. What responsibility do you accept for the low level of this campaign for the nation's highest office?

Carter

I think the major reason for a decrease in participation that we've experienced ever since 1960, has been the deep discouragement of the American people about the performance of public officials. When you've got seven and a half, eight million people out of work, when you've got three times as much inflation as you had during the last eight-year Democratic administration, when you have the highest deficits in history, when you have it uh– becoming increasingly difficult for a family to put a child through college or to own a home, there's a natural inclination to be turned off. Also, in the aftermath of Vietnam and Cambodia and uh– Watergate and uh– the C.I.A. revelations, people that feel, have felt that they've uh– been betrayed by public officials. I have to admit that in the uh– heat of a campaign–I've been in thirty primaries during the springtime, I've been campaigning for twenty-two months–I've made some mistakes. And I think this is uh– uh– part of uh– of just being a human being. I, I have to say that my campaign's been an open one. And uh– the *Playboy* thing has been of, of great, very great concern to me. I don't know how to deal with it exactly. Uh– I uh– agreed to give the interview uh– to *Playboy*. Other people have done it who are notable–uh– Governor Jerry Brown, uh– Walter Cronkite, uh– Albert Schweitzer, and Mr. Ford's own Secretary of Treasury, Mr. Simon, uh– William Buckley, many other people. But they weren't running for president. And, in retrospect, from hindsight, I would not have given that uh– interview had I do it, had I to do it over again. If I should ever decide in the future to discuss my, my deep Christian beliefs and uh– condemnation and sinfulness I'll use another forum besides *Playboy*. But I can say this. Uh– I'm doing the best I can to get away from that. And during the next uh– ten days the American people will not see the Carter campaign running uh– television advertisements and newspaper advertisements based on a personal attack on President Ford's character. I believe that the opposite is true with President Ford's campaign. And uh– I hope that we can leave those issues in this next ten days, about personalities and mistakes of the past–we've both made some mistakes–and talk about unemployment, inflation, housing, education, taxation, government organization, stripping away of secrecy, and the things that are crucial to the American people. I regret the things in my own long campaign that have been mistaken. But I'm trying to do away with those the last ten days.

Walters

Thank you, Governor Carter, President Ford, your response.

Ford

I believe that the uh– American people have been turned off in this election, uh– Mr. Maynard, for a variety of reasons. We have seen on Capitol Hill, in the Congress, uh– a great many uh– allegations of wrongdoing, of uh– alleged immorality. Uh– those are very disturbing to the American people. They wonder how an elected representative uh– can serve them and participate in such activities, uh– serving in the Congress of the United States. Yes, and I'm certain many, many Americans were turned off by the revelations of Watergate, a very, very uh– bad period of time in American political history. Yes, and thousands–maybe millions–of Americans were turned off because of the uh– problems that came out of our involvement in Vietnam. But, on the other hand, I found on July Fourth of this year, a new spirit born in America. We were celebrating our Bicentennial, and I find that uh– there is a, a movement as I travel around the country of greater interest in this campaign. Now like uh– any hardworking uh– person seeking public office uh– in the campaign, inevitably sometimes you will use uh— rather graphic language, and I'm guilty of that just like I think most others in the political arena. But I do make the pledge, that in the next ten days when we're asking the American people to make one of the most important decisions in their lifetime, because I think this election is one of the most vital in the history of America, that uh— we do, together, what we can to stimulate voter participation.

Walters

Thank you, President Ford. Mr. Nelson, your question to President Ford.

Nelson

Uh— Mr. President, you mentioned Watergate, and you became president because of Watergate. So don't you owe the American people a special obligation to explain in detail your role of limiting one of the original investigations of Watergate—that was the one by the House Banking Committee? And I know you've answered questions on this before, but there are questions that still remain, and I think people want to know what your role was. Will you name the persons you talked to in connection with that investigation? And since you say you have no recollection of talking to anyone from the White House, would you be willing to open for examination the White House tapes of conversations uh— during that period?

Ford

Well, Mr. uh— Nelson, uh— I testified before two committees, House and Senate, on precisely the questions that you have asked, and the testimony under oath, was to the effect that I did not talk to Mr. Nixon, to Mr. Haldeman, to Mr. Ehrlichman or to any of the people at the White House. I said I had no recollection whatsoever of talking with any of the White House legislative liaison people. I indicated under oath, that the initiative that I took was at the request of the ranking members of the House Banking and Currency Committee on the Republican side, which was a legitimate request and a proper response by me. Now that was gone into by two congressional committees, and following that investigation, both committees overwhelmingly approved me, and both the House and the Senate did likewise. Now, in the meantime, the special prosecutor within the last few days after an investigation himself, said there was no reason for him to get involved because he found nothing that would justify it. And then just a day or two ago, the Attorney General of the United States made a further investigation, and came to precisely the same conclusion. Now, after all of those investigations by objective, responsible people, I think the matter is closed once and for all. But to add one other feature, I don't control any of the tapes. Those tapes are in the jurisdiction of the courts, and I have no right to say yes or no. But all the committees, the Attorney General, the special prosecutor, all of them have given me a clean bill of health. I think the matter is settled once and for all.

Nelson

Well, Mr. President, if I do say so, though, the question is that I think you still have not gone into details about what your role in it was. And uh— I don't think there's any question about whether or not uh— there was a criminal prosecution, but whether, whether you had told the American people your entire involvement in it. And whether you would be willing, even though you don't control the tapes, whether you would be willing to ask that the tapes be released for examination.

Appendix F 287

Ford

That's for the uh— proper authorities who have control over those tapes to make that decision. I have given every bit of evidence, answered every question that's a— been asked me by any senator or any member of the House, plus the fact that the special prosecutor, on his own initiation, and the Attorney General on his initiation, the highest law enforcement official in this country—all of them have given me a clean bill of health. And I've told everything I know about it. I think the matter is settled once and for all.

Walters

Governor Carter, your response.

Carter

I don't have any response.

Walters

Thank you. Then we will have the next question from Mr. Kraft to Governor Carter.

Kraft

Uh— Governor Carter, the next big crisis spot in the world may be Yugoslavia. Uh— President Tito is old and sick and there are divisions in his country. Uh— it's pretty certain that the Russians are gonna do everything they possibly can after Tito dies to force Yugoslavia back into the Soviet camp. But last Saturday you said, and, and this is a quote, I would not go to war in Yugoslavia even if the Soviet Union sent in troops. Doesn't that statement practically invite the Russians to intervene in Yugoslavia? Uh— doesn't it discourage Yugoslavs who, who might be tempted to resist, and wouldn't it have been wiser on your part uh— to say nothing and to keep the Russians in the dark, as President Ford did, and as I think every president has done since, since President Truman.

Carter

In the last uh— two weeks I've had a chance to talk to uh— two men who have visited uh— the Soviet Union, Yugoslavia and China. One is Governor Averell, Averell Harriman, who visited the Soviet Union and Yugoslavia, and the other one is James Schlesinger, whom I think you accompanied to uh— China. I got a, a complete report back from those countries from these two distinguished uh— gentlemen. Mr. Harriman talked to the leaders in Yugoslavia, and I think it's accurate to say that there is no uh— prospect, in their opinion, of the Soviet Union invading uh— Yugoslavia should uh— Mr. Tito pass away. The present leadership uh— there is uh— is fairly uniform in, in their purpose. I think it's a close-knit group uh— and uh— I think it would be unwise for us to say that we will go to war uh— in Yugoslavia uh— if the Soviets should invade, which I think would be an extremely unlikely thing. I have maintained from the very beginning of my campaign—and this was a standard answer that I made in response to the Yugoslavian question—that I would never uh— go to war or become militarily involved in the internal affairs of another country, unless our own security was directly threatened, and uh— I don't believe that our security would be directly threatened if the Soviet Union went uh— into Yugoslavia. I don't believe it will happen, I certainly hope it won't. I would take eh— the strongest possible measures, short of uh— actual military uh— action there by our own troops. But I doubt that that would be an eventuality.

Kraft

One quick follow-up.

[Interruption 3]

Carter

Yes.

Kraft

Did you clear the response you made with Secretary Schlesinger and Governor Harriman?

Carter

No, I did not.

Walters

President Ford, your response.

Ford

Well I firmly believe, uh– Mr. Kraft, that it's unwise for a president to signal in advance what uh– options he might exercise if any uh– international problem arose. I think we all recall with some sadness that at uh– the period of the ninet– late 1940s, early 1950s, there were some indications that the United States would not include uh– South Korea in a area of defense. There are some who allege–I can't prove it true or untrue–that uh– such a statement uh– in effect invited the North Koreans to invade South Korea. It's a fact they did. But no president of the United States, in my opinion, should signal in advance to a prospective enemy what his uh– decision might be or what option wa– he might exercise. It's far better for a person sitting in the White House uh– who has a number of options, to make certain that the uh– other side so to speak, doesn't know precisely what you're going to do. And therefore that was the reason that I would not uh– identify any particular course of action uh– when I responded to a question a week or so ago.

Walters

Thank you. Mr. Maynard, your question to President Ford, please.

Maynard

Sir, this question concerns your administrative performance as president. The other day, General George Brown, the chairman of the Joint Chiefs of Staff, delivered his views on several sensitive subjects, among them Great Britain, one of this country's oldest allies. He said, and I quote him now, Great Britain, it's a pathetic thing. It just makes you cry. They're no longer a world power. All they have are generals, admirals, and bands, end quote. Since General Brown's comments have caused this country embarrassment in the past, why is he still this nation's leading military officer?

Appendix F

Ford

I have indicated to General Brown that uh— the words that he used in that interview, in that particular case and in several others, were very ill-advised. And General Brown has indicated uh— his apology, his regrets, and I think that will uh— in this situation, settle the matter. It is tragic that uh— the full transcript of that interview was not released, and that there were excerpts—some of the excerpts—taken out of context. Not this one, however, that you bring up. General Brown has an exempl'y record of military performance. He served this nation with great, great skill and courage and bravery for thirty-five years, and I think it's the consensus of the people who are knowledgeable in the military field, that he is probably the outstanding military leader and strategist that we have in America today. Now, he did use uh— ill-advised words. But I think in the fact that he apologized, that he was reprimanded, uh— does permit him to stay on and continue that kind of leadership that's we so badly need as we enter into uh— negotiations uh— under the SALT Two agreement or if we have operations that might be developing uh— in the Middle East or in southern Africa or in the Pacific. Uh— we need a man with that experience, that knowledge, that know-how and I think, in light of the fact that he has uh— apologized, uh— would not have justified my asking for his resignation.

Walters

Thank you. Governor Carter, your response.

Carter

Well, just briefly, I, I think this is uh— the second time that General Brown has made a statement at, for which he did have to apologize. And I know that everybody uh— makes mistakes. I think the first one was related to uh— the unwarranted influence of American Jews on the media and uh— on the Congress. This one concerned uh— Great Britain. I think he said that Israel was a, a military burden on us, and that Iran, uh— hoped to reestablish the Persian empire. Uh— I'm not uh— sure that I remembered earlier that President Ford had, had expressed uh— his concern about the statement or apologized for it. This is uh— something, though, that I think, uh— is uh— indicative of a need among the American people to know how the Commander in Chief, the president, feels. And, and, and I think the only criticism that I would have uh— o— of Mr. Ford is that uh— immediately when the statement was re—re—revealed, uh—perhaps a, a statement from the president would have been a clarifying and a very beneficial thing.

Walters

Mr. Nelson, your question now to Governor Carter.

Nelson

Governor, despite the fact that uh— you've been running for president a long time now, uh— many m— Americans uh— still seem to be uneasy about you. Uh— they don't feel that uh— they know you or the people around you. And one problem seems to be that you haven't reached out to bring people of broad background or national experience into your campaign or your presidential plans. Most of the people around you on a day-to-day basis are uh— people you've know— uh— known in Georgia, uh— many of them are young and relatively inexperienced in national affairs. And uh— doesn't this raise a serious question as to uh— whether you would bring into a Carter administration uh— people with the necessary background to run the federal government?

Carter

I don't believe it does. Uh— I began campaigning uh— twenty-two months ago. At that time nobody thought I had a chance to win. Uh— very few people knew who I was. I came from a tiny town, as you know, Plains, and didn't hold public office, didn't have very much money. And my first organization was just four or five people, plus my wife and my children—my three sons and their wives. And we won the nomination by going out into the streets, barber shops, beauty parlors, restaurants, stores, in factory shift lines, also in farmers' markets and livestock sale barns—and we talked a lot and we listened a lot. And we learned from the American people. And we built up uh— an awareness among the uh— voters of this country, particularly those in whose primaries—I entered thirty of them, nobody's ever done that before—about who I was and what I stood for. Now we have a very, very wide-ranging group of advisers who helped me prepare for these debates and who teach me about international economics and foreign affairs, defense matters, health, education, welfare, government reorganization—I'd say several hundred of them. And they are very fine, and very highly qualified. The one major decision that I have made since acquiring the nomination—and I share this with President Ford—is the choice of the vice-president. I think this would be indicative of the kind of leaders that I would choose to help me, if I am elected. I chose Senator Walter Mondale. And the only criterion that I ever put forward in my own mind, was who among the several million people in this country, would be the best person qualified to be president, if something should happen to me, and to join me in being vice-president if I should serve out my term. And I'm convinced now more than I was when I got the nomination, that Walter Mondale was the right choice. And I believe this is a good indication of the kind of people I would choose in the future. Mr. Ford has had that same choice to make. I don't want to say anything critical of Senator Dole. But I never heard Mr. Ford say that that was his pri— primary consideration—who is the best person I could choose in this country, to be president of the United States. I feel completely at ease knowing that some day Senator Mondale might very well be president. In the last five pres— uh— vice-presidential uh— uh— nominees, uh— incumbents, three of them have become president. But I think this is indicative of what I would do.

Walters

President Ford, your response, please.

Ford

The governor may not have heard my uh— established criteria for the selection of a vice-president, but uh— it was a well-established criteria that the person I selected would be fully qualified to be president of the United States, and Senator Bob Dole is so qualified— sixteen years in the House of Representatives and in the Senate, uh— very high responsibilities on important committees. I don't mean to be critical of uh— Senator Mondale, but uh— I was uh— very, very surprised when I read that uh— Senator Mondale made a very derogatory, very personal comment about General Brown uh— after the news story that uh— broke about General Brown. My recollection is correct, he indicated that uh— General Brown was not qualified to be a sewer commissioner. I don't think that's a proper way to describe a uh— chairman of the Joint Chiefs of Staff who has fought for his country for thirty-five years, and I'm sure the governor would agree with me on that. Uh— I think Senator Dole would show more good judgment and discretion than to so describe a, a heroic and brave and very outstanding leader of the military. So I think our selection of Bob Dole, as vice-president uh— is based on merit, and if he should ever become uh— the president of the United States with his vast experience as member of the House and a member of the Senate as well as a vice-president, I think he would do an outstanding job as president of the United States.

Appendix F 291

Walters

Mr. Kraft, your question to President Ford.

Kraft

Uh— Mr. President uh— uh— let me assure you and maybe some of the uh— viewing audience, that being on this panel hasn't been, as it may seem, all torture and agony. Uh— one of the heartening things is that uh— I and my colleagues have received uh— literally hundreds and maybe even thousands of suggested questions from ordinary citizens all across the country uh— who want answers.

[Interruption 4]

Ford

That's a tribute to their interest in this election.

Kraft

I'll give you that. Uh— but uh— let me go on, because one main subject on the minds of all of them has been the environment. Uh— and th— particularly curious about your record. People, people really want to know why you vetoed the strip-mining bill. They want to know why you worked against strong controls on auto emissions. They want to know why you aren't doing anything about pollution uh— of the Atlantic Ocean. Uh— they want to know why uh— a bipartisan organization such as the National League of Conservation Voters, says that when it comes to environmental issues you are, and I'm quoting, hopeless.

Ford

First uh— let me set the record straight. I vetoed the strip-mining bill, Mr. Kraft, because it was the overwhelming consensus, of knowledgeable people, that that strip-mining bill would have meant the loss of literally uh— thousands of jobs—something around a hundred and forty thousand jobs. Number two, that strip-mining bill would have severely set back our need for more coal, and Governor Carter has said repeatedly that coal is the resource that we need to use more in the effort to become independent of the um— Arab oil supply. So I vetoed it because of a loss of jobs and because it would have interfered with our energy independence program. The auto emission uh— it was agreed by Leonard Woodcock, the head of the U.A.W. and by the uh— heads of all of the automobile industry. We have labor and management together, saying that those auto emission standards had to be modified. But let's talk about what the Ford administration has done in the field of environment. I have increased, as president, by over sixty percent, the funding for water treatment plants in the United States, the federal contribution. I have fully funded the land and water conservation program. In fact, have recommended and the Congress approved a substantially increased land and water conservation program. Uh— I have uh— added in the current year budget the funds for the National Park Service. For example, we uh— proposed about twelve million dollars to add between four and five hundred more employees for the National Park Service and a month or so ago I did uh— likewise say over the next ten years we should expand double the uh— national parks, the wild wilderness areas, the scenic river areas and then, of course, the, the final thing, is that I have signed and approved of more scenic rivers, more wilderness areas eh— since I've been president, than any other president in the history of the United States.

Walters

Governor Carter.

Carter

Eh– well I might say that I think the League of Conservation Voters is absolutely right. This uh– administration's record on environment is very bad. Uh– I think it's accurate to say that the uh– strip-mining law which was passed twice by the Congress, uh– and was uh– only lacked two votes, I believe, of being overridden, would have been good for the country. The claim that it would have put hundred and forty thousand miners out of work is uh– hard to believe when at the time Mr. Ford vetoed it, the United Mine Workers was uh– supporting the bill. And I don't think they would have supported the uh– bill had they known that they would lose a hundred and forty thousand jobs. There's been a consistent policy on the part of this administration to lower or to delay enforcement of air pollution standards and water pollution standards. And under both President Nixon and Ford, moneys have been impounded that would have gone to uh– cities and others, to control uh– water pollution. We have no energy policy. We, I think, are the only developed nation in the world that has no comprehensive energy policy, to permit us to plan in an orderly way how to shift from increasingly scarce uh– energy uh– forms–oil–and have research and development concentrated on the increased use of coal, which I strongly favor. The research and development to be used primarily to make the coal burning uh– be clean. We need a heritage trust program similar to the one we had in Georgia to set aside additional lands, that have uh– geological and archeological importance uh– natural areas for enjoyment. Uh– the lands that Mr. Ford uh– brags about having approved are in Alaska and they are enormous in uh– in size, but as far as the accessibility of them by the American people, it's very uh– far in the future. We've n– taken no strong position in the uh– control of pollution of our oceans, and I would say the worst uh– threat to the environment of all is nuclear proliferation. And this administration, having been in office now for two years or more, has still not taken strong and bold action to stop the proliferation of nuclear waste around the world, particularly plutonium. Those are some brief remarks about the failures of this administration. I would do the opposite in every respect.

Walters

Mr. Maynard, to Governor Carter.

Maynard

Governor, federal policy in this country since World War Two has tended to favor the development of suburbs at the great expense of central cities. Does not the federal government now have an affirmative obligation to revitalize the American city? We have heard little in this campaign suggesting that you have an urban reconstruction program. Could you please outline your urban intentions for us tonight?

Carter

Yes, I'd be glad to. In the first place, uh– as is the case with the environmental policy and energy policies I just described, and the policy for nonproliferation of uh– of nuclear waste, this administration has no urban policy. It's impossible for mayors or governors to cooperate with the president because they can't anticipate what's gonna happen next. A mayor of a city like New York, for instance, needs to know uh– eighteen months, or two years ahead of time, what responsibility the city will have in administration and in financing, in things

Appendix F 293

like housing, uh— pollution control, uh— crime control, education, welfare and health. This has not been done, unfortunately. I remember the headline in the *Daily News* that said "Ford to New York: Drop Dead." I think it's very important, that our cities know that they have a partner in the federal government. Quite often Congress has passed laws in the past, designed to help people with uh— the ownership of homes, and with the control of crime, and with adequate health care and better education programs, and so forth. Uh— those uh— programs were designed to help those who need it most. And quite often this has been in the very poor people and neighborhoods in the downtown urban centers. Because of the uh— great—ly eh— greatly uh— advantaged uh— l— p— persons who live in the suburbs— better education, better organization, more articulate, more aware of what the laws are— quite often this money has been channeled out of the downtown centers where it's needed. Also, I favor all revenue-sharing money being used for local governments, and also to remove the prohibitions in the use of revenue-sharing money so that it can be used to improve education and health care. We have now, uh— for instance, only seven percent of the total education costs being financed by the federal government. When uh— the Nixon-Ford administration started, this was ten percent. That's a thirty percent reduction in the portion that the federal government contributes to education in just eight years, and as you know, the education costs have gone up uh— tremendously. The last point is that the major uh— thrust has got to be to put people back to work. We've got an extraordinarily high unemployment rate among downtown urban ghetto areas— uh— particularly among the very poor, and particularly among minority groups—sometimes fifty or sixty percent. And the concentration of employment opportunities in those areas would help greatly not only to res— establish the tax base, but also to help reduce the extraordinary welfare cost. One of the major responsibilities on the shoulders of uh— New York City is to, is to f— finance welfare, and I favor the shifting of the welfare cost away from the local governments altogether, and over a longer period of time, that the federal government begin to absorb part of it that's now paid by the state government. Those things would help a great deal of the cities, but we still have a w— a very serious problem there.

Walters

President Ford.

Ford

Let me um— speak out very strongly. The Ford administration does have a very comprehensive program to help uh— our major metropolitan areas. I fought for and the Congress finally went along with a general revenue-sharing program, whereby cities and uh— states um— the cities two-thirds and the states one-third—get over six billion dollars a year in cash for which they can uh— provide many, many services—whatever they really want. In addition we, uh— in the federal government, make available to uh— cities about uh— three billion, three hundred million dollars in what we call community development. In adush— in addition um— uh— as a result of my pressure on the Congress, we got a major mass-transit program uh— over a four-year period, eleven billion eight hundred million dollars. We have a good housing program uh— that uh— will result in cutting um— the down payments by fifty percent, and uh— having mortgage payments uh— lower at the beginning of any mortgage period. We're expanding our homestead uh— housing program. The net result is, uh— we think, under Carla Hills, who's the chairman of my uh— Urban Development and uh— Neighborhood Revitalization program, we will really do a first-class job in helping um— the communities throughout the country. Uh— as a matter of fact that committee under Secretary Hills released about a seventy-five page report with specific recommendations so we can do a better job uh— weeks ahead, and in addition, the tax program of the Ford administration, which provides an incentive for industry to move into our major uh— metropolitan areas, into the inner cities, will bring jobs where prople are, and help to revitalize those cities as they can be.

Walters

Mr. Nelson, your question next to President Ford.

Nelson

Um— Mr. President, your campaign has uh— run ads in black newspapers saying that quote, for black Americans, President Ford is quietly getting the job done. Yet study after study is shown little progress in desegregation, and in fact, actual increases in segregated schools and housing in the Northeast. Now, civil rights groups have complained repeatedly that there's been lack of progress and commitment to an integrated society uh— during uh— your administration. So how are you getting the job done for blacks and other minorities, and what programs do you have in mind for the next four years?

Ford

Let me say at the outset, uh— I'm very proud of the record of this administration. In the Cabinet, I have one of the outstanding, I think, administrators, is the Secretary of Transportation, Bill Coleman. Eh— you're familiar, I'm sure with the recognition given in the Air Force to uh— General James, and there was just uh— approved a three-star admiral, the first in the history of the United States Navy. So, uh— we are giving full recognition to individuals of quality in the Ford administration in positions of great responsibility. In addition, uh— the Department of Justice is fully enforcing, and enforcing effectively, the Voting Rights Act, the legislation that involves jobs, housing for minorities, not only blacks but all others. Uh— the Department of um— uh— H.U.D. is enforcing the new legislation that uh— outla— that takes care of redlining. Uh— what we're doing is saying that there are opportunities, business opportunities, educational opportunities, responsibility, uh— where people with talent, black or any other minority, uh— can fully qualify. The Office of Minority Business in the Department of Commerce, has made available more money in trying to help uh— black businessmen or other minority businessmen than any other administration since the office was established. The Office of Small Business under Mr. Kobelinski, has a very massive program trying to help the black community. The individual who wants to start a business or expand his business as a black businessman, is able to borrow, either directly or with guaranteed loans. I believe on the record that this administration has been responsive, and we have carried out the law to the letter. And I am proud of the record.

Walters

Governor Carter, your response please.

Carter

The uh— description just made of this administration's record is hard to uh— recognize. I think it's accurate to say that Mr. Ford voted against the uh— Voting Rights Act and against the civil rights acts in their uh— debative stage. I think once it was assured they were going to pass, he finally voted for it. This country uh— changed drastically in 1969, when the uh— terms of John Kennedy and Lyndon Johnson were over, and Richard Nixon and, and Gerald Ford became the presidents. There was a time when there was hope for those who were, were poor and downtrodden and who uh— are elderly or who uh— are ill or hu— who were

Appendix F 295

in minority groups. But that time has been gone. I think the greatest thing that ever happened to the South was the passage of the Civil Rights Act and the opening up of opportunities uh— to black people the chance to vote, to hold a job, to buy a house, to go to school, and to participate in public affairs. It not only liberated uh— black people, but it also liberated the whites. We've seen uh— in many instances in recent years in minority affairs uh— section of uh— Small Loan Administration uh— Small Business Administration lend uh— a black entrepreneur just enough money to get started, and then they go bankrupt. The bankruptcies have gone up uh— an extraordinary degree. Uh— Fe— F.H.A. which used to be a very responsible agency uh— that everyone looked to help own a home, lost six hundred million dollars last year. There've been over thirteen hundred indictments in HUD, over eight hundred convictions, relating just to home loans. And now the federal government has become the world's greatest slum landlord. We've got a thirty percent or forty percent unemployment rate among minority uh— young people. And there's been no concerted effort given to the needs of those who are both poor and black, or poor and who speak a foreign language. A— and that's where there's been a great uh— generation of despair and ill health and the lack of education, lack of purposefulness, and the lack of hope for the future. But it doesn't take just a kwy— or dole mon— uh— minimum enforcement of the law, it requires an aggressive searching out and reaching out to help people who especially need it. And that's been lacking in the last eight years.

Walters

Mr. Kraft to Governor Carter.

Kraft

Uh— Governor Carter uh— in the nearly two hundred year history of the Constitution, there have been only—uh— I think it's twenty-five amendments, uh— most of them on issues of the very broadest principle. Uh— now we have proposed amendments in many highly specialized causes like gun control, school busing, balanced budgets, school prayer, abortion, things like that. Do you think it's appropriate to the dignity of the Constitution to tack on amendments in a wholesale fashion, and which of the ones that I listed, that is uh— balanced budgets, school busing, school prayer, abortion, gun p— control—which of those would you really work hard to support, if you were president?

Carter

I would not work hard to support any of those. Uh— we've always had, I think, a lot of uh— constitutional amendments proposed. But the passage of 'em has been uh— fairly slow, and uh— few and far between. In the two hundred year history there's been a very uh— cautious approach to this. We quite often we have a transient problem. Uh— I'm strongly against in— abortion. Uh— I think abortion's wrong. I don't think the government ought to do anything to encourage abortion. But I don't favor a constitutional amendment on the subject. But short of a constitutional amendment, and within the confines of the Supreme Court rulings, I'll do everything I can to minimize the need for abortions with better sex education, family planning, with better doctor procedures. I personally don't believe that the federal government ought to finance abortions. But I, I draw the line and don't support constitutional amendment. However, I honor the right of people to seek the constitutional amendments on school busing, on uh— prayer in the schools and on abortion. But among those you named, I won't actively work for the passage of any of 'em.

Walters

President Ford, your response, please.

Ford

I support the uh— Republican uh— platform which calls for a constitutional amendment that would uh— outlaw abortion. I favor the particular constitutional amendment that would turn over to the states, the uh— individual right of the voters in those states, uh— the chance to make a decision by public referendum. Uh— I call that the people's amendment. I think if you really believe that the people of a state ought to make a decision on a matter of this kind uh— that uh— we ought to have a federal constitutional amendment that would permit each one of the fifty states to make the choice. Uh— I think this is a responsible and a proper way to proceed. Uh— I believe also that uh— there is some merit to a, an amendment that um— uh— Senator Everett Dirksen uh— proposed very frequently, an amendment that would uh— change the Court decision as far as voluntary prayer in public schools. Uh— it seems to me that there should had be an opportunity uh— as long as it's voluntary, as long as there is no uh— compulsion whatsoever, that uh— an individual ought to have that right. So in those two cases I think uh— such uh— a constitutional amendment would be proper, and I really don't think in either case they're trivial matters. I think they're matters of very deep conviction, as far as many, many people in this country believe. And therefore they shouldn't be treated lightly. But they're matters that are uh— important, and in those two cases I would favor them.

Walters

Mr. Maynard to President Ford.

Maynard

Mr. President, twice you have been the intended victim of would-be assassins using handguns. Yet, you remain a steadfast opponent of substantive handgun control. There are now some forty million handguns in this country, going up at the rate of two point five million a year, and tragically, those handguns are frequently purchased for self-protection and wind up being used against a relative or a friend. In light of that, why do you remain so adamant in your opposition to substantive gun control in this country?

Ford

Uh— Mr. Maynard uh— the record of gun control, whether it's in one city or another or in some state, does not show that the registration of a gun, handgun, or the registration of the gun owner, has in any way whatsoever decreased the crime rate or the use of that gun in the committing of a crime. The record just doesn't prove that such legislation or action by a local city council is effective. What we have to do, and this is the crux of the matter, is to make it very, very uh— difficult for a person who uses a gun, in the commission of a crime, to stay out of jail. If we make the use of a gun in the commission of a crime a serious criminal offense, and that person is prosecuted, then in my opinion, we are going after the person who uses the gun for the wrong reason. I don't believe in the registration of handguns or the registration of the handgun owner. That has not proven to be effective. And therefore I think a better way is to go after the criminal, the individual who commits a crime eh— in the possession of a gun and uses that gun for a part of his criminal activity. Those are the people who ought to be in jail, and the only way to do it is to pass strong legislation, so that once apprehended, indicted, convicted, they'll be in jail, and off the streets, and not using guns in the commission of a crime.

Appendix F 297

Maynard

But Mr. President, don't you think that the proliferation of the availability of handguns contributes to the possibility of those crimes being committed, and there's a second part to my follow-up, very quickly. There are as you know and as you've said, jurisdictions around the country with strong gun control laws. The police officials in those cities contend that if there were a national law, to prevent other jurisdictions from providing the weapons that then come in to places like New York, that they might have a better handle on the problem. Have you considered that in your analysis of the gu— the handgun proliferation problem?

Ford

Yes, I have, and uh— the individuals that uh— with whom I've consulted, have not uh— convinced me that uh— a national registration of handguns or handgun owners, will solve the problem you're talking about. The person who wants to use a gun for an illegal purpose, can get it whether it's registered or outlawed. They will be obtained. And they are the people who ought to go behind bars. You should not in the process penalize the legitimate handgun owner. And when you go through the process of registration, you in effect are penalizing that individual who uses his gun for a very legitimate purpose.

Walters

Governor Carter?

Carter

I, I think it's accurate to say that Mr. Ford's position on gun control has changed. Uh— earlier uh— Mr. Levi, his uh— Attorney General, put forward a gun control proposal, which Mr. Ford later, I believe, espoused. That called for the prohibition against the uh— sale o— of the uh— so-called Saturday night specials, and would have put uh— very strict uh— uh— control over who owned a handgun. I have been a hunter all my life and happen to own both shotguns, rifles and a handgun, and uh— the only purpose that I would see in registering uh— handguns and not long guns of any kind, would be to prohibit the uh— ownership of those guns by those who've used them in the commission of a crime, or who uh— have been proven to be mentally incompetent to own a gun. I believe that limited approach to the, to the question would be uh— advisable and, and I think, adequate. But that's as far as I would go with it.

Walters

Mr. Nelson to Governor Carter.

Nelson

Uh— Governor, you've said the S— uh— Supreme Court of today is uh— as you put it, moving back in a proper direction uh— in rulings that have limited the rights of criminal defendents, and you've compared the present Supreme Court under Chief Justice Burger very favorably with the more liberal court that we had under Chief Justice Warren. So exactly what are you getting at, and can you elaborate on the kind of Court you think this country should have, and can you tell us the kind of qualifications and philosophy you would look for as president in making Supreme Court appointments?

Carter

Uh— while I was governor of Georgia, although I'm not a lawyer, we had complete reform of the Georgia court system. We uh— streamlined the structure of the court, put in administrative officers, put a unified court system in, required that all uh— severe sentences be reviewed for uniformity, and in addition to that put forward a proposal that was adopted and used throughout my own term of office, of selection of uh— all judges and district attorneys—uh— prosecuting attorneys—on the basis of merit. Every time I had a vacancy on the Georgia Supreme Court—and I filled five of those vacancies out of seven, total, and about half the Court of Appeals judges, about thirty-five percent of the trial judges, I was given from an objective panel, the five most highly qualified persons in Georgia. And from those five I always chose the first or second one. So merit selection of judges, is the most important single criterion. And I would institute the same kind of procedure as president, not only in judicial appointments but also in diplomatic appointments. Secondly, I think that the Burger Court, has fairly well confirmed the major and, and most far-reaching and most controversial decisions of the Warren Court. Civil rights uh— has been confirmed by the Burger Court, hasn't been uh— reversed, and I don't think there's any inclination to reverse those basic decisions. The one man-one vote rule, which is a very important one that uh— s— struck down the unwarranted influence into legislature of parsely— sp—uh— populated areas of, of the states. The uh— right of indigent or very poor accused persons to uh— legal counsel, uh— I think the Burger Court has confirmed that basic and very controversial decision of the Warren Court. Also, the, the protection of an arrested person, against unwarranted persecution in trying to get a false uh— confession. But now I think there have been a couple of instances where the Burger Court has made techinical rulings, where an obviously guilty person was later found to be guilty. And I think that in that case uh— some of the more liberal uh— members of the uh— so-called Warren Court agreed with those decisions. But the only uh— thing that I uh— have pointed out was, what I've just said, and that there was a need to clarify the technicalities so that you couldn't be forced to release a person who is obviously guilty just because of a, of a small technicality in the law. An— and that's a uh— reversal of position uh— by the Burger Court with which I do agree.

Nelson

Mi— Governor, I don't believe you answered my, you answered my question, though, about the kinds of uh— people you would be looking for the Court, the type of philosophy uh— you would be looking for, if you were making . . .

[Interruption 5]

Carter

Of course.

Nelson

uh—appointments, to the Supreme Court as president.

Carter

OK. I thought I answered it by saying that it would be on the basis of merit. Once the uh— search and analysis procedure had been completed, and once I'm given a list of the five or seven or ten uh— best-qualified persons in the country, I would make a selection from among those uh— persons. If the uh— list was uh— in my opinion fairly uniform, if there

Appendix F 299

was no outstanding person, then I would undoubtedly choose someone who would most accurately reflect my own basic polisa— political philosophy, as best I could determine it. Which would be, uh— to continue the progress that has been made under the last two uh— Courts, the Warren Court and the Burger Court. I would also like to uh— completely revise our criminal justice system to do some of the things at the federal level in court reform that I've just described as has been done in Georgia and other states. And then I would like to appoint people who would be interested in helping with that. I know that uh— Chief Justice Burger is. He hasn't had help yet from the administration, from the Congress, to carry this out. The uh— emphasis I think, of the, of the court system uh— should be to interpret the uh— the Constitution and the laws uh— equally between property protection and, and personal protection. But when there's uh— a very narrow decision, which quite often is one that reaches the Supreme Court, I think the choice should be with human rights. And uh— that would be another factor that I would follow.

Walters

President Ford.

Ford

Well I think the answer uh— as to the kind of person that I would select uh— is obvious. I had one opportunity to nominate uh— an individual to the Supreme Court and I selected the Circuit Court of Appeals judge from Illinois uh— John Paul Stevens. I selected him because of his outstanding record as a Circuit Court of Appeals judge, and I was very pleased that uh— an overwhelmingly Democratic United States Senate, after going into his background, came to the conclusion that he was uh— fit and should serve, and the vote in his behalf was overwhelming. So I would say somebody in the format of uh— Justice Stevens would be the kind of an individual that I would uh— select in the future, as I did him in the past. I uh— believe however, a comment ought to be made about the direction of the uh— Burger Court vis-a-vis the uh— uh— Court uh— that preceded it. It seems to me that the *Miranda* case was a case that really made it very, very difficult for the uh— police, the law enforcement people in this country, to uh— do what they could to make certain that the victim of a crime was protected, and that those that commit crimes uh— were properly handled and uh— sent to jail. The *Miranda* case uh— the Burger Court uh— is gradually changing, and I'm pleased to see that there are some steps being made by the uh— Burger Court to modify the so-called *Miranda* decision. Uh— I might make a correction uh— of what uh— Governor Carter said uh— speaking of uh— uh— gun control. Uh— yes it is true, I believe that the sale of uh— Saturday night s— specials should be cut out, but he wants the registration of handguns.

Walters

Mr. Kraft.

Kraft

Uh— Mr. President, uh— the country is now uh— in um— in something that your uh— advisers call an economic pause. But I think to most Americans that sounds like a, a antiseptic term for uh— low growth, uh— unemployment, standstill at a high, high level of decline in take-home pay, uh— lower factory earnings, more layoffs, uh— isn't that really a rotten record, and doesn't your administration bear most of the blame for it?

Ford

Well Mr. Kraft, uh— I violently disagree with your assessment. And I don't think the record justifies the conclusion that you come to. Uh— let me uh— talk about uh— the economic announcements that were made just this past week. Yes, it was announced that the uh— G.N.P. real growth in the third quarter was at four percent. But do you realize that over the last ten years, that's a higher figure than the average growth, during that ten-year period. Now it's lower than the nine point two percent growth in the first quarter, and it's lower than the uh— five percent growth in the second quarter. But every economist, liberal conservative that I'm familiar with, recognizes that in the fourth quarter of this year and in the fifth quar— uh— the first quarter of next year, that we'll have an increase in real G.N.P. But now let's talk about the pluses that came out this week. We had an eighteen percent increase in housing starts. We had a substantial increase in new permits for housing. As a matter of fact, based on the announcement this week, there w— will be at an annual rate a million eight hundred and some thousand new houses built, which is a tremendous increase over last year and a substantial increase over the earlier part of this year. Now in addition, we had eh— a very, some very good news in the reduction in the rate of inflation, and inflation hits everybody, those who w— are working and those who are on welfare. The rate of inflation as announced just the other day, is under five percent, and the uh— four point four percent that was indicated at the time of the four percent G.N.P. was less than the five point four percent. It means that the American buyer is getting a better bargain today because inflation is less.

Kraft

Mr. President, let me ask you this. Uh— there has been an increase in layoffs, and that's something that bothers everybody because even people that have a job are afraid they're gonna be fired. Did you predict that layo— uh— that increase in layoffs. Didn't that take you by surprise? Hasn't the gu— hasn't the— your administration been surprised by this pause? Uh— t— in fact, haven't you not, haven't you been so obsessed with saving money uh— that you didn't even push the government to spend funds that were allocated?

Ford

Uh— Mr. Kraft uh— I think the record can be put in this uh— in this way, which i— is the way that uh— I think satisfies most Americans. Since the depths of the recession, we have added four million jobs. Im— most importantly, consumer confidence as surveyed by the reputable organization at the University of Michigan, is at the highest since 1972. In other words there is a growing public confidence in the strength of this economy, and that means that there will be more industrial activity. It means that there will be a reduction in the uh— unemployment. It means that there will be increased hires. It means that there will be increased employment. Now we've had this pause, but most economists, regardless of their political philosophy, uh— indicate that this pause for a month or two was healthy, because we could not have honestly sustained a nine point two percent rate of growth which we had in the first quarter of this year. Now uh— I'd like to point out as well, that the United States economic recovery from the recession of a year ago, is well ahead of the economic recovery of any major free industrial nation in the world today. We're ahead of all the Western European countries. We're ahead of Japan. The United States is leading the free world out of the recession that was serious a year, year and a half ago. We're going to see unemployment going down, more jobs available, and the rate of inflation going down. And I think this is a record that uh— the American people understand and will appreciate.

Appendix F *301*

Walters

Governor Carter.

Carter

Well, with all due respect to President Ford, I think he ought to be ashamed of making that statement because we have the highest unemployment rate now, than we had at any time between the Great Depression caused by Herbert Hoover, and the time President Ford took office. We've got seven and a half million people out of jobs. Since he's been in office, two and a half million more American people have lost their jobs. In the last four months alone five hundred thousand Americans have gone on the unemployment rolls. In the last month, we've had a net loss of a hundred and sixty-three thousand jobs. Anybody who says that the inflation rate is in good shape now, ought to talk to the housewives. One of the overwhelming results that I've seen in polls is that people feel that you can't plan any more. There's no way to make a prediction that my family might be able to own a home or to put my kid through college. Savings accounts are losing money instead of gaining money. Inflation is robbing us. Under the present administration, Nixon's and Ford's, we've had three times the inflation rate that we experienced under President Johnson and President Kennedy. The economic growth is less than half today, what it was at the beginning of this year. And housing starts—he compares the housing starts with last year. I don't blame him. Because in 1975 we had fewer housing starts in this country, fewer homes built, than any year since 1940. That's thirty-five years. And we've got a thirty-five percent unemployment rate in many areas of this country among construction workers. And Mr. Ford hasn't done anything about it. And I think this shows a callous indifference, to the families that have suffered so much. He has vetoed bills passed by Congress, within the congressional budget guidelines, job opportunities for two million Americans. We'll never have a balanced budget, we'll never meet the needs of our people, we'll never control the inflationary spiral, as long as we have seven and a half or eight million people out of work, who are looking for jobs. And we've probably got two and a half million more people who are not looking for jobs any more, because they're given up hope. That is a very serious indictment of this administration. It's probably the worst one of all.

Walters

Mr. Maynard.

Maynard

Governor Carter, you entered this race against President Ford with a twenty point lead or better in the polls. And now it appears that this campaign is headed for a photo finish. You said how difficult it is to run against a sitting president, but Mr. Ford was just as much an incumbent in July when you were twenty points ahead, as he is now. Can you tell us what caused the evaporation of that lead in your opinion?

Carter

Well that's not exactly an accurate description of what happened. When I was that far ahead, it was immediately following the Democratic convention, and before the Republican convention. At that time, uh— twenty-five or thirty percent of the Reagan supporters said that they would not support President Ford. But as occurred at the end of the con— Democratic convention, the Republican party unified itself. And I think immediately following the Republican convention there was about a ten point spread. I believe that, to be accurate,

I had forty-nine percent, President Ford had thirty-nine percent. Uh— the polls uh— are good indications of fluctuations, but they vary widely one from another. And the only poll that I've ever followed is the one that uh— you know is taken on election day. I was in uh— thirty primaries in the spring, and uh— at first it was obvious that I didn't have any standing in the polls. As a matter of fact I think when Gallup ran their first poll in December of 1975 they didn't put my name on the list. They had thirty-five people on the list, my name wasn't even there. And at the beginning of the year I had about two percent. So the polls to me are interesting, but they don't determine either my hopes or, or my despair. I campaign among people. I've never depended on powerful political figures to put me in office. I have a direct relationship with hundreds of people aroun— hu— hundreds of thousands of people around the country who actively campaign for me. In Georgia alone, for instance, I got eighty-four percent of the vote, and I think there were fourteen people uh— in addition to myself on the ballot. And Governor Wallace had been very strong in Georgia. That's an overwhelming support from my own people who know me best. And today, we have about five hundred Georgians, at their own expense, just working people who believe in me, spread around the country uh— involved in the political campaign. So, the polls are interesting, but uh— I don't know how to explain the fluctuations. I think a lot of it uh— depends on current events, uh— sometimes foreign affairs, som— s— times domestic affairs but I think our hold uh— our support among those who uh— are crucial to the election, has been fairly steady. And my success in the primary season, was I think notable for a newcomer from someone who's outside of Washington, who, who, never has been a part of the Washington establishment. And I think that we'll have good result uh— on November the second, for myself and I hope for the country.

Walters

President Ford, your response.

Ford

I think uh— the uh— increase in the uh— prospects as far as I'm concerned, and the l— less favorable prospects for Governor Carter, reflect that Governor Carter uh— is inconsistent in many of the positions that he takes. He tends to distort on a number of occasions. Uh— just a moment ago for example, uh— he uh— was indicating that uh— uh— in the 1950s for example uh— unemployment was very low. He fails to point out that uh— in the 1950s we were engaged in the war in Vietnam we— mean in uh— Korea. We had uh— three million five hundred thousand young men uh— in the Army, Navy, Air Force and Marines. That's not the way to end unemployment or to reduce unemployment. At the present time we're at peace. We have reduced the number of people in the Army, Navy, Air Force and Marines, from three million one hundred uh— t— three million five hundred thousand, to two million one hundred thousand. We are not at war, we have reduced the military manpower by a million, four hundred thousand. If we had that many more people in the Army, the Navy, the Air Force, and Marines, our unemployment figure would be considerably less. But this administration doesn't believe the way to reduce unemployment is to go to war, or to increase the number of people in the military. So you cannot compare unemployment—as you sought to uh— with the present time with the 1950s, because the then-administration had people in the military, they were at war, they were fighting overseas, and this administration has reduced the size of the military by a million four hundred thousand. They're in the civilian labor market and they're not fighting anywhere around the world today.

Appendix F 303

Walters

Thank you, gentlemen. This will complete our questioning for this debate. We don't have uh– time for more questions and uh– full answers, so now each candidate will be allowed up to four minutes for a closing statement. And at the original coin toss in Philadelphia a month ago, it was determined that President Ford would make the first closing statement tonight. President Ford.

Ford

For twenty-five years, I served in the Congress under five presidents. I saw them work. I saw them make very hard decisions. I didn't always agree with their decisions, whether they were Democratic or Republican presidents. For the last two years I've been the president. And I have found, from experience, that it's much more difficult to make those decisions, than it is to second-guess them. I became president at the time that the United States was in a very troubled time. We had inflation of over twelve percent. We were on the brink of the worst recession in the last forty years. We were still deeply involved in the problems of Vietnam. The American people had lost faith and trust and confidence in the presidency itself. That uh– situation called, for me to first put the United States on a steady course, and to keep our uh– keel eh– well balanced, because we had to face the difficult problems that had all of a sudden hit America. I think most people know that I did not seek the presidency, but I am asking for your help and assistance to be president for the next four years. During this campaign we've seen a lot of television shows, a lot of bumper stickers, and a great many uh– slogans of one kind or another. But those are not the things that count. What counts is that the United States celebrated its two hundredth birthday on July Fourth. As a result of that wonderful experience all over the United States, there is a new spirit in America. The American people are healed, are working together. The American people are moving again, and moving in the right direction. We have cut inflation by better than half. We have come out of the recession and we're well on the road to real prosperity in this country again. There has been a restoration of faith and confidence and trust in the presidency, because I've been open, candid, and forthright. I have never promised more than I could produce and I have produced everything that I promised. We are at peace. Not a single young American is fighting or dying on any foreign soil tonight. We have peace with freedom. I've been proud to be president of the United States during these very troubled times. I love America just as all of you love America. It would be the highest honor for me to have your support on November second and for you to say, Jerry Ford, you've done a good job, keep on doing it. Thank you, and good night.

Walters

Thank you, President Ford. Governor Carter.

Carter

Thank you Barbara. The major purpose of an election for president is to choose a leader, someone who can analyze the depth of feeling in our country, to set a standard for our people to follow, to inspire people to reach for greatness, to correct our defects, to answer difficult questions, to bind ourselves together in a spirit of unity. I don't believe the present administration has done that. We have been discouraged and we've been alienated, sometimes we've been embarrassed, and sometimes we've been ashamed that people are out of work and there's a sense of withdrawal. But our country is innately very strong. Mr. Ford is a good and decent man, but he's in, been in office now more than eight hundred days, approaching almost as long as John Kennedy was in office. I'd like to ask the American people what, what's been accomplished. A lot remains to be done. My own background is different from his. I was a school board member and a library board member, I served on a hospital authority and I was in the State Senate, I was governor and I'm an engineer, a naval officer, a farmer, a businessman. And I believe we require someone who can work harmoniously with the Congress, who can work closely with the people of this country and who can bring a new image and a new spirit to Washington. Our tax structure is a disgrace, it needs to be reformed. I was governor of Georgia for four years. We never increased sales taxes or income tax or property tax. As a matter of fact, the year before I went out of office we gave a fifty million dollar refund to the property taxpayers of Georgia. We spend six hundred dollars per person in this country, every man woman and child, for health care. We still rank fifteenth among all the nations of the world in infant mortality, and our cancer rate is uh– higher than any country in the world. We don't have good health care. We could have it. Employment ought to be restored to our people. We've become almost a welfare state. We spend now seven hundred percent more on unemployment compensation than we did eight years ago when the Republicans took over the White House. Our people want to go back to work. Our education system can be improved. Secrecy ought to be stripped away from government, and a maximum of personal privacy ought to be maintained. Our housing programs have uh– gone bad. It used to be that the average uh– family could own a house, but now less than a third of our people can afford to buy their own homes. The budget was more grossly out of balance last year than ever before in the history of our country–sixty-five billion dollars, primarily because our people are not at work. Inflation is robbing us, as we have already discussed, and the government bureaucracy is uh– just a horrible mess. This doesn't have to be. Uh– I don't know all the answers, nobody could, but I do know that if the president of the United States, and the Congress of the United States, and the people of the United States said, I believe our nation is greater than what we are now. I believe that if we are inspired, if we can achieve a degree of unity, if we can set our goals high enough and work toward recognized goals, with industry and labor and agriculture along with government at all levels, that we can achieve great things. We might have to do it slowly. There are no magic answers to it, but I believe together we can make great progress. We can correct our difficult mistakes, and answer those very tough questions. I believe in the greatness of our country. And I believe the American people are ready for a change in Washington. We've been drifting too long. We've been dormant too long. We've been discouraged too long. And we have not set an example for our own people. But I believe that we can now, establish in the White House, a good relationship with Congress, a good relationship with our people, set very high goals for our country, and with inspiration and hard work, we can achieve great things. And let the world know–that's very important–but more importantly let the people in our own country realize, that we still live in the greatest nation on earth. Thank you very much.

Walters

Thank you Governor Carter. And thank you President Ford. I also would like to thank the audience and my three colleagues Mr. Kraft, Mr. Maynard and Mr. Nelson who have been our questioners. This debate has of course been seen by millions of Americans and in addition, tonight it is being broadcast to one hundred and thirteen nations throughout the world. This concludes the 1976 presidential debates, a truly remarkable exercise in democracy. For this is the first time in sixteen years that the presidential candidates have debated. It is the first time ever that an incumbent president has debated his challenger. And the debate included the first between the two vice-presidential candidates. And President Ford and Governor Carter, we not only want to thank you but we commend you for agreeing to come together to discuss the issues before the American people. And our special thanks to the League of Women Voters for making these events possible. In sponsoring these events, the League of Women Voters' Education Fund has tried to provide you with the information

Appendix F

that you will need to choose wisely. The election is now only eleven days off. The candidates have participated in presenting their views in three ninety minute debates, and now it's up to the voters—now it is up to you—to participate. The League urges all registered voters to vote on November second, for the candidate of your choice. And now from Phi Beta Kappa Memorial Hall on the campus of the College of William and Mary, this is Barbara Walters, wishing you all a good evening.

BIBLIOGRAPHY

Abelson, Robert P., Eliot Aronson, William J. McGuire, Theodore M. Newcomb, Milton J. Rosenberg, and Percy H. Tannenbaum, eds. 1968. *Theories of Cognitive Consistency*. Chicago: Rand McNally.

Abramowitz, Alan. 1977. "The First Debate: A Study of Attitude Change." Williamsburg, Va.: College of William and Mary. Mimeographed.

Agranoff, Robert. 1976. *The Management of Election Campaigns*. Boston, Mass.: Holbrook Press.

Atkin, Charles K. 1972. "Anticipated Communication and Mass Media Information Seeking." *Public Opinion Quarterly* 36:188-99.

Becker, Lee B., Maxwell E.McCombs, and Jack M. McLeod. 1975. "The Development of Political Cognitions." In *Political Communication*, edited by Steven H. Chaffee, pp. 21-63. Beverly Hills, Calif.: Sage.

Becker, Lee B., David H. Weaver, Doris A. Graber, and Maxwell E. McCombs. Forthcoming. "Influence on Public Agendas." In *Great Debates, 1976—Ford vs. Carter*, edited by Sidney Kraus. Bloomington: Indiana University Press.

Becker, Samuel L., and Elmer W. Lower. 1962. "Broadcasting in Presidential Campaigns." In *Great Debates*, edited by Sidney Kraus, pp. 25-55. Bloomington: Indiana University Press.

Bennett, Stephen E. 1973. "Consistency among the Public's Social Welfare Policy Attitudes in the 1960s." *American Journal of Political Science* 17:544-71.

Bennett, Stephen E., and Robert W. Oldendick. 1977. "The Power of the Federal Government: The Case of the Changing Issue." Paper read at the annual conference of the Midwest Political Science Association, Chicago. Mimeographed.

Benton, Marc, and P. Jean Frazier. 1976. "The Agenda-Setting Function of the Mass Media at Three Levels of Information Holding." *Communication Research* 3:261-75.

Berelson, Bernard R., Paul F. Lazarsfeld, and William N. McPhee. 1954. *Voting*. Chicago: University of Chicago Press.

Bishop, George F., Robert W. Oldendick, and Alfred J. Tuchfarber. 1978. "Effects of Question Wording and Format on Political Attitude Consistency." *Public Opinion Quarterly*, in press.

Bishop, George F., Robert W. Oldendick, Alfred J. Tuchfarber, and Stephen E. Bennett. 1977. "The Changing Structure of Mass Belief Systems: Facts or Artifacts?" Paper read at the Biennial Meeting of the Inter-University Consortium for Political and Social Research, University of Michigan, Ann Arbor. Mimeographed.

Bishop, George F., Alfred J. Tuchfarber, and Robert W. Oldendick. 1978. "Change in the Structure of American Political Attitudes: The Nagging Question of Question Wording." *American Journal of Political Science*, in press.

Blumer, Herbert. 1959. "Suggestions for the Study of Mass Media Effects." In *American Voting Behavior*, edited by Eugene Burdick and Arthur J. Brodbeck, pp. 197-208. Glencoe, Ill.: Free Press.

Blumer, Jay G., and Denis McQuail. 1969. *Television in Politics*. Chicago: University of Chicago Press.

Broadcasting. 1977a. "From Primary to Post-Election, TV and Radio Were There." January 3, pp. 36-39.

———. 1977b. "Television: Medium of Choice and Necessity." January 3, pp. 73-76.

———. 1976. "Third and Fourth Debates Look to Be Almost Routine for the Networks." October 18, p. 26.

Brown, Steven R. 1974. "Intensive Analysis in Political Research." *Political Methodology*, 1:1-25.

Brunk, Gregory J. 1978, "The 1964 Attitude Consistency Leap Reconsidered." *Political Methodology*, forthcoming.

Campbell, Angus, Philip E. Converse, Warren E. Miller, and Donald E. Stokes. 1960. *The American Voter*. New York: John Wiley.

Campbell, Angus, Gerald Gurin, and Warren E. Miller. 1954. *The Voter Decides*. Evenston: Row, Peterson.

Campbell, Donald T., and Julian C. Stanley. 1963. *Experimental and Quasi-Experimental Designs for Research*. Chicago: Rand McNally.

Cantrall, William R., Michael A. Colella, and Alan D. Monroe. 1976. "The Great Debates of 1976: A Quasi-Experimental Analysis of Audience Effects." Paper read at the Annual Conference of the Midwest Association for Public Opinion Research, Chicago. Mimeographed.

Carter, Richard F. 1978. "A Journalistic Cybernetic." In *Communication and Control in Social Processes*, edited by Klaus Krippendorff. New York: American Elsevier, forthcoming.

———. 1977. "Theory for Researchers." Paper read at the Annual Conference of the Association for Education in Journalism, Madison, Wis. Mimeographed.

———. 1965. "Communication and Affective Relations." *Journalism Quarterly* 15:203-12.

―――. 1962. "Some Effects of the Great Debates." In *The Great Debates,* edited by Sidney Kraus, pp. 253-70. Bloomington: Indiana University Press.

Carter, Richard F., W. Lee Ruggels, Kenneth M. Jackson, and Beth M. Heffner. 1973. "Application of Signaled Stopping Technique to Communication Research." In *New Models for Communication Research*, edited by Peter Clarke, pp. 15-43. Beverly Hills, Calif.: Sage.

Carter, Richard F., and Ray L. Sweigert, Jr. 1963. "Rehearsal Dissonance and Selective Information Seeking." In *Paul J. Deutschmann Memorial Papers in Mass Communication Research*, edited by Wayne A. Danielson, pp. 25-33. Cincinnati: Scripps-Howard Research.

Catton, William R., Jr. 1960. "Changing Cognitive Structure as a Basis for the Sleeper Effect." *Social Forces* 38:348-54.

Chaffee, Steven H. 1975. "Asking New Questions about Communication and Politics." In *Political Communication*, edited by Steven H. Chaffee, pp. 13-20. Beverly Hills, Calif.: Sage.

Chaffee, Steven H., and Jack M. McLeod. 1973. "Individual vs. Social Predictors of Information Seeking." *Journalism Quarterly* 50:237-45.

Chaffee, Steven H., Keith R. Stamm, Jose L. Guerrero, and Leonard P. Tipton. 1969. *Experiments on Cognitive Discrepancies and Communication*, Journalism Monographs, no. 14. Baton Rouge: Louisiana State University Press.

Clevenger, Theodore, Jr., Donald W. Parson, and Jerome B. Polisky. 1962. "The Problem of Textual Accuracy." In *The Great Debates*, edited by Sidney Kraus, pp. 341-430. Bloomington: Indiana University Press.

Converse, Philip E. 1975. "Public Opinion and Voting Behavior." In *Handbook of Political Science,* vol. 4, edited by Fred I. Greenstein and Nelson W. Polsby, pp. 75-169. Reading, Mass.: Addison-Wesley.

―――. 1966. "The Concept of the Normal Vote." In *Elections and the Political Order*, edited by Angus Campbell, Philip E. Converse, Warren E. Miller, and Donald E. Stokes, pp. 9-39. New York: Wiley.

―――. 1964. "The Nature of Belief Systems in Mass Publics." In *Ideology and Discontent*, edited by David E. Apter, pp. 540-91. Glencoe, Ill.: Free Press.

―――. 1962. "Information Flow and the Stability of Paritsan Attitudes." *Public Opinion Quarterly* 26:578-99.

Darcy, Robert. 1977. "Consensus, Constraint and Political Polarization in Recent Presidential Elections." Paper read at the Annual Conference of the Midwest Association for Public Opinion Research, Chicago. Mimeographed.

Downs, Anthony. 1957. *An Economic Theory of Democracy*. New York: Harper & Row.

"Election Study Notes New Trends in Voter Behavior, Attributes Close Race to Well-Run Campaign." *IRS Newsletter*, Winter 1977, pp. 4-5.

Ellsworth, John W. 1965. "Rationality and Campaigning: A Content Analysis of the 1960 Presidential Campaign Debates." *Western Political Quarterly* 18:794-802.

Farley, Lawrence T., and John S. Marks. 1974. "Campaign Events and Electoral Outcomes." Paper read at the Annual Conference of the American Political Science Association, Chicago. Mimeographed.

Federal Election Commission, 1976. Policy Statement on Presidential Debates, August 30.

Frank, Robert S. 1973. *Message Dimensions of Television News*. Lexington, Mass: D. C. Heath.

Funkhouser, G. Ray. 1973. "The Issues of the Sixties: An Exploratory Study in the Dynamics of Public Opinion." *Public Opinion Quarterly* 37:62-75.

Gallup, George H. 1977. Oral remarks during the Conference on Polling and Survey Research, University of Michigan, Ann Arbor.

―――. 1976. *The Gallup Opinion Index*. Report no. 137, December.

―――. 1972. *The Gallup Poll: Public Opinion, 1935-71*, vol. 3. New York: Random House.

Gans, Herbert J. 1977. "Lessons 1976 Can Offer 1980." *Columbia Journalism Review* 15:25-28.

Graber, Doris A. 1971. "Press Coverage Patterns of Campaign News: The 1968 Presidential Race." *Journalism Quarterly*. 53:499-508.

Graber, Doris A., and Young Kim. 1978. "Why John Q. Voter Did Not Learn Much from the 1976 Presidential Debates." In *Communication Yearbook II*, edited by Bernard Ruben. New Brunswick, N.J.: Transaction-International Communication Association, forthcoming.

―――. 1977. "The 1976 Presidential Debates and Patterns of Political Learning." Paper read at the Annual Conference of the Association for Education in Journalism, Madison, Wis. Mimeographed.

Green, Bert F. 1954. "Attitude Measurement." In *The Handbook of Social Psychology*, vol. 1, edited by Gardner Lindzey, pp. 335-69. Reading Mass.: Addison-Wesley.

Hagner, Paul R., and John P. McIver. 1976. "Attitude Stability and Change in the 1976 Election: A Panel Study." Paper read at the Annual Conference of the Midwest Association for Public Opinion Research, Chicago. Mimeographed.

Hofstetter, C. Richard. 1976. *Bias in the News*, Columbus: Ohio State University Press.

Holsti, Ole R. 1969. *Content Analysis for the Social Sciences and Humanities*. Reading, Mass: Addison-Wesley.

Hovland, Carl I., Irving L. Janis, and Harold H. Kelley. 1953. *Communication and Persuasion*. New Haven, Conn.: Yale University Press.

Hovland, Carl I., A. A. Lumsdaine, and Fred D. Sheffield. 1949. *Experiments on Mass Communication*. Princeton, N.J.: Princeton University Press.

Hyman, Herbert H., Charles R. Wright, and John Shelton Reed. 1975. *The Enduring Effects of Education*. Chicago: University of Chicago Press.

Inter-University Consortium for Political and Social Research. 1976. *Continuity Guide to the American National Election Surveys: 1952-1974*. Ann Arbor: University of Michigan.

IRS Newsletter. 1977. "Election Study Notes New Trends in Voter Behavior, Attributes Close Race to Well-Run Campaign." 5(Winter): 4-5.

Jackson-Beeck, Marilyn, and Robert G. Meadow. 1977. "Issue Evolution: Parameters in Presidential Debate and Public Perceptions." Paper read at the Annual Conference of the Midwest Association for Public Opinion Research Convention, Chicago. Mimeographed.

Jacoubovitch, M. Daniel. 1977. "Differences in Orientation Behavior in One- and Two-Persons Situations." *Journalism Quarterly* 17:114-19.

Katz, Elihu, Jay G. Blumler, and Michael Gurevitch. 1974. "Uses and Gratifications Research." *Public Opinion Quarterly* 37:502-23.

Katz, Elihu, and Jacob. J. Feldman. 1962. "The Debates in the Light of Research: A Survey of Surveys." In *The Great Debates*, edited by Sidney Kraus, pp. 173-223. Bloomington: Indiana University Press.

Katz, Elihu, and Paul R. Lazarsfeld. 1955. *Personal Influence*. Glencoe, Ill.: Free Press.

Keniston, Kenneth. 1968. *Young Radicals*. New York: Harcourt, Brace and World.

Kerlinger, Fred N. 1972. "Q-Methodology in Behavioral Research." In *Science, Psychology, and Communication*, edited by Steven R. Brown and Donald J. Brenner, pp. 3-38. New York: Teachers College Press.

Key, V. O., Jr. 1966. *The Responsible Electorate*. Cambridge, Mass.: Harvard University Press.

Kirkpatrick, Samuel A., William Lyons, and Michael R. Fitzgerald. 1975. "Candidates, Parties and Issues in the American Electorate: Two Decades of Change." *American Politics Quarterly* 3:247-83.

Klapper, Joseph E. 1960. *The Effects of Mass Communication*. Glencoe, Ill.: Free Press.

Kraus, Robert E., and John B. McConahay. 1973. "How Being Interviewed Affects Voting." *Public Opinion Quarterly* 37:398-406.

Kraus, Sidney, ed. Forthcoming. *Great Debates, 1976: Ford Vs. Carter*. Bloomington: Indiana University Press.

Kraus, Sidney. 1962. *The Great Debates*. Bloomington: Indiana University Press.

Kraus, Sidney, and Dennis Davis. 1976. *The Effects of Mass Communication on Political Behavior*. University Park: Pennsylvania State University Press.

Kraus, Sidney, and Raymond G. Smith. 1962. "Issues and Images." In *The Great Debates*, edited by Sidney Kraus, pp. 289-312. Bloomington: Indiana University Press.

Kuhn, Thomas S. 1962. *The Structure of Scientific Revolutions*. Chicago: University of Chicago Press.

Lamb, Karl. 1975. *As Orange Goes: Twelve California Families and the Future of American Politics*. New York: W. W. Norton.

Lane, Robert E. 1962. *Political Ideology: Why the American Common Man Believes What He Does*. New York: The Free Press.

Lang, Kurt, and Gladys Engel Lang. 1968. *Television and Politics*. New York: Quadrangle.

———. 1968. *Voting and Nonvoting*. Boston: Blaisdell.

———. 1961. "Ordeal by Debate: Viewer Reactions." *Public Opinion Quarterly*. 25:277-88.

Lasswell, Harold D. 1962. "Introduction." In *The Great Debates*, edited by Sidney Kraus, pp. 19-24. Bloomington: Indiana University Press.

Lazarsfeld, Paul F., Bernard R. Berelson, and Hazel Gaudet. 1948. *The People's Choice*. New York: Columbia University Press.

League of Women Voters' Education Fund. 1977; "Effect of the Debates on the 1976 Campaign and Election." Washington, D.C. Mimeographed.

Levine, Myron A. 1976. "Reporting Ambiguous Events: Television Interprets the 1976 Iowa Democratic Presidential Caucuses." Paper read at the Annual Conference of the Midwest Association for Public Opinion Research, Chicago. Mimeographed.

Lewin, Kurt. 1935. *A Dynamic Theory of Personality*. New York: McGraw-Hill.

McCartney, James. 1977. "The Triumph of Junk News." *Columbia Journalism Review*. 15:17-21.

McClure, Robert D., and Thomas E. Patterson. 1973. "Television News and Voter Behavior in the 1972 Presidential Election." Paper read at the Annual Conference of the American Political Science Association, Washington, D.C. Mimeographed.

McCombs, Maxwell E. 1976. "Agenda Setting Research: A Bibliographic Essay." *Political Communication Review* 1:1-7.

McCombs, Maxwell E., and L. Edwards Mullins. 1973. "Consequences of Education: Media Exposure, Political Interest, and Information-Seeking Orientations." *Mass Communications Review* 1:27-31.

McCombs, Maxwell E., and Donald L. Shaw. 1972. "The Agenda-Setting Function of Mass Media." *Public Opinion Quarterly* 36:176-87.

McLeod, Jack M., and Lee B. Becker. 1974. "Testing the Validity of Gratification Measures through Political Effects Analysis." In *The Uses of Mass Communications*, edited by Jay G. Blumler and Elihu Katz, pp. 137-164. Beverly Hills, Calif.: Sage.

McLeod, Jack M., and Steven H. Chaffee. 1972. "The Construction of Social Reality." In *The Social Influence Processes*, edited by James T. Tedeschi, pp. 50-99. Chicago: Aldine-Atherton.

McLeod, Jack M., Lee B. Becker, and James E. Byrnes. 1974. "Another Look at the Agenda-Setting Function of the Press." *Communication Research* 1:131-66.

McLeod, Jack M., Carl R. Bybee, Jean A. Durall, and Dean A. Ziemke. 1977. "The 1976 Debates as Forms of Political Communication." Paper read at the Annual Conference of the Association for Education in Journalism, Madison, Wis. Mimeographed.

Margolis, Michael. 1977. "From Confusion to Confusion: Issues and the American Voter, 1956-1972." *American Political Science Review* 71:31-43.

Meadow, Robert G. 1976. "Issue Empahsis and Public Opinion: The Media during the 1972 Presidential Campaign." *American Politics Quarterly* 4:177-92.

―――. 1973. "Cross-Media Comparison of Coverage of the 1972 Presidential Campaign." *Journalism Quarterly* 50:482-88.

Mears, Walter R. 1977. "A View from the Inside." *Columbia Journalism Review* 15:21-25.

Mendelsohn, Harold, and Irving Crespi. 1970. *Polls, Television and the New Politics*. Scranton, Pa.: Chandler.

Mendelsohn, Harold, and Garrett J. O'Keefe. 1976. *The People Choose a President*. New York: Praeger.

Middleton, Russell. 1962. "National TV Debates and Presidential Voting Decisions." *Public Opinion Quarterly* 26:426-28.

Miller, Arthur H., and Michael MacKuen. 1977. "Who Saw What and Why: Media Effects in the 1976 Election." Paper read at the Annual Conference of the American Association for Public Opinion Research Convention, Buck Hill Falls, Pa. Mimeographed.

Miller, Arthur H., Warren E. Miller, Alden S. Raine, and Thad A. Brown. 1976. "A Majority Party in Disarray: Policy Polarization in the 1972 Election." *American Political Science Review* 70:753-78.

Miller, Warren E., and Teresa E. Levitin. 1976. *Leadership and Change*. Cambridge, Mass.: Winthrop.

Morrison, Andrew J., Frederick T. Steeper, and Susan C. Greendale. 1977. "The First 1976 Presidential Debate: The Voters Win." Paper read at the Annual Conference of the American Association for Public Opinion Research, Buck Hill Falls, Pa. Mimeographed.

New York *Times*, April 1, 1976.

Nie, Norman H., and Kristi Andersen. 1974. "Mass Belief Systems Revisited: Political Change and Attitude Structure." *Journal of Politics* 36:540-91.

Nie, Norman H., Sidney Verba, and John R. Petrocik. 1976. *The Changing American Voter*. Cambridge, Mass.: Harvard University Press.

Niemi, Robert G., and Herbert F. Weisberg. 1976. *Controversies in American Voting Behavior*. San Francisco: W. H. Freeman.

Nimmo, Dan, and Robert L. Savage. 1976. *Candidates and Their Images*. Pacific Palisades, Calif.: Goodyear Publishing Co.

O'Keefe, Garrett J. 1975. "Political Campaigns and Mass Communication Research." In *Political Communication*, edited by Steven H. Chaffee, pp. 129-64. Beverly Hills, Calif.: Sage.

Palmgreen, Philip, and Peter Clarke. 1977. "Agenda-Setting with Local and National Issues." *Communication Research* 4:435-52.

Parkinson, Hank. 1977. "Jumping on an Opponent's Blooper Nearly Always Works." *Campaign Insight* 3:13-15.

Patterson, Thomas E., and Robert D. McClure. 1976. *The Unseeing Eye*. New York: G. P. Putnam.

Patterson, Thomas E., Robert D. McClure, and Kenneth J. Meier. 1974. "Issue Voting and Voter Rationality: A Panel Analysis." Paper read at the Annual Conference of the American Political Science Association, Chicago. Mimeographed.

Phillips, Derek. 1973. *Abandoning Method*. San Francisco: Jossey-Bass.

Pomper, Gerald M. 1975. *Voters' Choice: Varieties of Electoral Behavior*. New York: Dodd, Mead & Company.

———. 1972. "From Confusion to Clarity: Issues and American Voters, 1956-1968." *American Political Science Review* 66:415-28.

"Presidential Forum Does Well in Rating." The New York *Times*, April 7, 1976.

Repass, David E. 1971. "Issue Salience and Party Choice." *American Political Science Review* 65:389-400.

Robinson, John P. 1976. "Interpersonal Influence in Election Campaigns: Two-Step Flow Hypotheses." *Public Opinion Quarterly* 40:304-19.

———. 1971. "Mass Media Usage by the College Graduate." In *A Degree and What Else? Correlates and Consequences of a College Education*, edited by Stephen B. Withey, pp. 95-109. New York: McGraw-Hill.

Robinson, Michael J. 1977. "Television and American Politics." *The Public Interest* 48:3-39.

Sears, David O. 1969. "Political Behavior." In *The Handbook of Social Psychology*, Vol. 5, edited by Gardner Lindzey and Elliot Aronson, pp. 315-458. Reading, Mass.: Addison-Wesley.

Sears, David O., and Jonathan L. Freedman. 1967. "Selective Exposure to Information: A Critical Review." *Public Opinion Quarterly* 31:194-213.

Seldes, Gilbert, 1962. "The Future of the National Debates." In *The Great Debates*, edited by Sidney Kraus, pp. 163-69. Bloomington: Indiana University Press.

Seymour-Ure, Colin. 1974. *The Political Impact of Mass Media*. Beverly Hills, Calif.: Sage.

Shaw, Donald L., and Maxwell E. McCombs. 1977. *The Emergence of American Political Issues*. St. Paul, Minn.: West Publishing Co.

Sherif, Carolyn W., Muzafer Sherif, and Roger E. Nebergall. 1965. *Attitudes and Attitude Change*. Philadelphia: W. B. Saunders.

Siepmann, Charles A. 1969. "Were They 'Great'?" In *The Great Debates*, edited by Sidney Kraus, pp. 132-41. Bloomington: Indiana University Press.

Sigel, Roberta. 1964. "Effects of Partisanship on the Perception of Political Candidates." *Public Opinion Quarterly* 28:483-96.

Skinner, B. F. 1974. *About Behaviorism*. New York: Alfred A. Knopf.

―――. 1953. *Science and Human Behavior*. New York: Macmillian.

―――. 1953. *The Study of Behavior: Q-Technique and Its Methodology*. Chicago: University of Chicago Press.

Sloan, Lloyd Reynolds. 1977. "Biasing Effects of News Analyses of the 1976 Presidential Debates." Paper read at the Annual Conference of the American Association for Public Opinion Research, Buck Hill Falls, Pa. Mimeographed.

Stephenson, William. 1967. *The Play Theory of Mass Communication*. Chicago: University of Chicago Press.

Sullivan, John L., James E. Piereson, and George Marcus. 1978. "Ideological Constraint in the Mass Public: A Methodological Critique and Some New Findings." *American Journal of Political Science*, in press.

Teeter, Robert. 1977. Oral remarks during the Conference on Polling and Survey Research, University of Michigan, Ann Arbor.

Tichenor, Phillip, J., George A. Donohue, and Clarice N. Olien. 1970. "Mass Media Flow and Differential Growth in Knowledge." *Public Opinion Quarterly* 34:159-70.

Tuchfarber, Alfred J., and William R. Klecka. 1976. *Random Digit Dialing*. Washington, D.C.: The Police Foundation.

Ungar, Sanford J. 1977. "By Trivia Obsessed." *Columbia Journalism Review* 15:16-17.

University of Michigan. 1976. *Continuity Guide to the American National Election Surveys: 1952-1974*. Ann Arbor: Inter-University Consortium for Political and Social Research.

Weiss, Walter. 1969. "Effects of the Mass Media of Communication." In the *Handbook of Social Psychology*, Vol. 5, 2nd ed., edited by Gardner Lindzey and Eliot Aronson, pp. 871-976. Reading, Mass.: Addison-Wesley.

Wiener, Norbert. 1950. *The Human Use of Human Beings*. New York: Houghton-Mifflin.

Wooten, James T. 1976. "Carter Says He Won Because of Exposure Gained in Three Debates." The New York *Times*, November 7, 1976, p.1.

Yalch, Richard F. 1976. "Pre-election Interview Effects on Voter Turnout." *Public Opinion Quarterly* 40:331-36.

Zajonc, Robert B. 1968. "Attitudinal Effects of Mere Exposure." *Journal of Personality and Social Psychology Monograph Supplement* 9:2-27.

AUTHOR INDEX

Abelson, Robert P., 179
Abramowitz, Alan, 193
Agranoff, Robert, 177
Atkin, Charles K., 194

Becker, Lee B., 4, 37, 38, 109, 126, 127, 194, 198
Becker, Samuel L., 7
Bennett, Stephen E., 180, 191
Benton, Marc, 37
Berelson, Bernard R., 36, 157, 179
Bishop, George F., 181, 198
Blumer, Herbert, 155
Blumler, Jay G., 179, 194
Brown, Steven R., 108
Brunk, Gregory J., 181
Byrnes, James E., 37

Campbell, Angus, 36, 179, 181, 191
Campbell, Donald T., 199
Cantrall, William R., 109
Carter, Richard F., 6, 8, 9, 10, 11, 12, 197
Catton, William R., Jr., 61
Chaffee, Steven H., 4, 10, 12, 194
Clarke, Peter, 127
Clevenger, Theodore, Jr., 39
Colella, Michael A., 109
Converse, Philip E., 92, 141, 157, 179, 181, 191
Crespi, Irving, 62, 181
Curry, James, 198

Darcy, Robert, 181
Davis, Dennis, 157, 180
Donohue, George A., 196

Ellsworth, John W., 38

Farley, Lawrence T., 157
Feldman, Jacob F., 14, 39, 127, 140, 189
Fitzgerald, Michael R., 180
Frank, Robert S., 37
Frazier, P. Jean, 37
Funkhouser, G. Ray, 37

Gallup, George H., 124, 130-31, 141, 196
Gans, Herbert J., 4
Gaudet, Hazel, 36, 157, 159, 179
Graber, Doris A., 37, 109, 199, 200
Green, Bert F., 8
Greendale, Susan C., 109
Gurevitch, Michael, 179, 194

Hagner, Paul, 122, 198
Hofstetter, C. Richard, 37
Holsti, Ole R., 41
Hovland, Carl I., 9, 61
Hyman, Herbert H., 194

Jackson-Beeck, Marilyn, 57, 197, 201
Jacoubovitch, M. Daniel, 9
Janis, Irving L., 9, 61

Katz, Elihu, 14, 37, 127, 140, 179-80, 189, 194
Kelley, Harold H., 9, 61
Keniston, Kenneth, 108
Kerlinger, Fred N., 108
Key, V.O., Jr., 36, 197
Kim, Young, 109
Kirkpatrick, Samuel H., 180
Klapper, Joseph E., 9, 180
Klecka, William R., 182
Kraus, Robert E., 195
Kraus, Sidney, 34, 37, 109, 140, 157, 172, 179-80
Kuhn, Thomas S., 9

Lamb, Karl, 108
Lane, Robert E., 108
Lang, Gladys Engel, 34, 35, 37, 62, 129, 140, 198-99
Lang, Kurt, 34, 35, 38, 62, 129, 140, 198-99
Lasswell, Harold D., 3, 13
Lazarsfeld, Paul F., 36, 157, 159, 179-80
League of Women Voters' Education Fund, 29
Levine, Myron A., 199

Levitin, Teresa E., 180
Lewin, Kurt, 10
Lower, Elmer W., 7
Lumsdaine, A. A., 61
Lyons, William, 180

McCartney, James, 3
McClure, Robert D., 110, 177, 181, 196
McCombs, Maxwell E., 4, 37, 126, 127, 179, 194
McConahay, John B., 195
McLeod, Jack M., 4, 12, 37, 109, 126, 127, 194
McPhee, William N., 36, 179
Mackuen, Michael, 109
Mansfield, Michael, 198
Marcus, George, 181
Marks, John S., 157
Meadow, Robert G., 37, 57, 197, 201
Mears, Walter R., 5, 15
Meier, Kenneth J., 181
Middleton, Russell, 172
Miller, Arthur H., 38, 109, 180
Miller, Warren E., 180
Monroe, Alan D., 109
Morrison, Andrew J., 109
Mullins, L. Edwards, 194

Nebergall, Roger E., 141
Nie, Norman H., 180
Niemi, Robert G., 179
Nimmo, Dan, 140, 141, 142, 145, 147, 198

O'Keefe, Garrett J., 4, 6, 181
Oldendick, Robert W., 181, 191, 198
Olien, Clarice N., 196

Palmgreen, Philip, 127
Parkinson, Hank, 81
Parson, Donald W., 39
Patterson, Thomas E., 110, 177, 181
Petrocik, John R., 180
Phillips, Derek, 197

Pierseon, James E., 181
Polisky, Jerome B., 39
Pomper, Gerald M., 180

Reed, John Shelton, 194
Repass, David E., 180
Rieselbach, Leroy N., 122, 198
Robinson, John P., 179, 194

Savage, Robert L., 140, 141, 142, 145, 147
Sears, David O., 126, 179
Seldes, Gilbert, 6
Shaw, Donald L., 37, 127, 179
Sheffield, Fred D., 61
Sherif, Carolyn W., 141
Sherif, Muzafer, 141
Segel, Roberta, 163
Siepmann, Charles A., 13, 34
Skinner, B. F., 11
Sloan, Lloyd Reynolds, 199
Smith, Raymond G., 140
Stanley, Julian C., 199
Steeper, Frederick T., 109, 115, 198, 199
Stephenson, William, 142
Sullivan, John L., 181
Sweigert, Ray L., Jr., 10

Teeter, Robert, 115, 124
Tichenor, Phillip J., 196
Tuchfarber, Alfred J., 181, 198

Ungar, Sanford J., 3

Verba, Sidney, 180

Weisberg, Herbert F., 179
Weiss, Walter, 78
Wiener, Norbert, 11
Wooten, James T., 30
Wright, Charles R., 194

Yalch, Richard F., 195

Zajonc, Robert B., 191

SUBJECT INDEX

Abel, Elie, 20
agenda setting (*see*, mass media)
Agnew, Spiro T., 35
Alexander, Shana, 196
American Independent party, 27
American party, 27
American national election studies: 1960 and 1976, 41
American voter: models of, 179-81
American Voter, The, 181
Anderson, Tom, 27
Annenberg School of Communications (*see*, presidential debates, research conference on)
Aspen Institute: program on communications and society, 19
Associated Press: poll by, 62 (*see also*, presidential debates, public opinion polls about)
attitude (*see*, candidate images, issues, presidential debates)
audience effects: methodological problems in studying, 105, 109-25

Bailey, Douglas, 28
Benton, Charles, 19
Benton, Marjorie, 19
Benton Foundation (*see*, William Benton Foundation)
Burger, Warren Earl, 27 (*see also*, Warren and Burger courts)

Caddell, Patrick, 30
California (*see*, primary)
Camejo, Peter, 27
campaign events: converting versus reinforcing effects of, 159-78; effects on political decision making, 157-58, 174-75 (*see also*, political campaigns, presidential debates)
candidate images: effects on evaluation of candidate performance in debates, 68-70, 169-72; ideal president and, 145-47; as personal constructions, 155-56; 1976 presidential nominees, 147-53; 1976 vice-presidential nominees, 153-55
CBS (*see*, Columbia Broadcasting System)
Center for Political Studies, University of Michigan, 200
"Checkers" speech, by Richard Nixon, 35
Christian Science Monitor, 25
Clausen, Ruth, 21, 24, 26
cognitive consistency: strain toward, 79; theories of attitude change, 179
Columbia Broadcasting System (CBS): 23; poll by, 31 (*see also*, presidential debates, public opinion polls about)
Columbia University Graduate School of Journalism, 20
communication process, 199
communications context: effects of, 198 (*see also*, presidential debates, mediated reactions to)
content analysis: of issues in the 1960 and 1976 presidential debates, 38-57 [problems in application, 205-07]

Deardouff, John, 28
debates (*see*, presidential debates)

Eastern Europe: Gerald Ford's remarks about, 82 [reactions to, 84-101]
education: effects on media use and political learning, 120-22, 137, 138, 194; and political involvement, 192-94
Eisenhower, Dwight D., 34
electoral process, 199
Evanston, Illinois: panel study in, 105-09

FCC (*see*, Federal Communications Commission)
FEC (*see*, Federal Election Commission)
Federal Communications Act of 1934:

Section 315 of, 18, 22, 23, 36
Federal Communications Commission, 18
Federal Corrupt Practices Act, 24
Federal Election Campaign Act of 1974, 22, 24
Federal Election Commission, 20, 24
Ford-Reagan debate, 20
Frank, Reuven, 23
Frankel, Max, 82

Gallup organization, 201
Gallup poll, 62, 130-31, 141 (see also, Gallup, George)
gap (see, twenty-seven minute gap)
Goldwater, Barry, 18
gratification (see, uses and gratifications hypothesis)
Greater Cincinnati: panel study of, 182

Harris organization, 201
Hauser, Rita, 23
Helsinki agreement (see, Eastern Europe, Gerald Ford's remarks about)
Humphrey, Hubert H., 18

ideology: and the American electorate, 179-80
images (see, candidate images)
Indiana University: panel study of 1976 election campaign with Knight-Ridder newspapers, 159
information-seeking patterns, 194
"instant news analysis," 62-63, 84-85
Inter-University Consortium for Political and Social Research, University of Michigan, 200
interviewing: effects of repeated, 130, 147, 195
issue evolution: and agenda-setting, 57-58; concept of, 37-38; from 1960 to 1976, 41-57; methodology of, 38-41
issues: effects on evaluation of candidate performance in debates, 74-76, 172-74; and elections, 36-37, 198; impact on voting, 189-92; mass media coverage of, 53; as unit of content analysis, 39-42

Johnson, Lyndon B., 19
Johnson, Nicholas, 26

Karayn, James, 19, 21
Kennedy, John F., 18, 23, 29, 35-36, 50-53, 77, 80, 140, 172, 180
Kennedy-Nixon debates (see, presidential debates, comparison of 1960 and 1976)
Kennedy, Robert F., 18, 180
Kilpatrick, James J., 196
King, Martin Luther, Jr., 180
"kitchen debate," Nixon with Khrushchev, 35
Knight-Ridder newspapers, study with Indiana University, 159
Korea, 34
Khrushchev, Nikita, 35

Lampl, Peggy, 21
League of Women Voters: and arrangement of the 1976 debates, 21-23; legal battles in staging of debates, 24-27; reaction of commercial networks to League sponsorship of 1976 debates, 23-24; study of local chapter members' candidate images, 142, 149-50, 153, 155-56 (see also, presidential forums, League of Women Voters' Education Fund)
Los Angeles *Times*, 25

McCarthy, Eugene, 18
McGovern, George, 19
Maddox, Lester, 27
Manchester *Union Leader*: building for, 81
Market Opinion Research, 83
mass communication: and electoral process, 105, 157; models of political effects, 179-80 (see also, mass media)
mass communication research (see, political communication research)
mass media: and agenda setting, 37, 126; gatekeeping function of, 30, 33, 36-37; informational versus persuasive function of, 126-28; and patterns of use, 194; power of, 58, 81-82, 101; "umpiring role" of, 199
Minnow, Newton, 23
Muskie, Edmund, 81

National Broadcasting Company (NBC), 23, 31
National Public Affairs Center for Television, 19

National Public Radio, 20
National Science Foundation, 200
National Security Council: incorrect reference to in debates, 206
NBC (*see*, National Broadcasting Company)
New Hampshire (*see*, primary)
Newman, Edwin, 34, 65
Newsday, 62
Newsweek, 41, 53, 58
New York *Times*, 20, 23, 25, 39, 41, 53, 58, 62, 82, 205-07
Nielsen, A. C. (*see*, presidential debates, Nielsen ratings of)
Nixon, Richard M., 18-19, 22, 23, 29, 34-35, 49-52, 53, 80, 81, 128, 140, 152
Nixon-Agnew administration, 62

Onondaga County, New York: panel study of, 128-29

paradigms: construction and reorientation, 11-14; orientation, 7-14; "rationalist," 3-4, 197 (*see also*, political communication research, paradigms in; presidential debates, future research on, policy implications for)
partisanship: effects on evaluation of candidate performance in the debates, 79, 92-94, 160-61, 162, 169, 171-72, 177; and voting, 137-38, 189-91
party identification (*see*, partisanship)
Pastore, John, 23
Pokorny, Gene, 19
Poland (*see*, Eastern Europe)
political campaigns: electoral college system and, 158; and electoral rationality, 3-4; as horse races, 4-7
political communication research: future of, 14-17, 79, 199; paradigms in, 7-14
political learning: effects of respondent factors on, 96-99, 120-21, 192-94; problems of defining, 111-15
polls (*see*, public opinion polls; presidential debates, public opinion polls about)
President Ford Committee, 83
presidential debates: as campaign events, 38, 157; and candidate images, 70-74, 81, 140-41, 159, 163-69; candidates preparation for, 34; candidate reactions to, 30; comparison of 1960 and 1976, 28-30, 33-34, 41-57; effects on cognitions, 31, 74-79, 85-86, 159, 163, 169, 185-92; effects on voting, 31, 84-101, 126-27, 137-38, 159, 174-76, 177; and electronic era of politics, 34; evaluation of candidates' performance in, 64-68, 159-63; evaluation of quality of, 68-70; financial incentives in, 28, 32; future research on, 14-17, 199-200; historical setting of, 18-19, 34-38; legal and political aspects of, 24-27, 31-32; mediated reactions to first debate, 67-68, 79-80; mediated reactions to second debate, 84-87, 101; methodological problems in studying, 78-79, 90, 91-92, 109-19, 124, 194-95; Nielsen ratings of, 20, 29; policy implications for, 14-16, 31-32, 57-58, 196, 200-02; political context of, 79-80, 117-19, 121-24; and political learning, 87-89, 105-06, 109-15, 127-28, 181, 194; and political rationality, 3-4, 179, 180-81; public opinion polls about, 31, 62; ratings of Nielsen, 20, 29; research conference on, 200; transcription of, 206-07 [research uses of, 207-08, 209-10] ; as vehicles for informing the electorate, 29-31, 34, 53, 56, 105, 126-27, 138, 181-82, 198; watching of, 29-30, 130, 183-85; winning of, 62, 130-31 (*see also*, campaign events, candidate images, presidential forums, vice-presidential debates)
presidential forums: League of Women Voters and, 19-20
primaries: regional and national, 202
primary: California, 20; New Hampshire, 81
Public Broadcasting System (PBS), 20
public opinion polls: effects on the electorate, 61-62; and future presidential debates, 201 (*see also*, presidential debates, public opinion polls about)

Q-methodology: and application to study of candidate images, 141-45
question wording: and artifacts in electoral research 181; problems in establishing psychological equivalence of, 115-17

Rafshoon, Gerald, 28

Subject Index

rationality: in American electoral behavior, 179-80 (*see also*, political campaigns, presidential debates)
Reagan, Ronald, 20, 35
Robinson, Aubrey E., Jr., 27
ROC paradigm (*see*, paradigms, reorientation, orientation, and construction)
Romania (*see*, Eastern Europe)
Romney, George, 81-82
"Romney rule," 81
Roper Poll, 62 (*see also*, presidential debates, public opinion polls about)

Seattle, Washington: panel study in, 83
selective exposure thesis, 179
sensitization effects, 109-11
sleeper effect, 61
Smith, Howard K., 34
social influence model, 179
Socialist Workers Party, 27
Soviet Union, 45, 82-83
"Stapel Scalometer": use of, 140
Stony Brook campus, State University of New York: study at, 63-64
Syracuse, New York (*see*, Onondaga County)

television (*see*, mass media)
Television News Archives, Vanderbilt University, 205
Time, 41, 53, 57
twenty-seven minute gap: in the first presidential debate, 62
two-step flow hypothesis, 179-80

United States Information Agency, 23

United States Supreme Court, 27
U.S. Chamber of Commerce, 26
U.S. Court of Appeals, District of Columbia, 27
U.S. District Court for the District of Columbia, 25
uses and gratifications hypothesis, 179, 194-95
USIA (*see*, United States Information Agency)
U.S. Senate Commerce Committee: Communications Subcommittee of, 23

Van Deerlin, Lionel, 23
Vandegrift, Benjamin M., 26
vice-presidential debate of 1976: effects on cognitions, 134-35; winning of, 131-34 (*see also*, candidate images, presidential debates)
Vietnam, South, 35, 81
Vladivostok meeting, 82
voting (*see*, presidential debates, effects on voting)

Walker, Charles, 23
Wallace, George C., 19, 20
Wall Street Journal, 25
Walnut Street Theatre, Philadelphia, 27
Warren, Earl, 52
Warren and Burger courts, 52
Washington *Post*, 25
Watergate, 35
William Benton Foundation, 19-20
Woods, Rosemary, 206

Yugoslavia (*see*, Eastern Europe)

ABOUT THE EDITORS AND CONTRIBUTORS

GEORGE F. BISHOP is a political social psychologist and Senior Research Associate at the Behavioral Sciences Laboratory of the University of Cincinnati. Dr. Bishop has published widely in the area of public opinion and political behavior. His articles and reviews have appeared in the *American Journal of Political Science, Comtemporary Sociology, Journal of Communication, Journal of Politics, Journal of Social Psychology, Public Opinion Quarterly, Psychological Reports*, and *Social Forces*. He was past president (1977-78) of the Midwest Association for Public Opinion Research and is currently a member of the editorial board of *Political Behavior Quarterly*.

Dr. Bishop received his Ph.D. in social psychology (1973) from Michigan State University and previously taught at the University of Notre Dame.

ROBERT G. MEADOW holds a joint appointment in Political Science and Communications at the University of California, San Diego. Formerly he was on the faculties of the Annenberg School of Communications, University of Pennsylvania, and the University of Kentucky, where he was founding Director of the University of Kentucky Survey Research Center. In addition to his recent book, *Politics as Communication*, Professor Meadow has contributed articles and reviews to *Public Opinion Quarterly, American Politics Quarterly, Political Science Quarterly, Journal of Communication, Communication Research, Presidential Studies Quarterly*, and *Journalism Quarterly*, as well as other professional journals. Currently he is completing a book on public opinion surveys and foreign policy. Professor Meadow completed his undergraduate and graduate studies at the University of Pennsylvania, receiving his Ph.D. in political science.

MARILYN JACKSON-BEECK is Assistant Professor of Communications at Cleveland State University. Her research focuses on the relationship between mass communication and politics, with interests encompassing televised presidential debates, political consequences of viewing prime-time television, and the role of mass media in children's political socialization. She is coauthor of annual research reports describing television content and linking television exposure to (mis)perceptions of social and political reality. Other research appears in the *Journal of Broadcasting, Journal of Communication,* and the *Handbook of Political Socialization*. Her bachelor's and master's degrees were completed at the University of Wisconsin, in political science and journalism; at the Universty of Pennsylvania she received her Ph.D. in communications.

HERBERT E. ALEXANDER is Professor of Political Science at the University of Southern California and Director of the Citizens' Research Foundation at U.S.C.

LEE B. BECKER is Associate Professor in the School of Journalism at Ohio State University.

RICHARD F. CARTER is Professor of Communication at the University of Washington.

ROBIN E. COBBEY is Manager of News and Circulation Research at Knight-Ridder Newspapers in Miami.

JAMES CURRY is Assistant Professor in the Department of Political Science, Baylor University.

CHAIM H. EYAL is completing post-doctoral studies at the S. I. Newhouse School of Public Communications at Syracuse University.

DORIS A. GRABER is Professor of Political Science at the University of Illinois, Chicago Circle.

PAUL R. HAGNER is Assistant Professor in the Department of Political Science at Washington State University.

GLADYS ENGEL LANG is Professor of Sociology, State University of New York, Stony Brook.

KURT LANG is Professor of Sociology, State University of New York, Stony Brook.

MICHAEL W. MANSFIELD is Associate Professor of Political Science at Baylor University.

JOEL MARGOLIS is a Political Scientist and former associate with the Citizens' Research Foundation.

DAN NIMMO is Professor of Political Science, University of Tennessee.

ROBERT W. OLDENDICK is a Research Associate in the Behavioral Sciences Laboratory at the University of Cincinnati.

LEROY N. RIESELBACH is Professor of Political Science at Indiana University.

IDOWU A. SOBOWALE is an Assistant Lecturer in the Department of Mass Communication at the University of Lagos, Nigeria.

FREDERICK STEEPER is Vice-President of political research at Market Opinion Research, Inc. in Detroit.

ALFRED J. TUCHFARBER is Director of the Behavioral Sciences Laboratory at the University of Cincinnati.

JK526 1976.P73 1978